ABRAHAM
JOSHUA
HESCHEL

ABRAHAM JOSHUA HESCHEL

THE CALL OF TRANSCENDENCE

SHAI HELD

INDIANA UNIVERSITY PRESS

Bloomington and Indianapolis

This book is a publication of

Indiana University Press
Office of Scholarly Publishing
Herman B Wells Library 350
1320 East 10th Street
Bloomington, Indiana 47405 USA
iupress.indiana.edu

Telephone orders 800-842-6796
Fax orders 812-855-7931

⊖ The paper used in this publication
meets the minimum requirements of the
American National Standard for Information Sciences—Permanence of Paper
for Printed Library Materials, ANSI
Z39.48–1992.

Manufactured in the United States of
America

Library of Congress
Cataloging-in-Publication Data

Held, Shai, [date] author.
    Abraham Joshua Heschel : the call of
transcendence / Shai Held.
        pages cm
    Includes bibliographical references and
index.
    ISBN 978-0-253-01126-8 (cloth :
alk. paper) — ISBN 978-0-253-01130-5
(e-book) 1. Heschel, Abraham Joshua,
1907–1972—Teachings. 2. Judaism—
Doctrines. 3. God (Judaism) I. Title.
    BM755.H37H45 2013
    296.3092—dc23

                                2013022925

1 2 3 4 5 18 17 16 15 14 13

To the Memory of
Moshe Held,
My Father

CONTENTS

ACKNOWLEDGMENTS

I have accumulated a great many debts in the long and drawn-out process of producing this book. I wish to offer especial thanks to the following teachers, colleagues, students, and friends.

Professor Jon Levenson has been a significant teacher, valued mentor, and cherished friend for two decades now. My thinking in general and this work in particular have been immeasurably enriched by his incisive questions, consistently original insights, and keenly critical eye. This book began as a dissertation, and I could not have asked for a more supportive and responsive advisor. Let me state at the outset: any errors, oversights, or lapses in judgment in this work are Jon's fault; any insights are entirely my own. Or something like that.

In recent years, Professor Michael Morgan has become an important teacher and a cherished friend. He is a philosopher in the truest sense of the word: a lover of wisdom—and a wonderful person to boot. My thinking, on Heschel and on much else, has been deepened by our exchanges and conversations.

Ken Koltun-Fromm and Robert Erlewine were kind enough to offer extensive feedback on the manuscript. Bob and I have since had a productive series of exchanges, and my thinking and writing about Heschel have grown in clarity and sophistication as a result. He has also been producing some of the best, most insightful work about Heschel, and I am honored by and grateful for his support of my work.

Professor Arthur Green opened up the world of Hasidic texts for me, and he has been unflagging in his encouragement of my work. Art has also served as an important model for me in integrating a life of scholarship with a deep commitment to serving the Jewish community and the broader world. Professor Khaled Anatolios was a skilled guide through the landscape of Christian theology in the twentieth century. Jonathan Boyarin graciously allowed me to consult his unpublished draft translation of *Kotzk: In Gerangl Far Emesdikeyt.*

In very different ways and in very different registers, Rabbi Yitz Greenberg and Rabbi Louis Jacobs opened up the world of Jewish theology to me. They both taught me never to fear questions, and never to apologize for them. My debt to Yitz is boundless, and I am honored to call him my teacher. Bernie Steinberg has given more to this study, and to my understanding of my work in the world, than he knows; he has been a model and an inspiration in countless ways. Bill Lebeau taught me how to be a rabbi. Barry Mesch gave me my first opportunity to teach Heschel some two decades ago.

A variety of friends made important contributions to this work, sometimes through explicit conversations about content, but far more often through the sheer delights of friendship and mutual support. I will not mention them all, but I thank a few in particular who have, in ways direct and indirect, shaped the content and vision of this work: Yehudah Mirsky, David Starr, Steve Greenberg, Jeremy Dauber, Jeffrey Wechselblatt, Michael Kress, David Hoffman, Marcie Lenk, Or Rose, Shaul Magid, and Mark Nussberger.

Elie Kaunfer, Ethan Tucker, and Avital Hochstein have been partners in building Mechon Hadar, an institution that embodies many of the values I hold most dear; we have worked together with a remarkable and all-too-rare spirit of *mentschlichkeit* and camaraderie. In countless ways, our shared work delayed this project, and in equally abundant ways, their encouragement and support helped move it forward. To them, and to all of my colleagues at Mechon Hadar: my profound thanks.

The countless hundreds of students with whom I have studied Heschel's writings and ideas have taught me more than I can ever hope to repay. Their often relentless questioning, their persistent challenges, and their frequently profound openness to new and provocative ideas have again and again inspired me to dig deeper and think harder. Thanks to all of you, and to each and every one of you.

Librarians (especially interlibrary loan librarians) at Harvard, Columbia, and Brown Universities, as well as at the Jewish Theological Seminary and Union Theological Seminary, have been patient, helpful, and resourceful. My thanks to them all.

Jaclyn Rubin and Gabriel Seed served as research assistants at various stages of my research, and I am grateful to them, both for their industriousness and for their *mentschlichkeit*. I am also thankful to Jaclyn for asking me questions, and then asking me some more, and then, well, you get the picture. Abby Phelps and Rachel Scheinerman provided extremely useful first rounds of copyediting with abundant good cheer. Rachel Druck also cast a careful eye on early drafts of several chapters.

Dee Mortensen, Sarah Jacobi, June Silay, and Dave Hulsey of Indiana University Press have shepherded the book to completion, and Eric Schramm provided meticulous copyediting. Rabbi Ben Kramer painstakingly prepared the index. I am grateful to them all.

My in-laws Bill and Francine Krasker have provided crucial support in a variety of ways, and I am profoundly in their debt.

My sister Dalith and brother-in-law Zeev have loved me and my family unconditionally, and it has meant more than I can say.

It is difficult to know what to say about Rachel, Lev, and Maya. I can imagine no greater blessing than the opportunity to share a life and a home with Rachel, one of the kindest and gentlest human beings one could ever hope to know. Rachel's love is my life's greatest privilege; her sense of humor and her generous tolerance of mine (most of the time, anyway) are among my life's treasures. Being with Rachel and Lev and Maya each day fills me with a sense of peace and wholeness like nothing I have ever experienced before. Lev, now three, and Maya, now one, teach me—day after day and hour after hour—about wonder and responsiveness (and about "transitive concern"), not to mention joy and laughter. May you, Lev and Maya, grow to embody the best ideals discussed in this work, and may you never let your capacity for wonder and gratitude wither or fade.

My late father, Moshe Held, died a mere month before my bar mitzvah, now almost three decades ago. In the short time we had together, he taught me a lot of things, among them how to love and be loved, how to live passionately, and how to really love a text, to read it closely, and to turn it over again and again. Rarely a day goes by when I do not think of him, and I am profoundly saddened by the thought that he will not hold this book in his hands. Theology was not his "cup of tea," as he would have said, but in his own way, Torah was. I trust that he would have appreciated how closely and carefully I have tried to read, and that he would have understood just how much I owe him. This book is dedicated to his memory, a small token of vast love.

ABBREVIATIONS:
WORKS BY ABRAHAM JOSHUA HESCHEL

AJHEW   *Abraham Joshua Heschel: Essential Writings.* Edited by Susannah Heschel. Maryknoll, N.Y.: Orbis, 2011.

EL   *The Earth Is the Lord's: The Inner Life of the Jew in Eastern Europe.* New York: Farrar, Straus & Giroux, 1950.

GSM   *God in Search of Man: A Philosophy of Judaism.* New York: Farrar, Straus & Giroux, 1955.

HT   *Heavenly Torah as Refracted through the Generations.* Translated by Gordon Tucker with Leonard Levin. New York: Crossroad, 2005.

IEE   *Israel: An Echo of Eternity.* New York: Farrar, Strauss & Giroux, 1967.

IF   *The Insecurity of Freedom: Essays on Human Existence.* Philadelphia: Jewish Publication Society, 1966.

INGM   *The Ineffable Name of God: Man.* Translated by Morton Leifman. New York: Continuum, 2005.

KGE   *Kotzk: In Gerangl Far Emesdikeyt* (Yiddish). 2 vols. Tel Aviv: Ha-Menorah, 1973.

MGSA   *Moral Grandeur and Spiritual Audacity: Essays.* Edited by Susannah Heschel. New York: Farrar, Straus & Giroux, 1996.

MNA   *Man Is Not Alone: A Philosophy of Religion.* New York: Farrar, Straus & Young, 1951.

MQ   *Man's Quest for God: Studies in Prayer and Symbolism.* New York: Scribner, 1954.

The Prophets,   *The Prophets: An Introduction.* 2 vols. New York: Harper,
   I & II   1962.
PT   *A Passion for Truth.* New York: Farrar, Straus & Giroux,
              1973.
TMHS   *Torah min ha-shamayim be-aspaklaryah shel ha-dorot.* 3
              vols. New York: Soncino, 1962 (vols. 1–2). New York: Jew-
              ish Theological Seminary, 1995 (vol. 3).
WM   *What Is Man?* Stanford: Stanford University Press, 1965.

ABRAHAM JOSHUA HESCHEL

INTRODUCTION

Abraham Joshua Heschel (1907–1972) was one of the most influential religious figures of the twentieth century. A prolific scholar, he wrote important works on the whole history of Jewish thought; an eloquent and impassioned theologian, he penned several classics of modern Jewish theology and spirituality; a prominent activist, he spoke out in theological terms on behalf of the civil rights movement and against American involvement in the Vietnam War.[1] Heschel has been hailed as a hero, honored as a visionary, and endlessly quoted as a devotional writer. His work has generated a large and growing corpus of secondary literature, some of it both incisive and insightful.[2] But unfortunately, many scholarly treatments have tended toward either uncritical adoration or overly facile dismissal. Thus, for the most part, Heschel's work has not received what it so clearly warrants: scholarly investigation that is at once genuinely sympathetic and unapologetically critical. This work is an attempt to provide just that, and thus to fill a significant lacuna in the scholarship on modern Jewish thought.

All interpreters of Heschel's work are indebted to Fritz Rothschild and John Merkle, who blazed the trail for Heschel scholarship by drawing out the philosophical and theological assumptions underlying his work, organizing his often meanderingly presented ideas into an orderly whole, and refusing to treat him as a mere fountain of devotional aphorisms and lapidary formulations.[3] Yet for all the insight Rothschild and Merkle offer into Heschel's theological world, a reader would search their works in vain for any critical perspective on Heschel's work. Both writers seek to present Heschel's thought in the best possible light and simply stop there, presumably leaving the task of constructive criticism to others. Even many more recent writers have tended toward reticence where criticism is concerned. To take but one example, Alexander Even-Chen has authored an important volume discussing many of the key themes in Heschel's work and engaging a broad range of Heschel's commentators and interpreters, but he, too, mostly shies away from sustained critique. Thus, some of the most problematic aspects of Heschel's thought—his notion of universal, pre-conceptual religious experiences, for instance, or his assumption that a separation of theology from chronology is in itself an adequate response to the challenges posed by historical criticism of the Bible—are presented without so much as a whiff of critical appraisal. At the other extreme are critics like William Kaufman, who makes the startlingly ungenerous claim that "on reading Heschel, one gets the impression that inconsistency is not only tolerated but is made a virtue,"[4] or Eliezer Berkovits, who portrays Heschel as a simple-minded literalist espousing a theology perilously close to Christianity.[5]

And yet a close perusal of Rothschild's study shows that something else is also missing. Reading Rothschild, one could almost come away with the impression that Heschel is, at bottom, a systematic philosopher, preoccupied above all with constructing an alternative to Western ways of approaching ontology and metaphysics. Conspicuously absent from the essay is any hint either of Heschel's lyrical prose or of his ardent piety. So striking is the omission that one wonders whether, despite his obvious achievement in exhibiting the internal coherence of Heschel's thought, Rothschild has not lost something of the heart of the latter's work. Heschel's evocative style is not somehow incidental to his project; he is emphatically not a systematic philosopher who just happens to write beautifully. On the contrary, Heschel communicates as he does because he wants to galvanize the heart as well as the mind; to rouse his readers from their existential slumber, not just to present them with a series of intriguing ideas or philosophical approaches. Moreover, Heschel's blazing fervor is not an adventitious aspect of his writing; it is not subsidiary to something else that is primary and more essential. For Heschel, the poetry, the piety, and the theology are all inextricably intertwined. Heschel is decidedly not a theologian *or* a devotional writer; on the contrary, he is both simultaneously. Indeed, he is to some extent one *because* he is the other.[6] For Heschel, the two projects cannot be disentangled—the goal of theology is not, ultimately, to know something about God, but to know God, and this demands passion, not just cognition. This is why the poetry is so integral to the writing: Heschel strives to (re)introduce his readers to the experience of wonder and the living reality of God, and for that, discursive, analytical prose alone simply will not do.

But the reader of Heschel must be careful to avoid the opposite extreme as well. When Jacob Petuchowski writes, for example, that what emerges from Heschel's writings is not a "ready-made philosophy of religion or of Judaism, but a feeling, a mood, powerful enough to carry us with it and heighten our religious sensitivity,"[7] he, too, loses the complex, multi-faceted Heschel, dilating on one aspect of the latter's project at the expense of the other. No doubt, Heschel does seek to move his readers, but he does not seek merely to move them. He also assays a broad-reaching theology and an interpretation of Judaism (and arguably of religion more generally), and for that task, poetry and piety alone are plainly insufficient. What I am suggesting, in other words, is that in Heschel, theology and spirituality are always interwoven; to attempt to separate them is, inevitably, to flatten and falsify his thought.

In light of all this, the first goal of this book is to explore the major issues in Heschel's thought with an eye toward the nexus of theology and spirituality, in a mode that is at once critical and sympathetic. The second goal is to offer a fresh perspective on what ultimately underlies and unifies Heschel's various writings. My contention is that Heschel's work is animated by a passion for self-transcendence, for moving beyond an exclusive focus on the ego and its needs and desires. Self-transcendence is both the dominant theme of Heschel's theology—God is, he argues, perfectly self-transcendent—and the paramount aspiration of his spirituality—to become truly human, he insists, is to progress from self-centeredness to God-centeredness. Heschel will try to convince us, but he will also attempt to move us, stir us, and reorient us in fundamental ways so that our conventional, egoistic ways of thinking, feeling, and acting can be replaced with something radically different— an approach to the world in which God is the hub and the radial point of our lives. As I show in this introduction, for Heschel, self-transcendence, both human and divine, is precisely what makes God's covenants with Israel and humanity possible.

* * *

"The greatest beauty grows," Heschel writes, "at the greatest distance from the ego."[8] This deceptively simple sentence could serve as an interpretive key for Heschel's entire approach to theology and spirituality. Both Heschel's understanding of God and his vision for humanity are grounded in a commitment to self-transcendence as the highest possible ideal. The God of Israel, Heschel repeatedly tells us, transcends Himself entirely, and the challenge placed before humanity is to follow suit. It is an aspiration as difficult to achieve as it is easy to articulate: to move from ego-centeredness to other-centeredness, to cultivate a posture of responsiveness to God and to others rather than remaining mired in the abyss of unrestrained self-assertion and self-regard.

Heschel is thus a theologian of self-transcendence. But what exactly does that mean? What, for Heschel, is the meaning of self-transcendence? Heschel distinguishes between "reflexive concern," or concern with the self and its future, on the one hand, and "transitive concern," or concern with the interests of others, on the other.[9] There is nothing inherently wrong with reflexive concern; it is constitutive, after all, of all organic existence.[10] But human life is more than mere organic life. Where human life goes astray—where it ceases, in fact, to be meaningfully human at all—is where reflexive concern becomes exclusive of any other. Authentic human personhood, Heschel tells us, is constituted by transitive concern: "A man entirely unconcerned with his self is dead," he writes, but "a man exclusively concerned with his self is a beast. . . . Human is he who is concerned with other selves."[11] Heschel consistently argues that human beings need to be "self-surpassing": perhaps paradoxically, he insists that "man cannot ever be in accord with his own self unless he serves something beyond himself." A human being, Heschel writes, "can never be truly self-sufficient, not only by what he must take in, *but also by what he must give out*."[12] According to Heschel, "A vital requirement of human life is transitive concern, a regard for others, in addition to a reflexive concern, an intense regard for itself."[13] Self-transcendence, then, is predicated upon (or perhaps simply *is*) transitive concern. The latter, of course, goes hand in hand with—may actually be synonymous with—a transformation from self-centeredness to God-centeredness. Thus, Heschel writes that "in its depths, egocentricity amounts to a demonic attempt to depose God and remake the world in the image of man."[14] Faith, in contrast, is "the beginning of the end of egocentricity."[15]

If human beings must strive for self-transcendence, God, in contrast, is always already self-transcendent. In contradistinction to created, organic existence, Heschel argues, God has no reflexive concern at all: "He does not have to be concerned about Himself, since there is no need of His being on guard against danger to His existence." God is, as it were, animated by concern, but exclusively by concern for others: "The only concern that may be ascribed to Him is a transitive concern, one which is implied in the very concept of creation." Indeed, since God's concern for others is untainted by self-concern, "God's care for His creatures is a pure concern."[16] Heschel maintains that "the decisive thought in the message of the prophets is not the presence of God to man but rather the presence of man to God. . . . The prophets speak not so much of man's concern for God as of God's concern for man. At the beginning is God's concern."[17] For the prophets, critically, this is not an abstract claim but a lived experience: "The primary content of the prophet's consciousness," Heschel writes, "is a divine attentiveness and concern."[18]

This is the crucial distinction, for Heschel, between biblical and Greek thinking. "The gods of mythology," he writes, "are self-centered, egotistic." They are driven only by "reflexive passions,"[19] and are thus no different from, and no better than, the most selfish of human beings. For Heschel, I would suggest, the God of Greek philosophy is really not much of an improvement over the gods of Greek mythology. To be sure, the former is perhaps more dignified than the cowardly Ares or the lustful Zeus, but where it matters most, He is in fact just like them: the God of Greek philosophy is totally aloof and impervious to everything but Himself. He is *utterly devoid of transitive concern*. As Heschel acidly puts it, "The God of the philosophers is all indifference, too sublime to possess a heart or to cast a glance at our world."[20] Since humanity is constituted by transitive concern, a God whose only concern is reflexive, and who is thus completely indifferent to anything but His own eternal perfection, is, for Heschel, less than a human being, not more. One can readily imagine Heschel asking: Do we really need a God even more self-absorbed than we are?[21]

In a striking passage in *The Prophets*, Heschel argues that when we speak of God as a "personal Being," we are speaking of His transitive concern. "The outstanding feature of a person," Heschel writes, "is his ability to transcend himself, his attention to the nonself. To be a person is to have a concern for the nonself. It is in this limited sense that we speak of God as a personal Being: He has concern for nondivine being."[22] A prophet, according to Heschel, is a human being who understands this truth about God and feels it in the very core of his being; he is "intoxicated with the awareness of God's relationship to His people and to all men."[23] Indeed, "what the prophets proclaim is God's intimate relatedness to man," so much so that "divine concern . . . is the stuff of which prophecy is made."[24] The prophet attempts to move Israel both to respond to God's concern, and ultimately, as we shall see, to share in it as well. As a result, Heschel avers, "Prophetic religion may be defined [as] *what man does with God's concern.*"[25]

Not surprisingly, Heschel's theology and his spirituality are inextricably intertwined. The God of Israel, on the one hand, is pure self-transcendence and transitive concern; He combines, Heschel argues, "absolute selflessness with supreme concern for the poor and exploited."[26] Human beings, on the other hand, face a complex task: we are asked to cultivate and deepen our transitive concern even as we cannot but persist in reflexive concern (else we cannot survive). Only thus, as we have seen, do we become worthy of being called human beings at all. For Heschel, God is both the perfect paradigm of self-transcendence and the voice that summons us to our own (necessarily imperfect) reflection thereof. The Bible, as we see in chapter 3, is the central manifestation of that voice in our world; according to Heschel, it seeks to awaken us to our responsibility for others, and especially for the oppressed and downtrodden. But something of this voice is discernible whenever we are stirred by wonder out of our usual self-enclosure. "Awareness of the divine," Heschel writes, ultimately "bristles with an unbearable concern that deprives us of complacency and peace of mind, forcing us to care for ends which we do not wish to care for, for ends which have no appeal to our personal interest." We resist this ineffable call "with all our might, pride and self-reliance," but it is an "enforced concern . . . a pressure that weighs upon us," and it "plants a question, a behest, in front of us, which our heart echoes like a bell, overpowering as if it were the only sound in endless stillness and we the only ones to answer it." The voice of God, Heschel tells us, demands "concern for the unregarded."[27] As we deepen our humanity, instead of seeing other human beings as means for the attainment of our own needs, we "begin to acknowledge . . . other selves as ends, to respond to their needs even regardless of personal expediency." We become, Heschel writes, "concerned with their concern; what is of importance to them becomes vital" to us. Heschel beautifully contrasts the biblical figures of Cain, who, "when asked about the whereabouts of his brother, gave answer: 'Am I my brother's keeper?' (Genesis 4:9)," and Abraham, who "unasked, unsolicited, pleaded for Sodom, the city of wickedness."[28] All of this can be stated quite simply: the heart of prophetic theology is the fact of a God who cares, and, consequently, the heart of prophetic spirituality is the mandate for human beings to do the same.

This elemental link between the nature of the God we believe in and the vision of the good life we espouse is critical for understanding Heschel's project as a writer and thinker. In a time of unprecedented cruelty and barbarism—in a time when, as we see in chapter 1, humanity has so fundamentally forfeited its capacity for self-transcendence and concern for others that we have become "callous to catastrophes"[29]—it is a matter of desperate urgency to reject worldviews which facilitate and even valorize indifference to the fate and well-being of others. Thus, Heschel remarks that he was led to study the prophets in depth by the realization that philosophy in academic environments "had become an isolated, self-subsisting, self-indulgent entity," that it had grown unconscionably "indifferent to a situation in which good and evil became irrelevant." What led Heschel away from abstract philosophizing, then, was "the realization that some of the terms, motivations, and concerns which dominate our thinking may prove destructive to the roots of human solidarity. . . . It was the realization that the right coins were not available in the common currency that drove me," Heschel writes, "to study the thought of the prophets."[30]

What is it about Western philosophical modes of thinking that Heschel finds so dangerous and damaging? First and foremost, as we have seen, according to Heschel Greek philosophy posited an abstract, indifferent deity, too transcendent to hear the cries or collect the tears of the innocent; in modern times, deists affirmed the same divine "detachment and apartness from the world."[31] The notion of a God who is apathetic and indifferent could not but give rise to a parallel conception of man. Hence, for example, the Stoic claim that "'apathy,' the subduing of the emotions . . . [is] the supreme moral task."[32] But Heschel contends, in contrast, that passions and desires can be directed to concern for God and other human beings; "neither in the legal nor in the prophetic writings," he writes, "is there a suggestion that [they] are to be negated." The key sentence for understanding what is at stake for Heschel in rejecting Greek theology and anthropology is perhaps this: "The source of evil is not in passion, in the throbbing heart, but rather in hardness of heart, in callousness and insensitivity."[33] On Heschel's account, then, the chasm between biblical thinking and Greek is that whereas the latter embraces the ideal of an apathetic man worshipping an apathetic God, the former valorizes the sympathetic man worshipping a God of pathos, a God whose very grandeur "implies the capacity to experience emotion."[34] The greatest lesson humanity can learn from the horrors of the twentieth century, according to Heschel, is that "indifference to evil is more insidious than evil itself; it is more universal, more contagious, more dangerous." And thus the most urgent response is to return to a God who refuses indifference, and to a vision of humanity that works against the ever-present temptation to succumb to its lures. As we see in chapter 4, this is, for Heschel, "one of the meanings of the anger of God: the end of indifference!"[35] Heschel's theology and spirituality merge in the shattering realization that "the thought of God and indifference to other people's suffering are mutually exclusive."[36]

The sentence that appears in Heschel's writings more frequently than any other—one encounters it countless times in his vast corpus—is a simple one: "God is in need of man." In a lecture to educators, Heschel says that "the idea of God being in need of man is central to Judaism and pervades all the pages of the Bible, of *Chazal* [the talmudic sages], of Talmudic literature."[37] Accordingly, it becomes the dominant motif in his theology. God will not redeem the world alone, Heschel insists, but instead waits for human beings to participate in that work. God is "in need of man," he writes, "in need of man's share in redemption";[38] this is, he argues, the fundamental meaning of covenant. Again, Heschel contrasts biblical and Hellenistic thinking: "In Greek theology, the highest power does not need man. Events are a monologue. But Jewish religion starts with the covenant: God *and* man."[39]

Every human being needs to be needed, and our ultimate need, Heschel maintains, is "to be needed by God." In fact, "every man is in need of God because God is in need of us. Our need of him is but an echo of His need of us."[40] As Heschel famously puts it, "*To be* is to *stand for,* and what man stands for is the great mystery of being [God's] partner. *God is in need of man.*"[41] If God is merely a human need, Heschel suggests, then He is really no more than idol, created by man "for the satisfaction of his needs and desires. . . . God must not be described as a human need. On the contrary, man must be understood as a need of God."[42]

Boldly, Heschel declares:

> There is only one way to define Jewish religion. It is the *awareness of God's interest in man,* the awareness of a *covenant,* of a responsibility that lies on Him as well as on us. Our task is to concur with His interest, to carry out His vision of our task. God is in need of man for the attainment of His ends, and religion, as Jewish tradition understands it, is a way of serving these ends, of which we are in need, even though we may not be aware of them, ends which we must learn to feel the need of.[43]

Life, Heschel tells us, is a "*partnership* of God and man"; indeed, "the essence of Judaism is the awareness of the reciprocity of God and man, of man's togetherness with Him who abides in eternal otherness."[44] Put simply again, God enters into covenant with man "because of His being in need of man."[45]

According to Heschel, God's need of man runs deeper than just His yearning for His ends to be fulfilled: even God's immanence depends, as it were, on humanity's making space for Him. Heschel maintains that "the *Shechinah,* the presence of God, is in exile. Our task is to bring God back into the world. . . . To have faith is to reveal what is concealed."[46] Again, Heschel writes that "God is hiding in the world and our task is to let the divine emerge from our deeds."[47] Indeed, as we see at length in chapters 6 and 7, according to Heschel, the core project of prayer is to transcend the self, and thus to let God in: "To worship is to expand the presence of God in the world. God is transcendent, but our worship makes Him Immanent. This is implied," he contends, "in the idea that God is in need of man: His being immanent depends on us."[48]

Crucially for Heschel, God's need is a "self-imposed concern. God is now in need of man, because He freely made him a partner in His enterprise, 'a partner in the work of creation.'"[49] God acts in this way because "God's dream is not to be alone, to have mankind as a partner in the drama of continuous creation."[50] As a result of this divine decision, "Man's relationship to God is not one of passive reliance on His Omnipotence but one of active assistance."[51] Heschel returns repeatedly to the idea that the God of Israel is not limited, but, as it were, self-limited.[52] God exercises self-restraint in order to make space for human freedom. The meaning of covenant is, at bottom, not that God needs man, but that *God has chosen to need man.*[53]

It is worth noting that some of Heschel's interpreters have been tripped up by this notion of divine self-limitation. Alexander Even-Chen, for example, argues—unconvincingly, in my view—that over time, in the shadow of the Shoah, Heschel came to abandon his belief in God's omnipotence. I see no evidence for this in Heschel's writings; on the contrary, the tragic drama of an omnipotent God granting freedom to humanity, only to see it exploited in unspeakable ways, persists throughout Heschel's oeuvre. Thus, Even-Chen is simply mistaken when he writes that, according to Heschel, "The exiled, suffering God cannot offer redemption,"[54] or when he suggests that by the time of *GSM*, "Heschel ha[d] already concluded that God is in exile, and therefore not omnipotent."[55] That this is not the case is evident from a decisive passage in *The Prophets* (published seven years after *GSM*), which Even-Chen misses. Heschel distinguishes between two types of divine suffering—divine passion on the one hand, and divine pathos on the other. Passion, he argues, is what befalls a limited God; pathos, an omnipotent One: "In passion, the divinity is thought of as a martyr, the basis of whose suffering lies, in the last analysis, in the powerlessness of God. In pathos [in contrast], God is thought of as the supreme Master of heaven and earth, Who is emotionally affected by the conduct of man."[56] There can be no doubt, then, that according to Heschel, God's sufferings in history should be understood as the travails of an omnipotent God.[57]

I can thus make no sense at all of Even-Chen's contention that Heschel's description in *MNA* of God's need of man as a "self-imposed concern" is "a very unusual assertion" for which he can find no parallels in Heschel's writings.[58] Contra Even-Chen, in *GSM*, Heschel speaks of God's "restrained omnipotence,"[59] not of his lack thereof (Even-Chen appears to miss this passage as well). In that same work, Heschel writes that the Bible "speak[s] in the name of a Being that combines justice with omnipotence."[60] Or again, Heschel says that "the omnipotence of God is not always perceptible"[61]—implicit in this, of course, is that the omnipotence of God is no less real for being imperceptible, or subject to self-limitation. As late as 1964, Heschel speaks of God's "self-imposed absence" from the world.[62] Consider also Heschel's famed PBS interview with Carl Stern days before his death. In the course of the conversation, Heschel says that God has given human beings essentially unlimited freedom: "If we understand the Bible properly," he says, "we discover that God shares life with man and He has given man freedom. A very questionable gift, and the most outstanding gift man has. Man can do anything. When the first son of the first couple decided to murder his brother, he did what he pleased. And God did not interfere."[63] This is not a description of a God limited in power—what, after all, would it mean for a limited God to give man freedom? That gift is only meaningful because it comes from a God who has the power to bestow it. Finally, the vein of protest against God's inaction in the face of immense human suffering (which, I argue in chapter 5, persists from Heschel's earliest poems to his last work on Menahem Mendl of Kotzk) would make no sense at all were God impotent and unable to act in history.[64]

There is really only one passage in Heschel that would at first glance seem to support Even-Chen's interpretation. Speaking to a group of educators in 1968, Heschel declares that "the whole conception of God's omnipotence, I suspect, was taken over from Islam. . . . I tell you that the idea of divine omnipotence, meaning, holding God responsible for everything, expecting Him to do the impossible, to defy human free-dom, is a non-Jewish idea."[65] Two responses to this passage are in order. First, even if we take it at its surface level, we should note that it would be a highly uncharacteristic statement for Heschel, and, in light of what we have already seen, it would be inconsistent with the overwhelming thrust of his writings on divine power. But second, and more fundamen-tally, we might ask what Heschel is trying to get at in this passage, since even here he appears to move between the position that God *cannot* redeem the world without man's help and the very different contention that God *will not* do so. Thus, when Heschel remarks that "God is not going to redeem Israel while Israel remains passive. God waits for Israel either to do *tshuvah* [repentance] or to help bring about the redemptive act of *geulah* [redemption],"[66] it seems that he is talking about a decision God has made, not an inherent limitation that He faces. Let us look for a moment at the one other passage in Heschel in which he compares the God of Israel to the God of Islam. In *The Prophets*, Heschel writes:

> The God of pathos may be contrasted with the God of Islam. For all the belief in divine mercy, Allah is essentially thought of as unqualified Omnipotence [*sic*], Whose will is absolute, not conditioned by anything man may do. He acts without regard to the specific situation of man. Since everything is determined by Him, it is a monologue that obtains between Allah and man, rather than a dialogue or a mutuality as in the biblical view. Not the relation between Allah and man, but simply Allah himself is central to Islam. . . . The power of God is not the ultimate object in the prophet's experience of the divine . . . but the divine Mind whose object of attention is man whose pathetic reactions reveal man as cause. Spirit, not power, is the ultimate reality for the prophetic con-sciousness.[67]

It is evident from this passage, I think, that the contrast between Islam and Judaism, according to Heschel, is a contrast between a the-ology in which God is the monological only actor, and a theology in which God is a dialogical covenantal partner. (Needless to say, I am interested here in the work Heschel's conception of Islam does for him, not in the historical accuracy of his portrayal.) I see nothing here to sug-gest that the issue between Judaism and Islam is how much power God inherently has; the issue, rather, is whether and how God chooses to use it—whether, that is, God is motivated by a concern for relationship or by an insistence on using His sheer, unadulterated power. Reading the passage from "Jewish Theology" in light of this one (written only six years earlier), I would suggest that in the former, Heschel is speaking in a kind of theological shorthand (and, admittedly, a potentially misleading one at that): what he means to suggest is that in contrast to Islam, Judaism does not believe in God's active, unrestrained omnipotence. It is the latter that is the uniquely Islamic idea. Judaism does not deny God's intrinsic omnipotence, but rather His active omnipotence in disregard of human freedom and agency. Thus, even this seemingly idiosyncratic passage in a late lecture can be integrated into our larger interpretation of Heschel's approach. Whatever limitations there are on God's power, they are ultimately self-imposed. Christian theologian Keith Ward captures this well when he asserts that, for Heschel, God's pathos is a manifestation not of "vulnerable weakness" but of "freely willed affectivity."[68]

I emphasize this point at length because something absolutely critical is at stake for Heschel, namely, God's interest in a relationship with humanity, and His *free decision to pursue it*. In order to render authentic mutuality possible, God must make space for human beings to act freely. In other words, Heschel's God seems to understand that one cannot bludgeon another into reciprocity and commitment. As biblical theologian Terence Fretheim has written, "Any relationship of integrity will entail a sharing of power. There can be no true relationship if one party has all the power. . . . [Consequently,] God has chosen not to be the only one in the world with power."[69] Divine-human relationship entails meaningful human freedom, and the latter, in turn, entails divine self-restraint. This, I am suggesting, is a dramatic form of divine self-transcendence.

In a similar vein, Heschel makes two entwined claims—first, that God's presence fills the world, and second, that that presence is less than fully manifest; indeed, that it is actively concealed. "The earth is filled with the glory [of God]," Heschel writes; "now the glory is *concealed*," whereas in the time to come it will be revealed to all.[70] More dramatically, Heschel maintains that "the God of Abraham, the Creator of heaven and earth, deemed it wise to conceal His presence in the world in which we live. He did not make it easy for us to have faith in Him, to remain faithful to Him."[71] There is a tragic dimension to this concealment. Indeed, Heschel writes, "the failure of perception, the inability to apprehend [God] directly is the sad paradox of our religious existence."[72] At times,

Heschel makes veiled reference to the kabbalistic notion of *tzimtzum*, or divine self-contraction. Heschel maintains, for example, that "God had to conceal His presence in order to bring the world into being. He had to make His absence possible in order to make room for the world's presence. Coming into being brought about along denial and defiance, absence, oblivion, and resistance."[73] Indeed, the spiritually perceptive are able to discern the paradox that "every moment is a carefully concealed act of His creation."[74] As we shall see, the meaning of performing a mitzvah is to reveal the God who is presently concealed.[75] Heschel goes so far as to suggest that sacred deeds are redemptive acts on the part of man: "The meaning of redemption is to reveal the holy that is concealed, to disclose the divine that is suppressed. Every man is called upon to be a redeemer, and redemption takes place every moment, every day."[76] This is another lens, then, through which to view covenant as Heschel understands it: the God who conceals His power and His presence waits for humanity to make Him known.

If God places limits on His power, human beings, in contrast, have utterly failed to circumscribe our own. The unmitigated horrors of the twentieth century, epitomized for Heschel by the ravages of Auschwitz and Hiroshima, are the ultimate manifestation of human power run amok, of humanity's seemingly infinite capacity to deal out devastation and destruction. What we have learned in modern times, Heschel avers, is "the dangerous greatness of man . . . his immense power and ability to destroy all life on earth. . . . Never before has the superhuman power of our existence been as clearly manifest as it is in our time."[77] According to Heschel, there is no overstating the danger of human power without trammels: "This is our predicament," Heschel writes, that "our power may become our undoing. We stand on a razor's edge. It is so easy to hurt, to destroy, to insult, to kill. Giving birth to one child is a mystery; bringing death to millions is a skill."[78] In consequence, "We are terrified at our own power. Our proud Western civilization has not withstood the stream of cruelty and crime that burst forth out of the undercurrents of evil in the human soul." It is hard to miss the sheer depth of Heschel's anguish as the world, he thinks, is overrun by a "flood of wretchedness. . . . What have we done with our power? What have we done to the world?"[79] Heschel describes the plight of modern man with haunting clarity: "Others may suffer from degradation by poverty; we are threatened by degradation through power."[80] As we see in chapter 1, humanity's obsessive focus on what Heschel terms "expediency"—that is, on viewing the world as nothing more than "material for the gratification of our desires"—cannot but end up consuming and dissolving humanity itself. Heschel writes,

> Not only do we distort our sight of the world by paying attention only to its aspect of power; we are reducing the status of man from that of a *person* to that of a *thing*. There is a strange cunning in the fact that when man looks only at that which is useful, he eventually becomes useless to himself. In reducing the world to an instrument, man himself becomes an instrument. . . . The instrumentalization of the world leads to the *disintegration of man*.[81]

According to Heschel, our very humanity depends on our suppressed capacity for self-restraint.

Never before has the challenge been clearer or more pressing: humanity needs to bring its unbridled self-assertion under control. "The more power [man] attains, the greater his need for an ability to master his power."[82] Heschel's prescription for a humanity drunk on power is a return to biblical religion. "Our civilization is in need of redemption," he writes; "there is a war to be waged against . . . the glorification of power; a war that is incessant, universal," and humanity's best weapon for that battle is "the radical wisdom, the sacrificial devotion" of our ancestors.[83] More fundamentally, as we see in chapter 3, what is needed is a new openness to the desperately urgent message of the Bible: "Unless history is a vagary of nonsense, there must be a counterpart to the immense power of man to destroy, there must be a voice that says NO to man, a voice not vague, faint and inward, like qualms of conscience, but equal in spiritual might to man's power to destroy."[84] The only hope for humanity is to curtail our own power, to make space for God by setting limits on ourselves. If humanity is not to obliterate the world, receptiveness to God and revelation is not an expendable luxury, but a burning necessity.

Again here we find a kind of mirror effect in Heschel's thinking: just as God restrains His omnipotence to make space for man, so must humanity in turn place limits on its power to make space for God. To respond to God, to enter into relationship with Him, is to relinquish our will to power. Self-restraint, we might say, is a form of *imitatio dei*. "The will to power and the will to believe are mutually exclusive," Heschel writes, because in the former "we arrogate to ourselves what belongs to God and suppress the claim of His presence," while in the latter we "learn how to let His will prevail."[85] Indeed, one of the paramount tasks before humanity is to learn that "the glory of man is not in his will to power, but in his power of compassion."[86] Heschel captures this in a striking passage in *WM*. "The acceptance of the sacred," he notes, "is an existential paradox: it is saying 'yes' to a 'no'; it is the antithesis of the will to power; it may contradict interests and stand in the way of satisfying inner drives."[87]

At bottom, I think, the self-transcendence for which Heschel advocates is a fundamental reorientation, at once theological and epistemological. As I argue in chapter 1, Heschel rejects the Cartesian *cogito* as just another form of self-assertion: as long as "I" is the first word in our vocabulary, God, the world, and other human beings will all be cognized—and ultimately treated—as objects. The first step in our transformation is the realization that life is a gift, that "I am what is not mine." That awareness leads us to understand that, in reality, "man is not a subject but an *object*."[88] It is God who is the subject: God is "the Knower and we are the known . . . to be means to be thought of by Him."[89] Thus, when we awaken to the wonder of existence, "when we are overtaken with the spirit of the ineffable, there is no logical self left to ask the question or the mental power to stand as the judge with God as an object, about the existence of whom I am to decide. . . . There is no self to say: I think that . . . "[90] With this comes the profoundly humbling recognition that "God can never become the mere object of our thought." What we seek when we pray, for example, is not "to be informed about Him, as if He were a fact among facts," but instead "to be wholly possessed by Him . . . not to know the unknown but to be penetrated with it; *not to know* but *to be known* to Him, to expose ourselves to Him rather than Him to us; not to judge and to assert but to listen and to be judged by Him."[91] In one of the most important passages in *GSM*, Heschel tells us that in moments of insight, we abandon the presumption of passing judgment on whether or not there is a God; "we realize" instead, he writes, "that the question we ask is a question we are being asked; that *man's question about God is God's question of man*."[92] What results is a brake on self-assertion, and what emerges in its place is a newfound consciousness of "indebtedness" and "requiredness," an openness to the reality that, as Heschel never tires of pointing out, "something is asked of us."[93] Heschel's subversion of Cartesian philosophy, on the one hand, and of the culture of expediency and self-assertion, on the other, is perhaps best encapsulated toward the end of *WM*: "Do I exist as a human being?" he asks. "My answer is: *I am commanded—therefore I am*."[94]

The three forms of human self-transcendence we have been discussing are, of course, inextricably linked: in (1) developing transitive concern for God as well as for others, we (2) set limits on the use of our own power. All of this is made possible, for Heschel, by (3) the rediscovery that life is a gift, and that something is asked of us. "I" is no longer our first and only word, and a sense of obligation and commandedness comes to replace our otherwise relentless self-assertion. As a result, our lives are animated by reciprocity and responsiveness, rather than acquisitiveness and consumption; expediency makes way for the return of wonder. All three dimensions of self-transcendence constitute an opening to the commanding yet vulnerable presence of God. In transcending ourselves, in other words, we make divine immanence possible.

* * *

Chapter 1 begins with an examination of the dynamics of wonder and awe in Heschel, and of the ways in which these existential postures elicit an awareness that "something is asked of us," and thereby make for the possibility of self-transcendence and receptivity. I probe the all-important contrast in Heschel between the "way of wonder," on the one hand, and the "way of expediency," on the other, and note the ways in which modernity's seemingly boundless emphasis on the latter has all but eliminated the former—with unspeakable consequences. The unique barbarism of modern times, Heschel argues, stems from self-assertion utterly without bounds, from callousness to the call of God and the reality of other selves; the only hope for humanity lies, consequently, in a rediscovery of wonder and a renewed openness to demands that come from outside of us. Not to put too fine a point on it, this is, for Heschel, a matter of life and death for humanity as a whole.

The second part of the chapter investigates Heschel's problematic insistence that the most fundamental religious experiences—or, better, religious intuitions and insights—are pre-linguistic and pre-conceptual, and, what is more, that they are universal. Concomitantly, I explore Heschel's ambivalent—one is tempted to say tortured—relationship with epistemology and the problem of certainty, and his sometimes hyperbolic denunciations of non-belief.

Chapter 2 deals with the intertwined questions of theological method on the one hand and theological anthropology on the other. I show that although there are important similarities between Heschel and Karl Barth, Heschel is decidedly not a Barthian, both because he is an optimist about the human capacity to know God and obey His will, and because he explicitly advocates the correlation of questions raised in human experience with answers provided by revelation, a procedure that was anathema to Barth. I compare Heschel's approach to correlation to Paul Tillich's, and I draw out crucial similarities between Heschel's approach to theology and anthropology and that of Karl Rahner. The latter's conceptions of mystagogy and poetic theology offer us an extremely useful lens through which to understand Heschel's project as a religious thinker and writer, and give the lie to a common misapprehension—namely, that Heschel is a poet *rather than* a theologian. As I show, Heschel is, on the contrary, a poet at least in part *because* he is a theologian.

In this chapter, again, self-transcendence is a major theme, now intensified to constitute a fundamental critique of modernity's turn to the self. In a strikingly paradoxical move, Heschel begins his theological reflections by focusing on the human self and its experiences, and in seemingly Tillichian terms, he imagines revelation providing answers to (now tragically suppressed) human questions. But the ostensible sovereignty of the self is soon subverted, as Heschel leads his readers to the realization that the most fundamental human awareness is of the reality that "something is asked of us." The quest to find out what is asked of us, and by whom, is already a portal to self-transcendence, since the self now realizes that long before it asks, it is already asked. This discovery makes possible a radical reorientation: the human project now becomes not to ask but to answer; not to assert but to respond; not to think, but to be thought of; not, finally, to know God, but to be known by Him.

Not surprisingly, according to Heschel, the human eagerness to know what is asked of us, and by whom, opens us to the possibility of receiving revelation. Chapter 3 is an extended treatment of Heschel's approach to revelation and its associated problems and complexities. I offer a fresh perspective on the crucial question of whether or not, for Heschel, revelation has content—that is, to borrow terms from the philosopher Michael Morgan, whether revelation "contains" meaning or merely "provokes" it[95]—and suggest that Heschel believes that the content of revelation is divine, even as the words are human. I then explore Heschel's (not fully satisfactory) strategy for managing the challenge posed to theology by historical criticism of the Bible. Over the course of the chapter, I pay close attention to the ways in which Heschel tries to clear away the obstacles many moderns face in confronting the possibility, let alone the reality, of revelation, as well as to what is undoubtedly one of the weakest and most disturbing aspects of Heschel's writing—namely, his insistence that what is self-evident to him ought to be self-evident to others, and his resulting propensity to blame (and castigate) non-believers for their lack of faith. Once again in this chapter, the importance of self-transcendence comes to the fore, as Heschel insists that the central tasks of biblical teachings are to orient us to the good and the holy, and to place a brake on our otherwise unbridled propensity for self-assertion and manipulation. To be open to the word of God, for Heschel, is to be willing to heed the divine NO that places limits on our exploitative, expediency-centered ways of thinking and acting.

Paying close attention to Heschel's words in *GSM*, we can discern an additional aspect of divine self-transcendence. On the one hand, Heschel tells us, God is fully capable of making His will known "unambiguously."[96] And yet, as I discuss at length in chapter 3, prophecy consists of what Heschel calls a "co-revelation" of God and man, and the latter's share is both substantial and significant. Indeed, as Heschel notes rather mutedly, "The share of the prophet manifested itself not only in what he was able to give but also in what he was unable to receive."[97] Thus, in choosing to reveal His will to the prophet, who is "a person, not a microphone,"[98] Heschel's God runs the risk of being heard less than perfectly. Moreover, in bestowing upon human beings the obligation to interpret His word, God faces the frightful possibility that we will "try to interpret the Bible in terms of paganism" and thus turn it to violent and abusive ends.[99]

If chapter 3 explores the question of what is revealed to humanity, chapter 4 addresses the conjoined question of "by whom." Here I analyze Heschel's insistence that the God of Greek metaphysics and the God of biblical revelation are incommensurable, and his attendant attack on the Hellenization of the God of Israel so common in the medieval philosophical tradition. Returning to themes we have already begun to consider, I survey Heschel's idea of the divine pathos and the meaning of divine concern, and I probe Heschel's response to the charge of anthropopathism. We also resume our exploration of another aspect of divine self-transcendence, the idea that God's pathos results from God's voluntarily restraining His own power. As we think through Heschel's claim that pathos tells us nothing at all about the divine essence, I show that Heschel's understanding of God is more informed by philosophical concerns than he was perhaps willing to see or admit. As we have seen, Heschel's God is so completely self-transcendent as to be "selfless." In chapter 4, we discover, in turn, that the prophetic demand entails human self-transcendence: to do justice, we learn, "demand[s] from everyone a certain abnegation of self, defiance of self-interest,"[100] while to love "means to transfer the center of one's inner life from the ego to the object of one's love."[101] Although some degree of self-transcendence is thus required of all, it is the prophet, we are told, who fully sympathizes with the divine pathos, and thus exemplifies the commitment to moving beyond self-centeredness. Transcendence of the self, Heschel tells us, is the very essence of prophecy. The chapter also includes an investigation of Heschel's presentation of Rabbi Akiva in TMHS and suggests that, for Heschel, the latter represents the rabbinic continuation (and even radicalization) of the prophetic tradition of sympathy with God's suffering. Through the image of Akiva, I suggest, Heschel flirts with his most radical image of self-transcendence—that of a people that transcends its own suffering by focusing exclusively on God's.

Taking chapters 3 and 4 together, we realize that both God and His Torah are vulnerable in the world precisely because God has elected the path of self-transcendence and vulnerability in the name of genuine relationship. But in chapter 5, the tragic dimensions of divine self-transcendence emerge in full force, as we discover, in the long shadow of the Shoah, that human callousness and brutality have the power to drive the divine into exile. Indeed, we hear both about God's "homelessness" and about humanity's refusal to take responsibility for what we have wrought. God's self-limitation means that human beings have the terrifying capacity to "silence" Him, and even, seemingly, to chase away His providential concern. But as I argue, the tragedy runs much deeper, as Heschel allows himself to confront—tentatively, haltingly—the underside of God's self-transcendence: perhaps divine self-limitation is necessary to allow for human freedom, but, nevertheless, there are times in which "defeat is all we face [and] horror is all that faith must bear." At these moments, human beings cry out with the psalmist, "Wherefore hidest thou thy face, and forgettest our afflictions and our oppression?" and beseech God to arise and help us "for Thy mercy's sake."[102] Implicit here is a question, a lament, and a challenge: how much divine self-transcendence is too much? What happens when self-transcendence becomes indistinguishable from abandonment? Are there not moments when decency would require God to exercise His omnipotence actively? In contrast with several other interpreters of Heschel's work, I contend that this excruciating question is left unresolved—muted, to be sure (a manifestation, perhaps, of self-transcendence on the part of Heschel, who feels that humanity's need for God is greater than his need to protest), but definitely not silenced.

Chapters 6 and 7 constitute an extended exploration of the meaning of prayer, which, for Heschel, encapsulates the spiritual life in all its richness and complexity. As we might expect by now, the dominant theme in Heschel's philosophy of prayer is the challenge of self-transcendence, the mandate to "shift the center of living from self-consciousness to self-surrender."[103] Indeed, Heschel tells us that "the essence of prayer lies in man's self-transcending."[104] As we shall see, this leads Heschel to insist that the heart of prayer lies in praise rather than in petition, and to argue that, seen phenomenologically, even ostensibly petitionary prayer is in fact less about petition than about praise. Crucially, however, Heschel distinguishes between self-transcendence and self-annihilation, and, correlatively, he rejects all talk of mystical union with God. Heschel is emphatic that there is no value in self-obliteration; on the contrary, the very possibility of covenant depends on robust human selfhood. To talk of mystical union is, for Heschel, to compromise both the transcendence of God and the integrity of the human self, and thereby to reduce the idea of covenant to incoherence. Thus, in contrast to thinkers such as Evelyn Underhill and Thomas Merton, for Heschel, the self that transcends itself always remains just that—a self open to the possibility of relationship and reciprocity. Chapter 7 examines the painful problem of prayer in a time of divine hiddenness, and takes stock of Heschel's notion of making space for God through prayer. For Heschel, I suggest, it is in prayer that the covenantal reciprocity of self-transcendence reaches its full flowering: as we have seen, God limits His power to such an extent that his very presence in the world depends on our receptivity and responsiveness to his call. How do we let God in? By decentering the self, by placing God and other selves at the center of our concern. "To pray," Heschel writes, "means to bring God back into the world, to establish his Kingship for a second at least. To pray means to expand his presence."[105] This, then, is the deepest truth of covenant: *God's immanence depends on human self-transcendence.*

I have chosen to analyze prayer rather than religious observance more broadly, because, for Heschel, prayer is the religious act par excellence. It is, he says, "the queen of all commandments." Prayer is, in fact, the barometer of our religious lives: "This is the way of finding out whether we serve God, or an idea of God—through prayer. It is the test of all we are doing." Indeed, Heschel interprets the very category of mitzvah (commandment) in light of prayer, rather than the other way around. As he famously puts it, "What is a *mitzvah*, a sacred act? A *Prayer in the form of a deed.* . . . No religious act is performed in which prayer is not present."[106] This means, I think, that according to Heschel the performance of a mitzvah is a moment of self-transcendence, a gesture of worship in which we strive to let God in. In exploring Heschel's concept of prayer, then, we are investigating the meaning of observance more generally, attempting to uncover the very pith of the religious life.

It is crucial to emphasize that for Heschel, prayer is "no substitute for action. It is, rather, like a beam thrown from a flashlight before us into the darkness. It is in this light that we who grope, stumble, and climb, discover where we stand, what surrounds us, and the course which we should choose."[107] In other words, prayer epitomizes the self-transcendence and responsiveness that ultimately ought to animate our every deed—indeed, the entirety of our lives. This is, I think, what Heschel meant when he famously said of his march in Selma with Dr. Martin Luther King Jr. that "my feet were praying": his participation in the struggle for civil rights was, he believed, a mitzvah in the highest sense—an attempt to bring God into the world through the pursuit of justice and concern for the oppressed and downtrodden. In an extremely important insight into Heschel's theology, Arthur Green traces his preoccupation with the idea of God in search of man to the classical Jewish mystical idea of "ha-ʿavodah tzorekh gavoah," worship fulfills a divine need,[108] and suggests that Heschel's "brilliant and transformative move" was to apply this sense of divine need "first and foremost to the . . . commandments that regard the way we treat our fellow humans." In other words, whereas the kabbalists had focused on the heavenly consequences of ritual performances, Heschel shifts emphasis to the realm of divine concern for humanity. God's need is thus more centered on interpersonal actions like visiting the sick or feeding the hungry than on theurgic unifications of "The Blessed Holy One and His Shekhinah" through actions like immersing in a ritual bath or blowing the ram's horn on the New Year.[109] Green's analysis offers us a remarkable window into the intertwining of profound theocentrism with radical ethical passion that so pervades the Heschelian corpus.[110]

It bears noting that the precise relationship in Heschel between theocentrism, on the one hand, and this-worldly ethical activism, on the other, has sometimes eluded his interpreters. Thus, for example, Rivka Horwitz can write that "there seems to me to be a contradiction. . . . It is surprising that Heschel himself was not aware of the discrepancy between these two directions in his thought: the one founded on the here and now and the other stressing the Beyond and which sees everything from the point of view of God."[111] But Heschel was more than aware, of course, of this purported dissonance. Indeed, one could argue that demonstrating that the discrepancy is only apparent is one of his central projects as a theologian. The believer turns to God, only to learn that, paradoxically, the transcendent, majestic God is intimately concerned with human life in general, and with the fate of the vulnerable and downtrodden, in particular. By placing so much emphasis on the divine pathos, in other words, Heschel overcomes the ostensible split between other-worldliness and groundedness in this-worldly reality.[112]

* * *

As we have seen, Heschel believes that given humanity's descent into callousness and indifference, and the unimaginable atrocities that have resulted, the need for repentance has never been more urgent. It behooves us to ask: How did Heschel understand his own role in bringing about this human turning and transformation? There is a telling passage in *GSM* that is as important as it is easy to miss. Heschel writes:

> God is not always silent, and man is not always blind. . . . Some of us have at least once experienced the momentous realness of God. Some of us have at least caught a glimpse of the beauty, peace, and power that flow through the souls of those who are devoted to Him. There may come a moment like a thunder in the soul, *when man is not only aided, but also taught how to aid, how to guide other beings.*[113]

It is difficult to avoid the sense that Heschel is here talking about himself, perhaps offering an uncharacteristic admission of his sense of divinely ordained purpose. With these words, Heschel allows us a rare glimpse into his own self-understanding—as a man whose task is to be not merely a theologian or an inspirational writer, but, much more momentously, a religious guide to his generation (and quite possibly to later ones as well). Eliezer Schweid speculates as to whether or not Heschel saw himself as a prophet, and arrives at the conclusion that "even if Heschel did not see himself as a prophet in the direct and immediate sense, he surely saw himself as a prophet of the prophets (*nevi ha-nevi'im*)"—in other words, just as the prophet brought the word of God to the people, Heschel now brings the words of the prophets to them. This, Schweid adds, is the paradox of "hidden prophecy": in order to render people receptive to the words of the prophets, one needs divine inspiration (*ruach ha-kodesh*), which, "even if it is not prophecy in the fullest sense of the term, nevertheless borders on it."[114] This question is, of course, unanswerable, and speculating about it will yield only so much fruit. More important, I think, one thing is absolutely clear: whatever else Heschel may have been—philosopher, theologian, poet, phenomenologist, historian—he was, first and foremost, a religious teacher (in Schweidian terms, we might add: in the prophetic tradition), one who understood himself to have a vital (and, again, perhaps even divinely appointed) role to play in reawakening humanity's sense of wonder, and thus in restoring its capacity for responsiveness and self-transcendence. Heschel saw himself as called to remind humanity that God is perpetually in search of man, and to revive its now dormant capacity to answer that divine summons. Everything else he did, I would suggest, was in service of that fundamental goal: in his scholarship on the Bible and the rabbis, Heschel sought to legitimate and ground his understanding of the divine pathos; in his lyrical evocations of the spiritual life, he aspired to restimulate humanity's abeyant sense for the piercing reality of God; in his phenomenological portrayal of the prophets, he endeavored to provide humanity with a taste of what the world looks like when beheld from the perspective of a loving God. Put very simply, Heschel wanted nothing less than to reorient human life away from self-centeredness and toward God-centeredness.[115] This, as we shall see, is the animating passion of everything that he wrote and taught.

* * *

Before turning to the heart of our exploration, a few brief methodological comments are in order. One of the most striking characteristics of Heschel's theology is its remarkable stability over time. In contrast to a figure like Martin Buber, for whom we can fairly sharply distinguish the early, mystical phase and the later, dialogical phase;[116] or Joseph Soloveitchik, for whom it is not clear whether, let alone how, the assumptions of various essays map onto one another; Heschel articulates a vision of Judaism that is notable, among other things, for its exceptional coherence and consistency. Thus, Alexander Even-Chen rightly notes that "it is difficult to identify an early and late phase in Heschel's writings, since his later writings evince conceptions already present in his earlier works."[117] And Michael Marmur observes that "it is . . . remarkable how little Heschel's theological program changes in the course of his life, considering the epoch-making events which dissected it."[118] In light of this, I have for the most part chosen to treat Heschel's work as a synchronic whole, freely integrating earlier writings and later ones in expositing or analyzing his ideas.

This brings us to another important feature of Heschel's writings. Although, as I have already indicated, I believe that Heschel did offer a lucid and consistent interpretation of Judaism, it is nevertheless apparent that systematic presentation was not his forte; Heschel simply was not a linear writer. Indeed, one is reminded of the talmudic sage Rabbi Nehemiah's dictum that "the words of Torah are sparse in one place, and enriched from another."[119] Thus, one who wishes to interpret Heschel's approach to wonder, for example, cannot rest content merely with analyzing the sections of Heschel's oeuvre in which he explicitly deals with wonder, because a stray thought here and a seemingly irrelevant line there may provide crucial insight not articulated or adequately expressed in its proper place. Or a later essay may offer an articulation that sheds helpful light on an earlier, more opaque aphoristic formulation. The first project of serious Heschel scholarship, therefore, is to cull appropriate passages from a variety of books and essays in order to shed light on the core themes of his theology. As Edward Kaplan succinctly puts it, "Given that Heschel scatters his analysis throughout several books, interpreters must gather the strands together and arrange them into some order."[120] Only then is critical analysis really possible. The fact that Heschel's writings are so consistent over time renders this procedure eminently defensible, and I have employed it throughout.

One final note. Despite some serious misgivings, out of a desire to represent Heschel's thought as accurately as possibly, I have chosen not to alter his heavily gendered language. Therefore, God is frequently referred to as "He" and humanity as "man," even when I am discussing Heschel in my own words rather than in his. Since God's personal aspects are so central to Heschel's theology, I have decided not to eschew personal pronouns for God altogether. I have little doubt that had Heschel lived longer, he would have been sensitive to the quest for more gender-inclusive language, but since he did not, and since the heart of the book consists of close and careful engagement with his own words, I have chosen to treat them as he wrote them. I am keenly aware that there is no fully satisfying solution to the problem I faced, but I trust that my readers will accord me—and, more important, Heschel—the benefit of the doubt.

ONE

WONDER, INTUITION,
AND THE PATH TO GOD

Abraham Joshua Heschel begins his discussion of wonder in *God in Search of Man* by declaring that "among the many things that religious tradition holds in store for us is *a legacy of wonder.*"[1] This opening sentence ends with something of a surprise: one might have expected Heschel to invoke a legacy of "fidelity," "commitment," or "piety." But *wonder*? Can a sense of wonder be passed from generation to generation? Can one, in fact, inherit a "legacy of wonder"? This perhaps counter-intuitive sentence can serve as an interpretive key to one of Heschel's primary projects as a religious writer: he seeks to subvert the views of those, like Martin Buber, who insist on an inherent tension between spontaneous religious expression and received tradition.

In one of his most famous early lectures, Buber paints a stark contrast between "religion" and "religiosity."[2] Religiosity, Buber writes, is "man's sense of wonder and adoration . . . an ever anew [*sic*] articulation and formulation of his feeling that, transcending his conditioned being yet bursting from its very core, there is something that is unconditioned." Religion, in contrast, is "the sum total of the customs and teachings articulated and formulated by the religiosity of a certain epoch in a people's life."[3] Although Buber recognizes that religion and religiosity can in theory go hand in hand, his profound skepticism about the former, and its potentially deadening effects on the latter, are evident throughout. Thus Paul Mendes-Flohr, Buber's foremost contemporary commentator, can write that, for the latter, "Religion is antithetical to religiosity."[4] Religion, Buber tells us, is governed by "rigidly determined . . . prescriptions and dogmas," and in thwarting authentic religiosity, it all too readily

28

becomes "uncreative and untrue."[5] In a rather dramatic formulation, Buber writes: "Religiosity induces sons, who want to find their own God, to rebel against their fathers; religion induces fathers to reject their sons, who will not let their fathers' God be forced upon them. Religion means preservation; religiosity, renewal."[6] Now, Heschel is well aware that religion can serve to undermine and even destroy authentic religious devotion and practice. He does, after all, polemicize against the stultifying state of the American synagogue, at one point even asking whether "the temple [has] become the graveyard where prayer is buried."[7] Moreover, he evinces an ongoing fascination with the Hasidic master R. Menahem Mendl of Kotzk, who was nothing if not suspicious of the role of habit and imitation in religion as it is all too often practiced.[8] But Heschel insists whole-heartedly that far from constituting an inevitable consequence of religion, the suppression of religiosity is, instead, the result of the dilution and falsification thereof. In fact, much of Heschel's work is an attempt to revitalize what he regards as the fruitful polarity of *qeva* and *kavvanah*, or fixed practice and inner devotion. As he puts it in consecutive chapter titles in *Man's Quest for God*, "Spontaneity is the goal . . . Continuity is the way."[9] If for Buber, modern man needs to break free from the shackles of inherited tradition, for Heschel, in stark contrast, he needs to be saved from the "callousness" induced by modernity—and his salvation may be found precisely in inherited tradition, and the commitment to wonder and responsiveness it transmits. According to Heschel, in other words, religious tradition holds out a legacy of wonder that can elicit and awaken our own. It is on this possibility, as we shall see, that he thinks the very future of humanity depends.

* * *

According to Heschel, all human beings have a natural proclivity to wonder, a sense of "unmitigated innate surprise."[10] A sense of wonder, of amazement and appreciation, is constitutive of who we are as human beings. Wonder, for Heschel, is not merely an emotion or an experience. It is more like an existential posture, a fundamental orientation to the world. All religious awareness and insight are rooted in wonder. As Heschel writes, "Wonder or radical amazement is the chief characteristic of the religious man's attitude toward history and nature. One attitude is alien to his spirit: taking things for granted."[11] Indeed, "The surest way to sup-press our ability to understand the meaning of God and the importance of worship is *to take things for granted*."[12]

And yet routinization is like spiritual poison: "This is the tragedy of every man: 'to dim all wonder by indifference.' Life is routine, and rou-tine is resistance to the wonder."[13] One of the crucial tasks of religion, Heschel therefore insists, is to struggle against the anesthetizing effects of our over-familiarization with life and reality, and to instill in us a sense of "perpetual surprise,"[14] a willingness to encounter the world again and again as if for the first time.[15] The fact that the sense of wonder can be so difficult to maintain renders the need for regular worship all the more urgent: "Every evening we recite: 'He creates light and makes the dark.' Twice a day we say: 'He is One.' What is the meaning of such repetition? A scientific theory, once it is announced and accepted, does not have to be repeated twice a day. The insights of wonder must be constantly kept alive. Since there is a need for daily wonder, there is a need for daily wor-ship."[16] Heschel contends, in other words, that "all worship and ritual are essentially attempts to remove our callousness to the mystery of our own existence and pursuits,"[17] and that "the main function of observance is in keeping us spiritually perceptive."[18]

In reading Heschel's writings, one often gets the impression that wonder and radical amazement are essentially synonyms; indeed, we have already seen Heschel speak of "wonder or radical amazement" as if the two were merely different terms for the same approach to reality. But at other times, it is clear that they are not completely overlapping categories. In an essay "On Prayer," Heschel writes that "we begin with a sense of wonder and arrive at radical amazement."[19] In general, I think, the distinction between them is that whereas wonder is essentially a state of surprise, radical amazement is reflexive wonder,[20] or wonder turned in upon itself and thereby intensified. "*Radical amazement*," Heschel writes, "has a wider scope than any other act of man. While any act of perception or cognition has as its object a selected segment of reality, radical amazement refers to all of reality; not only to what we see, but also to the very act of seeing as well as to our own selves, to the selves that see and are amazed at their ability to see."[21] Or, to put it somewhat differently, "Even our ability to wonder fills us with amazement."[22] In other words, for Heschel, all moments of radical amazement are also experiences of wonder, but not all experiences of wonder are moments of radical amazement. I suspect that Heschel would say that while the cultivation of a perpetual sense of wonder is the goal of much of ritual and worship, a continual sense of radical amazement, by contrast, is both impossible and undesirable, because it would lead, ultimately, to paralysis. While wonder is a form of thinking that ought to accompany all our acts of perception, radical amazement is more like a high-intensity religious experience, and is therefore necessarily both consuming and fleeting.[23]

Heschel writes:

> Wonder or radical amazement is the chief characteristic of the religious man's attitude toward history and nature. One attitude is alien to his spirit: taking things for granted, regarding events as a natural course to things. To find an approximate cause of a phenomenon is no answer to his ultimate wonder. He knows that there are laws that regulate the course of natural processes; he is aware of the regularity and pattern of things. However, such knowledge fails to mitigate his sense of perpetual surprise at the fact that there are facts at all. Looking at the world he would say, "This is the Lord's doing, it is marvelous in our eyes" (Psalms 118:23).[24]

According to Heschel, then, wonder is not a question in search of an answer; it is not "the same as curiosity," but a "form of thinking... an attitude that never ceases."[25] Religion thus has nothing to fear from science. The latter, Heschel writes, "extends rather than limits the scope of the ineffable, and our radical amazement is enhanced rather than reduced by the advancement of knowledge."[26] In light of this, Heschel warns that "the sense of wonder and transcendence must not become 'a cushion for the lazy intellect.' It must not be a substitute for analysis where analysis is possible; it must not stifle doubt where doubt is legitimate. It must, however, remain a constant awareness if man is to remain true to the dignity of God's creation, because such awareness is the spring of all creative thinking."[27] Here, of course, Heschel is concerned to combat the spurious contention that religious passions are dependent upon a lack of intellectual sophistication, as if wonder were merely the refuge of naive, underdeveloped minds. Science, he insists, is not inherently dangerous to religion, and the latter's well-being is in no way contingent upon the fear and eschewal of the former. Heschel seeks to demolish the assumption, ironically often shared both by religion's most vitriolic critics and some of its most spirited defenders, that wonder depends upon—or worse, is synonymous with—ignorance of science.

Implicit in all this, of course, is that Heschel's theology is not a search for "the God of the gaps"; God is not imagined to dwell in the lacunae of contemporary scientific understanding.[28] It is not so much specific facts that fill one with wonder, but rather, as Heschel puts it, "the fact that there are facts at all." In more philosophical terms, for Heschel, religious awareness begins with a sense of the sheer contingency of being. God is to be discerned, in other words, not primarily in interruptions of the natural order, but in the astounding fact that the natural order exists at all. "To the Biblical mind," Heschel writes, "nature, order are not an answer but a problem: why is there order, being, at all?"[29] At the root of Heschel's sense of wonder, then, is a preoccupation with this question: Why is there something rather than nothing?[30] "We are amazed," he writes, "at seeing anything at all; amazed not only at particular values and things but *at the unexpectedness of being as such,* at the fact that there is being at all."[31] But in the very question of why there is something rather than nothing, Denys Turner argues, there is already an implicit assertion: "It is a state of affairs which might not have been, that's the sort of world we have: that it exists at all has been *brought about.*"[32] For Turner, then, as for Heschel, in the very experience of wonder, one is already "beginning to say" that the world is created, that "existence comes to us as pure gift."[33] Or, as Heschel puts it, "Our question is in essence . . . an answer in disguise."[34] The notion that existence is a Russellian "brute fact" would be simply incomprehensible to Heschel; for him, existence is an irreducible mystery, and, as we shall see, all that exists alludes to its transcendent source.

Another way to think about wonder, according to Heschel, is as "our response to the sublime."[35] Crucially, however, for Heschel, the sublime is not to be identified with the vast or the terrible. On the contrary, "the sublime may be sensed in every grain of sand, in every drop of water." But what is it, exactly? The sublime, for Heschel, is "that which we see and are unable to convey. It is the silent allusion of things to a meaning greater than themselves. It is that which all things ultimately stand for."[36] This sense that all being is somehow allusive to inexpressible transcendent meaning is a pivotal piece of Heschel's conception of wonder; we can already see that according to Heschel, wonder necessarily involves sensitivity to transcendence.[37]

Heschel is careful to distinguish between "the sublime as such," and the sublime as biblical man perceives it: "To him the sublime is but a way in which things react to the presence of God."[38] Thus, biblical man's response to sensing the sublime is not horror, but rather "eagerness to exalt and to praise the Maker of the world."[39] Now, if wonder is the human response to the sublime, then for biblical man, the sense of wonder is already pregnant with perception of the divine. But for human beings more generally, we might say that wonder contains (or perhaps simply *is*) a perception that all of reality alludes to some transcendent meaning, though that meaning may remain, at least at first, anonymous and mysterious.

In general, I would suggest, for Heschel, wonder constitutes a kind of pre-apprehension of God. Although one can have a sense of wonder without an attendant conscious, explicit awareness of God, the former is already the first step toward the latter: "Awareness of the divine," Heschel writes, "begins with wonder. . . . Wonder or radical amazement, the state of maladjustment to words and notions, is . . . a prerequisite for an authentic awareness of that which is."[40] When wonder ripens into a full awareness of God, according to Heschel, we arrive at awe.[41] Thus, we might say that whereas wonder contains implicit reference to God, awe contains explicit reference to Him. Awe is, Heschel writes, "our relationship to God." Like wonder, awe, for Heschel, is not an emotion, but "a way of understanding . . . an act of insight into a meaning greater than ourselves."[42] Again, although Heschel can be less than consistent in his use of terms,[43] I think we can say in general that if, as we have seen, wonder is our response to the sense that reality alludes to something beyond it, awe, in turn, is our response to the realization that it is God to whom reality alludes. "Awe is," Heschel avers, "an intuition for the creaturely dignity of all things and their preciousness to God; a realization that things not only are what they are but also stand, however remotely, for something absolute. Awe is a sense for the transcendence, for the reference everywhere to Him who is beyond all things."[44]

Connected to the sublime is the reality of mystery. One of the central insights of biblical Wisdom literature, Heschel insists, is the realization that "what *is*, is more than what you see; what *is*, is 'far off and deep, exceedingly deep.' Being is mysterious."[45] The existence of the world is a mystery; the Wisdom writers teach that "the world of the known is a world unknown; hiddenness, mystery. What stirred their souls [says Heschel] was neither the hidden nor the apparent, but the hidden in the apparent; not the order but the mystery of the order that prevails in the universe."[46] Heschel is quick to emphasize that the term "mystery" describes not an aspect of human subjectivity, but rather an essential dimension of objective reality itself. "The mystery," Heschel states plainly, "is an ontological category."[47] It is an aspect of the world, in other words, rather than a construct of the perceiving mind. If wonder is a subjective state, the mystery is its objective correlative. Wonder, in other words, is a response to the mystery, which is a fact about the world itself. Indeed, just as wonder is primarily a response to reality as a whole, the mystery, according to Heschel, is not a limited corner of reality, "not an exception but an air that lies all about being, a spiritual setting of reality, not something apart, but a dimension of all existence."[48] Defying the subjectivist challenge, according to which what religion accesses is limited to the human mind, Heschel asserts unequivocally that he is speaking of the world, and not merely of human consciousness:

> What the sense of the ineffable perceives is something *objective* which cannot be conceived by the mind nor captured by imagination or feeling, something real which, by its very essence, is beyond the reach of thought and feeling. What we are primarily aware of is not our self, our inner mood, but a transubjective situation, in regard to which our ability fails. Subjective is the *manner*, not the *matter* of our perception. What we perceive is objective in the sense of being independent of and corresponding to our perception. Our radical amazement responds to the mystery, but does not produce it. You and I have not invented the grandeur of the sky nor endowed man with the mystery of birth and death. We do not create the ineffable, we encounter it.[49]

Mystery as such cannot be overcome: "The mysteries of nature and history challenged and often startled the Biblical man," Heschel writes, "but he knew that it was beyond his power to penetrate them."[50] Contra Hegel, who famously proclaimed that with the emergence of Greek religion, "the enigma is solved," Heschel insists that "to the Jewish mind the ultimate enigmas remain inscrutable."[51] Indeed, he writes, "The mystery of God remains for ever sealed to man."[52]

But Heschel wants to avoid a modern paganism which deifies mystery, or which worships a God who is perpetually shrouded in absolute mystery.[53] Thus, he assures his readers that *"God is a mystery, but the mystery is not God. He is a revealer of mysteries."*[54] In a passage to which we shall have occasion to return later, Heschel writes that although at one level "the extreme hiddenness of God is a fact of constant awareness[,] yet His concern, His guidance, His will, His commandment are revealed to man and capable of being experienced by him."[55] Thus, although we cannot penetrate the mystery, neither do we deify it. Instead, Heschel writes, "We worship Him who in His wisdom surpasses all mysteries."[56]

A central aspect of Heschel's theology begins to emerge here. On the one hand, human beings are capable of wonder, and with it, as we shall see, of profound religious insight. And yet there are limits to what insight alone, no matter how carefully cultivated, can achieve. In order to know the One who is beyond the mystery, we depend on divine assistance. Human beings can achieve first glimmers of the divine, but in order to know more, we need revelation. Now, to be sure, as we shall see in the next chapter, revelation does not solve the mystery, does not give us access to God's essence, but it does nevertheless provide us with both a window on the divine pathos and a path to living in accord with it.

Heschel's intuition that the world alludes to something beyond it is consonant with[57] the biblical insistence that "what is given is not the ultimate."[58] Nature itself is not ultimate, but is only an allusion to the ultimate: "The Biblical mind is deeply aware that the ultimate, God, is beyond the given. What is given is . . . created by Him Who is not given. . . . [In the Bible] a certainty prevails that for all its greatness the universe is as nothing compared with its Maker."[59] Indeed, Heschel tells us, "One of the great achievements of the prophets was the repudiation of nature as an object of adoration."[60] According to Heschel, there is thus an irreconcilable conflict between the Greek-Romantic legacy, with its "religious enthusiasm for nature," on the one hand, and the prophetic tradition, with its resolute desanctification of nature, on the other. We are thus faced with a stark choice: "The Western man must choose between the worship of God and the worship of nature."[61] According to Heschel, biblical theology is wholly incompatible with pantheism,[62] according to which nature itself *is* God, as opposed to an *allusion to* God. For pantheism, God is "essentially immanent and in no way transcendent"; for monotheism (both biblical and Heschelian), in contrast, God is "essentially transcendent and only accidentally immanent."[63] Nature is, according to Heschel, "not a part of God but rather a fulfillment of His will."[64] The task before humanity is to learn to "lift up your eyes on high and see who created these"[65] (Isaiah 40:26)—that is, to see through nature to the God who brought it into being.[66]

But the transcendent God is still immanent, even if "only accidentally." According to Heschel, "the glory" is the presence and goodness of God.[67] Tragically, although "the earth is filled with the glory . . . it is not filled with knowledge of the glory."[68] The messianic vision, however, is that one day "the earth shall *be filled with the knowledge of the glory of the Lord,* as the waters cover the sea."[69] In other words, Heschel maintains, the transcendent God to whom the world alludes is also immanent, even if His presence is currently concealed. And yet, Heschel insists, "The glory is not entirely unknown to us."[70] Indeed, the central reason we fail to perceive it is that "we fail to wonder, we fail to respond to the presence."[71] This last sentence contains a significant ambiguity: if, as seems to be the case, the two phrases are meant as appositives, then we have come upon a maximalist conception of wonder—the sense of wonder seems already to encompass within it an awareness of the presence of God, and is thus more than a mere pre-apprehension. The absence of wonder, conversely, is not the *cause of* the failure of perception; it is essentially *synonymous with* the failure of perception. But perhaps we should instead read the second phrase as a consequence of the first: we fail to respond to the presence *because* we fail to wonder. Wonder is thus what makes response possible, but it itself is not yet full awareness of—let alone response to—the divine presence.

Wonder, for Heschel, is decidedly "not a state of esthetic enjoyment." On the contrary, he insists, authentic wonder always carries a question and a challenge within it. "Endless wonder is endless tension,"[72] Heschel writes, because intrinsic to the experience of wonder is the sense that we are "being asked the ultimate question. . . . In spite of our pride, in spite of our acquisitiveness, we are driven by an awareness that something is asked of us."[73] That ineffable question "demands our whole being as an answer."[74] It is in awareness of this question, Heschel tells us, that religion is born.[75] If wonder is the state of being asked, then, crucially, "it is not a feeling for the mystery of living, or a sense of awe, wonder, or fear, which is at the root of religion; but rather the question of what to do with the feeling for the mystery of living, what to do with awe, wonder, and fear."[76] Wonder is the "state of our being asked."[77] When faced with the ultimate question, only "arrogance and callousness . . . would enable us to refuse" to answer.[78] This sense that "something is asked of us" is, for Heschel, the portal in human experience that opens us to the possibility of receiving revelation.

Interwoven with the sense of wonder, for Heschel, then, is the sense of what he calls "indebtedness": "The soul is endowed with a sense of indebtedness, and wonder, awe, and fear unlock that sense of indebtedness."[79] When human beings approach the world with wonder, Heschel suggests, we cannot but ask: "How shall we ever reciprocate for breathing and thinking, for sight and hearing, for love and achievement?"[80] The "content" of indebtedness is thus "gratitude for a gift received."[81] In general, Heschel may prefer the word "indebtedness" to "gratitude" because whereas the latter can be interpreted as a mere feeling, the former unequivocally conveys a sense of duty toward one's benefactor. As Heschel puts it in *WM*: "To the sense of indebtedness, the meaning of existence lies in reciprocity. In receiving a pleasure, we must return a prayer; in attaining a success, we radiate compassion. . . . The world is such that in its face one senses owingness rather than ownership."[82] According to Heschel, a sense of indebtedness is "a constitutive feature of being human. To eradicate it would be to destroy what is human in man."[83]

* * *

According to Heschel, there are two possible orientations to living, "the way of wonder" and "the way of expediency." In the latter approach, "we accumulate information in order to dominate"; in the former, "we deepen our appreciation in order to respond."[84] The way of expediency closes us off to what is outside us; the way of wonder, in contrast, awakens us to the reality of our "living in the great fellowship of all beings."[85] The former is animated by our mind, which "specializes in producing knives" that "cut . . . the world in two: in a thing and in a self; in an object and in a subject that conceives the object as distinct from itself."[86] The latter, in contrast, is guided by the soul, which leads us to commune rather than divide: "*To* our knowledge," Heschel writes, "the world and 'I' are two, an object and a subject; but *within* our wonder the world and the 'I' are one in being, in eternity."[87] Or, as Heschel also puts it, when we are attuned to the mystery that "lies about all being . . . we do not wonder *at* things any more; we wonder *with* all things."[88]

What this means is that for Heschel, all of life is a struggle between self-assertion (the way of expediency), on the one hand, and self-transcendence (the way of wonder), on the other: "There is . . . a perpetual tension in man between the focus of the self and the goal that lies beyond the self. . . . Animal in man is driven to concentrate on the satisfaction of needs; spiritual in man is the will to serve higher ends, and in serving ends he transcends his needs."[89] In life, Heschel avers, "we are attached to two centers: to the focus of our self and to the focus of God. Driven by two forces, we have both the impulse to acquire, to enjoy, to possess and the urge to respond, to yield, to give."[90] Crucially, human beings do have the momentous capacity to choose self-transcendence.[91] "*The grand premise of religion*," Heschel writes, is that "*man is able to surpass himself.*"[92] Indeed, the possibility of self-transcendence is already implicit in the experience of wonder. Through the latter, we learn "not to measure meaning in terms of our own mind, but to sense a meaning infinitely greater than ourselves."[93] In the experience of wonder, we focus not on finding answers to our questions, but rather on responding to the sense that "something is asked of us." Wonder, in other words, is very different from curiosity; if the latter allows us to remain at the center, as the questioning subject, the former decenters us, putting us in the position of responding to something outside us rather than fulfilling hungers within us. Wonder, then, "reflects a situation in which the mind stands face to face with the mystery rather than with its own concepts. . . . A genuine insight rends the enclosure of the heart and bestows on man the power to rise above himself."[94] There is an unbridgeable divide between these two ways of being: "The will to power and the will to believe are mutually exclusive. For in our striving for power we arrogate to ourselves what belongs to God and suppress the claim of His presence."[95] God's presence is a call to self-transcendence.[96] Blindness to God's presence, accordingly, at once stems from and leads to unbridled "self-assertion."

It is on this basis that Heschel declares that "indifference to the sublime wonder of living is the root of sin."[97] How does indifference to wonder lead to sin? Wonder, as we have seen, is a state in which I feel compelled by something other than myself. Indifference to wonder, in contrast, is a form of self-enclosure, in which the only criterion of value is what it useful for the fulfillment of my own desires and aspirations. In closing myself off to the possibility of wonder, in other words, I effectively shut out any claim that that which is outside me makes upon me. This process leads me to devalue everything other than myself, and gives me permission, as it were, to neglect—or worse, to manipulate and exploit—the other, and ultimately God as well.[98] It is this self-enclosure, for Heschel, which lies at the root of sin. Now, were Heschel a Christian theologian, he might well be tempted to say that "indifference to the sublime wonder of living [simply] *is* sin," but instead he says that such indifference is "*the root of* sin." Ever the Jewish thinker, Heschel wants sin to be an action rather than (merely) a state of being. Sin, in other words, is the manifestation of indifference to wonder (and thereby to that which is not me) in the actions that I undertake. If, as Heschel suggests, "religion is the result of what man does with his ultimate wonder,"[99] then sin, by implication, is what he does with his lack of wonder.

Let us look more closely at the nature of self-transcendence as Heschel imagines it. Heschel insists that "self-centeredness is the tragic misunderstanding of our destiny and existence. For man, to be human is an existential tautology. In order to be a man, man must be more than a man." Indeed, he writes, "A vital requirement of human life is transitive concern, a regard for others, in addition to a reflexive concern, an intense regard for itself."[100] Self-transcendence is constitutive of what it means to be human. "If man is not more than human," Heschel avers, "then he is less than human";[101] "A man exclusively concerned with his self is a beast."[102] Thus, without self-transcendence, we are in some sense not yet human: "The shift from the animal to the human dimension takes place when . . . [the human being] begins to acknowledge . . . other selves as ends, to respond to their needs *even regardless of personal expediency.*"[103] Accordingly, joy and fulfillment result from moments of achieving that potential: "There is no joy for the self within the self. Joy is found in giving rather than in acquiring; in serving rather than in taking."[104]

For Heschel, it is the sense of the ineffable that enables us to look "beyond the horizon of personal interests, helping us to realize the absurdity of regarding the ego as an end"; indeed, such consciousness has the potential to "tear selfishness to shreds."[105] When this happens, "conformity to the ego is no longer our exclusive concern, for we become concerned with another problem—how to fulfill what is asked of us."[106] The belief in our capacity for "eliminating self-regard" is rooted in the metaphysical realization that "the self is not the hub but a spoke, neither its own beginning nor its own end."[107]

Ultimately, for Heschel, self-transcendence entails a fundamental existential re-orientation, a new understanding of selfhood and subjectivity. The transformation begins when we admit that we are a mystery to ourselves: "What we are, we cannot say; what we become, we cannot grasp. . . . What we face in penetrating the self is the paradox of not knowing what we presume to know so well."[108] In being attentive to this reality, we discover that "the mystery is not there, while we are here. The truth is we are all steeped in it, imbibed with it; we are, partly, it."[109] We are, at bottom, not what we think: the self is not an "isolated entity, confined in itself." This common way of envisioning the self is a "monstrous deceit"; in reality, the self is "something transcendent in disguise."[110] My life is not my own creation, but rather a "transcendent loan" bestowed upon me;[111] existence is "not a property but a trust."[112] From these realizations, a new consciousness emerges: "I have neither initiated nor conceived [the] worth and meaning [of my life]. The essence of what I am is not mine. *I am what is not mine.*"[113]

Once our most deeply held assumptions about ourselves have been dislodged, we discover that, as Heschel puts it, "ultimately man is not a subject but an *object.*"[114] Turning Descartes on his head (without, however, ever mentioning his name), Heschel insists that "when we are overtaken with the spirit of the ineffable, there is no logical self left to ask the question or the mental power to stand as the judge with God as an object, about the existence of whom I am to decide. . . . There is no self to say: I think that . . . "[115] Our usual cognitive presuppositions are overturned as we come to understand that God "can never become the mere object of our thought." On the contrary: "In thinking of Him, we realize that it is through Him that we think of Him. Thus, we must think of Him as the subject of all, as the life of our life, as the mind of our mind." Whatever stature we have is not in being thinkers, but in being thought of: God is "the Knower and we are the known . . . to be means to be thought of by Him."[116]

Cartesian philosophy, in other words, is a form of self-assertion—it asserts the self and questions everything else. But true self-transcendence utterly rejects these premises: it begins with God and questions the self. God is the asker, and we are the asked; God is the thinker, and we are the thought-of; God is the subject, and we are the object of His knowledge and thought. The aspiration and task of prayer, for example, is thus "not to know but to be known to Him, to expose ourselves to Him rather than Him to us; not to judge and to assert but to listen and to be judged by Him."[117] More generally, Heschel writes, "God-awareness is not an act of God being known to man; it is the awareness of man's being known by God. In thinking about Him we are thought by Him."[118] The consequence of all this, Heschel insists, is that in moments of "radical insight . . . we realize that the question we ask is a question we are being asked; that man's question about God is God's question of man."[119]

On Heschel's account, then, the self has neither ontological nor epistemological priority: life and knowledge begin with God. To accept Descartes' assumptions is to lose the battle for self-transcendence before it has even begun. This is the transformation Heschel seeks to inspire: "The transition from obliviousness to an awareness of God . . . going behind self-consciousness and questioning the self and all its cognitive pretensions."[120] Humanity's cognitive pretensions, it seems, are part and parcel of its ethical and religious failures—in all the domains of our life, we are assertive rather than responsive. For the possibility of ethical and theological self-transcendence to gain any traction, ontological and epistemological self-transcendence are required as well. To borrow an image from Dror Bondi: just as the world is not an object to be exploited, so are we not subjects entitled to do the exploiting.[121]

For biblical man, as we have seen, wonder is the "starting point in facing reality."[122] But modern man, Heschel laments, has lost his sense of wonder; tragically, according to Heschel, "the awareness of grandeur and the sublime is all but gone from the modern mind."[123] Instead of cultivating a sense of appreciation for the sheer wondrousness of being, modern man simply takes the world for granted, and, what is worse, treats it as little more than a vast reservoir of information and opportunity for utilization. "Our age," Heschel laments, "is one in which usefulness is thought to be the chief merit of nature.... Man has ... become primarily a tool-making animal, and the world is now a gigantic tool box for the satisfaction of his needs."[124] "In our technological age," Heschel adds, "man could not conceive of this world as anything but material for his own fulfillment."[125] Indeed, a crucial mark of the religious emptiness of the modern world is the fact that "there is no education for the sublime. We teach the children how to measure, how to weigh. We fail to teach them how to revere, how to sense wonder and awe."[126]

Although Heschel does not make this point explicitly, I think that for him there are two stages in the death of wonder. The first, as we have seen, is "routinization" and the perennial temptation to "take the world for granted." This insidious snare is an ever-present danger in human life and is thus not an exclusively modern problem. The second stage, in contrast, is both distinctively modern (or so Heschel contends) and uniquely dangerous: human beings become crude instrumentalists who worship at the altar of expediency—the only question that interests them is whether and how the world can serve them. The deleterious consequences of the instrumentalization of the world are, for Heschel, not primarily esthetic, but rather ethical and theological. The decline of wonder spells the end of the sense for the transcendent, and this, in turn, means that modern man does not feel called or compelled by anything or anyone outside himself. "Forfeit your sense of awe, let your conceit diminish your ability to revere," Heschel writes, "and the universe becomes a marketplace for you."[127] It is this relentless self-assertion that has made unprecedented callousness and cruelty possible in modern times, and that has thus brought humanity such unimaginable devastation: the constant "expansion of man's needs which is . . . brought about by technological and social advancement . . . may sweep away civilization itself, since the pressure of needs turned into aggressive interests is the constant cause of wars and increases in direct proportion to technological progress."[128] Indeed, Heschel argues, the "essential predicament of man has assumed a peculiar urgency in our time, living as we do in a civilization where factories were established in order to exterminate millions of men, women, and children; where soap was made of human flesh. . . . Modern man may be characterized as a being who is callous to catastrophes."[129] This, I would suggest, is what Heschel has in mind when he warns that "mankind will not perish for want of information; but only for want of appreciation."[130]

Another way of characterizing the problem of modernity as Heschel sees it is to say that in a culture concerned with expediency and exploitation, "the sense of indebtedness is first blunted and then swept away by pride and the love of property and power."[131] When functioning properly, religion both emerges from and reinforces our all-too-precarious sense of indebtedness. Hence, again, modernity's need of religion, which can restore our sense of obligation and our willingness to serve "ends that are in need of us."[132] It is thus the sense of being called upon to respond, which lies at the very heart of religious awareness, that is also the best antidote to what ails modern man, in that it represents a fundamental alternative to our relentless self-assertion. To take the sense that "something is asked of us" seriously is to understand that at its deepest levels, life is not about *claims I make* so much as it is about responding to *claims made upon me.* This systematic re-orientation is arguably what is most distinctive about religion, which is why, according to Heschel, the latter is so urgent and indispensable if modern man is to overcome his imprisonment within the culture of expediency and self-assertion.[133]

But there is an additional danger to the culture of expediency: our treatment of the world as a vast toolbox ineluctably turns in on us, and we ourselves are abased by our relentless exploitation. "He who sets out to employ the realities of life as means for satisfying his own desires will soon forfeit his freedom and be degraded to a mere tool," Heschel writes. "Acquiring things, he becomes enslaved to them; in subduing others, he loses his own soul. It is as if unchecked covetousness were double-faced; a sneer and subtle vengeance behind a captivating smile."[134] There is something fundamental at work here: "My view of the world and my understanding of the self determine each other," and, as a result, "The complete manipulation of the world results in the complete instrumentalization of the self."[135] Uncurbed self-assertion, then, paradoxically but inexorably spells the ultimate dissolution of the self.

So low has modern man sunk, according to Heschel, that he has turned even religion into a mere resource for the fulfillment of his ends. "In a technological society," Heschel writes, "when religion becomes a function, piety too is an instrument to satisfy [man's] needs."[136] In modernity, God, too, has been reduced to a mere tool: modern man "postulated the existence of a Power that would serve as a guarantee for his self-fulfillment, as if God were a henchman to cater to man's aspirations and help him draw the utmost out of life."[137] Such religion is a sacrilege, a brazen attempt to turn God into an object rather than a subject: "He who seeks God to suit his doubts, to appease his skepticism or to satisfy his curiosity, fails to find the whereabouts of the issue."[138] Crucially, for Heschel, "God is not an explanation of the world's enigmas or a guarantee for our salvation. He is an eternal challenge, an urgent demand. He is not a problem to be solved but a question addressed to us as individuals, as nations, as mankind."[139] If human beings are to have any hope in modernity, they will have to be reminded that "the essence of religion does not lie in the satisfaction of a human need. As long as man sees religion as a source of satisfaction for his own needs, it is not God whom he serves but his own self."[140]

It is difficult to overstate this point: wonder, for Heschel, forces us to recognize that we are not the only source and judge of value in the world. The collapse of wonder, accordingly, can only have perilous consequences. A world without wonder is a world devoid of self-transcendence, and thus a world closed off to the presence of God:

> Out of a system of ideas where knowledge is power, where values are a synonym for needs, where the pyramid of being is turned upside down—it is hard to find a way to an awareness of God. If the world is only power to us and we are all

absorbed in a gold rush, then the only god we may come upon is the golden calf. Nature as a toolbox is a world that does not point beyond itself. It is when nature is sensed as mystery and grandeur that it calls upon us to look beyond it.[141]

A world without God, for Heschel, will have no brake on human exploitation and brutality: "Technological progress creates more problems than it solves. Efficiency experts or social engineering will not redeem humanity.... Religion, therefore, with its demands and visions, is not a luxury but a matter of life and death."[142] One might even say that according to Heschel, humanity's need for religion grows in direct proportion to its power to inflict pain and suffering: "Because of his immense power, man is potentially the most wicked of beings. He often has a passion for cruel deeds that only fear of God can soothe, suffocating flushes of envy that only holiness can ventilate."[143] It is religion alone, Heschel insists, that can rein in humanity's worst impulses: "Unless we make [the world] an altar to God, it is invaded by demons."[144]

According to Heschel, even philosophy, ostensibly a search for wisdom, is limited in that it is still a pursuit of answers to questions posed *by* human beings, rather than an attempt to respond to questions posed *to* them. Thus, Heschel implicitly argues, it is religion rather than philosophy that is needed in order to reorient human life:

> There is an ... essential difference between the issue of God in speculation and the issue of God in religion. The first is a question *about* God; the second is a question *from* God. The first is concerned with a solution to the problem, whether there is a God and, if there is a God, what is His nature? The second is concerned with our personal answer to the problem that is addressed to us in the facts and events of the world and our own experience.... To the speculative mind, the world is an enigma; to the religious mind, the world is a challenge.... The first is concerned with finding an answer to the question: what is the cause of being? The second, with giving an answer to the question: what is asked of us?[145]

But Heschel's anxiety runs deeper. On the one hand, as we have seen, he insists that humanity desperately needs religion in order to curb its cruelest impulses, in order to instill some shred of sensitivity to the reality and needs of the other. "Irreligion," he writes, "is not opiate but poison."[146] But on the other hand, Heschel is all too keenly aware that religion, too, can end up reinforcing rather than mitigating human selfishness:

> Even more frustrating than the fact that evil is real, mighty and tempting is the fact that it thrives so well in the disguise of the good, that it can draw its nutriment from the life of the holy. In this world, it seems, the holy and the unholy do not exist apart, but are mixed, interrelated and confounded. It is a world where idols may be rich in beauty, and where the worship of God may be tinged with wickedness. It was not the lack of religion but the perversion of it that the prophets of Israel denounced.[147]

"Even religion," Heschel laments, "can be fraud."[148] Indeed, in a late essay, Heschel pleads, "Let there be an end to the separation of church and God . . . of religion and justice, of prayer and compassion."[149] In the end, though, for Heschel, the desperate need for religion seems to outweigh its dangers, no matter how real. Religion is an urgent necessity, even if it must also be scrutinized for its own dangerous potentials.[150]

Heschel's distress in the face of technological modernity is to some extent resonant with Heidegger's. According to the latter, technology has dramatically changed the way human beings interact with the world. In the modern world, governed as it is by what Heidegger labels "calculative thinking," everything is available for manipulation and exploitation. Everything, in other words, is reduced to mere "standing-reserve."[151] As Richard Polt astutely observes:

> When we look at today's language, we can see that there is something to what Heidegger is saying. Natural things are routinely called 'natural resources.' . . . Human beings are 'human resources.' Books and artworks become 'information resources'; and writing becomes 'word processing,' as if language, too, were just a resource to be manipulated.[152]

Explaining the damage wrought by technological thinking, Heidegger comments: "The world now appears as an object open to the attacks of calculative thought. . . . Nature becomes a gigantic gasoline station, an energy source for modern technology and industry."[153] At the end of a famous passage describing a modern hydroelectric power plant on the Rhine, Heidegger laments that even the great river now appears before us as a mere resource, or, as he memorably puts it, "as an object on call for inspection by a tour group ordered there by the vacation industry."[154]

There is no *telos* to all this exploitation; it is, at some level, pure self-assertion. Thus unleashed, technology spins out of control, operating on a logic all its own: "The energy concealed in nature is unlocked, what is unlocked is transformed, what is transformed is stored up, what is stored up is distributed, and what is distributed is switched about ever anew." The consequence of all this is that "everywhere everything" is treated exclusively as resource. As a result, we lose our capacity to inter-act with the world in any other way. "Whatever stands by in the sense of standing-reserve," Heidegger warns, "no longer stands over against us as an object."[155]

It is vital to emphasize, however, that what is so problematic for Heidegger is not technology itself. Instead, as he puts it, "the *essence of technology* . . . is the danger."[156] This essence, which Heidegger labels "*Gestell*" (or "enframing"), is the insistence that there is nothing that can-not be subjected to calculative thinking.[157] The danger of technology lies, in other words, in the way it forces us to relate to the world: if, for Hei-degger, every "revealing" is also a concealing, the problem with *Gestell* is that it does not allow us to see the world through any lens besides the calculative-instrumental. The problem is thus not technology per se, but rather "the technological understanding of being,"[158] and the danger is that "calculative thinking may someday come to be accepted and prac-ticed as the only way of thinking."[159] This mode of thinking extends, as we have already seen Polt point out, far beyond technology as such, reaching into virtually every domain of life. To state this somewhat dif-ferently: for Heidegger, technology is, first and foremost, a way of "reveal-ing" things, not just of making them. It is a world-picture rather than a method. And it is the former that constitutes such a peril for humanity.

But why is the calculative approach so destructive? In our focus on exploiting and manipulating the world, we lose any sense of openness and receptivity, and we are no longer sensitive to meaning, to transcen-dence, and to the sheer mystery of Being.[160] We lose sight of any and all other ways we can encounter beings. Whatever else it is, *Gestell* is also, as George Pattison notes,

> necessarily a concealing, a continuous closing-down or covering-over of other possibilities of representing or living in the world. Despite the prodigious ex-planatory and technological success of science, it is, Heidegger believes, an essentially limiting, one-sided, and one-track way of approaching the world. In terms of enframing itself, the self-limitation is necessary, but when we forget that there is just such a limitation, that science's truth is also untruth, imagining that our one-sidedness is omnicompetence, then we are en route to a rapid im-poverishment of the world, of experience, of language.[161]

One inevitable outgrowth of all this is that man himself comes "to be taken as standing-reserve." Rather than standing outside the logic of technology, human beings are subsumed by it; we become, ineluctably, part of the very stockpile that we have been so busy building. Although we "posture as lord[s] of the earth," this is mere illusion—through the technological enframing, we lose not only the world, but ourselves as well.[162]

And yet despite the obvious similarities between Heschel's critique of modernity and Heidegger's—both lament the culture of expediency and manipulation (not technology itself, in other words, but the ulti-mately reductive technological way of seeing), and both point to another path, constituted by openness and receptivity—there are crucial differ-ences as well. For one thing, Heschel's attempt to restore wonder to its rightful place is aimed at generating responsiveness to the commanding presence of the biblical God; the openness Heidegger advocates is to Being, and to "divinities," surely not to the God of Israel.[163] But perhaps even more fundamentally, Heschel's critique of technological moder-nity is at once ethical and theological (the two, for him, are inextricably interwoven), whereas Heidegger's is . . . something else. For the latter, the true danger of calculative thinking is not "the manipulation of human beings," but rather the "obscuring of Being" it brings about.[164] However one wishes to characterize this concern, it is surely not about ethics. As John Caputo notes, Heidegger is seemingly unconcerned with "hospi-tality and justice"; instead, he is "monomaniacally preoccupied with a discourse on clearing and unconcealment, manifestation and shining beauty."[165] Or, as John Macquarrie states rather simply, "It could be com-plained with some justice that from his early thinking onward, [Hei-degger] consistently avoided ethical questions."[166] In other words, al-though their assessments of modernity in some ways mirror one another, the animating passions behind Heschel's and Heidegger's critiques are quite different, as are their answers to the ultimate question: openness to what? Whereas Heschel advocates a return to the God of the prophets, Heidegger gestures much more amorphously toward a new relationship to Being. Whereas the former is especially distraught over the ethical consequences of technological modernity, the latter seems consistently indifferent to them.

Heschel's suspicion of attempts to make God serve human needs is also reminiscent of Heidegger's critique of "onto-theology." In order to draw out this connection (however briefly), it is important first to achieve some clarity about what Heidegger does and does not mean by onto-theology. For Heidegger, onto-theology is a label for what happens when philosophy appeals to God as "a theme of its discourse on its terms and in the service of its project,"[167] or, as Heidegger himself puts it, the God of onto-theology is allowed in, as it were, "only insofar as philosophy of its own accord and by its own nature, requires and determines how the deity enters into it."[168] In other words, the God of onto-theology is enlisted to answer human philosophical questions, to serve as the ultimate explanation of the questions that perplex us. Merold Westphal puts it with characteristic lucidity when he writes that for Heidegger, God is not "The One Who Makes Our System Work."[169] It is not hard to see that in all such systems, God is made to serve human ends, rather than the other way around. Implicit in this is that the God of onto-theology is a mere human construct, little more than a metaphysical idol. Moreover, as Heidegger famously points out, human beings "can neither pray nor sacrifice to this god. Before the *causa sui,* man can neither fall to his knees in awe nor can he play music and dance before this god."[170] The god of onto-theology—an idolatrous projection of human reason—is thus religiously otiose.[171]

Now that we have some sense of what Heidegger does mean by onto-theology, we can say something about what he does *not* mean. It would be a fundamental mistake, as Westphal has pointed out in a variety of writings, to insist that Heidegger's critique of onto-theology is meant to sweep away any and all talk about a transcendent God. As he acidly puts it, in much of contemporary academic discourse,

> "onto-theology" becomes the abracadabra by which a triumphalist secularism makes the world immune to any God who resembles the personal Creator, Lawgiver, and Merciful Savior of Jewish, or Christian, or Muslim monotheism. The only religion that escapes the Lord High Executioners who speak as Heidegger's prophets is religion that is pagan/polytheistic, pantheistic, or a/theistic (with or without the slash).[172]

The problem with such readings of Heidegger, Westphal insists, is that his own writings simply do not support it. Heidegger is clearly dismissive of philosophical systems that invoke God in order to eliminate mystery, and thus provide us with a totally intelligible universe. But Westphal rightly notes that, as a rule, Christian theology—and, we should add, Jewish and Muslim—do not pretend to dissolve mystery and offer us total intelligibility. On the contrary, as we have already seen, according to Heschel, Jewish theology serves to restore and intensify the sense of ineffable mystery that is available everywhere and at all times. To state this somewhat differently: Heidegger's opponent when he rails against onto-theology is the Western metaphysical tradition as he imagines it, beginning with Aristotle. But the "Pascalian character" of Heidegger's critique is all too frequently "overlooked"; the latter offers "an invitation and challenge to theology to be itself, to refuse to sell its birthright for a mess of philosophical pottage."[173] As we shall see at length in chapter 4, it is precisely such a challenge that Heschel takes up. As Westphal writes, "One could quite legitimately have religious rather than secular motives for offering a critique like Heidegger's." Much of Christian theology—and, again, Jewish as well—affirms that "to posit God is to affirm mystery, not to make everything clear. . . . Christian [and Jewish] theology, taken as a . . . whole, is more a sustained critique of onto-theology than an instance of it."[174] In other words, Heidegger's attack on onto-theological thinking "neither presupposes nor argues for the unreality of an uncreated Creator."[175] To be absolutely clear: I am not suggesting that Heidegger was a biblical monotheist; far from it.[176] I am merely pointing out, following Westphal, that the former's dismissal of onto-theology need not entail the rejection of the God of Israel.[177] On the contrary, that very dismissal may be what enables a genuine return to the God of Israel—not least in that it would save that God from what Heschel thought of as the ravages of Greek metaphysics.[178]

One final point: for Heidegger, the critique of onto-theology is inextricably linked to the critique of technology. Just as modern technology places the world at humanity's practical disposal, so onto-theology places God at its conceptual disposal. As we have seen, this is very much the case for Heschel, too. When the latter insists that "God is not an explanation of the world's enigmas," or that He is not "a henchman to cater to man's aspirations and help him draw the utmost out of life," he is articulating a challenge to modern theology very much in line with Heidegger's own. And when Heschel heaps scorn on any notion of a God who offers "promises of salvation and immortality as a dessert to the pleasant repast on earth,"[179] he is dismissing something we might call a crude cousin of onto-theology—a God, in other words, who responds to our questions instead of our responding to His.

In ways strikingly reminiscent of Heschel, recent writers on wonder have emphasized the link between wonder, on the one hand, and the transcendence of instrumental thinking, on the other. Thus, for example, philosopher Martha Nussbaum writes that the emotion of wonder "responds to the pull of the object, and one might say that in it the subject is maximally aware of the value of the object and only minimally aware, if at all, of its relationship to her own plans."[180] Wonder is, thus, according to Nussbaum, "as non-eudaimonistic as an emotion can be," in that it makes no reference to "my important goals and projects."[181] Psychologist Robert Fuller focuses again and again on what he considers the twin functions of wonder—to "induce receptivity and openness,"[182] and to lead us to "suspend utilitarian calculations."[183] Wonder, he writes, can facilitate what Ernest Schactel characterizes as "allocentric" (that is, other-centered) rather than "androcentric" (self-centered) perception.[184] Taking us beyond "everyday utilitarian rationality,"[185] wonder leads both to a deeper sense of compassion and empathy for others,[186] and to an intensified search for "meanings that somehow lie just beyond sensory appearances."[187] Indeed, in a state of wonder, "the surrounding world appears to be appreciated rather than manipulated."[188] Sounding ever more Heschelian, Fuller even goes so far as to maintain that wonder can bring us to "delight in a nonegoistic contemplation of the causal power that might make . . . vitality, beauty, and truth possible."[189] What all of this means, of course, is that for Fuller, as for Heschel, wonder leads to self-transcendence, to an overcoming of exclusive fealty to the stubbornly selfish "I."

At one point in his study of wonder, however, Fuller writes: "You can surely get through life without a developed sense of wonder, but you would lack certain sensibilities that enrich the texture of human existence."[190] Such a formulation would no doubt have struck Heschel as woefully anemic. As we have seen, Heschel insists that a sense of wonder is imperative for far more than "enrichment." Without wonder, there is self-enclosure and therefore, inevitably, exploitation and sin. A life without wonder, according to Heschel, is a life devoid of responsiveness and responsibility, whether to God or to others. It is not, therefore, a luxury, but an urgent and indispensable necessity for healing humanity's metastasizing callousness.

It is worth noting, in concluding this part of our discussion, one linguistic anomaly in Heschel's discussions of wonder: on several occasions, he speaks of "acts of wonder," suggesting, for example, that *"acts of wonder* are signs or symbols of what all things stand for,"[191] and that the question of God comes alive in "acts in which we are astir beyond words."[192] Similarly, Heschel writes, "Awe is itself an act of insight into a meaning greater than ourselves."[193] Why all this talk of wonder and awe as acts, rather than experiences? The key here, I think, is that acts are subject to our will, whereas emotions and experiences are not. Heschel's point is that wonder is not something that happens to us, but is, at least to some extent, something that we actively choose: responding to the world with wonder and thus attaining insight into God requires an exercise of freedom and agency. In one passage, Heschel tells us that "faith is not a product of the will. It occurs without intention, without will. . . . A decision of the will, the desire to believe, will not secure it."[194] And yet wonder, the "antecedent" of faith,[195] can be willed. And it is the former that makes the latter possible. This is what Heschel has in mind when he declares that "what we lack is not a will to believe but a will to wonder."[196] We cannot will ourselves to believe, but we can will ourselves to wonder. It is on that act of will, according to Heschel, that the future of humanity depends.[197]

* * *

One of the foundational assumptions of Heschel's worldview is that human beings are capable of a "pre-conceptual awareness" of God:

> Beyond our reasoning and beyond our believing, [Heschel writes,] there is a *preconceptual* faculty that senses the glory, the presence of the Divine. We do not perceive it. We have no knowledge; we only have an awareness. . . . We have no concept, nor can we develop a theory. All we have is an awareness of something that can be neither conceptualized nor symbolized.[198]

The sense of transcendent meaning, Heschel tells us in a similar vein, is a "nondiscursive perception."[199] Indeed, on countless occasions in his writings, Heschel reiterates his conviction that religious concepts, categories,

and ideas are secondary representations of what is given immediately—
and pre-linguistically—to human experience and awareness:

> Ultimate insight takes place on the presymbolic, preconceptual level of think-
> ing. It is difficult, indeed, to transpose insights phrased in the presymbolic lan-
> guage of inner events into the symbolic language of concepts. . . . The soul rarely
> knows how to raise its deeper secrets to discursive levels of the mind. We must
> not, therefore, equate the act of faith with its expression.[200]
>
> The encounter with reality does not take place on the level of concepts
> through the channels of logical categories; concepts are second thoughts. All
> conceptualization is symbolization, an act of accommodation of reality to the
> human mind. The living encounter with reality takes place on a level that pre-
> cedes conceptualization, on a level that is responsive, *immediate, preconceptual
> and presymbolic.*[201]

Heschel's hope, it seems, is that an immediate awareness of God can
serve to bypass the limits Kant had placed on rational, discursive human
knowing.[202] Somewhat simplistically, we could say that whereas Karl
Barth thought he could get around Kant from above, Heschel thinks he
can get around him from above *and below*—that is, through both revelation and intuition.

Heschel is inconsistent about whether what is given to immediate
awareness can be considered "knowledge" or not. On the one hand, he
affirms that "we have a certainty without knowledge: it is real without
being expressible."[203] But on the other hand, he asserts that "any genuine
encounter with reality is an encounter with the unknown, is an intuition
in which an awareness of the object is won, a rudimentary, *preconceptual*
knowledge."[204] What Heschel is struggling with here is the question
of whether a purportedly pre-linguistic, pre-conceptual awareness can
properly be considered "knowledge," or whether the latter is an irreducibly conceptual-linguistic category. Of course, whether or not it makes
sense to speak of "certainty without knowledge" is an open question.[205]
In the end, though, what is important for Heschel is his insistence that
religious awareness takes place at a level that is prior to our usual, verbal-
conceptual mode of thinking.[206]

In *MNA,* Heschel usefully suggests that "the ideas we acquire in our
wrestling with the ineffable" are better described as "understanding"
than "knowledge." "We know through induction or inference," Heschel
writes; "we understand through intuition." Knowledge suggests a purely

cognitive, even analytical act; understanding, in contrast, suggests relationship and engagement. One can have disinterested knowledge, but
there is no such thing as disinterested understanding. As Heschel puts it,
"Knowledge implies familiarity with, or even the mastery of, something;
understanding is an act of interpreting something which we only know
by its expression and through inner agreement with it."[207] In a similar
vein, in describing the prophets' encounter with God, Heschel writes,
"The prophets had no theory or 'idea' of God. What they had was an *understanding*.... They had an intuitive grasp of hidden meanings, of an un-
spoken message.... They sensed the signs of God's presence in history."
This was not "speculative knowledge," but rather understanding made
possible by the "pensive-intuitive attitude of the prophet to God."[208] Understanding, for Heschel, is what emerges from an intuition rooted in
openness, relatedness, and receptivity.

It is critical that we understand what Heschel is *not* saying: he is emphatically not suggesting that we begin with the experience of wonder
and proceed from there to infer the existence of God. On the contrary,
as Heschel insists time and again, the reality of God is an immediate apprehension, an "intuition" or "insight" rather than a logical inference:[209]

> We are often guilty of misunderstanding the nature of an assertion such as "God
> is." Such an assertion would constitute a leap if the assertion constituted an ad-
> dition to our ineffable awareness of God. The truth, however, is that to say "God
> is" means less than what our immediate awareness contains. *The statement "God
> is" is an understatement.*
>
> Thus, the certainty of the realness of God does not come about as a corol-
> lary of logical premises, as a leap from the realm of logic to the realm of ontology,
> from an assumption to a fact. It is, on the contrary, a transition from an imme-
> diate apprehension to a thought, from a preconceptual awareness to a definite
> assurance, from being overwhelmed by the presence of God to an awareness of
> His existence. What we attempt to do in the act of reflection is to raise the pre-
> conceptual awareness to the level of understanding....
>
> Our belief in the reality of God is not a case of first possessing an idea and
> then postulating the ontal counterpart of it; or, to use a Kantian phrase, of first
> having the idea of a hundred dollars and then claiming to possess them on the
> basis of the idea. What obtains here is first the actual possession of the dollars
> and then the attempt to count the sum. There are possibilities of error in count-
> ing the notes, but the notes themselves are there.[210]

According to Heschel, in other words, faith in God is not the consequence of discursive reasoning or argumentation: "To Jewish thinkers

of the past, the evidence for their certainty of the existence of God was neither a syllogism derived from abstract premises nor any physical experience but *an insight.*"[211]

For a religious thinker, one of the central dangers of beginning with human experience is the gnawing anxiety that perhaps one is always only talking about just that—human experience, and nothing more. Human beings may sense or feel that they are experiencing or interacting with something (or someone) objectively real, but can we ever be confident about that, or are we destined to live in the shadow of Feuerbach, endlessly questioning whether what we encounter is merely our own projection? This is what Heschel means, I think, when he claims that our sense for the realness of God is rooted in an "ontological presupposition." How, Heschel wonders, can we move from our presumably fallible pre-conceptual awareness to the confident assertion that the God we intuit is "trans-subjectively real"? His response is to insist, as we have just seen, that the realness of God is already a constituent part of our immediate awareness. To ask the question, in other words, is already to belie the fullness of what is given to our pre-conceptual awareness. Heschel writes: "In the depth of human thinking we all presuppose some ultimate reality which on the level of discursive thinking is crystallized into the concept of a power, a principle or structure. This, then, is the order in our thinking and existence: the ultimate or God comes first and our reasoning about Him second."[212] Now, as a phenomenological portrayal of how the religious person thinks, this may be both accurate and compelling. But as anything more—as an argument for why the experience should be trusted by someone who has not had it, for example, or by someone who has had it but is nevertheless plagued by epistemological doubts—it obviously fails, essentially sidestepping a question by re-asserting a conviction. One cannot successfully respond to an epistemological challenge to an experience simply by reaffirming the intensity of the experience itself; to do so is merely to beg the question of whether the intensity of the experience is any guarantee of its veracity.[213] At most, one can appeal to such intensity as the basis solely for one's own necessarily subjective confidence.[214]

This pattern—an expression of epistemological anxiety followed by a reassertion of certainty being *given with experience*—repeats itself again and again in Heschel's writings, and especially in *MNA*. On one occasion, Heschel briefly considers the question: in depicting the human sense for the mystery, perhaps all he has done is describe an internal psychological state? We all know, after all, that "a psychological reaction is no evidence for an ontological fact, and we can never infer an object itself from a feeling a person has about it." Heschel readily admits that this objection is valid, but he then proceeds to insist that in this case, "what we infer from is not the actual feeling of awe but the intellectual certainty that in the face of nature's grandeur and mystery we must respond with awe; what we infer from is not a psychological state but a fundamental norm of human consciousness, a *categorical imperative*." Again, the nature and intensity of the experience seems to trump epistemological interrogation thereof. Now waxing hyperbolic, Heschel concludes: "The validity and requiredness of awe enjoy a degree of certainty that is not even surpassed by the axiomatic certainty of geometry."[215]

What we find in this paragraph is indicative of a move Heschel makes time and time again. He begins by acknowledging that epistemologically speaking, there is ample room to doubt the veracity of the intuitions he conveys, but he then proceeds to characterize the experience as so forceful, so utterly compelling, that one cannot legitimately or coherently entertain doubts about it. Heschel's descriptions of these experiences are often moving, even captivating, and they go a long way toward explaining why someone who has had such experiences might well decide to trust in them. And yet it is unclear how effective he expects these evocations to be either in persuading non-believers or in buttressing the wavering certitude of many believers. The fact that he returns to this pattern of doubt and affirmation so consistently raises the question of what work he thinks it does, or fails to do, for him.

What Heschel betrays in all this back and forth motion, I think, is a profound ambivalence about epistemology in general, and about the extent to which he feels compelled to engage it on its own terms. Heschel's fundamental impatience with epistemological discourse in the face of what to him was the almost tangible reality of God is most clearly expressed in a passage recalling his student days in Berlin. Speaking of his professors at the university, he maintains that they were hopelessly mired in a "Greek-German way of thinking," and that, consequently, for them God was at best an idea or a "logical possibility," not a reality:

"To assume He had existence would have been a crime against epistemology."[216] Moreover, since epistemology deals in concepts, it cannot access the heart of religious awareness (which, as we have seen, is
pre-conceptual according to Heschel), let alone pass judgment upon
it. As Heschel warns, "By proceeding from awareness to knowledge we
gain in clarity and lose in immediacy. What we gain in distinctness by
going from experience to expression we lose in genuineness. . . . Religious thinking is in perpetual danger of giving primacy to concepts
and dogmas and to forfeit the immediacy of insights, to forget that the
known is but a reminder of God."[217] For Heschel, then, epistemology is
always a moment too late; it presumes to analyze that which has already
slipped through its fingers. Fully convincing or not, Heschel's claim is
that awareness of God is simply impervious to the stubborn conceptu-
ality of a great deal of philosophical discourse.

And yet Heschel cannot seem to cast epistemology aside. On the
one hand, he holds that for one who has experienced the overwhelming reality of God, the question of how to justify belief according to the
canons of Western philosophy is at best an afterthought, and at worst an
irrelevance. The experience of God is so absolute that it simply overrides
the philosopher's hesitations and objections. On the other hand, Heschel
is aware that for better or (mostly) for worse, modern man is plagued by
doubts; the legacies of Kant, and of Nietzsche, Feuerbach, and Freud
cannot simply be ignored or swept away. Heschel's impulse is obviously
to affirm the believer's confidence that God's reality is simply given to experience, and yet he worries that his readers (and, one can be permitted
to speculate, perhaps some part of himself as well) need to be engaged on
the skeptical terms more familiar to them, and to their cultural setting.
What results is a seesaw-like movement in Heschel's thought: he raises
epistemological questions again and again, only to invalidate them or
swat them away.

There is another way to get at this: we can ask whether, for Heschel,
certainty is an epistemological category or a phenomenological one. In
other words, does certainty describe a subjective state of mind or a claim
about conformity to philosophical criteria? Heschel is at his strongest, I
think, when he is willing to simply evoke and affirm the sheer power of
the former; he is less successful when he allows himself to be dragged

into a mode of discourse for which, as is palpable to any sensitive reader, he ultimately has no patience. Rather than explicitly refusing the terms of philosophical epistemology, Heschel repeatedly gestures toward them, only to attempt to override them with the force of his own conviction.

One additional lens may be helpful here: as we have already seen, Heschel wants to jolt readers out of the abyss of self-assertion, including what he considers the dead end of self-assertive Cartesian anxieties and preoccupations. His underlying project is therefore to educe an awareness that he insists is prior to, and deeper than, the worries of the isolated "I." From Heschel's vantage point, then, precisely because it places the solitary "I" on a kind of cognitive pedestal, epistemology conventionally understood is part and parcel of modern man's religious and ethical problems, not a path toward their solution. Hence the disdain Heschel seems to have for it. And yet, as we have seen, whether in response to other people's doubts or to his own, he cannot quite let go of epistemology's challenges and concerns. And so, again, we witness the recurring push and pull between rejecting epistemology and being lured by it. Perhaps we can put this one final way: Heschel gets bogged down in the quagmire of trying to accommodate a discourse he ultimately wants to overcome. What results is a double-edged deficiency in his writing—he neither fully repudiates epistemological criteria nor successfully meets them.

In the end, Heschel fails to reckon explicitly with the reality that evocations of experience, no matter how vigorous and robust, will never be fully persuasive to one who is not on some level already persuaded. Heschel could have responded to this challenge with a gesture of epistemological humility, conceding that all he has shown is that his intuitions and experiences are sufficient grounds to justify his own belief—and the belief of those who recognize themselves in his descriptions. But he is not content with that. On several occasions, he insists that a sense for the ineffable and all that it entails is universal. "The sense of the ineffable," he writes, "is not an esoteric faculty but an ability with which all men are endowed."[218] What Heschel describes is not merely a potential sensitivity, but one that is always to some extent actualized. Indeed, he asserts, all human beings share a "universal nondiscursive perception of the ineffable,"[219] and "this is why all words that hint at the ineffable are understandable to everybody."[220] Furthermore, "the intuition of God is universal,"[221] even though modes of characterizing it vary; in truth, "each of us has at least once experienced the momentous reality of God."[222] But Heschel goes even further: after describing a high-intensity experience of God's presence as "a power, a marvel beyond us, tearing the world apart," Heschel states matter-of-factly that "there is no man who is not shaken for an instant by the eternal. And if we claim we have no heart to feel, no soul to hear, let us pray for tears or a feeling of shame."[223] Or, just as strongly, Heschel writes: "No one can be a witness to the non-existence of God without laying a perjury upon his soul, for those who abscond, those who are always absent when God is present, have only the right to establish their alibi for their not being able to bear witness."[224] So persuaded is Heschel of the ontological reality of the God he intuits in these moments that he allows himself to declare that "there can be no honest denial of the existence of God. There can only be faith or the honest confession of inability to believe—or arrogance."[225]

Heschel here makes two problematic moves. He begins with a questionable assumption—the insistence that the religious experiences he describes are universal; and he follows with what appears to be a rather presumptuous conclusion—that the failure of some people to have them is a culpable failure to sense and respond to the presence of God. Not surprisingly, a variety of critics have responded harshly to this latter point. In reviewing *MNA*, for example, Emil Fackenheim famously noted that Heschel "lacks understanding for the tragedy of unbelief,"[226] and, in more impassioned tones, Arthur Cohen accused Heschel of "deficient sympathy and compassion for those who are trapped in their unknowing and disbelief. . . . It would appear, [he writes,] if we accredit the underlying assumption on Heschel's writing, that unbelief is sheer dishonesty."[227] Heschel goes even further than Cohen realizes, at one point declaring that "in the spirit of biblical tradition, we must speak not of the foolishness of faith but rather of the *foolishness of unbelief,* of the *scandal of indifference to God.* What is called in the English language an atheist, the language of the Bible calls a *fool.*"[228]

Heschel's insistence that atheists and deniers are arrogant, dishonest, and just plain foolish is jarring, to say the least. Such accusations are also somewhat odd coming from a thinker who, as we shall see in chapters 5 and 7, speaks at length about God's hiddenness, and who describes his own time as "a spiritual blackout, a blackout of God." Can a twentieth-century theologian who agonizes over the "wall" separating humanity and God[229] really insist that only a fool can be an atheist? Heschel's formulations are so extreme that we ought to stop and ask what he is trying to accomplish with such statements. What work does he hope they will do for his project as a religious writer? (We should ask these questions not necessarily to justify Heschel's pronouncements, but simply to better understand them.)

The question, of course—and there is no way to answer it definitively—is how Heschel means these accusations against non-believers to be taken: are they meant as straightforward declarations of his position, or as rhetorical attempts to shake his readers free of their assumptions, to jolt them into another quality of awareness? In other words, though passages like these may well fall flat (I agree with Fackenheim and Cohen on that score), I am nevertheless not certain that they should be taken at face value, such that we can simply assume that Heschel would have insisted, even speaking in a more sober, discursive mode, that non-believers are little more than liars or fools.

I am not suggesting that Heschel does not mean these dramatic declarations at all. I am suggesting, rather, that he does not intend for them to be taken too literally. In his condemnatory descriptions of non-believers, in other words, Heschel is speaking hyperbolically. A hyperbole, of course, is an extravagant statement not intended to be taken literally. Hyperbole goes too far, but it goes too far in order to make a point the writer feels needs to be heard. As Robert Fogelin puts it, "Hyperbole is an exaggeration on the side of truth."[230] Fackenheim and Cohen are reacting to something real in Heschel. He does seem to think that even in our disenchanted, expediency-driven world, there is a degree of culpability in non-belief. As we have already seen, according to Heschel "the universe is an immense allusion,"[231] and thus sensitive souls are able to perceive "the silent allusion of things to a meaning greater than themselves"[232]—even, ostensibly, in thoroughly secularized modernity. On Heschel's account, therefore, total failure to sense the ways in which reality points beyond itself must to some extent be accounted culpable blindness. For Heschel, in other words, non-belief is not (or is not just) tragedy; it is also, to some extent, failure. Now, one can surely debate this point and accept or reject it, but it is not a crazy or unimaginable position for an impassioned believer to hold. What is more problematic—because more outlandish—is a full-scale assault accusing (all?) non-believers of arrogance or deceit. It is just these accusations, which cause critics like Cohen and Fackenheim to bristle, that I suggest we avoid taking at face value.

Why does Heschel feel he needs to write, at least at moments, in such a rhetorically charged mode? Robert Erlewine insightfully invokes the work of philosopher Charles Taylor to explain what Heschel is doing in his work.[233] According to Taylor, what divides modernity from what came before is the transition from the "porous self" to the "buffered self." Whereas with the porous self, "emotions which are in the very depths of human life exist in a space which takes us beyond ourselves, which is porous to some outside power, a person-like power,"[234] with the buffered self, in contrast, a sense of self-containedness emerges, such that "the possibility exists of taking a distance from, disengaging from everything outside the mind." The consequence of this momentous transition, Taylor writes, is that in modern times "my ultimate purposes are those which arise within me, the crucial meanings of things are those defined in my responses to them."[235] All this gives rise to what Taylor calls the "immanent frame," which is the uniquely modern possibility of seeing and experiencing the world as sufficient unto itself, so that "one can speak of the natural world, of existence as such, without any necessary reference to a beyond."[236] As Erlewine astutely notes, Heschel does not want to argue within this frame but to resist and subvert it altogether. Thus,

> While [many of] Heschel's critics remain within the immanent frame in their critiques of his work, Heschel himself seeks to challenge this very structure.... Heschel uses the sensibilities of the porous self to challenge the assumptions of (modern) reason, and thus the buffered self, asking if rather than emancipating the human being from a world of superstition, it has not instead walled the mind up in a trap such that it is no longer in touch with reality.[237]

Taylor's work offers us another way to think both about Heschel's tortured relationship to epistemology and about his most extravagant statements. In order to understand Heschel, it is crucial to keep in mind the depth of the damage that secular, technological modernity has wrought.

The culture of expediency and self-enclosure, he argues, has brought unimaginably devastating consequences. For those with eyes to see, Heschel insists, modernity's illusions had been painfully shattered: "The problem of man is more grave than we were able to realize a generation ago. What we used to sense in our worst fears turned out to be a utopia compared with what has happened in our own days. We have discovered that reason alone may be perverse, that science is no security."[238] So terrifying are the events of the twentieth century that "life in our time has become a nightmare for many of us."[239] Indeed, as Heschel poignantly puts it, "We have once lived in a civilized world, rich in trust and expectation. Then we all died, were condemned to dwell in hell. Now we are living in hell."[240] The depths of modern man's predicament are such that "our civilization is in need of redemption. The evil, the falsehood, the vulgarity of our way of living cry to high heaven."[241]

Left to their own devices, human beings have built societies "plagued by three maladies: dishonesty, egocentricity, and avarice."[242] Never before, Heschel insists, has humanity so desperately needed religion to help bridle its self-assertion, to tame its ghastly propensity for violence and brutality. And yet instead of helping break through man's self-enclosure, modern philosophy, Heschel fears, only buttresses it. With their brazen contempt for religion and faith, philosophers all too often dismiss the one reality that has the potential to contain humanity's seemingly unquenchable thirst for violence and bloodshed.

Faced with a theological and moral impasse—humanity needs religion more than ever, but it refuses even to consider the urgent claims religion makes—Heschel pulls out all the rhetorical stops. In attempting to understand what he is doing, it is useful to consider a comment of Friedrich Nietzsche's. Like Heschel, Nietzsche believed he was living in a time of deep crisis. Speaking of abuses in the political sphere, Nietzsche notes, "When the description of an emergency . . . is greatly exaggerated, it does of course have less of an effect on insightful people, but it has all the greater effect on the uninsightful (who would have remained indifferent to a careful, measured presentation). To that extent *it is useful to exaggerate in describing emergencies.*"[243] Interpreting Nietzsche's often outrageous style, Stephen Webb observes, "Because of the rocklike hardness of his culture's ignorances and prejudices, Nietzsche had to philosophize with the hammer of hyperbole."[244] Heschel, too, takes up the hammer of hyperbole when he runs up against what he considers the ignorances and prejudices of modern society: a triumphalist secularity bolstered by stubborn self-assertion, and a willful blindness to the moral and spiritual perils of the buffered self, trapped in the immanent—that is, godless—frame. When one wants to work within the epistemological and ontological assumptions of one's readers, one can argue with them; when, in contrast, one wants to shake those assumptions to their very foundations, one might decide to shock them, to assault what one assumes is their implacable complacency. At a certain point, when evocation and argumentation have run their course, Heschel attempts something else: he tries to break through modern man's buffer with the sheer force of his words, and thus to pierce his otherwise impregnable defenses against incursions of the transcendent.

This is, at any rate, what Heschel wants to accomplish. Why, then, do these passages fall flat with so many readers? Literary theorist Louis Wirth Marvick's comments about hyperbole can help us understand Heschel's failure here: "Hyperbole is so passionate and naïve," Marvick argues, "that only an audience that wants to be uplifted and overcome will take it seriously.... The enthusiasm of hyperbole must be shared by the audience or else it will look pretentious or ridiculous."[245] In other words, increasingly extreme formulations intended to jolt the reader can only be successful if the reader is already open to being stirred; as an attempt to elicit that first opening, such statements will too often seem strident and overbearing—hence, for example, the deep offense Cohen takes at Heschel's words. Here, then, is Heschel's bind: he cannot argue with his often stubbornly secularized readers on their terms, since the very heart of his religious vision is a renunciation of the one thing to which they are most committed—the kind of thinking that begins with the sovereign, self-enclosed self. So he starts by trying to evoke wonder rather than arguing toward it, but, as we have seen, he senses that even those who share his sense of wonder may be beset by epistemological doubts, uncertain that their experiences point to anything real beyond themselves. So Heschel takes another tack and engages in an ambivalent dance with epistemology. But he no doubt realizes that his epistemological arguments are likely to be persuasive only to the already persuaded.

Out of options, as it were, Heschel turns to extravagant statements meant to shake the reader and thus enable her to see realities to which modern culture and philosophy have blinded her. But these formulations are a double-edged sword in that they undoubtedly alienate as many readers as they inspire.[246] As Webb puts it, "Hyperbole attracts some readers with the same intensity and power with which it repels others—or leaves yet others alternating between comprehension and confusion."[247] Instead of stirring the reader, extravagant statements like Heschel's sometimes only convey the impression that he and his readers inhabit different universes, and that the gap between them is simply too vast to be bridged. To take two further examples: "The nonsense of denial is too monstrous to be conceivable,"[248] Heschel writes; "How is it possible not to believe? How is it possible not to sense the presence of God in the world?"[249] The impassioned certainty of such passages no doubt captivates and enthralls some readers, even as it leaves others wondering how any modern person can be so metaphysically overconfident. Heschel's hypercharged formulations no doubt charm some even as they alienate others. Heschel's hyperbole, then, can obviously have the opposite of its intended effect.

One of the most fundamental problems in Heschel's writing is that he often loses sight of the difference between an intuition, on the one hand, and an argument, on the other.[250] In other words, Heschel cannot always distinguish between an argument *for* faith and a description *of* faith. Heschel is, I would suggest, immensely skilled at the latter, but much less so at the former. But he is manifestly not content to portray what faith and its antecedents look like from the inside; again and again, he evokes the life of faith with enormous power and depth, only to assume that his evocations are somehow more than what they are—that they are demonstrations rather than evocations, arguments rather than portrayals. The flattest, weakest moments in Heschel's writing are those in which he overreaches, seemingly convinced that he has led the reader to an unavoidable conclusion when all he has done—and this is actually a great deal, but again, from Heschel's perspective, apparently not enough—is to evoke with often stunning eloquence the inner life of the person of faith. This methodological confusion—the lack of clarity about what he is or is not doing—contributes greatly to those moments in Heschel where he descends from forceful and compelling to dogmatic and shrill.

Why is it so important to Heschel to imagine that his portrayals of faith and its antecedents are somehow universal? What is it about the possibility that his perceptions are not universally shared that is so unacceptable to Heschel? The source of the problem here is Heschel's preoccupation with certainty. Already in his 1941 study of Saadia, Heschel noted that books of philosophy should be regarded not as "mirrors, reflecting other people's problems, but rather as windows, allowing us to view the author's soul."[251] Saadia, Heschel argues, was plagued by "the worm of uncertainty."[252] Accordingly, "we may . . . regard Saadia's philosophy as a personal quest of certainty, as an effort to reach evidence about the main issues of thinking."[253] It does not require much of a stretch to suggest that Heschel is, consciously or not, talking as much about himself as about Saadia. While he ultimately rejects Saadia's philosophical project,[254] he remains preoccupied with certainty—and subjective certainty, it must be emphasized, does not seem to satisfy him. (One wonders at times whether a dose of Kierkegaardian uncertainty would have served Heschel well.) It is the anxious quest for objective certainty that, one suspects, leads Heschel both to raise epistemological challenges and, just as quickly, to thwart them. Similarly, Heschel's insistence on the universality of his experiences may be regarded as an attempt, however quixotic, to generate what I would call "universal subjective certainty," which is as good, for his purposes, as objective certainty.

Coming at the same problem from another angle: Heschel is either unable or unwilling to confront the fact that even many of his most basic perceptions of the world are in fact culturally conditioned. He does not entertain the possibility, for example, that one can have a robust sense of wonder and "perpetual surprise" without an attendant sense that the whole world is a vast allusion to the transcendent mystery beyond it; even an elementary exploration of much of the history of Buddhism would sever that ostensible link. Or one could take note of the fact that some of the most passionate contemporary advocates of wonder are often fiercely atheistic scientists.[255] For the Western theist, wonder may well always already constitute a pre-awareness of God, but in many cultural and historical contexts it would constitute no such thing. Heschel's fails even to engage with such questions, and his writing suffers seriously as a result.

All of this, of course, calls Heschel's assumptions about pre-linguistic, pre-conceptual awareness of God into question. If I am correct in my assessment, Heschel is not sufficiently aware of the ways in which his most primary experiences are already deeply shaped by the language, texts, and ideas of the Jewish tradition—and are thus unlikely to be universally recognizable, let alone shared.[256] For the careful reader, Heschel's writings consistently point to this very issue—to be sure, despite the author's own intentions. In part I of *GSM*, Heschel often intersperses phenomenological evocations of wonder, amazement, awe, etc. with citations of biblical verses that describe similar experiences of, and responses to, the world. From Heschel's perspective, I think, the verses serve to demonstrate the extent to which these intuitions and perceptions are central to Jewish religious experience, and to point to the way Jewish tradition gives language and voice to these fundamentally ineffable experiences. But one cannot help but wonder: might it not be the case that these verses and concepts *shape* Heschel's perceptions, rather than merely *describing* or reflecting them after the fact? What I am suggesting is that Heschel's insistence on pre-conceptual awareness, and his assumption that his experiences are somehow universal, are in fact two sides of the same coin. Both claims depend on the implausible assumption that intuitions about transcendence and ultimacy, about indebtedness and obligation, are somehow independent of cultural context.[257]

Read as a description-evocation of faith from the inside, part I of *GSM* stands as one of the monuments of twentieth-century religious writing. Read as something else—as a set of defensible assumptions and unassailable arguments, for example—it is far less compelling. Heschel was enormously successful at giving language to the theistically tinged experience of wonder and amazement; he was much less successful—as one must necessarily be—in attempting to suggest that the very experience of wonder is always already implicitly theistic. Put differently, Heschel was far more skilled at what he in fact did than in what he aspired to do.

In his *Varieties of Religious Experience,* William James defended the religious beliefs of mystics even as he insisted that the latter had no right, and indeed no grounds, to coerce others to share in their convictions. James argued, on the one hand, that "mystical states, when well developed, usually are, and have the right to be, absolutely authoritative over the individuals to whom they come.... The mystic is, in short, invulnerable, and must be left ... in undisturbed enjoyment of his creed."[258] But he was quick to assert the converse as well: "No authority emanates from them which should make it a duty for those who stand outside of them to accept their revelations uncritically."[259] Reiterating the point, James wrote that "non-mystics are under no obligation to acknowledge in mystical states a superior authority."[260] In a recent study, Gordon Tucker links James and Heschel, arguing that the latter's approach to religious certainty should be understood against the "backdrop of the incommensurability of religious *experience,* on the one hand, and religious *philosophy* on the other." According to Tucker, Heschel "was, of course, well aware of the frustrating lack of power of religious experience to convince."[261] As he admits in *MNA,* "There are indeed no credentials in our possession by which we could demonstrate to others that the endless concern in which we were initiated is not the outpouring of our own heart."[262] And yet, Heschel repeatedly insists, one has the right to believe—not, as we have seen, because of an argument, but because of an "immediate apprehension" that cannot be refuted (any more than it can be proven).

So far, so good. But in correctly pointing to the parallels between Heschel and James, Tucker overlooks the crucial differences between them. According to James, although many people have had mystical experiences, many others have not; indeed, James notes wistfully, "My own constitution shuts me out from their enjoyment almost entirely, and I can speak of them only at second hand."[263] There is no sense in James that those who are not blessed with such experiences are somehow to be blamed for their failures. For Heschel, in stark contrast, those who are devoid of wonder are at least to some degree responsible for their own failing. As we have seen, Heschel has a difficult time admitting to the possibility of non-culpable non-belief, and a lack of wonder can only be rooted, ultimately, in a failure of character. (Again, although I think Heschel consciously overstates the point he wants to make, he still does very much want to make the point.) Because Heschel's appeal is usually to a kind of religious experiencing that he imagines is anything but extraordinary—it is available, he insists, to any human being who has not become entirely mired in a culture of expediency—he lacks patience for the possibility that one can fail to share his intuitions and yet not be at least somewhat (morally, spiritually) blameworthy. Thus, while Tucker is right that Heschel at moments seems to learn the lessons that James has taught him, it is also the case that he tends just as quickly to forget them. Whereas James is consistent in his call for epistemological humility—as we have seen, the faith of the mystic can neither be denied by, nor coerced upon, the non-mystic—Heschel is more erratic, at moments taking a posture of humility, but then just as readily lambasting the non-believer who fails to share his religious perceptions. At times, then, Heschel succumbs to the very "dogmatism" which Tucker argues he eschews.[264] It is as if Heschel feels, as I have suggested, that subjective certainty is not enough: he is not content to have his intuitions immune to refutation, but wants to establish their superiority—morally and spiritually—to other, less theistic, more secular intuitions.[265] It is this gnawing need for a more-than-subjective certainty that gives rise to some of Heschel's least convincing—and least generous—passages.

Let us take one more tack in exploring the most vulnerable points in Heschel's thought. As we have seen, Heschel's theology operates on the assumption that experiences, even experiences of the transcendent, can be pre-verbal, pre-conceptual, and, by implication, unconditioned by culture. But this kind of approach to experience has largely been abandoned in light of linguistic philosophy and hermeneutical theory, which together have taught us that "the human subject exists within a world of language and a tradition of cultural meaning."[266] What is at stake here, as Francis Schüssler Fiorenza points out, is the relationship between experience and language. Whereas "transcendental theology appeals to religious experience that underlies creedal and doctrinal formulations" and thus "views language as expressive" of a prior "basic religious experience,"[267] hermeneutical theology, in contrast, reminds us of "the degree to which language does not just express but also constitutes experience.

WONDER, INTUITION, AND THE PATH TO GOD   69

Therefore, religious language is not only expressive, but also constitutive of religious experience."[268] Contemporary theologians tend to be much more conscious than were many in the past of "the experience-forming dimension of interpretive frameworks."[269] In other words, "religions produce religious experience rather than merely being the expression of it."[270] One cannot stand immersed in a particular cultural context and purport to have or describe a foundational experience that lies behind or beneath it; the experience, and thus the view from nowhere, is simply not available. Not to put too fine a point on it, the underlying problem of part I of *GSM* is that Heschel does not realize the extent to which his experiences are always already Jewish—they are not precursors of Judaism but rather manifestations of it.[271]

What to do with a transcendentalist Heschel in a time dominated by hermeneutical theology?[272] What is necessary, I think, is to articulate a revised understanding of what Heschel is doing as a theologian—to understand him, in other words, differently than he understood himself. On such an account, Heschel would be seen as providing us with a profoundly learned and often startlingly eloquent "thick description" of what Jewish faith looks like from the inside. Jewish theology would be seen as generating—indeed, constituting—experiences, not just reflecting upon them after the fact. The appeals to pre-conceptual experience and the pretensions to universality, so prevalent in Heschel's work, simply cannot survive the challenges put to them by the post-modern realization of the linguistically and culturally conditioned nature of experience. In other words, if Heschel is to be of more than historical interest, one must move to a neo-Heschelian paradigm, one which understands Heschel's project in far more modest terms than Heschel himself understood it.[273]

* * *

In general, Heschel seems less interested in intense religious experiences than in the more commonly available religious perceptions of the mystery and the allusiveness of reality to the transcendent God. In other words, it seems, Heschel is frequently more interested in *religious experiencing* than in *religious experiences*—that is, in the religious dimension of all experiencing of the world, rather than in discrete experiences one might label "religious." And yet, Heschel writes, a deeper "understanding for the realness of God" is only available at "moments"; ultimate insights are "events, rather than a permanent state of mind." When it comes to the full flowering of always-available perceptions of the mystery into full-blown awareness of God, in other words, Heschel moves into an illuminationist mode. "Our understanding of the greatness of God comes about as an act of illumination," he writes; "what is clear at one moment may subsequently be obscured."[274] Similarly, Heschel maintains that "faith . . . is *an event,* something that happens rather than something that is stored away; it is *a moment* in which the soul of man communes with the glory of God."[275] I would suggest, in light of all this, that for Heschel, there are three stages in religious awareness, each of which is preparatory for the next. First is the posture of wonder and amazement, attunement to the mystery, and awareness of the ineffable reality that something is asked of us. For the sensitive, non-calloused soul, this orientation and its attendant intuitions are perennially possible. Second are moments of "ultimate insight" into the "momentous reality" of God, which are "rare events."[276] Wonder and amazement are necessary but not sufficient for achieving this type of "understanding" of God. Third are events in history in which God reveals His will for humanity, which we consider in chapter 3. "Private insights and inspirations," Heschel writes, "prepare us to accept what the prophets convey."[277]

According to Heschel, then, the spiritual life is animated by a combination of human initiative, on the one hand, and divine assistance, on the other. Though humanity's efforts are vital, they are not enough to get us to God. Even insight—ostensibly prior to revelation—is, at least in part, a manifestation of divine grace: "It is within man's power to seek Him; it is not within his power to find Him. All Abraham had was wonder, and all he could achieve on his own was readiness to perceive. The answer was disclosed to him; it was not found by him. But the initiative, we believe, is with man."[278] Again, Heschel writes: "The truth is that for all our aspirations we remain spiritually blind unless we are assisted."[279]

But even divinely assisted insight is by itself insufficient. According to Heschel, the sense of wonder and the insights it makes possible are indispensable for a relationship with God, but, he repeatedly emphasizes, by themselves they are not equal to the task of fully establishing that relationship. Wonder leads to an awareness of God, but it alone cannot bring us to a fully developed relationship with Him. It alone cannot tell me who God is, or what God expects of me.[280] An intuition, no matter how important, will only get us so far. As Heschel writes:

> The God whose presence in the world we sense is anonymous, mysterious. We may sense that He is, not what He is. What is His name, His will, His hope for me? How should I serve Him, how should I worship Him? The sense of wonder, awe, and mystery is necessary, but not sufficient to find the way from wonder to worship, from willingness to realization, from awe to action.[281]

Thus, wonder and its consequences prepare us for revelation, but they can never take its place:[282]

> In thinking about the world, we cannot proceed without guidance, supplied by logic and scientific method. In thinking about the living God we must look to the prophets for guidance. Those who share in the heritage of Israel believe that God is not always evasive. He confided Himself at rare moments to those who were chosen to be His guides. We cannot express God, yet God expresses His will to us.
>
> Private insights and inspirations prepare us to accept what the prophets convey. They enable us to understand the question to which revelation is an answer. For our faith does not derive its full substance from private insights. . . .
>
> It is through the prophets that we may be able to encounter Him as a Being who is beyond the mystery. In the prophets the ineffable became a voice. . . . He is not the Unknown; He is the Father, the God of Abraham.[283]

The relationship between the pre-revelational human receptivity to the divine, on the one hand, and the contents of divine revelation, on the other, should be clear. Human intuition leads us to the sense that "something is asked of us." Revelation, in turn, comes to answer the two attendant questions: *What* is asked of us? And *by whom*? Chapters 3 and 4 consider each of these questions in turn.

TWO

THEOLOGICAL METHOD AND
RELIGIOUS ANTHROPOLOGY:
HESCHEL AMONG THE
CHRISTIANS

What kind of theologian was Heschel? Since, like many Jewish thinkers, Heschel talks very little about theological method, it falls to us to
piece together what he is doing. With his strong theocentric thrust,
Heschel can at moments sound very much like his contemporary, the
neo-Orthodox Protestant theologian Karl Barth (1886–1968). Consider,
for example, Heschel's insistence that "the Bible is primarily not man's
vision of God but God's vision of man. The Bible is not man's theology
but God's anthropology, dealing with man and what He asks of him."[1]
In a strikingly similar vein, Barth declares that "it is not the right human thoughts about God which form the content of the Bible, but the
right divine thoughts about men."[2] But Heschel's theocentrism should
not blind us to the fact that, in the tradition of modern liberal theology,
he begins his theology not with divine revelation, but with human experience. He commences not by asking what it is that God has revealed,
but rather, as we have seen, by asking what aspects of human nature and
experience can render us receptive to revelation. Or, to put it somewhat
differently, Heschel begins not already within the contents of revelation,
but rather with anthropological prolegomena, with a "critical, transcendental inquiry into the possibility of . . . belief."[3] Although it most assur-
edly does not end there, Heschel's theology begins in anthropology. In
what follows, I bring Heschel into conversation with some of the major
figures in twentieth-century Christian theology as a basis for exploring
Heschel's approach to the intertwined issues of theological method and
theological anthropology.[4]

It will be useful to begin our discussion by briefly considering the theological approaches of Karl Barth and Emil Brunner, and the rather acrimonious (at least from Barth's side) breach between them. No twentieth-century theologian was more emphatic in his rejection of a natural human capacity for knowing God than Karl Barth, who argued relentlessly in his writings that theology could brook no compromise at all between nature and grace; all knowledge of God is rooted in the latter rather than the former. Any form of natural theology constitutes an "abyss" that one must avoid at all costs; it is a "serpent," and the theologian must "hit it and kill it as soon as [he] see[s] it."[5] Barth insists that to talk about an inherent human capacity to know God, or even merely to receive revelation, is effectively to affirm that human beings aid in their own salvation, and thus to run afoul of the related Reformation principles of *sola scriptura* and *sola gratia*.[6] Barth is absolutely unyielding in his opposition to the notion that human beings can know anything at all of God outside of what they learn through revelation; the only God one can know through nature, he avers, is "a creature of man's philosophical phantasy,"[7] and thus nothing but an idol.[8] For Barth, this resolute rejection of natural knowledge is only the consequence of taking seriously humanity's total depravity after the Fall.[9]

Emil Brunner famously attempted to offer a more nuanced—and thus, from Barth's perspective, irredeemably compromised—approach to nature and grace. Brunner agrees with Barth (or purports to) that "the original image of God in man has been destroyed"[10] by Adam's sin, and that, as a result, the human being is "a sinner through and through . . . there is nothing in him which is not defiled by sin."[11] But he insists that even after the Fall, human beings retain an *"Anknüpfungspunkt,"* or "point of contact," that enables grace to reach them, and makes it possible for them to receive the Word of God. The latter, he tells us, "could not reach a man who had lost his consciousness of God entirely."[12] Brunner distinguishes between the formal image of God, which he insists survives after the Fall, and the material image, which he claims has been obliterated by it. The formal image is what makes human beings capable of language, and thus of being addressed; it is, in other words, the source of our responsibility.[13] For Brunner, I think, the formal image of God *is* the

Anknüpfungspunkt: "No one who agrees that only human subjects but not sticks and stones can receive the Word of God and the Holy Spirit," he writes, "can deny that there is such a thing as a point of contact for the divine grace of redemption."[14]

But Brunner is less than fully consistent in fleshing out the point of contact. On the one hand, he insists that the receptivity that constitutes the formal image "is the purely formal possibility of [man's] being addressed."[15] But as we have just seen, he then goes on to say—and here Barth rightly points out the contradiction—that "the Word of God could not reach a man who had lost his consciousness of God entirely.... What the natural man knows of God, of the law and of his own dependence upon God, may be very confused and distorted. But even so it is the necessary, indispensable point of contact for divine grace."[16] In other words, and perhaps despite himself, Brunner has smuggled some degree of material content into his supposedly purely formal definition of the image of God. To borrow language from Trevor Hart, Brunner seems at times to "trespass beyond" his own distinction, and to move from speaking of a purely passive capacity to talking about something more like an "aptitude" or "predisposition" to revelation.[17] It is no surprise, then, given Barth's strictures against even the slightest hint of natural theology, that Brunner here incurs his wrath.[18]

We can already note just how far Heschel's theological and epistemological assumptions are from anything articulated by either Barth or Brunner. On Heschel's account, as I have shown at length, human beings are in fact capable of achieving some knowledge (or at least "understanding") of God before revelation. Wonder and its attendant intuitions lead, as we have seen, to an immediate awareness of God, and to a sense that "something is asked of us." Revelation, in other words, comes to answer a question that arises in pre-revelational human experience, and that very question, as Heschel points out, already contains an implicit answer within it.[19] Heschel's theology of revelation, then, is not at all focused on the discontinuities between pre-revelational knowledge and what is disclosed in revelation. On the contrary, according to Heschel, the health of the former is a precondition for receptivity to the latter. Far from representing a rupture with human insight and intuition, revelation comes to extend, and expand upon, what is known through them. To be sure, as I show in the next chapter, according to Heschel human beings do learn things from revelation that they would not otherwise know. But where revelation and intuition are concerned, Heschel is unmistakably a theologian of continuity rather than rupture.

If Barth and Brunner share the conviction that "nature is not, in its historical state, predisposed towards grace, but resists it,"[20] Heschel insists that, on the contrary, there is a natural human responsiveness to God, and that even when it has been obscured by self-assertion and self-enclosure, the resulting "God-shaped hole" in human consciousness has the potential to reawaken it. To use Christian imagery, we can say that, for Heschel, grace completes nature. In a passage with somewhat Brunnerian resonances, Heschel insists that in order to recognize the divine, "we would have to know it. But if our knowledge were contingent upon acts of a divine communication, we might never be able to identify such a communication as divine."[21] In stark contradistinction from Barth, there is no hint in Heschel of humanity's acceptance of revelation requiring any kind of epistemological miracle;[22] humanity recognizes the word of God because of an inner sense of, and attunement to, the divine. In fact, even our personal insights and inner experiences depend on us having "an a priori idea of the divine . . . by which we would be able to identify it when given to us."[23]

To come at this from another angle: it is surely telling that Heschel's harshest criticisms are directed toward those who admit to no experiences of wonder and amazement, and who—out of callousness and arrogance, he insists—deny the reality of God. All of this, of course, stands in pronounced contradiction to Barth, who directs his indignation precisely at those who would suggest any possibility of natural, pre-revelational knowledge of God. For Heschel, the failure to perceive God in the natural world is, in a sense, rooted in sin; for Barth, in contrast, the very suggestion that such perception is possible is a manifestation of sin and rebellion. In taking aim at those who have the audacity to deny that God is given to pre-revelational awareness, then, Heschel is not only not a Barthian; he is a full-blown anti-Barthian.[24]

The contrast between Heschel and the Dialectical theologians can be drawn out even further. When he insists upon the reality of general revelation, Brunner points out that God "leaves the imprint of his nature upon what he does" and that therefore "creation of the world is at the same time a revelation."[25] But, ever mindful of humanity's fallen state, he is quick to add that "sin blinds human beings, and renders them incapable of recognizing or responding appropriately to this self-giving, unable to see what is there."[26] Thus "only the Christian, i.e. the man who stands within the revelation in Christ, has the true natural knowledge of God."[27] It hardly needs stating that Heschel would passionately affirm Brunner's first claim and utterly reject his second; in fact, it would not be an overstatement to say that Heschel's whole theological project depends upon a rejection thereof. After all, according to Heschel, the whole world alludes to the transcendent God, and is itself filled with the presence of God. Crucially, and contra both Barth and Brunner, *human beings are fully capable of discerning this; the religious life is rooted in, and dependent upon these intuitions.* To put the matter differently: according to Heschel, human beings have much more than a merely passive capacity for revelation. They have an intuition of the ineffable, and with it an innate capacity to respond to the call of God. Where a point of contact between God and humanity is concerned, Heschel is anything but a Brunnerian minimalist, let alone a Barthian.

These fundamental theological disagreements are inextricably bound up with anthropological differences. Both Barth and Brunner consistently underscore the burden of original sin and its utterly destructive epistemological consequences: sin has "destroyed" and "spoilt" the image of God, and thus eradicated any potential humanity has for knowing God apart from revelation. In fact, we might say that according to Barth, the damage done by Brunner's insistence on a "point of contact" is that it renders humanity's depravity less than total.[28] In Heschel, ever the Jewish theologian, one will find no trace of this—no original sin, and thus no irrevocable epistemological consequences thereof.[29] As he puts it, "Judaism is not committed to a doctrine of original sin and knows nothing of the inherent depravity of human nature."[30] What one finds in Heschel is a focus on the failings of modern man—beginning, as we have seen, with his loss of wonder, and thus of his openness to God—but no argument at all that humanity is somehow incapable of rediscovering the immediate awareness of God that comes with wonder. On the contrary, one of Heschel's central projects is precisely to re-evoke and re-elicit that always-available awareness. One step further: both Barth and Brunner agree that since the Fall, humanity has lost its freedom even as it retains responsibility. One of the wages of original sin, Brunner writes, is that "the possibility of doing or even of willing to do that which is good in the sight of God" has been irretrievably lost.[31] Heschel, of course, disagrees vigorously: "What is decisive" in responding to God, he writes, "is not the existential moment of despair, the acceptance of our own bankruptcy, but, on the contrary, the realization of our great spiritual power, the power to heal what is broken in the world, the realization of our capacity to answer God's question."[32]

In the end, Barth and Brunner's disagreement can perhaps be characterized as a dispute over whether theology should recognize "another task," namely anthropology. In "The Other Task of Theology,"[33] published in 1929, Brunner had argued precisely that. Theology, he averred, could not be content merely to articulate its message, but had also to be aware of the recipient; the theologian, in other words, had to do the work of relating revelation to human consciousness. Barth, of course, would have none of this: theology had one task, and one task only. To suggest otherwise was already to take the first step down a perilous slope. In a letter to Eduard Thurneysen, he wrote: "'The other task...?' No, just the *one* task all the more."[34] Heschel, of course, falls out on Brunner's side of this debate—only without any of Brunner's ambivalence or hesitations. As we have seen, *GSM* begins with an extended consideration of human beings and their capacity both for an immediate awareness of God and for intuiting God's question to them. Moreover, Heschel devotes a great deal of attention to identifying those aspects of modern culture that stand in the way of openness to revelation, and attempts to restore some of that now dimmed receptivity. For Heschel, in other words, *theology cannot but begin in anthropology.*

Now, Heschel too wants to avoid the trap of suggesting that human beings can know God by their own power alone. This is why, despite beginning in anthropology, and with a robust sense that human beings can begin to know God before revelation, Heschel tells us that the knowledge of God available through intuition is inadequate and incomplete, and goes on to insist (as we see in the next chapter) that revelation reveals truths about God and God's expectations that would otherwise be unavailable to us, and which God reveals on His own terms—that is, since God is a living God, God always maintains the freedom to reveal or remain silent as He chooses. And yet as important as all of this is, it does not determine the starting point of Heschel's theology. Like countless modern theologians, Heschel begins with the subject and proceeds to emphasize the human capacity to know God, intuitively and immediately.

One of Heschel's most consistent laments is that revelation is an answer to a question that human beings have stopped asking. In this very lament we can see again just how far Heschel is from Barth's contention that revelation reaches humanity by dint of a miracle. On the contrary, according to Heschel, part of the vulnerability of God lies in the fact that human beings must *open themselves* to hearing the divine Word, or it will fall on deaf ears; revelation does not create its own hearers (which is what renders Heschel's task in re-awakening human receptivity all the more urgent). Thus, we can say that whereas for Barth, revelation is an occasion to accentuate God's absolute, unmitigated sovereignty, for Heschel, it is a locus of a mix of God's majesty and vulnerability—an emphatic call from the transcendent God that depends for its force, nevertheless, on whether human beings are willing to listen.

One final—and fundamental—note of discord between Heschel and Barth: Heschel would likely have pointed out that Barth's theology was surprisingly, if unconsciously, indebted precisely to the modern secular worldview that he sought to combat. By insisting that absolutely no knowledge of God is available in and through nature, Barth was in effect embracing the secularizing assumptions of modernity whereby the world is a closed system,[35] and God is to be found, if anywhere, far above and beyond it. As Colin Grant puts it, Barth "is taking modern naturalism for granted as the way the world is."[36] For Heschel, in contrast, all of reality is an allusion to the transcendent God, and all of it is shot through with the presence of God.[37] In other words, Heschel's "natural theology," he would no doubt contend, stands as a much more complete counter-position to modern naturalism than does Barth's natural world plus a totally inaccessible transcendent God. In contrast to Barth, Heschel simply will not countenance a fully disenchanted world, because to do so, according to him, is to lose the battle for humanity's soul before it has even started.

Given Barth's willingness to condemn Brunner for engaging (so he insisted) in natural theology, there can be no doubt that he would have readily hurled the same charge at Heschel. Recall that for Barth, "natural theology" is not a technical term for a philosophical attempt to reason toward or about God, but rather a term of opprobrium for any theology that takes upon itself the "other task" of exploring those aspects of human life that make receiving revelation possible. But what would Heschel have made of being thus labeled? Would he have recognized himself in the term (stated derogatorily or not) "natural theologian"? Put another way: did Heschel believe that human beings are capable of "natural knowledge" of God? Now, on the surface, the very question seems preposterous—the burden of the last chapter, after all, was ostensibly to demonstrate precisely that. Does Heschel not repeatedly affirm that human beings are capable of immediate apprehension and pre-conceptual knowledge of God—and this, obviously, before revelation? Surely the apprehension-intuition-insight-certainty that we have been discussing constitutes natural knowledge?

And yet, self-evident as this conclusion may seem, I believe it is also profoundly mistaken. Let us look a little more closely at Heschel's understanding of the divine-human dynamics at work in pre-revelational knowledge. Although we surely have the freedom to turn astray, Heschel says, we are "attached to the ultimate at the root of [our] being";[38] the human being "stands in a relation to God which he may betray but not sever. . . . He is the knot in which heaven and earth are interlaced."[39] In other words, a connection to God is not something we must (or even can) achieve, but rather something that is always already planted within us by dint of our being human. This intrinsic conjunction with God has crucial consequences for the possibility of divine-human contact: "Recondite is the dimension where God and man meet," Heschel writes, "and yet not entirely impenetrable. He placed within man something of His spirit (see Isaiah 63:10), and 'it is the spirit in a man, the breath of the Almighty, that makes him understand' (Job 32:8)."[40] In a similar vein, Heschel adds: "There is a divine light in every soul, it is dormant and eclipsed by the follies of this world. We must first awaken this light, then the upper light will come upon us. In thy light which is within us will we see light."[41] Or again: "There is a breath of God in every man, a force lying deeper than the stratum of will, and which may be stirred to become an aspiration strong enough to give direction and even to run counter to all winds."[42] Heschel's contention, then, is not that we have some "natural capacity" that discovers God, but rather that we are created with that "discovery," as it were, already made. "We do not have to discover the world of faith," Heschel writes; "we only have to recover it. It is not a *terra incognita,* an unknown land; it is a forgotten land." What this means is that "our quest for God is a return to God; our thinking of Him is a recall, an attempt to draw out the depth of our suppressed attachment."[43] Heschel offers a startling pair of images that bring us to the heart of his approach. On the one hand, he says, "Man's walled mind has no access to a ladder upon which he can, of his own strength, rise to knowledge of God." And yet, he adds, "His soul is endowed with translucent windows that open to the beyond."[44] In other words, according to Heschel, human beings do not, and cannot, arrive at knowledge of God through our own powers, but in our very humanity we are already open toward the transcendent.[45] What God completes, then, it is God who also began. A moment of insight into God is the sprouting, in other words, of a seed that God has already planted within us. In fact, it is impossible to disentangle human effort from the workings of the divine spirit. "The stirring in man to turn to God is actually a 'reminder by God to man.' It is a call that man's physical sense does not capture, yet the 'spiritual soul' in him perceives the call."[46] To articulate this a bit differently: for Heschel there is no desacralized human nature that somehow manages to reach out to God. Instead, there is, we might say, a created human nature that is always already infused with an indestructible attachment to the divine. It is this divine spirit within us that prods and enables us to discover—or better, to recover—God: "Man is akin to the divine by what he is, not only by what he attains. . . . If his spirit ever rises to reach out for Him, it is the divine in man that accounts for his exaltation."[47] Heschel encapsulates all of this as follows: "What is behind our soul is beyond our spirit; what is at the source of our selves is at the goal of our ways."[48]

* * *

In light of all this, if we seek kindred spirits to Heschel in the Christian world, we would do better, I think, to turn to some central voices in twentieth-century Catholic theology than to their neo-Orthodox counterparts. In the face of Neo-Scholasticism's complete separation of the natural and the supernatural, and its attendant insistence on the extrinsic character of divine grace, the Jesuit theologian Henri de Lubac reminded Catholic theology, first, that God is "the creator of both nature and grace," and, second, that God created nature "with a view towards grace." To dilate exclusively upon divine transcendence is effectively "to cut the Divine off from the human" and thus to contribute, however unwittingly, to a loss of a sense for the sacred.[49] Appealing to what he insisted was a better reading of Thomas Aquinas than the one accepted by the Neo-Scholastics, de Lubac argued that part of what it means to be created in the image of God is to have a desire for a vision of God. In other words, de Lubac rejected what the Neo-Scholastics had come to call "pure nature"; as he wrote in a letter to Maurice Blondel, "This concept of a pure nature runs into great difficulties, the principal one of which seems to me to be the following: how can a conscious spirit be anything other than an absolute desire for God?"[50] For Catholic theology, de Lubac taught, there is no nature that is not already graced. Accordingly, nature and grace should be understood as related not extrinsically, but intrinsically.

Fergus Kerr sums up de Lubac's "most characteristic, if also most controversial thesis" with words that could just as easily apply to Heschel: "The vision of God is a free gift, and yet the desire for it is at the root of every soul."[51] De Lubac forcefully insisted that, ironically, the very notion of an autonomous individual—seemingly the foundation of atheistic humanism—was in fact the invention of Neo-Scholastic theologians, so preoccupied with protecting the supernatural that they effectively created a secularized conception of human nature.[52] To return to itself, Catholic thought needed to recover Thomas's teaching that "the nature of a human being, created in the image of God . . . is directed beyond itself to a supernatural destiny—which so transcends its natural possibilities, however, that it cannot achieve this destiny by its natural powers."[53] Thus, for de Lubac, theology begins with a soul already oriented toward the divine, even as that soul still needs divine grace and revelation in order to reach its ultimate end.

Karl Rahner moved in a similar direction in arguing against "extrinsicism," and for the inextricability of nature and grace. Creation, Rahner insists, is "an element in the fundamental miracle of divine love" and thus cannot be understood apart from grace. "Despite its supernatural character," Rahner writes, "the order of grace is not in respect of the world a supplementary orientation added afterwards, directing towards higher but extrinsic goals. It is the world's innermost characteristic from the outset."[54] By extension, "God's will or God's decree to endow human beings with grace cannot be understood in a purely external or extrinsic way."[55]

> On the contrary, must not what God decrees for man be *eo ipso* an interior ontological constituent of his concrete quiddity 'terminative,' even if it is not a constituent of his 'nature'? For an ontology which grasps the truth that man's concrete quiddity depends utterly on God, is not his binding disposition *eo ipso* not just a juridical decree of God but precisely what man *is*, hence not just an imperative proceeding from God but man's most inward depths?[56]

Rahner wants at once to affirm that grace is intrinsic to the human person, and to safeguard the freedom of God and the gratuity of grace.[57] He achieves this delicate balance through his notion of the "supernatural existential," arguably the "central concept" of his theology.[58] An existential, in the language of Heidegger, is something that is constitutive of human existence; for Rahner, then, the offer of grace is a key component of what makes human existence human. But this offer is also "supernatural," in that it is, always, a gift from God. The term supernatural existential suggests that human beings are not created and then invited into relationship with God; on the contrary, that invitation is always already present within us. We are thus, consciously or not, always oriented toward God. Rahner writes, "In every human being there is something like an anonymous, unthematic, perhaps repressed basic experience of being oriented to God (which is constitutive of man in his concrete make-up of nature and grace) and which can easily be repressed but not destroyed."[59]

Closely intertwined with the supernatural-existential is Rahner's notion of the *Vorgriff auf esse*, or pre-apprehension of being. Briefly summarized: according to Rahner, "in every human act of knowing and willing there is a pre-apprehension of infinite being, and therefore of God."[60] God cannot be known directly—the contrast with Heschel on this point should be obvious; infinite being is, rather, the horizon of our knowledge of all particular things. The implication of this latter claim is that, according to Rahner, every human being is aware of God—even if only implicitly or "pre-thematically." Thus, as Karen Kilby notes, "if Rahner is right, then everyone, whether they describe themselves as agnostic or atheist or indifferent, is actually on some level aware of God."[61]

Rahner's claim is similar to Heschel's: attachment to and knowledge of God are always present within us, even if not yet explicitly. Although as a Catholic theologian, Rahner obviously affirms the doctrine of original sin, his theology bears none of the attendant epistemological pessimism we find in someone like Barth. For Rahner, as for Heschel, the divine is always present in the world, and in human experience within it.

Rahner was arguably the most influential figure in turning twentieth-century Catholic theology toward human experience as a source for theological reflection. The dichotomy between theocentrism and anthropocentrism, he insisted, is ultimately false and unhelpful; the two are, he contended, "strictly the same reality understood from two perspectives which mutually render each other intelligible."[62] Despite the various ways his theology changed and evolved over time, Rahner always remained committed to a theology "which explores the intrinsic relationship of revelation with man's experience and self-understanding."[63] Since human nature, as we have seen, is always already graced, human experience is already reflective of the divine at work within it. Thus, for Rahner, theology "presupposes a common ground between the kerygma and the human subject."[64] The goal, he insists, is not to "deduce" theology from experience, but rather "to discover inherent relationships between the two."[65]

Heschel's project is in many ways much simpler and more straightforward than Rahner's. In contrast to the latter, the former does not seek to identify correspondences between transcendental human experience, on the one hand, and the dogmas of theology, on the other. His aim is more modest—to point to those aspects of human experience that open human beings to the possibility of receiving divine revelation, and thus to show how revelation is an answer to an ineffable question of which every human being has the capacity to become aware.

As we would expect, Heschel does not share the distinctively Christian preoccupation with how nature and grace are related. Moreover, it goes without saying that the content of revelation for Heschel is dramatically different from what it is for de Lubac and Rahner. And yet, there are striking similarities between his theological anthropology and theirs. For Heschel, as for de Lubac, there can be no such thing as "pure nature,"[66] because in actuality, as we have seen, human beings are always already connected to God at the very root of their being. A human being may be conscious of God's call or not, may be responsive to God's call or not, but that call always remains constitutive of what it means to be human. Recall Heschel's insistence that the relationship between God and the human being cannot be jettisoned or discarded; it can, he argues, be "betrayed but not severed." What all of this means is that for Heschel, Barth's unrelenting dichotomization between nature and grace is ultimately pernicious, because it loses sight of—seems to deny, in fact—the unbreakable bond between God and humanity, and the fact that the latter is always, consciously or not, oriented toward the former.

* * *

In dramatic contrast to Barth, the existentialist theologian Paul Tillich (1886–1965) insisted that theology must speak to the "situation" in which it finds itself—that is, to "the totality of man's creative self-interpretation in a [specific] period."[67] Theology cannot be exclusively kerygmatic; because theology needs to address human beings and their existential concerns, "kerygmatic theology needs apologetic theology for its completion." Apologetic theology is thus "answering theology,"[68] in that it seeks to answer questions implied in human existence with the content of divine revelation. Tillich is quick to point out that an "answering theology... must answer the questions implied in the general human and the special historical situation"[69] (ST, 31). In other words, Tillich is suggesting that theology must respond to the eternal questions implied in human existence generally, but it must do so in conversation and interdependence with the particular cultural and historical manifestations of these questions. Now, to be sure, apologetic theology needs to exercise caution lest it "lose itself in the relativities of the 'situation,'"[70] but the solution is not to avoid apologetics, but rather "to seek a theological method in which message and situation are related in such a way that neither of them is obliterated."[71] The method Tillich proposes seeks to explain "the contents of the Christian faith through existential questions and theological answers in mutual interdependence." Consciously or not, Tillich insists, theology has always employed this "method of correlation."[72] As Tillich clarifies, his method

> tries to correlate the questions implied in the situation with the answers implied in the message. It does not derive the answers from the questions as a self-defying apologetic theology does. Nor does it elaborate answers without relating them to the questions as a self-defying kerygmatic theology does. It correlates questions and answers, situation and message, human existence and divine manifestation.[73]

Tillich had little patience for Barth's refusal to acknowledge "any common ground with those outside the 'theological circle,'"[74] and for his insistence that apologetic theology is but "a surrender of the kerygma, of the immovable truth." Barth's theology, Tillich argues, effectively insists that "the message must be thrown at those in the situation—thrown like a stone."[75] But such a procedure can never be successful. As Tillich puts it: "Man cannot receive answers to questions he never has asked."[76] Of course, Tillich readily concedes that God is "in no way dependent on man," but he nevertheless maintains that "God in his self-manifestation to man is dependent on the way man receives his manifestation."[77] In the end, Tillich argues, any theology that purports to be purely kerygmatic essentially lies to itself, because it must, even if only despite itself, make use of "the conceptual tools of its period. It cannot simply repeat biblical passages."[78] Like it or not, theology simply cannot escape the "situation." To pretend otherwise, Tillich contends, is to be guilty of both self-deception and "religious arrogance."[79]

Heschel's method is in significant ways parallel to, and perhaps derived from, Tillich's.[80] According to the former, "Religion is an answer to man's ultimate questions."[81] We must pay attention not only to these questions, Heschel insists, but also to the "situation" in which we ask them: "We cannot succeed in understanding the reasons that force us to attach ourselves to a certainty of God's realness, unless we understand the situation in which we are concerned with the ultimate question." As a result, "We must, therefore, not deal with the ultimate question, apart from the situation in which it exists."[82] So far, so Tillichian: religion seeks to answer the questions implied in the human situation. But Heschel takes all this in a unique and innovative direction, because the problem of modernity, as he sees it, is precisely that *human beings have stopped asking the ultimate questions to which revelation is an answer.* The task of the theologian, therefore, is not simply to answer the questions human beings are asking, but rather to answer the questions *they are no longer asking.* In order to avoid falling on deaf ears, then, theology must first help modern people to recover the ultimate questions, and only then provide the answers thereto.

I would suggest that this is a helpful way of understanding the relationship between parts I and II of *God in Search of Man.* By re-eliciting wonder and amazement, and the attendant sense that "something is asked of us," part I seeks to restore the ultimate questions—the central one is, What is asked of us?—to which part II, as we see in the next chapter, provides the answer. Although he does not elaborate upon it, Heschel is explicit about this point. After telling us at the very beginning of *GSM* that "religion is an answer to man's ultimate questions," he immediately adds, "The moment we become oblivious to ultimate questions, religion becomes irrelevant, and its crisis sets in. The primary task of philosophy of religion is to rediscover the questions to which religion is an answer."[83] Then, when introducing revelation at the beginning of part II, Heschel writes: "The Bible is an answer to the supreme question: *what does God demand of us?* Yet the question has gone out of the world."[84] The Bible, Heschel asserts, is "a sublime answer, but we do not know the question any more."[85] More than a decade later, during an interview at Notre Dame University, Heschel explained again that, in his words, "We must lay bare what is involved in religious existence: we must recover the situations that both precede and correspond to the theological formulations. We must recall the questions that religious doctrines are trying to answer. . . . A major task of philosophy of religion is . . . to rediscover the questions to which religion is an answer."[86]

But if religion is an answer to man's questions, have we not fallen back into the trap we saw both Heschel and Heidegger warn about? Is theology just another "resource," this one aimed at making sense of, and providing meaning to, our lives? It is here, I think, that Heschel's approach is most daring and original. On the one hand, he is convinced that theology must begin with the human beings who are to be the recipients of revelation. Indeed, as we have seen, as a modern theologian, he must lay the groundwork for religion by restoring the ultimate human questions now dormant as a result of the death of wonder. Then, and only then, can human beings receive the answers to their questions—or, in more traditional theological language, hear the word of God. But, seeking to avoid a theology that turns to the subject and effectively remains there, Heschel formulates the ultimate question not so much as a question human beings ask as one that we *are asked*. The fundamental question of human life, as we have repeatedly seen, is rooted in the awareness that "something is asked of us." And the content of the "supreme question," as we have just seen, is simply this: "*What does God demand of us?*" In other words, the question human beings ask is, at its core, not so much a human question as it is a human readiness to respond to a question posed by God: "What gives birth to religion is not intellectual curiosity but the fact and experience of our being asked."[87]

To state this a bit differently: for Heschel, religion is born of a human question. But if this is the case, there is a perennial danger that religion will become just another resource at our disposal. Rather than turn to a Barthian approach as an alternative, however, Heschel offers his own: the ultimate question that the human subject asks is already the question of a self seeking to transcend itself. In other words, the very question I ask already pushes me out of the center, and places God there instead: "Man's anxiety about meaning is not a question, an impulse, but an answer, a response to a challenge. The Bible maintains that the question about God is a question of God."[88] The ultimate human question is thus not a form of self-assertion; on the contrary, it signals receptivity and responsiveness—and, thus, an eagerness for self-transcendence. As Heschel puts it, "Faith is *the response* to the mystery, shot through with meaning; the response to a challenge which no one can for ever ignore. . . . Faith is an act of man who *transcending himself* responds to Him who *transcends the world*."[89]

Theology can only begin with anthropology, in other words, if that anthropology is animated by a focus on responsiveness. Heschel's theology turns to the subject only to enable her to transcend herself. Stephen Duffy's characterization of Rahner's project could apply, mutatis mutandis, to Heschel's:

Rahner [Duffy writes] makes the modern turn to the subject, but all the while insisting that the human being in all aspects of its existence is referred to the absolute mystery, God. Reductionism, "mere humanism," results not from starting with the human, but from a failure to probe it deeply enough. The human creature is essentially open to the absolute and inevitably related to it. One does not find a place for the absolute only after analyzing humanity in a purely natural way. Concrete humans are from the beginning immersed in the absolute mystery.[90]

In *MNA* and *WM,* Heschel sets up another pairing of an existential question and a religious answer. He begins by describing an anxiety endemic to the human condition: "Animals are content when their needs are satisfied," he writes, whereas "man insists not only on being satisfied but also on being able to satisfy, on *being a need* not only on *having needs.* Personal needs come and go, but one anxiety remains: *Am I needed?* There is no man who has not been moved by that anxiety."[91] For human beings, Heschel insists, life is not meaningful unless we are engaged in serving something beyond ourselves. Indeed, he writes, "The only way to avoid despair is to be a need. . . . Happiness, in fact, may be defined as the *certainty of being needed.*"[92] Intertwined with the yearning to be needed is a longing to get beyond a preoccupation with fulfilling desires, which are at best ephemeral, and to cleave to the lasting. "There is not a soul on this earth," Heschel writes, "which, however vaguely or rarely, has not realized that life is dismal if not mirrored in something which is lasting. . . . There is not a soul which has not felt a craving to know of something that outlasts life, strife and agony."[93]

In other words: the human being needs to be needed, and needs to be needed by something abiding. Religion answers this quest-question: "There is a need for our lives, and in living we satisfy it. Lasting is not our desire, but our answer to that need, an agreement not an impulse. Our needs are temporal, while our being needed is lasting."[94] What all this amounts to is the realization that "man is needed, he is *a need of God.*"[95] Note carefully what Heschel has done here: he has constructed a correlation between what he insists is the deepest and most universal human hunger, on the one hand—the need to be needed, and the most fundamental truth of Judaism, on the other, namely, the fact that "God is in need of man."[96] Implicit in Heschel's mode of presentation—a human hunger first, divine revelation second—is, again, the assumption that revelation has to be correlated to some aspect of human life if it is not to fall on deaf ears. So Heschel begins by establishing a human hunger to be needed, and a receptivity to being needed by something ultimate, and only then announces that we are, in fact, needed by God.

Now, again, the reader might worry about religion being reduced here to mere resource, just another means for providing human beings with what we want. But note how Heschel incorporates and responds to that worry: the human need he is interested in is not the surface need for power, or wealth, or social status. It is, rather, the much deeper (and often more hidden and inaccessible) hunger to "break out of the circle of the self"[97]—the hunger, that is, for self-transcendence: "Unlike all other needs, the need of being needed is a striving to give rather than to obtain satisfaction."[98] Religion, then, does answer a human need, but the human need it answers is precisely the deep-seated need to orient our lives around something other than our own needs. Again, it is the questions of the self in search of self-transcendence that religion seeks to answer. Religion is not just another resource, but rather a call to service.

None of this should be taken to mean that religion is uninterested in the meaning of an individual's life. On the contrary, the paradox with which it works is the fact that, according to Heschel, meaning is found precisely in self-transcendence: "It is a most significant fact that man is not sufficient to himself, that life is not meaningful to him unless it is serving an end beyond itself, unless it is of value to someone else."[99] What this means is that "the meaning of existence is not naturally given; it is not an endowment but an art. It . . . depends on whether we respond or refuse to respond to God who is in search of man."[100]

Tillich's method of correlation has been criticized for being insufficiently attentive to the challenges modernity raises for received traditions. Francis Schüssler Fiorenza, for example, writes:

> The method of correlation does not sufficiently take into account the need for a critique of tradition. The critique I refer to is not simply a matter of criticizing the formulations of tradition in order that the underlying experience or affirmations of the tradition might more readily shine forth. Rather this critique is one that reexamines the experiences and affirmations themselves.[101]

If Tillich's theology is vulnerable to this challenge—and, of course, the option of rejecting its premise is available to those who would avail themselves of it—then, at first glance, it would seem, all the more so is Heschel's. Recall that according to Heschel, the sense of wonder comes entwined with a question to which revelation provides the answer. On this model, of course, modern man asks an open-ended question, and revelation ostensibly bestows an encompassing answer. As a result of this approach, there is no explicit consideration in Heschel of whether and when (or how) received tradition might be subject to critique based on modern values and assumptions. And yet, as we see in chapter 3, Heschel explicitly argues against an overly passive and submissive posture toward received understandings, and advocates for what he calls "creative dissent" in religion.[102] Like Abraham at Sodom, Heschel insists, "We too have the right to challenge the harsh statements of the prophets."[103] But this is obviously a far cry from David Tracy's description of what he calls the revisionist, or critical correlation, model of theology. "The central task of contemporary Christian theology," according to Tracy, is "the dramatic confrontation, the mutual illuminations and corrections, the possible basic reconciliation between the principal values, cognitive claims, and existential faiths of both a reinterpreted post-modern consciousness and a reinterpreted Christianity."[104] The modern theologian, Tracy insists, does not offer a "simple defense" or an "orthodox reinterpretation" of traditional belief, but rather "assume[s] a critical posture towards his own and the tradition's beliefs."[105] Heschel may well engage in such a critique *de facto* and without calling attention to it (in his presentation of the tradition, there is, for example, no trace of covenantal triumphalism or of an ontologically essentialist conception of Jewishness). But to the best of my knowledge, there is no explicit engagement of a give-and-take (to put it crudely) between tradition and modernity. On the other hand, Heschel may feel that such an explicit confrontation is unnecessary in a Jewish context precisely because the Jewish tradition has always encouraged other modes of reading than the purely submissive.[106]

I hasten to point out that the flipside of this non-engagement is that Heschel is much less vulnerable than Tillich (or the critical correlation school, for that matter) to the charge that he has essentially warped revelation's answer by forcing it into language determined by modern, secular culture. Another way of getting at this is to notice that the human question to which revelation is the answer is, as Heschel understands it, fundamentally open-ended: "What is asked of us?" It is, in other words, an invitation to revelation to speak on its own terms rather than to translate itself into some pre-determined idiom.[107]

* * *

Rahner and Heschel shared a similar distress over the "eclipse of mystery"[108] in modern times, and both sought to return human beings to the foundational awareness that lies, they believed, at the heart of all religion. To be sure, there are significant differences between their approaches: whereas Rahner appeals to the depth dimension of all human willing and knowing, and suggests that a transcendental awareness of God as ultimate mystery is present in all self-experiencing, Heschel focuses, as we have seen at length, on the sense of wonder and surprise at the fact that anything exists at all, and on the attendant sensitivity for the mystery that pervades all reality. But there are also crucial similarities: as we have seen, both Rahner and Heschel are convinced that human beings are connected to God at the very root of their being, and accordingly, both insist that one of the central tasks of the theologian is to recover and awaken for others an awareness that is already implicitly present within them. On various occasions Rahner referred to this task as "mystagogy"[109]—that is, the task of leading human beings back to the mystery, to a conscious, reflective awareness of that which is, especially in our time, unconscious and pre-reflective. James Bacik describes this task as "'maieutic,' taken in its common meaning of bringing latent ideas into explicit consciousness. Thus, mystagogy is not an initiation into something external or the production of a new experience, but rather the disclosure of an experience that is already present, although in a hidden way."[110] What this means, Bacik suggests, is that the mystagogue has no choice but to "make use of evocative language in order to disclose mystery effectively. It is a matter . . . of trying to describe the experience of mystery in the hope that the listeners will then discover it in themselves."[111] In a similar vein, Rudolf Otto had written of the "numinous":

> While it admits of being discussed, it cannot be strictly defined. There is only one way to help another to an understanding of it. He must be guided and led on by consideration and discussion of the matter through the ways of his own mind,

until he reach the point at which "the numinous" in him perforce begins to stir, to start into life and consciousness. . . . In other words our X cannot, strictly speaking, be taught, it can only be evoked, awakened in the mind; as everything that comes "of the spirit" must be awakened.[112]

In a little-known essay (which post-dates Bacik's study), Rahner links "the verbal or literary arts like poetry, drama and the novel" with theology, pointing out that the arts can be characterized "from a theological point of view by saying that they succeed, each in its own unique way, in putting a person in touch with those depths of human existence wherein religious experience takes place." In contrast to "reflexive, purely conceptual and rational theology," which often falls flat, these media may "perhaps evoke in me my own experience of the religious," and are thus enormously fruitful in stirring dormant religious awareness. Rahner complains that modern theologians have largely lost the capacity to connect conceptual theology to religious experience, and argues that we today lack what he calls a "poetic theology"; this he unequivocally portrays as "a defect in our theology."[113] To be sure, he admits, there is room for carefully reasoned conceptual theological thinking, and one cannot judge a theology merely by whether or not it "lead[s] immediately to some kind of religious or mystical experience." But nevertheless, he observes, one of the deleterious consequences of the rationalistic mode of theology is that "theology has lost so much of its poetry." This, Rahner writes, is one of the meanings of mystagogical theology: "It must not speak only in abstract concepts about theological questions, but must also introduce people to a real and original experience of the reality being talked about in these concepts." Thus, all theology must be "subjective"—not in the sense of being arbitrary or relativistic, but rather in that "ultimately, whether directly or indirectly, it must describe, evoke and introduce one mystagogically to this personal and spiritual relationship between man and God."[114]

Rahner's call for a mystagogically oriented poetic theology provides an extremely useful window, I think, into Heschel's style as a religious writer, and into the ways that form and content are so deeply intertwined in his thinking.[115] Recall that Heschel emphasizes faith over creed, depth theology over dogma; his first goal, as we have seen, is to "recover the situations that both precede and correspond to the theological formulations" and to "recall the questions that religious doctrines are trying to answer." My suggestion is that these commitments led Heschel almost ineluctably to a poetic, evocative mode of presentation. Heschel is keenly aware that his task may well be better served by the evocative mode than by the argumentative. One cannot, after all, argue for a purportedly universal, pre-conceptual experience; one can only strive to re-elicit and re-awaken it. It is this aspiration, it seems to me, that animates much of Heschel's writing.

To ask, as some have, whether Heschel is a philosopher *or* a poet is thus to insist on a dichotomy that is ultimately antithetical to Heschel's spirit as a thinker.[116] Heschel speaks in a poetic vein precisely because this is what he thinks is necessary for his theological project—first, as we have seen, because his cardinal task is to re-awaken a now quiescent sense of wonder, and second, as we shall see in the next chapter, because religious language is always "indicative" rather than "descriptive," and thus to speak about the mystery is to gesture toward it, and not to presume to capture it fully, thereby succumbing to the perennial temptations of epistemological arrogance and literal-mindedness. In other words, as I have suggested in the introduction, Heschel is a theologian *and* a poet, and to some extent he is the latter *precisely because* he is the former.[117]

THREE

REVELATION AND
CO-REVELATION

If wonder leads to a sense that "something is asked of us," revelation
seeks to address the obvious next question: *what,* precisely, is asked of
us? "The Bible," Heschel writes, "is an answer to the supreme question:
what does God demand of us? Yet the question has gone out of the world."[1]
In a spiritually robust environment, in other words, the experience of
wonder would elicit from humanity an openness to, indeed, an eagerness for the message of revelation. But our world, Heschel is at pains to
insist, is anything but spiritually robust: in casting off its capacity for
wonder, humanity has closed itself off from, and abandoned all interest
in, God's expectations. The Bible is thus rendered mute, irrelevant; it is
an answer to a question long since silenced and forgotten. If, as I have
suggested, the project of part I of *God in Search of Man* is to restore humanity to a wonder-filled response to the world as a whole, the project
of part II is to accomplish something similar in regards to the Bible—to
reactivate humanity's appreciation for, and receptivity toward, God's
revelation. Put differently: whereas part I seeks to re-elicit an interest
in "the supreme question," part II seeks to inspire a commitment to the
ultimate answer as Heschel conceives it—the revelation of God as found
in the Hebrew Bible.

In the modern world, Heschel laments, human thinking is dominated by a naturalism as impoverished as it is overconfident. If part I
of *GSM* bemoaned humanity's blindness to the wondrous allusiveness
of all reality, part II in turn rues its deafness to the awe-inspiring message of the Bible. But Heschel's ultimate purpose, it bears reiterating, is
not castigation, but transformation. His goal is to stir the reader from

his complacent naturalism, to remind him that another approach, profoundly attuned to the ways that both nature and scripture point beyond themselves, is both possible and necessary. Indeed, Michael Morgan has astutely characterized Heschel's approach in GSM as at least partly "therapeutic, aimed at reinvigorating Jewish life by diagnosing in detail the spiritual sickness of modern Judaism and then detailing a regimen of revitalization."[2] I might add that something similar is at play in part III of GSM as well: rather than seeing the commandments as mere actions to be performed by rote (and thereby succumbing to the perils of what Heschel calls "religious behaviorism"), the reader is encouraged to discover the divine meaning hidden within them. Whether dealing with nature, with scripture, or with divinely sanctioned deeds, Heschel's purpose is the same: to broaden humanity's horizons, to elicit from it a capacity to look and see more deeply, so that conventional, secularizing perspectives may be overcome—so that, in other words, the transcendent may come into clearer view.

* * *

Modern thinkers resisted revelation, Heschel writes, because of "two diametrically opposed conceptions of man: one maintained that man was too great to be in need of divine guidance, and the other maintained that man was too small to be worthy of divine guidance."[3] The first approach, rooted in social science, celebrated humanity's purported self-sufficiency, and thus labored under the illusion that technology could solve every problem. The second approach, rooted in natural science, insisted, in contrast, that humanity is "insignificantly small . . . in relation to the universe" and thus found it "preposterous" to assume that the infinite and eternal would commune with "the feeble, finite mind of man."[4] Another version of this second approach stems not from humanity's cosmic insignificance, but from its lack of moral stature: how could a species capable of genocide be considered worthy of divine communication? Given his powerful sense of modern man's massive moral failings, Heschel feels no small degree of sympathy with this question: "If man can remain callous to the horror of exterminating millions of men, women, and children; if man can be bloodstained and self-righteous, distort what his conscience tells, make soap of human flesh, then how can we assume that he is worthy of being apprehended and guided by the infinite God?"[5]

But over time, Heschel avers, it has become harder to dismiss the possibility of revelation on any of these grounds. The illusion of human self-sufficiency has been exposed as precisely that; the fantasy was no less false for being so widely accepted. Indeed, Heschel writes, "We have finally discovered what prophets and saints have always known: bread and power alone will not save humanity." The only thing that can stanch humanity's impulses toward violence and malice is God: "There is a passion and drive for cruel deeds which only the awe and fear of God can soothe; there is a suffocating selfishness in man which only holiness can ventilate."[6] Conversely, the insistence that humanity is too inconsequential to receive revelation has also been exposed as a sham:

> The realization of the dangerous greatness of man, of his immense power and ability to destroy all life on earth, must completely change our conception of man's place and role in the divine scheme. If this great world of ours is not a trifle in the eyes of God, if the Creator is at all concerned with His creation, then man—who has the power to devise both culture and crime, but who is also able to be a proxy for divine justice—is important enough to be the recipient of spiritual light at the rare dawns of his history.[7]

In other words, if the barbarisms of the twentieth century have taught us, on the one hand, that humanity lacks the capacity to cure its own ills, they have also shown, on the other hand, that it does have seemingly limitless potential to wreak havoc and devastation. If in one sense human beings have been exposed as having too little power, in another they have been shown to have too much. Thus, implicitly, Heschel replies to the moral challenge: though humanity may well be morally unworthy of receiving revelation, the extent of its power renders revelation an urgent necessity, since revelation alone (Heschel thinks) has the potential to place a brake on human callousness and brutality. Humanity's awesome dangerousness, we might say, trumps its moral unworthiness. Or, more positively, we can assert that God's concern for the world means that God must turn to humanity even in the face of its savagery and destructiveness. "Unless history is a vagary of nonsense," Heschel writes, "there must be a counterpart to the immense power of man to destroy, there must be a voice that says NO to man, a voice not vague, faint and inward, like qualms of conscience, but equal in spiritual might to man's power to destroy."[8]

That voice, of course, is the Bible's—and specifically, Heschel would no doubt add, that of the prophets. Heschel's theology of scripture thus assumes not only that God spoke in the past, but also that God continues to speak even now through the record of His past speech. It is thus a mistake to assume that for Heschel, the Bible is only a *record* of revelations past; on the contrary, it is also a *locus* of revelation in the present day. The Bible, in other words, is "living and active," addressing humanity even, and perhaps especially, amidst the depravity and malignity of modern times: "The Bible, speaking in the name of a Being that combines justice with omnipotence, is the never-ceasing outcry of 'No' to humanity. In the midst of our applauding the feats of civilization, the Bible flings itself like a knife slashing our complacency, reminding us that God, too, has a voice in history."[9]

Just as modern conceptions of humanity can be invoked to rule out revelation, so, too, can contemporary conceptions of God. For many, Heschel suggests, God is thought of only as "an immense unconscious mass of mystery" who remains shrouded always in "eternal mysteriousness."[10] This God, they contend, cannot speak or convey His will to humanity. But to maintain that God is total, unmitigated mystery, Heschel insists, is to lapse into a kind of presumptuous paganism which overconfidently maintains that God is the "Great Unknower. . . . Even having accepted the God of creation we still cling to the assumption that He who has the power to create a world is never able to utter a word."[11] But why, Heschel asks, should we make such an assumption? "If the world is the work of God, isn't it conceivable that there would be within His work signs of His expression?"[12] There is no legitimate theological reason, Heschel concludes, to constrain the Creator in a prison of silence. If creation, Heschel argues, then why not revelation?

* * *

Heschel suggests important points of continuity between the prophet's full-blooded experience of revelation, on the one hand, and our own often faint sense of divine beckoning, on the other. "When living true to the wonder of the steadily unfolding wisdom," Heschel writes, "we feel at times as if the echo of an echo of a voice were piercing the silence, trying in vain to reach our attention." This ever-so-subtle voice calls to us and reminds us of "the power invested in our words, in our deeds, in our thoughts." God's voice is so still and small that it can often be understood only retrospectively. Looking back on earlier experiences, we perceive a divine message encoded within them: "In our own lives the voice of God speaks slowly, a syllable at a time. Reaching the peak of years, dispelling some of our intimate illusions, and learning how to spell the meaning of life-experiences backwards, some of us discover how the scattered syllables form a single phrase."[13] Consciously or not, Heschel actually evokes two different types of divine communication here: first, a sense of God speaking through the tiny pricks of conscience that prod us to live better, holier lives; and second, a sense of God imparting to us—again, ever so subtly—the meaning of our lives. To be sure, these two types of divine-human intercourse are continuous with one another, but they should not be confused for the same experience.

A sense of wonder, an awareness of the mystery that pervades reality —a sense, in other words, of the allusiveness of all reality—leads human beings to ask, "Is there anything wherein His voice is not suppressed? Is there anything wherein His creation is not concealed?"[14] Note the paradox: God is speaking everywhere and at all times, and yet God's voice remains, in crucial ways, "suppressed." God is in search of man and thus beckons to human beings, but they must cultivate a discerning ear in order to hear the indistinct divine call. Now, we ought to pause for a moment to examine this elusive word, "suppressed." Something can be said to be suppressed if it is blocked either by an internal decision of the actor (in which case, "suppressed" is understood as akin to "repressed"), or by an external force; thus, one can suppress a smile, in the first sense, or suppress a political movement, in the second. What Heschel means here is, unfortunately, not fully clear: is God's speech suppressed by a decision on God's part, or by actions taken by human beings? In other words, does God swallow His own words, as it were, or are they somehow thwarted by human deafness and insensitivity? Perhaps, in an act of self-transcendence, God has decided to allow human beings the power to drown out His voice? Precisely what it is that stands between divine speaking and human hearing is left uncertain. We will have occasion to return to these questions when we consider the dialectic of divine hiding (God's decision), on the one hand, and divine exile (humanity's action), on the other, in chapters 5 and 7. For now, we can speculate that perhaps Heschel intends this ambiguity: God *is* speaking, but something—again, precisely what is left unclarified—stands in the way of humanity's hearing.

Some human beings "have sensed the sound of *Let There Be*, in the fullness of being," but for others the voice is a bit louder and more distinct, "lifting the curtain of unknowableness." Such people, Heschel insists, will be receptive to the possibility of divine revelation:

> Those who know that the grace of guidance may be ultimately bestowed upon those who pray for it, that in spite of their unworthiness and lowliness they may be enlightened by a spark that comes unexpectedly but in far-reaching wisdom, undeserved, yet saving, will not feel alien to the minds that perceived not a spark but a flame.[15]

In other words, one who discerns the voice of God in his own life will grow increasingly open to the possibility of divine address in the lives of the prophets. If we reject the notion that God seeks relationship with each and every human being—that is, if we remain deaf to the voice of God suing for humanity's attention—then we will rule out the possibility of revelation as an "absurdity." But the sensitive soul, attuned to the voice that rings slowly and subtly in his own life, "will find it impossible to remain certain of the impossibility of revelation."[16]

It is crucial that we understand what is going on here. In dealing with the question of revelation, the religious thinker has two options before him: either to insist on the absolutely *sui generis* nature of revelation and prophecy—that is, to emphasize the profound discontinuities between prophetic experience, on the one hand, and more general human experience, on the other—or to point instead to the ways in which revelation merely expands upon and intensifies that which is given to more ordinary human experience. In these passages, Heschel is a theologian of continuity, one who wants to draw attention to the ways each of us is a potential recipient of a kind of proto-revelation in which God speaks to us through conscience or through conveying of the meaning of our lives. Even though the two are decidedly not the same, there is a crucial continuity between the subtle experience of the sensitive person,[17] on the one hand, and the overwhelming experience of the prophet, on the other.[18]

In a sense, what Heschel says here about "proto-revelation" (the clumsy term is mine, not his) in everyday human experience is akin to something Buber had said three decades earlier. In a well-known lecture, Buber sought to bridge the chasm between "The Man of Today and the Jewish Bible" (1926). Acknowledging the fundamental "strangeness" of biblical categories to modern ears, Buber nevertheless insisted that an "approach" to the realities of creation, revelation, and redemption remains within humanity's reach.[19] Speaking of revelation, Buber writes:

> Sometimes we have a personal experience related to those recorded as revelations and capable of opening the way for them. We may unexpectedly grow aware of a certain apperception within ourselves, which was lacking but a moment ago, and whose origin we are unable to discover. . . . What occurred to me was otherness, the touch of the other. . . . I think that as we take, it is of the utmost importance to know that someone is giving. He who takes what is given him, and does not experience it as a gift, is not really receiving; and so the gift turns into theft. But when we do experience the giving, we find that revelation exists. . . . This path is the approach. It is on this path that we shall meet with the major experience that is of the same kind as our minor experience.[20]

We must pay careful attention to what Buber says: this experience of an apperception bestowed by another is not revelation but an anticipation thereof, and an approach thereto. I suspect that Heschel would say something similar about the human being who learns to read God's messages one syllable at a time. Such an attunement to God's voice, for Heschel, would constitute an approach to revelation, but not yet revelation itself. Note that Heschel calls this experience a personal "analogy"[21] to revelation—and an analogy to something, for all its similarity and comparability, is not the thing itself. But it is, as Buber says, "an approach,"[22] and "a beginning."[23]

* * *

According to philosopher Basil Mitchell, to believe in revelation is to believe that "God has found ways of communicating to his creatures fundamental truths about his nature and purposes which they would otherwise not know";[24] according to theologian William Placher, to speak of revelation is to be confident that "we have a way of talking about God appropriate to who God is, a way that is not something we can figure out by our reason."[25] These are robust definitions of revelation—they would not be content to affirm, for example, that in revelation all that is revealed is God's presence; instead, they assume that even if revelation discloses God's presence, it also discloses more—namely, information about God that we otherwise would not have, and that would be beyond our human capacities to acquire. With this definition in mind, we ought to ask: according to Heschel, does Judaism need a revelation?[26] That is, is there something Jews need to learn *about* God *from* God, and if so, what is it?

In order to interpret Heschel correctly, it is crucial to understand that for him, revelation is always, first and foremost, an act of God. In contrast to the mystic, the prophet does not seek out experiences of God; on the contrary, he attempts to escape them. To the prophet, Heschel writes, "Revelation is not an act of his seeking, but of his being sought after, an act of God's search of man." Revelation is a matter of divine pursuit rather than human discovery: "God's search of man, not man's quest for God, was conceived to have been the main event in Israel's history. This is at the core of all Biblical thoughts: God is not a being detached from man to be sought after, but a power that seeks, pursues and calls upon man." In a sense, then, the fundamental insight of revelation is that the divine quest is prior to the human. Judaism is born, Heschel insists, not out of a human insight, but rather out of a divine gesture: "Israel's religion originated in the initiative of God rather than in the efforts of man. It was not an invention of man but a creation of God; not a product of civilization, but a realm of its own."[27] Thus, as we shall see, although much of the Jewish tradition may have been shaped by human hands, its point of origin, according to Heschel, is in a divine call: "At Sinai we have learned that spiritual values are not only aspirations in us but a response to a transcendent appeal addressed to us."[28] I think we can say, then, that for Heschel, the form and the core content of revelation are, in crucial ways, the same: the fact of God's search for man.

Heschel takes all of this a step further. Sounding a Barthian note, he writes that all human knowledge of God is derived from, and dependent upon, God's revelation: "Man would not have known Him if He had not approached man. God's relation to man precedes man's relation to Him."[29] But this requires clarification, since at first glance it seems to undermine the very project of part I of *GSM*. There, as we have seen, Heschel tied an awareness of God to the basic human experiences of wonder, amazement, and the like. Can a thinker who begins his theologizing with a focus on human experience and its inherent God-connectedness then turn around and insist that humanity can only know God through revelation? In Christian terms, we might ask: can one begin as Rahner and end as Barth?

A proper interpretation of this sentence in Heschel is key to understanding his theology as a whole (as well as his theological method). While general human experience can point toward God as transcendent Creator, it tells us nothing about God's personality or about the depths of God's relationship to humanity. While Heschel's phenomenological approach to wonder leads him to speak of a transcendent Creator, his understanding of revelation yields a very different conception—namely, of a God who cares, and is in search of man. "Revelation means that the thick silence which fills the endless distance between God and the human mind was pierced, and man was told that God is concerned with the affairs of man; that not only does man need God, God is also in need of man."[30] What this means is that, for Heschel, a phenomenology of basic human experience, on the one hand, and an interpretation of the data of revelation, on the other, generate what I am suggesting is a core polarity in his theology—a God who is at once transcendent and in need, a God, in other words, both majestic and vulnerable.

Heschel is elusive—perhaps inconsistent is the more apt term—on this point. On the one hand, as we have just seen, he tells us that it is through revelation that we learn of God's concern for humanity. Yet, on the other hand, at times Heschel suggests that the divine concern is something that we can discover and discern in moments of insight: "At the climax of such moments," he writes, "we attain the certainty that life has meaning, that time is more than evanescence, that beyond all being there is someone who cares."[31] In light of this ostensible contradiction, one cannot help but wonder: is the fact of God's concern available to pre-revelational awareness, or not? Perhaps Heschel gestures toward an answer when he writes that "the extreme hiddenness of God is a fact of constant awareness. Yet His concern, His guidance, His will, His commandment, are revealed to man and capable of being experienced by him."[32] Now, of course, this sentence can be read in one of two ways: either to suggest that the fact of God's concern is knowable though two discrete paths—via revelation and via experience—or that it is available to experience only after, and in light of, what is taught through revelation. For all intents and purposes, in our post-Sinaitic age, the consequences may be the same—for those whose consciousness has been shaped by revelation, God's concern for humanity is discernible in our experience. But as a question of religious epistemology, a great deal is at stake: can humanity know about God's care without that fact being revealed to us? Inconsistencies in his approach notwithstanding, I would contend that as a rule, for Heschel, the answer is that it cannot: "Just as it is impossible to conceive of God without the world," he writes, "so it is impossible to conceive of His concern without the Bible. . . . The Bible disclose[s] the love of God for man."[33] One thing, at any rate, is absolutely clear: according to Heschel, the divine pathos (which we shall discuss at length in the next chapter) is not *perceived* by humanity in moments of insight generated by wonder and radical amazement. It is, rather, *revealed* by God to the human being who is open (through wonder and amazement) to receiving revelation.

That Heschel thinks Judaism needs a revelation is made abundantly clear by the following passage:

> The answer to the ultimate question is not found in the notion that the foundations of the world lie amid impenetrable fog. Fog is no substitute for light, and the totally unknown God is not a god but a name for cosmic darkness. The God whose presence in the world we sense is anonymous, mysterious. We may sense that He is, not what He is. What is His name, His will, His hope for me? How should I serve Him, how should I worship Him? The sense of wonder, awe, and mystery is necessary, but not sufficient to find the way from wonder to worship, from willingness to realization, from awe to action.[34]

Wonder, in other words, is necessary for knowledge of God, but it is not sufficient for it. Without wonder, a human being cannot receive revelation. But even a human being who has a sense of wonder, but lacks the contents of revelation, will remain in perpetual darkness as to God's "name, will, and hope." That knowledge depends upon revelation, rather than "perception"[35] or "insight."

Consider also how part I of *GSM* ends. Here again, Heschel makes explicit his assumption that the knowledge of God that is attendant upon wonder can only go so far—and, ultimately, for a Jewish theology, not far enough. One can get to the God of Mystery through wonder, but one can only get to the God of Israel through revelation. As Heschel writes:

> In thinking about the world, we cannot proceed without guidance, supplied by logic and scientific method. In thinking about the living God we must look to the prophets for guidance.... Private insights and inspirations prepare us to accept what the prophets convey. They enable us to understand the question to which revelation is an answer.... It is through the prophets that we may be able to encounter Him as a Being who is beyond the mystery. In the prophets the ineffable became a voice.... He is not the unknown; He is the Father, the God of Abraham.[36]

It is not just theology, but also anthropology that is shaped by the data of revelation. According to Heschel, it is through the Bible that human beings learn of their "independence of nature, [their] superiority to conditions, and [are] called on . . . to realize the tremendous implications of simple acts." The fact, in other words, that human life is not a tale signifying nothing, but rather a response to a divine call, is known to us only through the Bible. "The insight into the divine implications of human life is the distinct message of the Bible," Heschel writes, and thus, he insists, "The degree of our appreciation of the Bible is . . . determined by the degree of our sensitivity to the divine dignity of human deeds."[37] For Heschel, the Bible bestows upon us both a distinctive theology, and its correlative anthropology: a God who cares, and a human being who matters.

Beyond theology and anthropology, revelation also reveals God's way. If wonder leads us to an awareness that something is being asked of us, revelation comes to answer the obvious next question: "*What* does God demand of us?"[38] Implicitly countering Buber and Rosenzweig, Heschel writes: "God does not reveal Himself; he only reveals His way. Judaism does not speak of God's self-revelation, but of the revelation of His teaching for man." In other words, Heschel insists that revelation does include norms, and he thus seeks to give Jewish law a divine rather than a merely human sanction. Now, taken in isolation, this passage can be quite misleading, as it might suggest that, for Heschel, the fundamental—indeed, the exclusive—content of revelation is norms. At one level, Heschel does seem to be suggesting precisely that ("He *only* reveals His way"). But recall what we have just seen, namely, that for Heschel, through revelation we discover not just how God wants us to live, but also something crucial about God's relationship to human history—namely, the pathos and vulnerability of God. Thus, the next sentence in Heschel is critical: "The Bible reflects God's revelation of His relation to history, rather than of a revelation of His very self."[39] Here we come upon a significant theological polarity in Heschel, one which we have occasion to explore much more fully in chapter 4: on the one hand, an insistence that the God of Israel cares about the world to the point of suffering; on the other, the crucial caveat that this is a claim about God's relationship to history, and not an over-reaching assertion about God's own inner life.[40] I would suggest, in other words, that although he never articulates his position in quite this way, Heschel thinks that there are two components to revelation—a fact about God's relation to history and humanity, and a set of divine expectations for how the Jewish people should live. Judaism needs a revelation, we can say, because the latter teaches humanity both about God (and, by implication, about humanity itself), and about His expectations.

* * *

But what is the nature of God's revelation? Is the Torah verbally revealed, such that its words are ultimately, perhaps even literally, God's? Or is it a human document composed of human words? Could it somehow be both?

In beginning to address these vexed questions, it is important to keep in mind a point that Heschel returns to again and again, namely, that religious language is inherently inadequate to its task—that it tries, valiantly if also paradoxically, to speak of that which cannot be expressed by language. In chapter 18 of *GSM*, for example, the burden of Heschel's argument is his insistence that the prophetic word must never be confused with the plain words of everyday human speech. Heschel insists that words used in a religious context contain much more than they convey at a surface level; famously, he reminds us that "the cardinal sin in thinking about ultimate issues is literal-mindedness."[41] Thus, while the

words of scripture are true, they are not literally true; they contain a surplus of meaning that can never be conveyed by their literal meanings. It
is crucial that the listener (or reader) not miss the "unique connotations"
that words have when used in religious contexts. Religious language, for
Heschel, is in some sense antithetical to scientific language—whereas
the latter "must be clear, distinct, unambiguous, conveying the same concept to all people," the former must be suggestive, evocative, a *pointing to*
rather than a *capturing of*. Crucial for Heschel is the distinction between
what he calls "descriptive" and "indicative" words. Whereas the former
"stand in a fixed relation to conventional and definite meanings, such
as the concrete nouns, chair, table, or the terms of science," the latter, in
contrast, "stand in a fluid relation to ineffable meanings and, instead of
describing, merely intimate something which we intuit but cannot fully
comprehend."[42] Indicative words serve not to call up a definition in our
minds, but rather to introduce us to a reality that they signify. Religious
words, for Heschel, are pointers to that which is beyond expression; they
are gestures toward the ineffable. And since it is the ineffable toward
which they are gesturing, they must remain always only that—gestures,
rather than accurate or adequate portrayals.

According to Heschel, consciousness of the indicative nature of
religious language calls forth a mode of human "responsiveness" to it.
Whereas descriptive words may be taken literally, indicative words are to
be taken "responsively"—that is, they make us "part with preconceived
meanings," and they serve as "clues" and "guides" to the unknown, never
capturing but always pointing toward religious meanings. Thus, for example, the appropriate response to the idea that "God spoke" is not to
interpret it literally, but to shape our minds to "a meaning unheard of
before, [where] the word is but a clue; the real burden of understanding
is upon the mind and soul of the reader."[43] Only one who is entirely tone-
deaf to poetry (or metaphor) will assume that the exclusive options in
confronting religious language are literalism or dismissal of the words
as less than literally true. On the contrary, says Heschel: "The speech of
God is not less but more than literally real."[44]

What Heschel means by this evocative sentence, I think, is that one
can still be a theological realist without being a theological literalist;[45]
for Heschel, it would be at once scandalous and foolhardy to assume

that rejecting the latter somehow entails abandoning the former. Put somewhat differently, Heschel's warnings about the dangers of literal-mindedness are in no way meant to suggest that God (or God's revelation) is just a metaphor or symbol for purely human realities or aspirations. In a now classic essay, theologian Janet Martin Soskice points to

> a very real and important debate in modern theology. . . . The debate centres not on *whether* religious language is ineradicably metaphorical, but *what follows* if this is so. To put this in an extreme form, some theologians and philosophers of religion who agree that talk of God is metaphorical may be reflecting, in the mode of the prophets, psalmists, and mystics, on the inability of human thought or speech to comprehend the Diety [*sic*], while others mean something much more like "Christian language is merely metaphorical, a powerful if somewhat archaic system of images but not to be taken as somehow speaking about a world-transcending God in any sense."

Needless to say, Heschel would resile from the latter position and whole-heartedly embrace the former. Soskice's description of realists applies perfectly to Heschel: "While aware of the inability of any theological formulation to catch the divine realities, [theological realists] none the less accept that there are divine realities that theologians, however ham-fistedly, are trying to catch."[46] Heschel wants to argue against both literalists and fundamentalists (God is literally X), on the one hand, and against liberal reductionists (God is merely a metaphor for Y), on the other; his task is to chart a path that is at once robustly realist and fervently non-literalist. To misunderstand this is to miss the very heart of Heschel's theological project.

All this means that for Heschel, the key to approaching revelation lies in not presuming to understand too much. Revelation is, above all, a mystery, and any attempt fully to describe or convey the experience is doomed to failure. Since it is "an event in the realm of the ineffable . . . something which words cannot spell,"[47] revelation cannot be captured or portrayed by language. All words about revelation are indicative, rather than descriptive; they are "not photographs but illustrations, not descriptions but songs."[48] What is true about theological language in general is true about revelation in particular: "Like all terms that express the ultimate, ['revelation'] points to its meaning rather than fully rendering it."[49]

One of Heschel's most-cited sentences appears in this context: "As a report about revelation," he writes, "The Bible itself is *a midrash*."[50] It is important to understand exactly what Heschel intends here: contrary to popular interpretation,[51] he is not referring primarily to the humanity—as opposed to the divinity—of the Torah's language, but rather to the fact that its language is, necessarily, allusive and suggestive rather than literal or exhaustive. In other words, as is clear from context, the meaning of this sentence is not that the words of the Torah are, at bottom, human, but rather that they cannot ultimately provide for a full understanding of that which is inherently ineffable. Now, one could argue that these two meanings shade off into one another (words necessarily fail, one might suggest, precisely because they are human attempts to convey divine realities), but Heschel's concern here is with the nature of language rather than the problem of authorship.

Since, like the God it discloses, revelation always remains shrouded in mystery, a full-blown theory of revelation is an impossibility. "This is why," Heschel states, "all the Bible does is to state *that* revelation happened; *how* it happened is something they [*sic*] could only convey in words that are evocative and suggestive."[52] Just as God eludes language, so also does revelation: "Revelation can only be described *via negationis*; we can only say what it is not.... Never is our mind so inadequate as in trying to describe God. The same applies to the idea of revelation. When defined, described, it completely eludes us."[53] Thus, taking what he understands as the Bible's lead, Heschel abstains from offering a philosophy of revelation; to purport to describe the indescribable is, after all, to fail by definition. The implication of all of this, of course, is that there is no need—no justification, in fact—for taking the "sounds" and words of Sinai literally: "It was not essential that [God's] will be transmitted as sound," Heschel writes; "it was essential that it be made known to us."[54] Revelation, like the world itself, is available only to those who are mystery-minded:

> Our goal [in engaging the Bible, Heschel writes] must not be to find a definition, but to learn how to sense, how to intuit the will of God in the words. The essence of intuition is not in grasping what is describable but in sensing what is ineffable. The goal is to train the reason for the appreciation of what which lies beyond reason. It is only through our sense of the ineffable that we may intuit the mystery of revelation.[55]

So, *does* Heschel believe in verbal revelation—that is, did God speak actual words at Sinai? I should state at the outset that Heschel is elusive on this point, and a variety of passages can be marshaled from his writings in the service of widely divergent interpretations.[56] At times, Heschel sounds as if he believes that God revealed distinct words to Moses at Sinai. He writes, for example, that "out of God went the mystery of His utterance, and a word, a sound, reached the ear of man."[57] (Even here, though, we should be careful. What comes forth from God, according to Heschel, is "the mystery of His utterance"; "a word, a sound" is what reaches the human being in that encounter. Might Heschel be subtly suggesting that words are what human beings hear, but not necessarily what God "speaks"?) Heschel suggests that at Sinai there was "a show of thunder and lightning with a mysterious voice coming through the clouds";[58] he asserts that God spoke while Moses heard;[59] he extols the prophets for caring "intensely . . . [and] exclusively for what God has to say";[60] and he speaks unapologetically of the "divine language" of the Bible.[61] His ostensible embrace of the idea that God spoke actual words is also manifest in the following lengthy passage:

> Some people may wonder: why was the light of God given in the form of language? How is it conceivable that the divine should be contained in such brittle vessels as consonants and vowels? This question betrays the sins of our age: to treat lightly the ether which carries the light-waves of the spirit. What else in the world is as capable of bringing man and man together over the distances in space and in time? Of all things on earth, words alone never die. They have so little matter and so much meaning.
>
> The Bible does not deal with divinity but with humanity. Addressing human beings about human affairs, whose language should be employed if not man's? And yet, it is as if God took these Hebrew words and breathed into them His power, and the words became a live wire charged with His spirit. To this very day they are hyphens between heaven and earth.
>
> What other medium could have been employed to convey the divine? Pictures enameled on the moon? Statues hewn out of the Rockies? What is wrong with the human ancestry of scriptural vocabulary?[62]

And yet, in light of what we have seen of Heschel's admonitions against literalism, we should be at least somewhat wary about taking his own invocation of divine words too literally. For Heschel, to affirm that revelation takes places in concrete words would be to compromise God's transcendence and ineffability; recall his explicit contention that revelation is "an event in the realm of the ineffable . . . something which words cannot spell."[63] It is not surprising, then, that Heschel also makes a variety of statements that point away from an affirmation of verbal revelation. "It was not essential," he writes, "that [God's] will be transmitted as sound; it was essential that it be made known to us."[64] Indeed, Heschel tells us, "the leading exponents of Jewish thought exhort us not to imagine that God speaks, or that a sound is produced by Him through organs of speech."[65] The Torah, it seems, is thus the product of human hands:

> The prophets bear witness to an event. The event is divine, but the formulation is done by the individual prophet. According to this conception, the idea is revealed; the expression is coined by the prophet. The expression 'the word of God' would not refer to the word as a sound or a combination of sounds. Indeed, it has often been maintained that what reached the ear of man was not identical with what has come out of the spirit of the eternal God.... Out of the experience of the prophets came the words, words that try to interpret what they perceived.... The Bible reflects its divine as well as its human authorship.[66]

In view of these rather discordant formulations, it is easy to be led astray in interpreting Heschel; indeed, it is tempting to privilege one set of formulations while insisting that the other is somehow less reflective of Heschel's "real" position. In successive editions of a popular textbook on Conservative Judaism, Elliot Dorff offers disparate interpretations of Heschel's intent. In the first edition of *Conservative Judaism: Our Ancestors to Our Descendants*, Dorff describes Heschel as "the most famous modern proponent" of the view that "God uttered words during acts of revelation,"[67] and therefore categorizes him as a thinker who "retains a direct, verbal revelation at Sinai . . . [and] claims that God communicated His will to Moses in a direct, verbal way."[68] In the second edition, however, Dorff admits that his first interpretation was in error, and now suggests that for Heschel, "the Bible's citations of God's words should not be understood literally as God speaking physical, audible words, but rather such language in the Bible is only a human retelling of the experience of God in human terms."[69] On Dorff's more recent reading of Heschel, then, the Bible is a *human* document made up of thoroughly *human* words. More recently, Dorff has stated this position even more starkly: a "theory that proposes that the Revelation at Mount Sinai lacked all content," he writes, "is that of Abraham Joshua Heschel." According to Heschel, Dorff claims, "human beings created the contents of Jewish sacred texts."[70] Unfortunately, I fear that Dorff gets Heschel wrong both times—in the first edition, because he assumes that according to Heschel, God spoke literal words at Sinai (which, as I have already suggested, is not a sustainable interpretation of Heschel's view); and in the second, because he insists that for Heschel the contents of Torah are a human creation. Dorff is led astray, I think, by his implicit assumption that (for Heschel) "verbal revelation" and "revelation with content" are overlapping categories, and that to reject the former is necessarily to deny the latter. But this is, I think, fundamentally incorrect; on the contrary, I would suggest that Heschel wants to disentangle these two concepts from one another. For Heschel, I would argue, revelation conveys *divine content* in *human words*. Returning with new eyes to a passage we have just seen, we can see that Heschel explicitly says as much: "The event is divine," he writes, "but the formulation is done by the individual prophet.... The idea is revealed; the expression is coined by the prophet."[71]

Consider also another previously mentioned passage: "It was not essential that [God's] will be transmitted as sound; it was essential that it be made known to us."[72] God's will, Heschel says, is conveyed to the prophet, even if not necessarily in human words. And at one point in *The Prophets*, Heschel observes that "prophecy consists in the inspired communication of *divine attitudes* to the prophetic consciousness."[73] This formulation is potentially quite revealing: the phrase "divine attitudes," after all, suggests content, but not necessarily actual words.[74] We have already seen that Heschel needs revelation to answer two questions—first, what God asks of us, and second, what kind of God it is who does the asking. Or, as Heschel himself puts it, "At stake in our discussion is ... the question of either accepting or rejecting the Bible's formidable claim that God really is such as the prophets proclaim [2]; that His will really is such as the prophets maintain [1]." In order to supply answers to these questions, Heschel thinks, revelation must contain positive content—again, even if the concrete formulations are the prophet's rather than God's.

All of this makes sense only if we carefully recall something that we have already seen in the previous chapters—namely that for Heschel, not all thought is irreducibly linguistic. On the contrary, as David Novak astutely notes in his discussion of revelation in modern Jewish thought,

"Heschel seems to be implying that all language is essentially responsive and never truly original per se. Language, for him, seems to presuppose a form of thought that is metalinguistic, that transcends language while still making language possible."[75] As we have seen, the language that emerges from the moment of revelation will always be allusive rather than exhaustive, indicative rather than descriptive, but—and this is the crucial point for our purposes—the humanness of the words does not entail, for Heschel, the sheer humanness of the ideas conveyed.

* * *

In order to understand Heschel more clearly, it is fruitful to compare his approach to revelation with those of some other major figures in twentieth-century Jewish thought. According to Martin Buber, in revelation, "man receives, and what he receives is not a 'content' but a presence.... The word of revelation is: I am there as whoever I am there. That which reveals is that which reveals. That which has being is there, nothing more."[76] In a similar vein, Franz Rosenzweig writes that "all that God ever reveals in revelation is—revelation. Or, to express it differently, he reveals nothing but himself to man. The relation of this accusative and dative to each other is the one and only content of revelation."[77] It should be obvious by now that Heschel's view of revelation differs in significant ways from Buber's and Rosenzweig's. Whereas for them revelation lacks content—any content one is tempted to ascribe to it is in fact already a human response to the revelation of the divine presence[78]—for Heschel, as we have seen, revelation does have content, and of two kinds: God reveals both His will and the fact of His pathos. Heschel writes, "God does not reveal Himself; he only reveals His way.... The Bible reflects God's revelation of His relation to history, rather than of a revelation of His very self."[79] With these words, Heschel may very well have had a critique of Buber and Rosenzweig in mind. But to be fair, it should be pointed out that neither Buber nor Rosenzweig believed that God reveals His essence in revelation—a revelation of God's presence, after all, is not the same as a revelation of His essence. Nevertheless, if Heschel does have Buber and Rosenzweig in mind here, then one can say that (however inaccurate his reading of them) from his perspective, on their approach God reveals both too much and too little in the moment of revelation—too much in that God reveals His very self (thus compromising God's transcendence), and too little in that God fails to reveal His will and His way of relating and responding to human history.

With that in mind, it is equally important to distinguish clearly between Heschel's approach and those of certain Orthodox thinkers who unabashedly affirm the verbal revelation of the Torah, and insist, with Norman Lamm, that God's will was "communicated in discrete words and letters."[80] As we have already seen in some depth, both Heschel's focus on the ineffability of religious experience and his desire to protect God's transcendence against crude anthropomorphizing militate against his acceptance of such an approach.

Finally, to the reader familiar with even the barest outlines of their thought, it will hardly be surprising that Heschel's approach to revelation and Mordecai Kaplan's are light years apart. Recall that for Heschel, revelation is dependent, first and foremost, upon the decision of the transcendent God of Israel to reach out to humanity. According to Kaplan, in stark contrast:

> When our forefathers declared an idea to be revealed, it was because they were convinced, in light of their faith in God and of their conception of Him, that the idea was somehow related to God's purpose in having created them, and to the fulfillment of their destiny as individuals, as Jews, and as human beings. We today, who look upon God as the Power that prods man to become fully human, must regard as revealed any idea that helps individuals and groups to achieve the full stature of their humanity. Man's discovery of religious truth is God's revelation of it, since the very process of that discovery implies an activity of God.[81]

Note that Kaplan himself emphasizes that his naturalistic approach to revelation is rooted in his naturalistic understanding of God. Heschel's approach to revelation, I hasten to point out, shares a great deal with the position Kaplan assigns to "our forefathers" and their now purportedly outdated conceptions: Heschel, too, took ideas to be revealed because he was convinced, in light of his faith in God and of his conception of Him, that the idea of divine pathos, for example, was somehow related to God's purpose in having created human beings, and to the fulfillment of their destiny as individuals, as Jews, and as human beings. Although revelation may come to expression in human words, it begins, always, in divine initiative, and conveys (however inadequately) a message that is

God's. In the words of Christian theologian Jeff Astley, which Heschel would no doubt have endorsed: "'Reveal' and 'disclose,' in a theological context, are verbs taking God as their subject. . . . It is God who pulls back the curtain, not man. . . . It is [a] *divine act*."[82] For Heschel, then, one cannot simply reduce divine revelation to human discovery without embracing a thoroughgoing naturalism, and thus vitiating, to his mind, the very theological core of the Jewish tradition.

Against Buber and Rosenzweig, then, Heschel affirms that beyond mere presence, God reveals content; against Lamm, he maintains that the primary content of revelation is not verbal but metalinguistic—the text of the Torah, in other words, is the result of revelation, rather than the very content thereof; and against Kaplan, he insists that revelation begins with the transcendent God who seeks to communicate His will and to share His pathos with humanity.

In a series of essays, Neil Gillman has made the highly idiosyncratic claim that "the only genuine theological dividing line among contemporary Jews is verbal revelation, and on this issue, one can be only for or against."[83] Since, Gillman insists, Heschel is against, his approach to revelation can be clustered with the very different and (as we have seen) themselves quite varied approaches of Buber, Rosenzweig, and Kaplan.[84] Now, on one level, Gillman's contention is accurate as far as it goes—like the other three figures mentioned, Heschel did not believe that the Torah was revealed in discrete words and letters. But Gillman's presentation surely obscures as much as it reveals: as we have seen, in insisting that revelation does contain positive content, Heschel has articulated a view of revelation that is a far cry indeed from Buber's or Rosenzweig's. And, needless to say, in its focus on the initiative of the transcendent God, Heschel's perspective on revelation bears almost nothing in common with Mordecai Kaplan's naturalism. But even more fundamentally, one wonders whether any coherent sense can be made of Gillman's insistence that verbal revelation "is the only genuine theological dividing line among contemporary Jews." Think, for example, of Heschel and Kaplan on the nature of God: whereas the former would undoubtedly regard the latter's naturalism as tantamount to atheism, the latter would have forcefully charged the former with holding to theological perspectives that were naïve and antiquated at best. Heschel, I suspect, might well have argued that such differences about God have implications that are at least as critical as disagreements about the nature and content of revelation. In contrast to Gillman, Heschel might have said that the most important theological dividing line among contemporary Jews is God—specifically, the question of whether or not one speaks of a God who possesses will and consciousness, and on this issue, there can only be for or against. Along these lines, then, one could divide Jewish theologians thus: while many thinkers—ranging from Joseph Soloveitchik and Norman Lamm to Abraham Heschel and Franz Rosenzweig—profess faith in a God who cares for humanity and has a will He wants us to obey, others, like Mordecai Kaplan, do not. Thus, Gillman's essays go astray on two counts—first, they place revelation at the exclusive center of Jewish theology in a way that is not defensible; and second, they focus so single-mindedly on one aspect of revelation—whether or not it is verbal—that they thereby overlook or simply ignore both crucial nuances *within* each perspective and core disagreements *among* them.

An approach to the question of revelation that is similar to the one I have suggested above is implicit in the work of Heschel's contemporary, Reform theologian Jacob Petuchowski. According to Petuchowski, a meaningful notion of divine revelation is inextricably linked to, and dependent upon, an affirmation of the transcendent, personal God of classical Judaism. The fate of the one is inextricably woven with the fate of the other—in order to speak coherently of revelation, in other words, one must be able to invoke a personal, purposive God who serves as the revealer. Since the transcendent God did not fare well in modernity, Petuchowski argues, neither did traditional notions of revelation as God's incursion into history. In Hegel's system, for example, God "became an immanent Absolute, and proud man self-consciously became His bearer. Such a God does not reveal Himself to man—neither from above nor from outside. The very basis of the biblical concept of revelation had now disappeared." The collapse of the transcendent God meant that "modern Judaism, too, twisted revelation to inspiration."[85] More broadly, Petuchowski insists that many modern understandings of God simply cannot generate robust notions of revelation: "The Deists of the 17th and 18th centuries . . . the rationalists of the 19th, and the naturalists of the 20th" have all offered "God concepts' that, though they may indeed serve an important function . . . are [nevertheless] substitutes for, not restatements of, the biblical God of Israel."[86] However, Petuchowski contends, times have changed, and with them the religious situation: modernist illusions that God and humanity are one have faded, and as a result, "the religious person of today finds himself or herself again in the situation of biblical man: God is God, and man is man. . . . [As a consequence,] the biblical concept of revelation . . . has likewise become accessible again to people of today."[87] It is evident from all this that Petuchowski would divide Jewish thinkers quite differently from Gillman—for the former, the pivotal question on which all else turns is whether or not one speaks of a personal God. If so, Petuchowski is confident, then one can speak of revelation, and of God as revealer; if not, then one cannot really speak of revelation at all without contorting the word beyond recognition and ultimately reducing it to "inspiration." "It was left to our own time to rediscover the personal God," Petuchowski writes; "Kierkegaard, Barth, and Niebuhr have their Jewish counterparts in Buber, Rosenzweig, and Abraham J. Heschel." One of the crucial consequences of this rediscovery, Petuchowski insists, is that "modern Jews can again speak seriously about Revelation." To be sure, modern Jews remain modern, and "they cannot close their eyes to the findings of biblical criticism," but they nevertheless "can believe—and some of them *do* believe—that God really reveals Himself."[88]

* * *

In dealing with the Bible, Heschel seeks to steer a course between the Scylla of what he calls "fundamentalism" and the Charybdis of what he terms "rationalism." Heschel's task as a religious thinker is, in his words, "to winnow false notions of the fundamentalist[s]" while simultaneously "dampen[ing] the over-confidence of the rationalists."[89] Nowhere does he feel this imperative more keenly than in his attempts to confront the challenges posed to traditional notions of revelation by the findings of historical criticism. Acknowledging biblical criticism while simultaneously fighting its potentially lethal implications for theology, Heschel distinguishes between Mosaic authorship on the one hand and divine revelation on the other. Historical criticism may necessitate surrender of the former, but Heschel insists that it cannot touch the latter;

to presume that it can is to be guilty of a category mistake, since, after all, "revelation is not a matter of chronology," and "we accept the authority of the Pentateuch not because it is Mosaic, but because Moses was a prophet."[90] In other words: biblical criticism can force believers to revisit assumptions about the dating of the human text before them, but it cannot compel them to jettison their faith in God's involvement in its origins. "Divine inspiration," Heschel writes, refers to a "mystery," whereas Mosaic authorship refers to a "historic[al] fact"; whereas the latter can be "analyzed, examined, and conveyed in terms of chronological information," the former "can only be alluded to and expressed in terms of grandeur and amazement."[91] "The truth is," Heschel writes, "that revelation is a problem that eludes scientific inquiry. . . . Biblical criticism may have succeeded in . . . compelling us to modify our conception of how the text was transmitted, but the act of revelation remains beyond its scope."[92] Put differently, Heschel argues that while biblical scholarship can impact upon matters of "creed"—that is, on our "relation to the date of the Biblical books," it ought to have no say at all in matters of "faith"—that is, in our "relation to the prophetic event."[93] This, then, is how Heschel negotiates the challenge posed by critical scholarship on the Bible: he will relinquish his belief in the text's Mosaic origins (while downplaying the importance of the idea to traditional theology), but passionately uphold its divine provenance (even as he insists that the latter not be understood in crudely literalistic ways). Thus, Heschel all but explicitly assures us, the sophisticated believer can accept the critical findings of biblical scholars but still rest assured that the divinity of the text remains beyond the reach of even the most overweening of skeptics.

In both GSM and (at much greater length) in TMHS, Heschel employs his vast erudition to demonstrate the extraordinary diversity of rabbinic opinion regarding revelation and its contents, and thus, I suggest, to imply that the revisions to theology induced by biblical criticism are in fact less radical than they at first appear. The rabbis, Heschel is at pains to show, were not all revelational maximalists, and some would presumably have been less troubled by historical criticism than others.[94]

In an important series of essays on revelation, Petuchowski adopts a similar approach to the one espoused by Heschel. Questions about Mosaic authorship of the Pentateuch, Petuchowski insists, need not be translated into doubts about divine revelation. Whereas Mosaic author-ship is, in Petuchowski's terms, a *literary* question, divine revelation, in contrast, is a *theological one,* and the former cannot really touch, let alone undermine, the latter: "The theological problem of Revelation, and the literary problem of the evolution and transmission of the Text," Petu-chowski writes, "are, and must be retained as, quite separate."[95] Indeed, "the 'dating' of biblical materials, one way or the other, leaves the basic theological issues completely unaffected."[96] In other words, Petuchowski argues, "What does *not* necessarily follow [from the findings of critical scholars] is the widespread notion that, because Moses did not write the Torah, the Torah cannot be Divine Revelation. For, conceivably, God could have made use of J,E,P,D, and all the rest, in very much the same way in which it was traditionally believed that He had made use of Moses alone."[97] This distinction between the literary, on the one hand, and the theological, on the other, is not as new as one may be inclined to think; indeed, Petuchowski claims, it is already implicit in rabbinic literature. After all, he avers, "the dogma of 'Torah from Heaven,' at the time of its original formulation, did not carry with it any one canonized version of the Torah's literary history."[98] For the rabbis, divine revelation—and not Mosaic authorship—held the status of dogma. "Strange as it may seem," Petuchowski writes, "'the *Mosaic* authorship of the Pentateuch,' though generally assumed by Jews throughout the centuries, was not at all what really mattered to Judaism. What was emphasized was the fact that the Torah came from *God!*"[99] As with Heschel, so Petuchowski: each seeks to disentangle Mosaic authorship from divine revelation, and each, in turn, insists that the former notion was always less important to Jewish thought than is popularly assumed.[100]

With all that is compelling in Heschel and Petuchowski's approaches —surely there are some theological questions on which historians simply cannot pass judgment—it should be pointed out that similar limitations bedevil each of them. Both Heschel and Petuchowski write as if the central challenge posed by historical criticism of the Bible is the dating of texts, rather than the contention that different sources from different authors and periods express very different ideological and theological perspectives. What Frederick Grant has written of the New Testament applies with equal force, *mutatis mutandis,* to the Hebrew Bible. The diversity within cannot be "limited to choice of language, as if the New Testament writers all meant the same thing but selected different words for saying it. The diversity involves some of the basic ideas of New Testament theology: the religious attitude, ethos, and approach of quite different groups."[101] Thus, to rest content with saying, as Heschel does, that whether a text is written by Moses or another prophet is immaterial, is, in a sense, to evade the more difficult question of whether and in what ways multiple sources that understand God (and God's will) in radically divergent ways can all be said to be products of divine revelation. At one point, Heschel tellingly insists that there are only "relatively minor discrepancies within the Bible,"[102] but nowhere argues or defends this contention. It is fair to conclude, I suggest, that Heschel (and Petuchowski) fail to meet the depth of the historicist challenge to scripture.[103]

It is worth noting that Heschel could have taken a different tack and maintained that historical criticism of the Bible is based on a set of unargued-for assumptions about the nature of the text. He could have insisted, in other words, that historical criticism simply *assumes* what it purports to *find,* namely, that the biblical text can be studied like any other human text. But Heschel obviously did not find such an approach compelling, and he likely worried that it could be used to legitimate all kinds of intellectual evasion and obscurantism.

* * *

There is a crucial tension in Heschel's approach to the Bible. On the one hand, he insists that the Jewish people have faith that the Bible conveys the will of God: "The essence of our faith in the sanctity of the Bible," he writes, "is that its words contain that which God wants us to know and to fulfill."[104] But, on the other hand, he admits that "the share of the prophet [in revelation] manifested itself not only in what he was able to give but also in what he was unable to receive."[105] In other words, even as Heschel insists that in some ways the text is more perfect as a result of the "co-revelation"[106] of God and humanity, he also subtly acknowledges that in other respects the text is rendered less perfect by the limitations of the human partner.[107] This latter, of course, is a huge admission, and one that drives a potential wedge between the will of God, on the one hand, and the contents of scripture, on the other. Heschel comes close to saying so explicitly when he reminds his readers that "the words of scripture . . . are neither identical with, nor the eternally adequate rendering of, the divine wisdom." But immediately after making this point, Heschel feels the need to assert that "in its present form, the text contains that which God wishes us to know."[108] Heschel is here attempting to hold onto both poles of an important dialectic: God allows human beings to determine the content of the text, and yet providence still serves as a guarantor that the text does reflect what God wants us to know. This dialectical move recognizes the humanity of the text even as it works to uphold its divinity. Or, to put it differently, Heschel's invocation of providence enables him to acknowledge the gap between God's will and the biblical text without allowing the gap to open into a chasm.[109]

Building on a famous passage in the Palestinian Talmud,[110] Heschel reminds his readers that "[God's] will or [God's] wisdom is not completely expressed through the prophets. Prophecy is superior to human wisdom, and God's love is superior to prophecy."[111] Thus, again, Heschel is willing to entertain, and here even to accentuate, the possibility that what is written in the Torah may in some way fall short of the divine wisdom (and, implicitly, of the divine compassion). "God is infinitely more sublime than what the prophets were able to comprehend," Heschel writes, "and the heavenly wisdom is more profound than what the Torah contains in its present form."[112]

All of this has crucial implications for Heschel's approach to dealing with "harsh passages" in scripture. In confronting this vexed issue, Heschel begins by reminding us that "in analyzing this extremely difficult problem, we must first of all keep in mind that the standards by which those passages are criticized are impressed upon us by the Bible, which is the main factor in ennobling our conscience and in endowing us with the sensitivity that rebels against all cruelty."[113] Beginning in this way serves two separate purposes—first, it defends scripture from its critics by insisting that our very impulse to recoil at its ostensible cruelty has been inculcated in us by scripture itself. But second, it also provides sanction for those who want to read such passages creatively, or even resistantly, since their unwillingness to submit to a particular biblical passage is seen as growing out of a more fundamental commitment to the broader message of the Bible itself. In one crucial sentence, then, Heschel manages both to safeguard the dignity of scripture and to empower those who would interpret it boldly.

Still seeking to fend off attacks upon the Bible, Heschel emphasizes that harsh passages therein "describ[e] actions which were taken *at particular moments*," and contrasts them with "the compassion, justice and wisdom of the laws that were legislated *for all times*." But then he adds, even more starkly than before, that "we must not equate prophecy with God. Prophecy is superior to human wisdom, and God's love is superior to prophecy. Not every utterance contained in the Bible is to be regarded as a norm or a standard of behavior."[114] All of this leads Heschel to an explicit willingness to countenance, and even to encourage, human challenges to the biblical text. "Resignation and acceptance of the inscrutable will of God," Heschel writes, "are expressions of normal piety. In contrast, though *not* in contradiction, stands the prophet who, instead of being unquestioning and submissive in the face of God, dares to challenge His judgment, to remind Him of His covenant and to plead for His mercy."[115] The implication is clear: fidelity to the text need not always mean passive submission to it. More dramatically: fidelity to God may at times necessitate active resistance to His word—let alone, it would seem, to the biblical text, which, as we have seen, cannot be unequivocally equated with God's own word. Thus, to reiterate, at the same time that he defends scripture against charges of barbarism or cruelty, Heschel unambiguously champions "the independence of human understanding and its power to challenge a prophet's claim."[116] For Heschel, these two commitments are inextricably intertwined.

Heschel warns against servility as an exclusive religious posture and rails against "the obscurantism of a mechanical deference to the Bible." The biblical words are there to be engaged with, not passively submitted to. Heschel writes:

> The prophetic words were given to us to be understood, not merely to be mechanically repeated. The Bible is to be understood by the spirit that grows with it, wrestles with it, and prays with it. . . . To disregard the importance of continuous understanding is an evasion of the living challenge of the prophets, an

escape from the urgency of responsible experience of every man, a denial of the
deeper meaning of "the oral Torah."[117]

Not to put too fine a point on it: Heschel is here suggesting not merely
that it is *permissible* to read the text resistantly (or, what may amount to
the same thing, to read the text with greater fidelity to God's wisdom
than to the words of a particular verse), but also that at times it is actively
required of us to do so. To read with an overabundance of deference,
and thereby to silence the very conscience that has been nurtured by
the Bible's ideals, is, as he puts it, to deny "the deeper meaning of the
oral Torah." Faithfulness to the plain meaning of a particular verse can
amount to faithlessness with the broader covenantal process of reading
scripture. Conversely, sometimes readings that might appear rebellious
on the surface are in fact manifestations of deep faithfulness to God
and text.

Now, to be sure, Heschel was neither a legal theorist nor a legal deci-
sor, and nowhere does he offer a guide to how—or, for that matter, by
whom—such creative-resistant readings should be undertaken. But the
direction of his thinking is clear: passive surrender is unbecoming of
God's covenantal partner. A God who takes humanity seriously enough
to engage and speak with it seeks to cultivate active readers rather than
passive slaves. According to Heschel, then, human self-transcendence
should not be conflated with excessive submissiveness or abandonment
of conscience.

Heschel takes his commitment to active reading one step further.
The mandate for continuous understanding means not only that Israel
must sometimes read scripture resistantly, but also that it must sometimes read expansively. Revelation, Heschel writes, is not "vicarious thinking," and one cannot blithely assume that the prophets, or the rabbis,
have done all the thinking we need for us:

> The prophets tried to extend the horizon of our conscience and to impart to us
> a sense of the divine partnership in our dealings with good and evil and in our
> wrestling with life's enigmas. They tried to teach us how to think in the cate-
> gories of God: His holiness, justice and compassion. The appropriation of these
> categories, far from exempting us from the obligation to gain new insights in our
> own time, is a challenge to look for ways of translating Biblical commandments
> into programs required by our own conditions.[118]

Heschel does not spell out or offer examples of what he has in mind here, but I think he intends something like this: biblical laws are to be understood not merely as concrete norms, but also as paradigms. They invite each generation to develop contemporary commitments that apply the eternal essence of the laws to particular times. Thus, for example, a modern reader who learns of the biblical requirement to build a parapet around one's roof (Deuteronomy 22:8) will discern from the concrete norm that the Torah is concerned with a broader commitment to public safety; or one who reads of Amos's passion on behalf of the poor will concern himself with how the latter are treated in his own society. This principle should apply to theological commandments, and not just to ethical or interpersonal ones. Thus, one who understands that to observe the Sabbath is to offer testimony that God is creator, while human beings are mere creatures, may conclude that in a time of unprecedented technological power, additional forms of Sabbath-like acknowledgment of the divine-human divide are called for. And so on.

What all of this means, Heschel says in one of his frequently cited formulations, is that "Judaism is based upon a minimum of revelation and a maximum of interpretation, upon the will of God and upon the understanding of Israel."[119] It bears reiterating that for Heschel this is not—or, in any case, it is not merely—an argument for the centrality of the Oral Torah alongside the Written Torah, but more fundamentally (and potentially more radically) an argument for seeing the Oral Torah as an ongoing process. Just as the rabbis do not read the Bible passively or submissively, so also must contemporary Jews not read the Bible and the rabbis passively or submissively. Heschel writes, "There is a partnership of God and Israel in regard to both the world and the Torah: He created the earth and we till the soil; He gave us the text and we refine and complete it." But crucially, he continues: "The Bible is a seed, God is the sun, but we are the soil. Every generation is expected to bring forth new understanding and new realization. The word is the word of God, and its understanding He gave unto man."[120]

The refusal of servility and the cultivation of active reading are of a piece with the broader religious ethos Heschel seeks to instill. "To have faith," he writes, "does not mean . . . to dwell in the shadow of old ideas conceived by prophets and sages, to live off an inherited estate of doctrines and dogmas. In the realm of the spirit, only he who is a pioneer is able to be an heir."[121] In his Yiddish-language presentation of the Hasidic master Rabbi Menahem Mendl of Kotzk, Heschel repeatedly emphasizes that imitation, whether of others or of oneself, is a grave sin.[122] On this point Heschel manifests deep sympathy for the Kotzker; as he himself puts it in *MNA*, "The wages of spiritual plagiarism is the loss of spiritual integrity. . . . Authentic faith is more than an echo of a tradition. It is a creative situation, an event."[123]

And yet all too often religious traditions ossify, becoming "heirlooms" rather than "living fountains."[124] "Inherent to all traditional religion," Heschel states, "is the peril of stagnation. What has become settled and established may easily turn foul. Insight is replaced by clichés, elasticity by obstinacy, spontaneity by habit."[125] In such circumstances, when religion grows "irrelevant, dull, oppressive, insipid,"[126] when it is reduced to lifeless "customs and ceremonies,"[127] what is needed are courageous people willing to think, feel, and act differently. "Acts of dissent," Heschel writes, "prove to be acts of renewal."[128] The kind of "creative dissent" Heschel values, which "comes out of love and faith," is exceedingly rare, since it requires an exquisite combination of "deep caring, concern, untrammeled radical thinking informed by rich learning, a degree of audacity and courage, and the power of the word."[129] In other words, creative dissenters need to be thoroughly immersed in tradition without, however, being slaves to it; they have to combine deep faithfulness with profound audacity. Such souls are scarce, Heschel realizes, and yet they are indispensable if religion is to remain vital and avoid decay.

Heschel's insistence that God's love goes beyond what any text can adequately convey; his attendant disallowance of "mechanical deference" to received tradition; and his urging that people of faith sometimes need to read resistantly, actively, and expansively thus grow out of a more fundamental commitment to the religious value of human agency and responsibility. A God who is in search of man is not interested in groveling or obsequiousness but in courage, audacity, and even dissent.

* * *

As in his discussion of God's existence, so also in his consideration of revelation Heschel's thinking is marred by his refusal to allow any place for doubt. In place of argumentation, the skeptic is met only with impatience and impassioned re-assertion.[130] Heschel heaps scorn upon those who question whether revelation was in fact what the prophets thought and taught it was. Indeed, he is indignant at the very fact that such theories are entertained at all. Thus, responding to the crucial question of whether or not the prophets are "reliable" and their testimony "trustworthy," Heschel writes:

> In calling upon the prophets to stand before the bar of our critical judgment, we are like dwarfs undertaking to measure the heights of giants. How could our spiritual attainments be a yardstick with which to measure what they achieved, if their strivings were so completely above our own? Are we as open to God as they were? Do we care as intensely, as exclusively for what God has to say as they did?[131]

Heschel's harsh words for doubters persist throughout his "Examination of the Prophets" (chapter 24 of *GSM*) and his discussion of "The Bible and the World" (chapter 25): "If God had anything to do with the prophets," he writes, "then the prophets were neither liars nor impostors. And yet, we, Philistines, continue to insist upon intellectual clichés, upon setting up our own life as a model and measure of what prophets could possibly attain." Moderns, Heschel laments, subscribe to the "principle of fools: what is unattainable to us is unattainable to others."[132] Jon Levenson is thus understandably led to conclude that "in Heschel's theology, our very exercise critical judgment upon the prophets [constitutes] an act of hubris."[133]

Ultimately, Heschel insists, the Bible's singularity and sanctity are self-evident; since "genius identifies itself . . . the Bible is its own witness."[134] Heschel showers the Bible with (purportedly self-evident) superlatives: "Set the Bible beside any of the truly great books produced by the genius of man," he suggests, "and see how they are diminished in stature." Further, he insists, "The plummet line of scholarship cannot probe its depth nor will critical analysis ever grasp its essence. Other books you can estimate, you can measure, compare; the Bible you can only extol. . . . There is nothing greater."[135] The problem with such sentiments, of course, is that they impress only those who are already convinced; as attempts to move those as yet unpersuaded, they fall remarkably flat. Waxing rhapsodic, Heschel suggests a thought-experiment: "Use your imagination and try to conceive of a book that would excel the Bible, and you will admit that the power of the spirit has never gone further than the Bible."[136] But Heschel's claim is beset by obvious difficulties. As Levenson has written in response:

> Who is the 'you' in this sentence? It is obviously not the billions of Christians in the world who believe that they do indeed know a book that excels the Jewish Bible and in which the spirit has revealed itself in greater depth: it is called the New Testament. Nor can the 'you' refer to the hundreds of millions of Muslims who revere a book that is the final revelation of the God of Abraham to mankind, the Qur'an, the Word of God communicated to the consummation of all prophets, Muhammad. And when members of communities that revere the Bhagavad Gita, the Tao Te Ching, or the Book of Mormon come upon the Hebrew Bible, do they then throw out these inferior books and admit that Heschel was right?[137]

Here, just as in chapter 1, Heschel does not evince any awareness that his own assumptions and experiences may be culturally conditioned. So convinced is he that the Bible is an "incomparable marvel"[138] that he simply takes for granted that any truly honest person must share his perspective. Levenson rightly points out that Heschel does not "seem to suspect that his views on the matter may be colored by his identity as a practicing Jew, a rabbi, and a professor at a Jewish seminary." Here as elsewhere, therefore, Heschel's work suffers from a crucial "lack of critical reflexiveness."[139]

To be sure, at moments Heschel adopts a more modest tone: "Revelation can be either doubted or affirmed," he writes, "but neither denied nor proved."[140] But the epistemological humility of this statement is belied by both the tone and the content of the discussion surrounding it. Implying that all doubt is a function of flawed character, Heschel insists that "there are no proofs for demonstrating the beauty of music to man who is both deaf and insensitive, and there are not proofs for the veracity of the prophet's claims to a man who is spiritually deaf and without faith or wisdom."[141] Those who are unmoved by the Bible, Heschel asserts, only reveal the calloused state of their own souls: "No sadder proof can be given by a man of his own spiritual opacity than his insensitiveness to the Bible."[142] What is strange is that for all of Heschel's attentiveness to the spiritual crises of modernity, in these passages he comes across as unable to muster any sympathy at all for the predicament of the non-believer; it is as if for Heschel the inability to believe must always and everywhere be ultimately attributable to arrogance, or callousness, or bad faith (or some unattractive combination of the three). It is thus not surprising that Arthur Cohen charges Heschel with "deficient sympathy and compassion for those who are trapped in their unknowing and disbelief."[143]

Again, the generous reader is forced to ask: what is Heschel attempting to do with such extravagant and accusatory formulations? Robert Erlewine is undoubtedly correct that, in these passages, Heschel is again trying to reorient human life and thought by decentering the human self as the first and final arbiter of value. "By setting the prophets as standards for our experience," Erlewine writes, "rather than making our experience the standard for what is or is not feasible for the prophets, Heschel is attempting nothing less than to reverse the anthropocentric tendencies of the modern West."[144] And yet, consciously or not, Heschel finds himself in a difficult bind: on the one hand, he wants his readers to consider approaching this text differently from how they approach most (or all) others—that is, with a posture of humility and reverence rather than critical detachment. But on the other hand, in making that demand so forcefully and dogmatically, he conveys the impression that the reader is expected to surrender his critical faculties as part of the price of self-transcendence. Needless to say, for most modern readers not already committed to the sanctity of the Bible—and even for many who are—this is far too high a price to pay for piety.

Recall our discussion of Heschel's overheated condemnations of non-belief in chapter 1. It may well be that here again, Heschel wants to shake the reader, to startle her into seeing realities to which secular modernity has heretofore blinded her. Heschel's first task, as he understands it, is to remove the scales from his readers' eyes so that they can discover a world that both points to and contains the presence of God. His second task—to his mind, dependent on the first[145]—is to enable them to encounter a book that is an "ocean of meaning," replete with the presence of God.[146]

As we saw in chapter 1, Heschel's first choice is to inspire and enchant his readers, but when that fails he will attempt to jolt them into considering possibilities that modernity has ruled out of hand. And yet here again, his overwrought formulations run up against Louis Marvick's warning: "The enthusiasm of hyperbole must be shared by the audience or else it will look pretentious or ridiculous."[147] Heschel's statements may inspire some readers, but they likely alienate many others, who are left with the sense that he cannot possibly understand them, and that an unbridgeable chasm separates his assumptions from their own.

Without excusing Heschel's frequently intemperate criticisms of non-believers, we would nevertheless do well to understand just how much is at stake for him in his concern that we not "ignore, belittle, or traduce" the claim of the prophets to have been addressed by God.[148] Heschel is distressed by the deleterious consequences of denial: "Consider," Heschel warns, "what such denial [of the divine origin of the Bible] implies. If Moses and Isaiah have failed to find out what the will of God is, who will? If God is not found in the Bible, where should we seek Him? . . . If God had nothing to do with the prophets, then He has nothing to do with mankind."[149] These passages suggest that Heschel's attacks on revelational skeptics are rooted in a core existential-theological anxiety: "Sinai broke the cosmic silence that thickens our blood with despair," he writes; it is the Bible that conveys "the assurance that beyond all evil is the compassion of God."[150] In other words, for Heschel, the only way humanity can know that God is concerned with our individual and collective fates is through the message God reveals through the prophets. Without confidence in this message, Heschel insists, everything—the theological truth that sustains us, our openness to the voice that seeks to rein in our most barbarous impulses—all of it is lost. We ought to be careful when we play with the idea that the Bible is a book like any other, Heschel warns, lest "we gamble away . . . our tie to God."[151]

In a much lower register, Heschel writes that "proofs cannot open the gates of mystery for all men to behold. The only thing we can do is to open the gates of our own soul for God to behold us, to open the gates of our minds and to respond to the words of the prophets."[152] In other words, the key to faith in revelation is found not in reasoning, but in receptiveness and responsiveness.[153] This realization of the limits of reason gives rise both to the best and the worst of Heschel's prose: the best, because Heschel the poet-theologian can arguably stir his readers' religious impulses like no other Jewish writer in modern times; the worst, because Heschel at times seems unwilling to consider that what seems self-evident to him is utterly foreign to others[154]—and not because of obvious or culpable failure on their part.

* * *

One of the most striking aspects of Heschel's thought about revelation is the tension between his affirmation, on the one hand, that Judaism is rooted in unique events that happen at particular moments in time (Exodus, Sinai, etc.), and his insistence, on the other, that at Sinai, "the word of God entered the world of man ... [as] a perpetual event."[155] Like many a Jewish theologian, Heschel is torn between emphasizing the historicity of Sinai and dilating upon the eternality thereof. This tension persists unresolved in *God in Search of Man,* and in Heschel's writings more broadly.

In parts of *GSM,* Heschel emphasizes the absolute singularity of the revelation at Sinai. He goes so far as to suggest, in fact, that one of the greatest obstacles to belief in revelation is precisely the fact that (modern?) human beings lack a "sense of discretion for the diversity of time,"[156] and have been trained "to explain all that happens as a manifestation of a general law, every phenomenon as an example of a type"[157]— to assimilate the particular, that is, into a mere example of the universal. Such a relentless commitment to generalization militates against openness to the "extraordinary"[158] and "unprecedented,"[159] and Heschel suggests that "we find it hard to believe that an event which does not happen *all the time* or from time to time should have happened only *once, at one time.*"[160] All of this means, unfortunately, that we find the idea of revelation "unacceptable,"[161] since the latter is "an event that does not happen all the time but at a particular time, at a unique moment of time."[162]

Along the same lines, Heschel insists that Sinai is "an event without parallel in human history," and notes that "important to the Biblical understanding of history is not only the concept of a chosen people but also the concept of a chosen time; the election of a day, not only of a people."[163] Indeed, Heschel emphatically rejects the idea that "every age is equally near to God." On the contrary, "Jewish tradition claims that there is a hierarchy of moments within time, that all ages are not alike. Man may pray to God equally at all places, but God does not speak to man equally at all times.[164] At a certain moment, for example, the spirit of prophecy departed from Israel."[165]

Heschel offers another way to get at the same idea. "Prophetic inspiration," he argues, "must be understood as *an event*, not as *a process*." A process, he writes, "happens regularly, following a relatively permanent pattern." An event, in contrast, "is extraordinary, irregular." Whereas the former may be "continuous, steady, uniform," the latter occurs "suddenly, intermittently, occasionally." Or, to use terms familiar from what we have just seen, whereas "processes are typical ... events are unique."[166] Although the mind is conditioned to embrace the typical, in order to understand (let alone to affirm) revelation, one must be open to the radically atypical. While "nature is made up of processes," Heschel writes, "history consists primarily of events."[167] Moments of revelation are distinctive events of divine-human encounter, not processes—or even culminations of processes—by which human beings discover something about God or human destiny. But more important for our present purposes, revelation takes place at particular moments, and not in some sort of eternal process. This is, of course, Heschel's way of forcefully rejecting notions of continuous or progressive revelation.[168]

In more properly theological terms, Heschel notes that coming to know God requires both human effort and divine consent:

> If we assume God is not a passive object but a Being endowed with at least as much life and will as ourselves, understanding Him cannot be a process that goes on regardless of His agreement. If God is alive, we must assume that He plays a part in our acts of trying to understand Him; that our understanding of God depends not only on man's readiness to approach Him but also on God's willingness to be approached.[169]

In other words, God is not a passive object waiting to be cognized or understood, but an active subject who may choose to reveal or conceal at any time. Thus, the believer does not possess God, cannot take Him out to look at Him, as it were, but must constantly seek God anew. Discovery of God thus requires not will alone, but also grace. For, "if God is not thought of in terms of inanimate being, in terms of a Being that is not endowed with either will or freedom, then we must assume that He is not at all times at our disposal. There are times when he goes out to meet us, and there [are] moments when He hides His face from us."[170] All of this means that, for Heschel, not all moments are equally revelatory. Revelation is, after all, a function of divine decision rather than (mere) human effort, and therefore, as we have seen, an event rather than a process.

And yet, Heschel also says that "Sinai is both an event that happened once and for all, and an event that happens all the time. What God does, happens both in time and in eternity. Seen from our vantage-point, it happened once; seen from His vantage-point, it happens all the time."[171] Viewed from this perspective, the ostensible historicity of Sinai is a function of human epistemological limits; from God's perspective, Sinai is eternal. This stands in stark contrast (not to say contradiction) with what we have just seen: where previously Sinai was described as a distinct moment in historical time, now it is portrayed as a kind of abiding cosmic reality. The perceived historicity of Sinai is, in other words, precisely that—a human *perception*, rather than an accurate reflection of truth at its deepest levels.

Now, just a few sentences later, yet a third position slips in, perhaps intended as an attempt to compromise between the first two: "The day of giving the Torah can never become past; that day is this day, every day. The Torah, whenever we study it, must be to us 'as if it were given us today.'"[172] Here we have moved from an ontological-theological claim—Sinai is always happening—to a normative one: we must engage Torah in such a way that it is "*as if*" it were revealed this very day. To recapitulate: reading Heschel carefully, we have discovered an unresolved ambivalence in his understanding of Sinai: Does it take place at a particular time, or does it happen all the time? Is it a historical moment or, as it were, an eternal event? One possible attempt at a middle ground is Heschel's transposition of Sinai's purported eternality from the realm of ontology to that of phenomenology—it *is* historical, but we can (and ought to) *experience it* as eternal.[173] I am not at all sure that these three positions can be successfully synthesized, but one can at least gesture toward integration: if we bring together the various passages we have examined, we can say that for Heschel, from God's perspective revelation is an eternally occurring event, and our goal in studying it is to adopt

God's perspective. Although Heschel cannot bring himself to say these words, implicit in this insistence is the possibility that the ostensible historicity of Sinai can be overcome through the deepening of human perception. To see from God's vantage point is to discover the eternity of Sinai. Heschel may have something like this in mind when, in another context, he cites the Zohar: "The acts of God are eternal and continue for ever. Every day he who is worthy receives the Torah standing at Sinai; he hears the Torah from the mouth of the Lord as Israel did when they stood at Sinai. Every Israelite is able to attain that level, the level of standing at Sinai."[174]

So much for Sinai. But what of revelation more broadly; does it cease, or does God continue to speak? As is his wont, Heschel nowhere offers a systematic consideration of this question. But I think we can nevertheless establish the contours of an answer. Let us return to a crucial passage that we have already encountered: "Jewish tradition claims that there is a hierarchy of moments within time, that all ages are not alike. Man may pray to God equally at all places, but God does not speak to man equally at all times. At a certain moment, for example, the spirit of prophecy departed from Israel."[175] Heschel writes not that "God does not speak to man at all times," but rather that "God does not speak to man *equally* at all times." And he goes on to note that the spirit of *prophecy* departed from Israel—but not necessarily other, subtler forms of revelation and divine communication. Earlier in *GSM*, Heschel says explicitly that although "Sinai does not happen every day. . . . This does not mean that God is utterly silent in our age. . . . There are many ways and many levels on which the will of God communicates itself to man."[176] And he approvingly cites the Mishnah in Avot: "Every day a heavenly voice resounds from Mount Horeb."[177] Further, as we have seen, he points out that through the Bible God speaks with great urgency to contemporary times.[178] Recall, finally, Heschel's suggestion that God speaks in faint, understated ways even "in our own lives"[179]—what I have dubbed "proto-revelation." Of course, Heschel does not attempt a taxonomy of modes of divine communication, nor does he offer a clear line of demarcation between what he would consider "revelation" and what he would regard as lesser forms of divine communication (remember, for example, that Heschel describes "the echo of an echo of a voice" in our lives as analogous to revelation, but not as revelation proper). If pressed, he would have been quick to remind us that one cannot hope to classify, let alone to analyze exhaustively, phenomena which are inherently mysterious, and which we can only indicate, but never adequately describe. One thing, however, is clear: according to Heschel, even long after the age of prophecy has passed, "God is not always silent."[180]

* * *

Let us return, in closing, to the polarity of God's majesty and vulnerability, and to the dynamics of divine self-transcendence. On the one hand, as we have seen, Heschel affirms that in revelation, the transcendent God reveals His will to the Jewish people. But on the other hand, recall that, according to Heschel, God also reveals something else, namely, the fact of His intimate concern with human history, and the reality of His pathos. Through revelation, then, human beings learn that their obtuseness and indifference to the divine call lead, as we shall see at length in the next chapter, to divine suffering. In revelation, in other words, the transcendent God paradoxically conveys both His majestic will and His profound vulnerability.

Upon deeper reflection, we discover that even the seemingly majestic side of revelation is in fact more complicated than might appear at first glance. Recall Heschel's contention, made almost in passing, that "the share of the prophet [in revelation] manifested itself not only in what he was able to give but also in what he was unable to receive."[181] In other words, even as the transcendent God seeks to make His will known, He is vulnerable to the inevitable shortcomings of His human hearers. We have already encountered Norman Lamm's insistence that the will of God was "communicated in discrete words and letters." Lamm goes on to dismiss those who doubt that God can communicate His will unambiguously, averring that "to deny that God can make His will clearly known is to impose upon Him a limitation of dumbness that would insult the least of His human creatures."[182] Heschel would have responded, I suspect, along these lines: to posit a gap between God's will, on the one hand, and what the prophet hears, on the other, is to attribute to God not dumbness, but relational vulnerability. Note, in this context, that on at least two occasions Heschel tells us that "if God is real, then He is able to express His will unambiguously."[183] But Heschel goes even further, declaring that "the voice of God is unambiguous; it is the confusion of man, of the best of us, that creates the ambiguity."[184] Any human teacher worth her salt is well aware that her students—even the very best ones—will often fail to grasp all that she seeks to communicate. In choosing to engage with human beings, God takes the same risk upon Himself. In speaking to all-too-human prophets, the majestic God makes Himself vulnerable to their very real limitations and thus risks being inadequately understood. Revelation, in other words, is a covenantal act, rather than a purely majestic one, and thus entails self-limitation and self-transcendence. God does not dictate words to His servants, or treat them as mere recording devices. On the contrary, He summons them to participate in the moment of revelation, and in so doing renders Himself vulnerable to misinterpretation.

But God's vulnerability in revelation extends still further. Even—or perhaps especially—after the text has come into being, it can all too easily fall into the wrong hands. When read with jaundiced eyes, or heard by calloused ears, Heschel warns, the Bible can be interpreted "in terms of paganism" (by which he seems to mean theologically sanctioned immorality). The word of God, remains vulnerable to "false understanding. It is possible to commit murder in the name of the Torah; one may be a scoundrel and act within the letter of the law (Nahmanides)."[185] Wryly, Heschel concludes, "There has indeed been so much pious abuse that the Bible is often in need of being saved from the hands of its admirers."[186] Like God Himself, God's word is vulnerable in the world.

FOUR

THE PATHOS OF THE
SELF-TRANSCENDENT GOD

In talking to a group of Jewish educators in 1968, Heschel warned of an "insidious danger" that constituted nothing less than a "block to Jewish theology"; "I refer," he said, "to the Hellenization of Jewish theology."[1] This process, which began as early as Philo (20 BCE–50 CE), was based on the dangerously misleading assumption that, at bottom, "Plato and Moses"—that is, Greek and biblical thinking—"say the same thing. Only, Plato would say it in Greek and Moses in Hebrew. Consequently, you can say that Moses was a sort of Hebrew Plato." This conflation of two very different modes of thinking dominated the world of medieval Jewish philosophy, Heschel insists, and, as a result, Jewish philosophers too often "talk about God in the language of the Greeks."[2]

Heschel is careful to note that he is not opposed to Jewish students being exposed to the non-Jewish world and its ideas. But he worries that in thinking in "non-Jewish terms," Jews run the very real risk of losing what is most distinctive and original about Jewish thought. Whatever the strengths of non-Jewish thought, Heschel argues,

> it is not biblical thinking. It is not rabbinic thinking. It is not Hasidic thinking. It is non-Jewish thinking. A non-Jewish philosophy is fine. But we would also like to have in our thinking a Jewish view of things. We would like to apply the Bible and *Hazal* [the sages of the talmudic period], and they are often incongruent [with Greek thought]. If you take biblical passages or biblical documents or rabbinic statements, and submit them to a Greek mind, they often are absurd. They make no sense. But we do want to educate Jews. We wish to maintain Judaism. What can we do about it?

Here Heschel offers an important window into his own theological and educational project:

> May I say to you personally that this has been my major challenge, ever since
> I began working on my dissertation, that is: How to maintain a Jewish way of
> thinking? This was the major concern and the major thesis of my dissertation
> *Die Prophetie*. Since that day I consider this to be my major effort. It is not an
> easy enterprise.[3]

More concretely, Heschel insists that Jewish theology is rooted in the claim that *"God is in search of man."* This statement, which "summarize[s] all of human history as seen in the Bible . . . is *the* fundamental statement about God in Judaism."[4] Why is God in search of man? Because, Heschel maintains, "God is *in need* of man. The idea of God being in need of man is central to Judaism and pervades all the pages of the Bible, of *Hazal,* of Talmudic literature."[5] But the "simple formula: *God in search of man,"* Heschel points out, is "not a Hellenistic formula. It is a biblical formula. It is a rabbinic formula."[6] As we shall see, according to Heschel Greek thought cannot permit or make space for such a claim. And yet, Heschel argues, it is the very heart of Jewish theology. Jewish thought must proclaim its truths rather than surrendering them on the altar of Greek notions of philosophical respectability.

Why is Heschel so insistent that the biblical and rabbinic idea of God in search of man is incompatible with Hellenistic (and by extension, Hellenized Jewish) philosophy? Consider the case of Maimonides (1135–1204).[7] The towering philosopher and legist is known as perhaps the most uncompromising proponent of negative theology in the Middle Ages. According to Maimonides, we can never say what God is, but only what God is not; and to say that God is not "dumb," for example, is, at its deepest level, to say something quite radical: namely, that dumbness and smartness do not apply to God at all. Thus, any term that we use in speaking both of God and of human beings must be understood "equivocally"—that is, as a homonym. Despite appearances, then, to say both that God is wise and that a person is wise is not to assert any commonality or even analogy between them. No such analogy is possible, since no shared scale of wisdom (or any other virtue), of which God could be said to be at the top and we at the very bottom, could possibly exist. The very notion of such a scale violates the fundamental truth of theology: God is absolutely other, and incomparable to creation in every way.[8] As students of Maimonides, we must always be on guard lest, instead of worshipping God, we merely worship a glorified version of ourselves. So far from monotheism, such worship would in fact constitute little more than idolatry.

According to Maimonides, then, God is a completely unknowable mystery, and the only ultimately appropriate human posture toward the divine is silent adoration: in the words of the psalmist, "Silence is praise to Thee."[9] Technically, Maimonides does permit us to talk about God's "attributes of action," but the discerning student quickly realizes that these are permissible precisely because they are not really attributes at all. They say something about what God *does,* but nothing at all about what God *is.* And even in terms of what God does, what these "attributes" tell us is extremely circumscribed: God can be said to be merciful, for example, in the sense that if we did things similar to the ones God does, we would be doing them as a result of the moral quality of mercy within us, but God, strictly speaking, cannot be described as merciful.

So God is, for Maimonides, the supremely perfect Being (though, again, perfect in a way that bears no relation to any human perfection)—absolutely transcendent, eternally unchanging. Maimonides is relentless in drawing out the implications of his approach: God cannot enter into relation with any created thing, including, it bears emphasizing, human beings. He writes:

> How . . . can a relation be represented between Him and what is other than He when there is no notion comprising in any respect both of the two, inasmuch as existence is, in our opinion, affirmed of Him, may He be exalted, and of what is other than He merely by way of equivocation. *There is, in truth, no relation in any respect between Him and any of His creatures.*[10]

The consequences of all this philosophical austerity are dramatic, and—thinkers such as Heschel have been eager to argue—devastating to the very possibility of biblical faith. If we accept Maimonides' philosophical assumptions and their attendant conclusions, then we can no longer say that God "cares," or "loves," or bears any relationship to us at all. Even more fundamentally, we cannot speak of a "personal" God at all, since any attribution of personality to God is, in the end, a human projection, and is thus tantamount to idolatry. But if we cannot say that God cares, or loves, or that He enters into relationship with human beings, are we still talking about anything recognizable as the God of the

Bible and the rabbis? Heschel's argument, as passionately held as it is eloquently articulated, is that we are not. The God of Israel, revealed in scripture as a "living God," and, as we shall soon see, a God of pathos, simply cannot be reconciled or synthesized with the God of Greek philosophy. Attempts to force such synthesis do violence to the legacy of the prophets, Heschel insists, and lead to the dissolution of all that is distinctive and compelling in Jewish theology. Whatever their intensions, in purporting somehow to integrate the God of Israel with the God of Aristotle, Heschel contends, medieval philosophers effectively liquidated the former in the name of the latter. It is this kind of surrender masquerading as synthesis that Heschel seeks to combat. The "major concern" and "major challenge" of which we have seen Heschel speak, then, is to restore their proper dignity both to the Bible and to the God revealed therein.[11]

A year before his conversation with the educators, Heschel had been invited to address a conference of Catholic scholars on the question of "the God of Israel and Christian Renewal." "On the way to the printer," he reports, "the power of the title was emasculated. The magnificent biblical saying 'the God of Israel' was replaced by a scholastic mis-saying, 'the Jewish notion of God.'" This seemingly small error, Heschel observes, is in fact extremely telling: "Realism was replaced by notionalism." But "'The God of Israel,'" he points out, "is a *name*, not a notion, and the difference between the two is perhaps the difference between Jerusalem and Athens."[12] A notion can be arrived at by "abstraction and generalization"; a name, in contrast, "is learned through acquaintance.... A notion is conceived; a name is called." Pointedly, Heschel remarks: "The terms 'notion' and 'the God of Israel' are profoundly incompatible. All notions crumble when applied to Him. A more appropriate title might be: 'The Jewish Experience of the Collapse of All Notions in Relation to God.'"[13]

One of the dangers of abstract thinking is that it often fosters "a split between situation and idea." Such a split makes it possible for us to limit God to the realm of thinking, to maintain theoretical ideas that do not involve us at the core of our being. Thus, Heschel warns, "An idea or a theory of God can easily become a substitute for God, impressive to the mind when God as a living reality is absent from the soul."[14] The phrase

"God of Israel" is different, Heschel argues, from phrases such as "the God of Aristotle" or "the God of Kant," in that the first "does not mean a doctrine of God conceived of or taught by Israel. It means God with whom Israel is vitally, intimately involved, an involvement transcending the realm of thinking."[15] The term "God of Israel" points not to a notion, but to a covenantal relationship.

Already a decade and a half earlier, in *MNA*, Heschel had dismissed the speculative proofs of God's existence on related grounds. Even if such proofs could be successful, he argued, they would nevertheless remain irrelevant to the life of the believer:

> Granted that the existence of a being endowed with supreme genius and wisdom has been demonstrated, the question remains: Why should we, poor creatures, be concerned about Him, the most perfect? We may, indeed, accept the idea that there is a supreme designer and still say: "So what?" As long as a concept of God does not overpower us, as long as we can say: "So what?"—it is not God that we talk about but something else.[16]

One can believe in a supreme designer and yet "not cease to be haunted by a fear of futility, a fear that could not be overcome by a belief that, somewhere in the infinite recesses of the Divinity, there is a well of wisdom."[17] All that the God of philosophy can offer is order, but the deepest human hungers are for something very different: "We are more anxious to know whether there is a God of justice than to learn whether there is a God of order. Is there a God who collects the tears, who honors hope and rewards the ordeals of the guiltless?"[18] It is to this God, the God who cares for the vulnerable and downtrodden, that biblical revelation attests. In stark contrast, "The God of the philosophers is all indifference, too sublime to possess a heart or to cast a glance at our world."[19]

In similar terms, in *GSM*, Heschel dismisses the notion of God as first cause as religiously uninteresting: "A first cause or an idea of the absolute—devoid of freedom, devoid of life—is an issue for science or metaphysics rather than a concern of the soul or the conscience." What animates a "living soul" is not a "dead cause, but . . . a living God. Our goal is to ascertain the existence of a Being to whom we may confess our sins, of a God who loves, of a God who is not above concern with our inquiry and search for Him; a father, not an absolute."[20] Thus, a God who matters to human beings must be, at minimum, "alive" and "not inferior to us in the order of being"—which, for Heschel, means a God who is able to enter into dynamic relationship with human beings. A God who is "inanimate" is also irrelevant. In other words, Heschel insists, "A being that lacks the attributes of personal existence is not our problem."[21] A living God, for Heschel, is a God who cares.

There is thus, according to Heschel, a vast and unbridgeable chasm between the God of Israel and the God of philosophy, and Heschel none-too-subtly evinces his disdain for the latter. The purportedly exalted God of the philosophers, Heschel writes, "consists in being conscious of Himself and oblivious to the world." In contrast, the "God of the prophets is all concern, too merciful to remain aloof to His creation." Heschel characterizes the God of Israel in poignant and memorable terms:

> God does not judge the deeds of man impassively, in a spirit of cool detachment. His judgment is imbued with a feeling of intimate concern. He is the father of all men, not only a judge; He is a lover engaged to His people, not only a king. God stands in passionate relationship to man. His love or anger, His mercy or disappointment is an expression of His profound participation in the history of Israel and all men.[22]

What is most unforgivable about Hellenistic thought, from Heschel's perspective, is thus the fact that the God of Aristotle (and Maimonides) is utterly indifferent to the fate of other selves. This God manifests no transitive concern (which, recall, Heschel defines as "a regard for others," in contrast to reflexive concern, which he understands as "an intense regard for [one]self")[23] and is thus incapable of self-transcendence. In contrast, according to Heschel, *the only concern that can be ascribed to the God of Israel is transitive concern.* (After all, Heschel contends, attributing reflexive concern to God would make no sense: "He does not have to be concerned about Himself, since there is no need of His being on guard against danger to His existence.")[24] God's concern is exclusively for others: "While man's concern for others is often tainted with concern for his own self... God's care for His creatures is a pure concern."[25] Implicit in Heschel is an interesting hierarchy: the God of Israel is all transitive concern, the human being is an alloy of transitive and reflexive concern (not to mention bald egocentrism and self-assertion), and the

God of Aristotle is nothing but reflexive concern (or perhaps better: no concern at all). In the ways that matter most to Heschel, then, Aristotle's God is less than a human being, not more.

To return to where we began: Heschel reminds us that both philosophy and religion "claim to offer ideas about ultimate problems." Thus, philosophy of religion must "revolve around two foci: philosophy and religion." It cannot simply collapse the one into the other. In fact, Heschel argues, "The failure to sense the profound tension of philosophical and religious categories has been the cause of much confusion,"[26] a confusion which, in Heschel's mind, bedevils the whole medieval philosophical project. "The Bible," Heschel tells us, "like the philosophy of Aristotle ... represents *a way of thinking* ... a form of orientation; not only a mental fabric but also a certain disposition or manner of interweaving and interrelating intuitions and perceptions, a unique loom of thoughts."[27] But instead of focusing on the distinctiveness of biblical teaching, Philo and his heirs "were mainly interested in pointing to the common elements in reason and revelation and desired to equalize what was different in them."[28] In the process, they lost sight of what is most fundamental to revelation:

> What they failed to see is the unique wealth of spiritual insight contained in the prophetic ideas of the divine pathos. Hebrew thinking operates within categories different from those of Plato or Aristotle, and the disagreements between their respective teachings are not merely a matter of different ways of expression but of different ways of thinking. By dwelling upon the common elements of reason and revelation, a synthesis of the two spiritual powers was attained at the price of sacrificing some of their unique insights.[29]

On Heschel's account, then, Jewish theology must open itself to concepts and ideas from other cultures and traditions of thought, all the while remaining vigilant lest it forfeit, consciously or not, what is most distinctive to biblical ways of thinking. It must steer a course, in other words, between the Scylla of ghettoization and the Charybdis of self-liquidation. Heschel cautions that no matter how important it is for Judaism to absorb elements from outside it, this "must not be done at the price of giving up its intellectual integrity."[30] Implicit in all this is an uncompromising attack on medieval philosophy, which (so Heschel thinks) effectively reduced religious truths to philosophical abstractions. "The result of such an inquiry, is usually," Heschel notes rather acidly, "a highly rarefied religion. What begins as a philosophy of religion ends as a *religion of philosophy.*"[31]

Although Heschel often invokes Philo as the paradigmatic case of a philosopher dissolving the contents of revelation in the name of synthesis with Greek philosophy, it is clear, I think, that his ultimate target is Maimonides. For all his prodigious intellectual and spiritual achievements,[32] the great sage was still guilty, in Heschel's eyes, of having excessively Hellenized Jewish theology, and thus of having deviated from the heart of prophetic teaching. On multiple occasions in Heschel's writings, Maimonides is criticized for privileging the abstract over the concrete, and for thereby falsifying the spirit of Judaism. In discussing Maimonides' thirteen articles of faith, for example, Heschel notes that all but four of the articles "refer to principles or to the realm of ideas, rather than to events or to the realm of history." This reflects Maimonides' assumption that "it is in ideas that ultimate reality comes to expression." And yet, Heschel points out, "To the Biblical man ... it is in events, not only in ideas that ultimate reality comes to expression. The substance of Judaism is given both in history and in thought. We accept ideas and recall events. The Jew says, 'I believe,' and is told, 'Remember.'"[33]

Of course, as we have already seen, Maimonides' predilection for abstract thinking had profound ramifications for his notion of God. Having already expressed his reservations about Maimonides' list of dogmas, Heschel turns to Maimonides' abstract, Hellenized God. "To the Jewish mind," he writes, "the understanding of God is not achieved by referring in a Greek way to timeless qualities of a Supreme Being, to ideas of goodness or perfection, but rather by sensing the living acts of His concern, to His dynamic attentiveness to man." God is not abstract but personal. And God has a will, and the freedom to engage in concrete relationships with humanity. As Heschel writes, "We speak not of His goodness in general, but of His compassion for the individual man in a particular situation. God's goodness is not a cosmic force but a specific act of compassion."[34] Mark the subtle harshness of Heschel's words: in discussing Maimonides' articles of faith, Heschel contrasted Maimonidean thinking with "Biblical." Now, in rejecting Maimonides' conception of God,

Heschel contrasts the Maimonidean approach with that characteristic of "the Jewish mind." What can we conclude from this?

> Different are the problems when we accept such an approach [one based on God's concern]. The problem is no longer how to reconcile the Bible with Aristotle's view of the universe and of man, but rather: what is the Biblical view of the universe and of man's position in it? How should we understand ourselves in terms of Biblical thinking?[35]

Recall Heschel's remarks to the Jewish educators about how his central concern over the course of his career has been "to maintain a Jewish way of thinking. . . . It is not an easy enterprise."[36] In light of what we have just seen, we can formulate Heschel's project somewhat differently. Heschel's challenge, as he sees it, is to rescue Jewish theology from the ravages of Greek thinking as exemplified by Philo and Maimonides, and to allow the biblical and rabbinic traditions to speak once again in their own voice.[37]

For Heschel, the foreignness of Greek conceptions of God is rooted in the foreignness (and wrong-headedness) of Greek metaphysical assumptions. Heschel insists, for example, that Maimonides' notion of perfection is entirely rooted in alien soil, and thus cannot but distort biblical thinking. For the Bible, as John Merkle aptly notes, "pure actuality is no synonym for divine perfection." On the contrary, "mutability is no sign of imperfection, just as immutability is no sign of perfection."[38] Responsiveness rather than immutability is at the heart of the biblical conception of God.

But on Heschel's account, Greek thought is not content to affirm God's immutability; it goes farther, and embraces an absolute dichotomy between reason and emotion, and, as a result, valorizes the former and denigrates the latter.[39] But Heschel, in contrast, warns that "the ideas that dominate the Hellenistic understanding of the emotional life of man must not affect our understanding of Hebrew thinking."[40] The Bible does not share "the view that passions are disturbances or weaknesses of the soul, and much less the premise that passion itself is evil, that passion as such is incompatible with right thinking or right living."[41] Consequently, Heschel notes, "With no stigma attached to pathos, there was no reason [for the Bible] to shun the idea of pathos in the understanding of God."[42] According to Heschel, "The static idea of divinity is [thus] the outcome of two strands of thought: the ontological notion of stability and the psychological view of emotions as disturbances of the soul."[43] Both, Heschel insists, are incompatible with a biblical worldview and must be rejected.

To be clear, Heschel does not offer a systematic essay in metaphysics. But, it bears emphasizing, this was not his intention—he gestures toward what an alternative, biblically based metaphysics might look like,[44] but does not regard its full articulation as his (or, for that matter, Judaism's) project. He is content, instead, to point out that the metaphysical principles Maimonides simply took for granted are in fact historically conditioned—of Greek rather than biblical provenance. Now, as we have seen, according to Heschel, there is nothing intrinsically wrong with admitting foreign elements into Jewish thinking, but the Greek celebration of stasis and *apatheia* is profoundly problematic and antithetical to biblical thinking, and as such, it must be rejected.

Heschel is thus heir to a venerable tradition of insistence that, in Pascal's famous words, the God of Abraham, Isaac, and Jacob is not the God of the Philosophers. Time and again, Heschel draws our attention to the irreducible tension between scriptural, covenantal faith, on the one hand, and abstract, philosophical monotheism, on the other.[45] "The notion of God as a perfect being," he writes, "is not of biblical extraction. It is the product not of prophetic religion but of Greek philosophy; a postulate of reason rather than a direct, compelling, initial answer of man to His reality."[46] Again, he tells us that "a God of abstraction . . . a high and mighty First Cause . . . dwelling in the lonely splendor of eternity" is a far cry indeed from the God the prophets, "involved in human history and affected by human acts."[47] The God of the philosophers is, Heschel insists, "unknown and indifferent to man; He thinks, but does not speak; He is conscious of Himself, but oblivious of the world"; the God of Israel, in contrast, is "a God who loves, a God who is known to, and concerned with, man."[48]

* * *

One of the central implications of the concept of God in search of man, Heschel points out, is the idea of the divine pathos, which he characterizes simply at one point as "an explication of the idea of God in search of man."[49] The God of Israel, Heschel writes, is not "a Supreme Being, apathetic and indifferent to man,"[50] but rather a relational God, One who enters into relationship with human beings and depends upon them to help accomplish His goals. "For the accomplishment of His grand design, the Lord waits for the help of man."[51] "Not only is redemption a necessity for man," Heschel writes elsewhere, but "man is a necessity to redemption."[52]

God's need means that He may be hurt and disappointed. God is in search of man, but man maintains the freedom to turn away. The consequences of human freedom are such that God's ideals may be flouted and His aspirations thwarted. God may thus be afflicted with "pain and disappointment,"[53] "sorrow,"[54] and even "anguish."[55] God's words, at times, can be "plaintive and disconsolate";[56] "the heart of melancholy" beats within them.[57] God is, in other words, a God of pathos, afflicted by humanity's going astray. According to Heschel, this idea, that God "can be intimately affected, that He possesses not merely intelligence and will, but also pathos, basically defines the prophetic consciousness of God."[58] At the very heart of prophetic theology, then, is the paradoxical insistence that the Creator of heaven and earth is also a profoundly vulnerable Being. The cost of real relationship, it seems, is emotional vulnerability, even for an all-powerful God.

Although this is not the central theological concern of *The Prophets,* Heschel does point out that God is pained not only by Israel's waywardness, but also by its sufferings. Speaking of the theology of the prophet Jeremiah, Heschel writes that "Israel's distress was more than a human tragedy. With Israel's distress came the affliction of God, His displacement, His homelessness in the land, in the world."[59] Speaking of Second Isaiah, Heschel points out that "Israel's suffering is God's grief,"[60] and that, in the prophet's own words, "In all their affliction He was afflicted" (Isaiah 63:9). Thus God seems to suffer not only from disappointment with Israel, but also out of emotional solidarity with it.

Heschel savors the audacity of prophetic images that describe the intensity of God's suffering. Jeremiah worries that God is "like a stranger in the land, like a wayfarer who turns aside to tarry for a night" (Jeremiah 14:8). The prophet laments: "Thus says the Lord: . . . O my dear people, gird on sackcloth, and roll in ashes; make mourning as for an only son, most bitter lamentation, for suddenly the destroyer will come upon us"

(Jeremiah 6:22, 26). Perhaps too readily retrojecting rabbinic imagery into biblical literature, Heschel interprets Jeremiah as calling upon his listeners to mourn not only for Israel, but also for God Himself. God, Heschel declares, is "mourning Himself. God's sorrow rises again and again to unconcealed heights of expression."[61] "Cry," God pleads, "for Israel and Me."[62] In what Heschel describes as "the boldest figure used by any prophet," Second Isaiah reports God's declaration that although He has heretofore shown restraint, now He "will cry out like a woman in travail.... [He] will gasp and pant" (Isaiah 42:14).[63] Heschel consistently interprets the prophets as struggling valiantly to convey the profound depths of God's pain.

It is critical to emphasize, however, that for Heschel, God's pain and suffering do not result from external constraints or limits on His power. Although it would be easy, and for some perhaps tempting, to misread Heschel in this way, nowhere does he suggest that the God of Israel is a weak or limited Being. On the contrary: for Heschel, any limits on God's power are *self-imposed*. God's vulnerability is a consequence of His self-transcendence, not of some intrinsic divine limit or weakness. The God of Israel has *chosen* to enter into covenant and relationship with human beings—to need human partners and to respect human agency. In history as it is currently unfolding, God chooses not to exercise His omnipotence, but in the end of days, it is God who will redeem the world.[64] As we have already noted in the Introduction, in a critical passage in *The Prophets*, Heschel distinguishes between divine passion on the one hand and divine pathos on the other. The former, he insists, is something that happens to a limited God; the latter, in contrast, is an event in the life of an omnipotent One: "In passion, the divinity is thought of as a martyr, the basis of whose suffering lies, in the last analysis, in the powerless-ness of God. In pathos [in contrast], God is thought of as the supreme Master of heaven and earth, Who is emotionally affected by the conduct of man."[65] God's sufferings in history should thus be understood as the travails of an omnipotent God.

It therefore makes sense that for Heschel, divine pathos is a "free reaction of the Lord to the conduct of man."[66] To affirm divine pathos, Heschel emphasizes, is not to suggest that God is subject to involuntary emotional changes or mood swings. Divine emotion, Heschel contends, is inextricably bound up with divine freedom. In the world of the prophets, he writes, "Pathos was understood not as unreasoned emotion, but as an act formed with intention, depending on free will, the result of decision and determination."[67] God's emotions, Heschel insists, are also "always morally conditioned,"[68] never a mere function of divine whim. God is, in other words, utterly free, but also devoid of caprice.

According to Heschel, "the cardinal, fundamental" divine emotion is love.[69] It is perhaps the prophet Hosea who most eloquently expresses God's undying love for Israel. Hosea, Heschel tells us, "came to spell out the astonishing fact of God's love for man. God is not only the Lord who demands justice; he is also a God Who is in love with his people."[70] Indeed, according to Hosea, "the decisive motive behind God's strategy in history is love."[71] There may be moments of genuine anger and disappointment, but at bottom there is always love:

> Going beyond the description of momentary conditions, Hosea reaches an awareness of the basic feeling of the latent subjective meaning in all individual announcements and decisions. . . . The historically conditioned expressions of pathos and the immediate situation between God and man are set in the light of the eternal background. At the beginning "when Israel was a child I loved him" (Hosea 11:1).[72]

One of the central tasks of the prophet, Heschel reminds us, is thus to instill in the people the "sacred certainty" of God's abiding love for them.[73]

But God's love is inextricably interwoven with God's wrath. Far from being mutually exclusive, love and anger function in reciprocal relation in the life of God; the latter ultimately emerges from the very heart of the former.[74] It is God the disappointed parent, the spurned lover, who is revealed most vividly in the words of the prophets. On Heschel's interpretation, then, God's anger is a function of God's disappointed love. "Man is rebellious and full of iniquity, and yet so cherished is he that God, the Creator of heaven and earth, is saddened when forsaken by him. Profound and intimate is God's love for man, and . . . [therefore] harsh and dreadful can be His wrath."[75] God turns to the prophets to help Israel turn back, and thus to assuage His anger. God "so loves man that He does not tire of uttering through the prophets His outrage at the wrongs done unto man."[76] The prophet thus conveys not only God's love, but also God's frequently thwarted expectations.

Ultimately, Heschel insists, the possibility of divine wrath is implicit in the affirmation of divine personhood. "God is not only the Judge, Guardian, and Lawgiver," he writes, "but also the loving Father Who is intimately affected by what man does."[77] God, who has been abundantly gracious to Israel, is spurned by it. Interpreting the prophet Jeremiah, Heschel writes: "This people whose destiny was to be a witness to the living God and a light unto the nations, betrayed His teachings, turned to idols, and abandoned Him. The Judge of the world cried His protest again and again. But the people remained deaf to the prophets. Then came a moment when His patience turned to anger."[78] Anger is thus "the personal dimension of God's justice."[79] God's relationship to humanity is not an "indiscriminate outpouring of goodness,"[80] but the genuine relatedness of a personal being.

Heschel is quick to emphasize that divine wrath, like divine emotion in general, is neither "inscrutable" nor "irrational,"[81] but is, instead, explicable as God's "voluntary and purposeful" response to egregious human misconduct.[82] God's anger is not "impulsive" or "automatic,"[83] but is rooted instead in divine decision; it is always "conditional and subject to [God's] will."[84] Divine wrath is "an instrument rather than a force, transitive rather than spontaneous . . . a means of achieving 'the intents of [God's] mind.'"[85] In other words, although Heschel's God is described as "all-personal,"[86] He is nevertheless not subject to the idiosyncrasies of "temperament or propensity. . . . [Anger] comes about in the light of moral judgment rather than in the darkness of passion."[87] God, we see again, is free, but not capricious or impulsive. Anger is conditioned by ethics.

Anger, for Heschel, is not a "basic disposition" or a "quality inherent in the nature of God."[88] It is, rather, "a state of mind or soul" which emerges in response to human behavior: "An essential feature of anger as proclaimed by the prophets is its contingency and nonfinality. . . . It is man who provokes it, and it is man who may revoke it."[89] In this sense, God's anger thus stands in stark contrast to God's love: "Anger is always described as a moment, something that happens rather than something that abides. . . . His anger passes, His love goes on for ever."[90]

Anger, in other words, is a "tragic necessity" in the life of God, something God "deplores" but also finds indispensable.[91] God's baseline emotion, as it were, is love; anger emerges only when the situation calls for it. "As a mode of pathos," Heschel writes, "it may be necessary to characterize the anger of the Lord as *suspended* love, as mercy withheld, as mercy in concealment."[92] Otto's assertion that God's love is "nothing but quenched wrath"[93] thus constitutes an "extreme misinterpretation of biblical thought"; the God of the Hebrew Bible, Heschel is at pains to demonstrate, is characterized most fundamentally by love and mercy. "The normal and original pathos is love or mercy. Anger is preceded as well as followed by compassion."[94]

God's wrath, for Heschel, has no "spite, recklessness, . . . [or] iniquity" to it. Divine anger, he emphasizes, is a function of divine concern: "It is because [God] cares for man that His anger may be kindled against man."[95] Indeed, Heschel writes, it is "divine sympathy for the victims of cruelty [that] is the motive of anger."[96] God's responsiveness thus constitutes a dramatic contrast to human indifference: while human beings may remain unmoved in the face of callousness and brutality, God is different, always "personally affected by what man does to man."[97] This is one of divine anger's most important implications: "the end of indifference!" Here Heschel's own post-Holocaust voice emerges with clarity:

> To a generation afflicted by the fury of cruel men, by the outrage of abandoning God, no condemnation is too harrowing. . . . The message of wrath is frightful, indeed. But for those who have been driven to the brink of despair by the sight of what malice and ruthlessness can do, comfort will be found in the thought that evil is not the end, that evil is not the climax of history.[98]

If "indifference to evil is more insidious than evil itself,"[99] then divine anger constitutes a form of paradoxical consolation—it assures the victims that their sufferings are not forgotten, that the unspeakable pain they endure does not go unnoticed. Indeed, although anger may be "reprehensible when associated with malice," it can be a blessing as well—"morally necessary as resistance to malice."[100]

Hovering in the background here is the spirit of Marcion, the anathematized second-century Christian who insisted upon the "radical disparity and absolute discontinuity" between the Old Testament and the New,[101] and who thus taught that "Christianity has no relation to the Judaism from which it sprang."[102] Insistent upon a Christianity "free from every vestige of Judaism,"[103] Marcion based his teaching on a set of complete oppositions—between Law and Gospel, between the Old Testament and the New—and taught, ultimately, that there were two Gods, the just creator god (of the Old Testament) and the gracious redeeming God (of the New). "To Marcion," in Ermin Micka's words, "the god of the Old Law, though just, is likewise ignorant, cruel, the creator of evil, angry, remorseful, inconsistent, and mutable."[104] Marcion's position as described by Tertullian was that the God of the Old Testament is "judicial, harsh, mighty in war"; the God of the New, in contrast, is "mild, placid, and simply good and excellent."[105]

Marcion's bias against the God of Israel, Heschel laments, "has been stubbornly preserved in the mind of Western man to this day."[106] All too often the God of Israel is portrayed as vengeful, raging, and out of control—and thus, it goes without saying, as morally inferior. Consider Herbert Joseph Muller, for example, who describes the God of the Old Testament as "stern, arbitrary, inscrutable, unaccountable";[107] or Paul Volz, who characterizes Him as "sinister, dangerous, and unaccountably angered," and insists that He "punishes without mercy, demands cruelty and creates evil."[108] Although in the history of anti-Judaic scholarship the spirit of Marcion most often went unacknowledged, in the work of church historian and liberal theologian Adolf von Harnack it was brought to clear and unapologetic expression. As part of his war on "literalistic biblicism" and the excessive shackles of theological dogmatism, Harnack advocated that modern Protestantism deny canonical status to the Old Testament.[109] To have rejected the Old Testament in the second century, Harnack famously wrote, would have undoubtedly been a "mistake," but, equally, "still to preserve it in Protestantism as a canonical document since the nineteenth century is the consequence of religious and ecclesiastical crippling."[110] Marcion's greatest failing, it seems, is that he was too far ahead of his time.

Heschel's own writings on divine anger stand in stark polemical contrast with Marcion and his contemporary champions. As we have seen, Heschel insists that divine wrath in the Hebrew Bible is anything but inscrutable; it is, on the contrary, the mere flipside of God's love and concern. God's anger as described in the Hebrew Bible thus renders Him—and the Bible that tells of Him—more rather than less praiseworthy. For Heschel, there is no goodness without indignation, and it is thus Marcion's God—and not the God of the Hebrew Bible—who is morally inadequate. Heschel here does a brilliant job here of polemically "reversing the gaze": rather than allow Judaism to be seen and evaluated through the calumniatory lens of traditional Christian anti-Judaism (whether Marcionite or not), Heschel instead subjects Christianity (especially in its Marcion-inflected forms) to Judaism's critical eye and finds the former wanting.[111]

Heschel has thus set for himself a kind of dialectical task here—to affirm the reality and moral necessity of divine anger on the one hand, and to insist on its transitory nature on the other. Better an angry God than an indifferent One, Heschel seems to say, but better still an angry God whose wrath is ultimately transcended by His love. Indeed, the very grandeur of divine compassion is that it is "a love that transcends the most intense anger, a love that abides in full recognition of human weakness."[112] "Even in moments of indignation," Heschel assures us, God's "love remains alive."[113]

As a rule, as we have already noted, Heschel opposes extreme formulations according to which God is totally other. "The God of the prophets is not the Wholly Other . . . shrouded in unfathomable darkness,"[114] but is, rather, the God of covenant and relationship, reaching out to the prophets, and through them, to Israel as a whole:

> The divine pathos is like a bridge over the abyss that separates man from God. It implies that the relationship between God and man is not dialectic, characterized by opposition and tension. Man in his essence is not the antithesis of the divine. . . . [On the contrary,] the fact that the attitudes of man may affect the life of God, that God stands in an intimate relationship to the world, implies a certain analogy between creator and creature.[115]

The God of covenant is a God of "reciprocity" and "engagement,"[116] and thus cannot be totally Other. Indeed, Heschel asserts definitively, "Absolute antithesis is alien to the Hebrew mind."[117]

But when he gets to the vexed topic of God's anger, Heschel abruptly shifts gears, introducing a sharp blast of Maimonideanism. "The major difficulty in our attempt to understand the issue [of divine wrath]," he writes, lies in "the failure to sense the ambiguity and the *homonymous aspect* of the terms denoting the pathos of anger."[118] On this formulation, God's anger is totally unlike human anger; this is, after all, the meaning of a homonym—"anger" in one case means something totally different from "anger" in the other. Even more strongly, Heschel adds, "Just as God is absolutely different from man, so is divine anger different from human anger."[119] In general, then, Heschel embraces an analogical theology, according to which certain emotions may be predicated, however tenuously, of both God and humanity; indeed, as we have seen, he explicitly rejects theologies that insist uncompromisingly on God's total otherness. But in this instance, Heschel reverses course (seemingly without self-consciousness) and asserts precisely the opposite—that God is Wholly Other, and that predications can be made of both God and humanity only homonymously (and thus, of course, not at all).

Now, the interpreter faces two choices here—either to assume that Heschel is hopelessly self-contradictory, or to suggest that he is groping (however clumsily) for a complex philosophical point. A careful reading of *The Prophets* as a whole leads us down the latter path. On the one hand, as we have seen, Heschel contends that anger is central to the divine life; indeed, it is a morally necessary component of God's relationship with humanity. But on the other hand, there are good reasons to hesitate about attributing anger to God—in human beings, anyway, anger is deeply entwined with impulsiveness and loss of self-control, qualities any theologian would be reluctant to associate with God. Heschel thus finds himself in a bind—needing to affirm divine anger, and yet sensing the obvious difficulties therewith. In affirming a heavily qualified theory of divine anger, Heschel is attempting to swim in what he knows are morally ambiguous waters.

Paul Gavrilyuk's discussion of anger and impassibility in the Church Fathers can be helpful here.[120] Theologians like Arnobius (third century, North Africa) insisted that anger was a passion that rendered human beings "insane," and made them resemble "wild animals." Anger was inherently connected to "loss of reason," and it led, horrifically, to "lust for revenge" and to "revel[ing] in the torture of another's grief." Obviously, such a base and degrading emotion could not be properly attributed to God.[121] In contrast, some Church Fathers, like Irenaeus and Tertullian, found this approach simplistic and one-sided. "Far from being a conscience-blinding perturbation of the mind," divine anger, according to them, "manifests God's righteous indignation at human disobedience." Anticipating some of what we have already seen in Heschel, these Fathers insisted that divine anger was "intimately related to divine justice,"[122] and showed that theologians like Marcion had been far too quick to relegate divine wrath to the theological dustbin.

And yet the Fathers were understandably uneasy about the underside of anger, and they insisted, therefore, that God experiences it only "in a carefully qualified sense. . . . God is fully in control of his anger and he never becomes angry arbitrarily." God's anger, is always "rationally directed," and He never surrenders His "sovereign freedom and total control over [H]is emotions." This, Gavrilyuk shows, is what the Fathers meant when they spoke of divine impassibility—not that no emotions could be attributed to God, but that such attributions could be undertaken only with great care. Impassibility thus functions as "a negative qualifier that limits the analogical application of anger to God in a way that is God-befitting."[123] Impassibility, in other words, introduces a note of apophasis as a counterweight to the attribution of (seemingly all too human) emotions to God.

I want to suggest that protestations of God's utter otherness function in Heschel in just the way that impassibility functions in the Fathers, as a kind of "apophatic qualifier" that serves to ensure that "God experiences [emotions] in the manner appropriate to him alone."[124] If we subject Heschel to a rigorous philosophical examination, we will have to dismiss his invocation of homonymy as a way of distinguishing human anger from divine—this is more apophasis than Heschel's theology needs or can sustain. But we can nevertheless readily grasp the point that Heschel is trying to make: God does experience anger. Indeed, it is morally critical for God to do so. And yet divine freedom and morality mean that God's anger is vastly different from its human counterpart, and that God's anger is not morally compromised in the ways that human anger all too frequently is.[125] God experiences anger, both Heschel and the Church Fathers insist, but only in qualified, God-befitting ways.

As we have seen, in exploring the divine pathos, Heschel speaks frequently of God's "sorrow," "grief," and "affliction." God is, he says, "moved and affected by what happens in the world. . . . Man's deeds can move him, affect Him, grieve Him, or, on the other hand, gladden and please Him."[126] And, of course, Heschel places great emphasis on the ongoing interplay of divine love and divine anger. Indeed, he maintains, "The grandeur of God implies the capacity to experience emotion."[127] Thus, it is not surprising to hear Heschel assert elsewhere that "the prophets spoke of God's participation as emotional reaction, as feeling."[128] And yet we should tread carefully, lest in haste we interpret Heschel's discussions of divine emotions in straightforward, univocal terms. The "essential meaning" of the divine pathos, Heschel writes, "is not to be seen in its psychological dimension, as standing for the soul, but in its theological connotation, signifying God as involved in history, as intimately affected by events in history, as living care."[129]

According to Heschel, the radical difference between God and humanity meant that in prophetic theology, divine emotions were understood as something other than mere human emotions projected upward. "Since the human could never be regarded as divine," Heschel writes, "there was no danger that the language of pathos would distort the difference between God and man." Thus, Heschel notes, "We are inclined to question the legitimacy of applying the term anthropopathy to the prophetic statements about the divine pathos." To be sure, anthropopathism is a very real danger where there is an "unawareness of the transcendence and uniqueness of God," or where human beings presume "to picture or to describe God in His own existence, unrelated to man." Indeed, theology is in peril when it assumes that there is "no discrepancy between imagination and expression: the gods are conceived of as human beings and described as human beings."[130] But biblical texts, Heschel insists, are keenly aware of the difference between "anthropomorphic conceptions," on the one hand, and "anthropomorphic expressions," on the other; "The use of the latter," he reminds us, "does not necessarily prove belief in the former." In other words, the language of pathos serves not to "project human traits into the divinity" but rather to offer "genuine insight into God's relatedness to man."[131] All of this is encapsulated by Heschel's assertion, building on Isaiah 55:8–9, that "My pathos is not your pathos, neither are your ways My ways, says the Lord. For as the heavens are higher than the earth so are My ways higher than your ways, and My pathos than your pathos."[132]

Indeed, according to Heschel—and it is easy to miss this point—the very importance of divine pathos depends precisely on God's remaining, always, other. As he puts it, "Regarded as a form of humanization of God, the profound significance of this fundamental category [of pathos] is lost."[133] What this means, I think, is that for Heschel, what is crucial is not that *someone* cares about human life, but that *God* cares. But if divine caring is interpreted in excessively anthropopathic terms, then, paradoxically, it is no longer God who cares. Thus, the tenuous balance must consistently be struck between the unavoidable employment of human language and the necessarily vigilant awareness of its ultimate inadequacy.

Perhaps another way of getting at this point is to say that for Heschel, speech that at first glance appears anthropopathic in fact intends not to bring God down so much as to raise language up. "The greatest challenge to the biblical language," he writes, "was how to reconcile in words the awareness of God's transcendence with His overwhelming livingness and concern." The prophets had no alternative but "to use anthropomorphic language in order to convey His nonanthropomorphic Being."[134] Thus, "statements about pathos," Heschel maintains, are "the accommodation of words to higher meanings. Words of psychological denotations are endowed with a theological connotation. In the biblical expressions of divine emotions . . . the religious consciousness experiences a sense of superhuman power rather than a conception of resemblance to man." When the prophets speak of God's pathos, then, what is being evoked is something decidedly non-human: "The idea of the divine pathos combining absolute selflessness with supreme concern for the poor and the exploited can hardly be regarded as the attribution of human characteristics. Where is the man who is endowed with such characteristics?"[135] This combination of morality as "supreme, impartial demand" and "object of personal preoccupation and ultimate concern," Heschel contends, is much more plausibly described as divine than as human. More forcefully, Heschel wryly states: "The belief that ultimately there is . . . a God whose concern is for justice is anthropomorphic in the sense in which the idea of transcendence or eternity is anthropomorphic."[136] Thus, he concludes, "God's unconditional concern for justice is not an anthropomorphism. Rather, man's concern for justice is a theomorphism."[137]

We have already seen that divine pathos should not be understood in crudely anthropopathic terms, as a recognizable divine version of human feelings. But Heschel goes further, repeatedly emphasizing that pathos is not essence. "The divine pathos," he writes, "is not conceived of as an essential attribute of God . . . but as an expression of God's will . . . not an absolute content of divine Being, but rather a situation or the personal implication in His acts."[138] No matter how "precious" the prophetic realization of God's "attentiveness and concern," Heschel avers, "*we must not think that we reach God's essence.* Transcendent attentiveness merely defines the limits of the prophet's understanding of God. God in Himself, His Being, is a problem for metaphysics"—not for theology or faith.[139] Again, Heschel writes that "God can be understood by man only in conjunction with the human situation. For of God we know only what He means and does in relation to man. . . . Revelation means, not that God makes Himself known, but that He makes His will known; not God's disclosure of His Being, His self-manifestation, but a disclosure of the divine will and pathos, of the ways in which He relates Himself to man."[140] Note carefully that pathos is not God's being or self-manifestation, but rather an aspect of God's relationship to humanity. As Heschel says straightforwardly: "A subject of pathos, God Himself is not pathos."[141]

In light of everything we have just seen, it is difficult to make sense of Eliezer Berkovits's blistering condemnation of Heschel's discussion of the divine pathos as hopelessly and inexcusably literalistic.[142] Heschel repeatedly disavows literalistic understandings of religious language, both in *The Prophets*, as we have just seen, and elsewhere. In *GSM*, for example, he writes that "the cardinal sin in thinking about ultimate issues is literal-mindedness. The error of literal-mindedness is in assuming that things and words have only one meaning."[143] Yet Berkovits definitively declares that "the boldness of Dr. Heschel's thought consists . . . in taking literally all biblical expressions that ascribe to God emotions of love and hatred, joy and sorrow, suffering and pleasure."[144] Berkovits adds, quoting verbatim words borrowed from Heschel himself (!), that Heschel has "completely ignored" the problem of "how to reconcile in words the awareness of God's transcendence with His overwhelming livingness and concern."[145] To be sure, Berkovits is aware of Heschel's frequent insistence that expressions of pathos should be taken as "allusions rather than descriptions," but he forcefully insists that Heschel has failed to confront the dangers of literalism seriously enough. It soon becomes evident, however, that for Berkovits, anything short of a full-blown Maimonidean negative theology must be repudiated as crudely literalistic. "The distinction between the Infinite and the finite, between the Creator and the creation," is, he writes, "an absolute one."[146]

Here, two responses are in order: first, it is critical to remember that, as we have already seen at length, Heschel explicitly rejects the Maimonidean insistence on the absolute otherness of God, pointing out that it renders biblical notions of covenant (and pathos) meaningless and incoherent. Second, it is worth noting that Berkovits himself fails to reckon with just how radical Maimonides' views really are. He asserts, for example, that "God's care and concern for His creation . . . are, of course, familiar thoughts, well understood by all who have some knowledge of biblical theology or religious philosophy."[147] Yet if one takes Maimonides as the norm for philosophically defensible theology, it is not at all clear what sense can be made of the notion of "God's concern" for humanity and the world; the concept is, at any rate, surely not "well understood" by any serious Maimonidean. Berkovits thus fails to engage seriously with Heschel's critique of Maimonides, and to notice that his own theological ideas are themselves undercut by the very philosophical norm he purports to champion.[148]

And yet an unresolved—and perhaps irresolvable—tension does remain in Heschel's understanding of divine pathos. Can Heschel's persistent contrasting of the God of Israel and the God of philosophy, on the one hand, and his equally ardent insistence that an emphasis on pathos tells us nothing at all about God's essence, on the other, be fully integrated? If there is a divine essence utterly untouched by pathos, then why insist on such an absolute distinction between the God of the prophets and the God of the Stoics? Conversely, if dynamism is really to be privileged over stasis, and pathos over indifference, then why pull back and deny dynamism and pathos in the divine essence?[149] Now, perhaps Heschel would say that what he denies is not dynamism in the divine essence so much as the possibility of human beings knowing anything at all about that essence. But one wonders: does the tradition of Greek philosophy not exercise more of an influence on Heschel than he realizes?[150] And is that necessarily a bad thing? It is imperative, as Heschel tells us time and again, that religion not simply surrender its claims in the face of whatever philosophy is regnant at the time, but neither must it always defiantly reject philosophy's potentially sophisticating influence.[151] After all, in *GSM*, Heschel himself advocates (at least theoretically) a kind of "elliptical thinking" in which philosophy and religion provide "enrichment" to one-another.[152] My suggestion, then, is that Heschel engages in just such elliptical thinking in *The Prophets*, even though he feels compelled (consciously or otherwise) to deny it. The core point Heschel wishes to make about God, however stammeringly, is that, contra Maimonides and the Greeks, He does love and care and otherwise react emotionally; and that, against coarse literalists of every stripe, those emotions are radically different from anything human beings can comprehend, let alone embody themselves. The capacity to fully refine that claim may ultimately lie beyond the reach of human thought and language. This is why Heschel consistently insists that religious speech indicates but does not describe, points to but cannot capture, its transcendent subject.[153]

* * *

Heschel is interested not merely in "prophetic theology"—that is, in the question of divine pathos, but also in "prophetic religion"—that is, in the prophets' response to God's pathos. The latter is characterized most fundamentally by a sense of "sympathy," of feeling with (and, as we shall see, *for*) God. "The fundamental experience of the prophet," Heschel writes, "is a fellowship with the feelings of God, a sympathy with the divine pathos, a communion with the divine consciousness which comes about through the prophet's reflection of, or participation in, the divine pathos."[154] To be sure, the prophet encounters the word and will of God, but what most deeply moves him is the divine pathos: "To the prophet," Heschel says, "the pathos is the predominant and staggering aspect in what he encounters," and "the inner personal identification of the prophet with the divine pathos is ... the essential feature of his ... life.[155]

The thorny problem of anthropopathism emerges here again: if God's pathos is so radically different from ours, what does it mean to suggest that the prophet's life is animated by sympathy with it, indeed, that he "participates" in it? As Maurice Friedman comments, "When one talks of God's pathos and the prophet's sympathy with it, it is difficult not to attribute feelings to God in a way very like those of man, even if infinitely greater than his."[156] Whether or not his strategy is fully effective, what Heschel seeks is a way to talk about God and the prophet in a way that couples relational closeness with an unbridgeable metaphysical gap.

Here again, Heschel posits a stark divide between biblical thinking and Greek. In contrast with Greek religion, which denigrates the passions, prophetic religion is a characterized by "an awareness of the unity of the psychical life." Therefore, "an unemotional sobriety could not be the form of religious consciousness" taught by it. Heschel writes: "In contrast to the Stoic sage who is a *homo apathetikos*, the prophet may be characterized as a *homo sympathetikos*."[157] In utter contrast to the Greek philosopher, the biblical prophet is a man of feeling. Prophecy demands "not self-conquest but self-dedication; not the suppression of emotion but its redirection."[158]

Following Max Scheler, Heschel speaks of two types of sympathy—sympathy *with* someone and sympathy *for* them.[159] The former involves two persons sharing an experience, feeling the "same" sorrow or anguish, and thus generating a "community of feeling." In this case, the prophets stand with God, observing "the spiritual and moral plight" of Israel, and feeling the resultant "sorrow or indignation . . . love or anger." The latter, in contrast, involves one person observing another and directing his attention to the latter's experience—in this case, the prophet intuits the divine pathos in a given situation and is moved to commiserate with it. In this second case, in other words, God's pathos and the prophet's sympathy are phenomenologically not one fact, but two—God experiences love or anger, and the prophet directs his sympathy toward God. Here, instead of imagining God and the prophet looking together at Israel's waywardness, one can picture the prophet focused on God: "The prophet is guided, not by what he feels, but rather by what God feels. In moments of intense sympathy for God, the prophet is moved by the pathos of God, Who is disillusioned by His people."[160] In other words, we might say, the prophet displays transitive concern for God, who evinces transitive concern for Israel. Or, to put it somewhat differently: the prophet transcends himself by turning to God, who transcends Himself by turning to Israel. And thus, of course, the prophet is turned back to Israel himself. In sum: the prophet can look *with* God, or, as it were, he can look *at* God. In either case, what he feels is intense sympathy that is at once rooted in, and generative of, transitive concern.

The prophetic call emerges from a mix of "attraction" and "coercion"; the prophet is "conscious of both voluntary identification [with God] and forced capitulation [to Him]." The initial prophetic call, Heschel insists, comes from God; the prophet is at once enticed and overpowered by Him.[161] Thus, at base, prophetic sympathy is a "response, not a manifestation of pure spontaneity."[162] Nevertheless, Heschel emphasizes, true sympathy is "an act of will,"[163] a choice on the part of the prophet to identify with what God feels. Prophecy is thus a complex weave of freedom and compulsion.

Crucially for Heschel, all of this is based in the dynamics of interpersonal relationship. Sympathy "means living with another person." The prophet shares a profound intimacy with God, and sympathy therefore "has a dialogical structure. . . . Unlike the experience of the numinous or the feeling of sheer awe or fear," Heschel writes, "sympathy always refers to a person or to persons."[164] In contrast to the mystic, what the prophet seeks is not "*unio mystica*," but "*unio sympathetica*"—that is, "an intimate harmony [with God] in will and feeling."[165] The prophet does not aspire to union with the Being of God, but to "harmony of the soul with the concern of God."[166] "The modes of prophetic sympathy," Heschel writes, "are determined by the modes of the divine pathos."[167] What the prophet feels, in other words, is determined by what God feels. Thus, the prophet must be capable of "polarity of emotion," of both deep love and intense anger.[168]

At bottom, then, the prophets are concerned with God before they are concerned with injustice;[169] it is because the latter causes such suffering to the former that the prophets are enraged by it. "The [prophets'] preoccupation with justice," Heschel writes, "the passion with which the[y] condemn injustice, is rooted in their sympathy with divine pathos."[170] Those who wish to translate "prophetic ethics" into largely secular terms thus cannot in good faith turn to Heschel for inspiration. According to Heschel, "Since the prophets do not speak in the name of the moral law, it is inaccurate to characterize them as proclaimers of justice." On the contrary, "It is more accurate to see them as proclaimers of God's pathos, speaking not for the idea of justice, but for the God of justice, for God's concern for justice." The Bible's passion for social justice is inextricably intertwined with its passion for God: "Divine concern remembered in sympathy is the stuff of which prophecy is made."[171] To be clear: in the prophetic conception of the world, there can be no relationship with God devoid of, or divorced from, a passion for justice.[172] On the contrary, "the chief characteristic of prophetic thought is the primacy of God's involvement in history."[173] But neither does the prophetic world offer any model for a passion for justice devoid of, or divorced from, a relationship with God. To assert the one without the other is to dissipate the very heart of prophetic religion.[174]

* * *

As we have seen, these two themes—the pathos of God, and the sympathy of the prophets—constitute the core of Heschel's interpretation of the prophets. But these themes emerge in full force in Heschel's study of the rabbis as well. In *Torah min ha-shamayim*, Heschel portrays what he sees as the two central strands in rabbinic theology—the boldly paradoxical, unabashedly imaginative school of Rabbi Akiva, and the much more sober, rationalistic school of Rabbi Ishmael[175]—and suggests that a great deal of what is debated and discussed in later Jewish theology can be traced back to the positions of these two paradigmatic figures.[176] I am in agreement with Gordon Tucker that, as a rule, Heschel "is not asking us to choose between the two theological approaches that he persistently presents to us. Indeed . . . Heschel did not want to 'choose sides' but rather to effect some synthesis for himself."[177] This is perhaps most evident in Heschel's discussion of "Duties of the Heart."[178] Whereas Ishmael, who believed in a majestic and transcendent God, understands the duties to love and cleave to God in ethical terms—we are to cleave to God by living up to Judaism's interpersonal norms and aspirations— Akiva, who conceived of God in far more personal, almost human terms, interprets the same duties in more straightforwardly emotional terms. As Tucker astutely notes in his introduction to the chapter, Heschel "obviously valued both approaches. His lifelong pursuit of social justice followed the Ishmaelian view that love of God must be expressed by doing God's work in this world. But his studies of the phenomenology of prophetic experience, of Hasidism, of prayer, and of rabbinic theology sought to see the divine-human encounter as a reality through which God meets every one of us directly on a personal level."[179] While I would quibble with Tucker's characterization of Heschel's study of the prophets—what is true of God's relationship with the prophets cannot necessarily be transposed to God's relationship to "every one of us"—I think the broader point is correct. One might even go further, and say that for Heschel, the very power of prophecy is in its merging of the Akivan and Ishmaelian approaches—the prophet meets God in a direct personal encounter and is led thereby to a radical ethical concern for the world.

Nevertheless, on a variety of issues, it is possible to discern Heschel's Ishmaelian leanings. Heschel argues that in the history of Jewish thought, Akiva was, in the main, victorious over Ishmael, and it is fair to say, I think, that on many issues Heschel sought to "recover" Ishmael and give him his due.[180] But on one issue, at least, Heschel's passions and convictions clearly lie with Akiva: where the question of divine suffering is concerned, Heschel has strong Akivan tendencies.[181] Indeed, there is much in Akiva's theology of divine suffering that resonates with Heschel's own.[182]

In the chapter entitled "Teachings Concerning the Shekhinah," Akiva emerges as the great heir to the prophets, continuing and developing their central teaching. Heschel tells us plainly that "Rabbi Akiva saw the world through the lens of the divine pathos,"[183] and thus, implicitly, that his vision was that of a prophet. But Akiva went beyond the prophets in his daring theological approach: whereas the prophets affirmed God's empathy with Israel's suffering, Akiva and his cohorts spoke of God's active *suffering with Israel,* His full participation in their afflictions. "The prophets spoke of God's participation as emotional reaction, as feeling," Heschel writes, "but the Tannaim described God's participation in the woes of Israel in terms such as: 'The Shekhinah descended into exile with them.'"[184] As Heschel describes it, Akiva taught that

> the participation of the Holy and Blessed One in the life of Israel is not merely a mental nod, a measure of compassion born of relationship to God's people. The pain of compassion amounts to pain only at a distance; it is the pain of the onlooker. But the participation of the Holy and Blessed One is that of total iden-

tification, something that touches God's very essence,[185] God's majestic being. As it were, the afflictions of the nation inflict wounds on God.[186]

In other words, then, Akiva was not shy about attributing emotions to God;[187] God's profound vulnerability lay at the very core of his teaching. Indeed, God, like Israel, finds Himself in need. Interpreting 2 Samuel 7:23—" . . . whom you have redeemed for yourself from Egypt, peoples and their gods (asher padita lekha mi-Mitzrayim goyim v'elohav)," Akiva boldly declared, "What, then, is the intention of 'whom you have redeemed for Yourself from Egypt?' As it were, You have redeemed Yourself."[188] Or, similarly, "God redeemed Himself, not us, for it was said: 'whom you have redeemed for yourself from Egypt, a people and its God.'"[189] In a similar vein, Akiva's student Eliezer b. Jacob suggests that Exodus 14:30—"Thus the Lord delivered [Vayyosha'] Israel that day"— should be read (using the same letters but with an alternate vocalization) as "Thus the Lord was delivered" [Vayyivasha']. The God of Israel is thus a Redeemer who Himself stands in need of redemption.[190]

Akiva's teaching, according to Heschel, is both old and new—old, in that "this concept has a powerful parentage in the soul of Israel, permeated with faith and burdened with suffering"; new, in that "it is as though it had lain dormant . . . in the deepest strata of thought, and then suddenly burst forth out of the depths, to illuminate the whole world."[191] Akiva's teaching thus constitutes at once a continuation and an intensification of the prophetic worldview.

But note the subtle change in Heschel's presentation of the prophets here, as opposed to in *The Prophets* itself. As we have seen, in that book, God's emotional life is characterized by a "dramatic tension"[192] between love and anger, the latter of which is God's response to Israel's waywardness. Only secondarily, and on rare occasions,[193] does Heschel speak of the divine pathos as God's suffering *with* Israel; more often, in the prophetic books, God suffers *on account of* Israel. Here in *TMHS*, in contrast, divine anger has disappeared, and the prophets are described as presenting a theology of divine fellow-suffering. Divine pathos here means God's *suffering-with* rather than *suffering-on-account-of*.[194] In emphasizing the theological continuity between Akiva and the prophets, Heschel paints the prophets in a very different light from the one presented in *The Prophets* itself.

If Akiva himself is a (perhaps not fully conscious) follower of the prophets, he has his own followers and continuators, in turn. Akiva and his cohorts promote the idea that Israel has the power "to diminish or enhance God's might."[195] This notion, Heschel tells us, will become a "cornerstone" of kabbalistic teaching.[196] Similarly, the idea that human beings should share in God's sorrow will function as a "cornerstone" in the Hasidism of the Baal Shem Tov and his followers.[197] Now, we might stop to ask: what is Heschel doing here? Why is it so important for him to draw lines of continuity backward from Akiva to the prophets, and forward from Akiva to the kabbalists? Heschel's project seems clear: he wants to emphasize that the vulnerability of the God of Israel—so central to his own constructive theological efforts—is not an obscure minority opinion in Jewish teaching. On the contrary, it lies at the very heart of Judaism and pervades its classical sources. In other words, Heschel seeks to mainstream the idea of divine suffering by showing that its provenance lies not in the purportedly obscure corners of the Kabbalah, but in the very fundamental sources of biblical and rabbinic tradition.[198]

In order better to understand Akiva, let us turn back for a moment to the prophet Hosea. Keep in mind that Heschel was likely writing about both at more or less the same time.[199] In contrast to Amos, who limits himself to reporting God's emotional reactions to specific situations, Hosea goes much further and "flashes a glimpse into the inner life of God as He ponders His relationship to Israel." God's "decisive motive" in history "is love."[200] God is in love with His people, and "Hosea is able," Heschel insists, "to express as no other prophet the love of God for Israel in its most varied forms."[201]

But God's love, as we have already seen, entails vulnerability. In the face of Israel's deception and betrayal, Hosea's God "goes on pleading for loyalty, uttering a longing for a reunion, a passionate desire for reconciliation."[202] Hosea's prophecy is characterized most strongly by his "emotional solidarity"[203] with God; Hosea sees the world from God's perspective, and he is angry on God's behalf.

For Hosea, the most apt image for God's relationship to Israel is that of marriage.[204] But Hosea's purpose in evoking marriage is not to "celebrate the grandeur of that relationship," but rather to expose the damage done, and the pain caused, by waywardness and infidelity. "Idolatry is adultery. . . . More than stupidity, it is lewdness. Israel is like a wanton wife, the Lord like a faithful, loving, but forsaken husband." God's threats are thus colored by a profound sense of disappointment and "disillusionment" with Israel.[205]

What of Hosea's own, earthly marriage? God tells the prophet to marry a woman named Gomer. When the latter's promiscuity and unfaithfulness are revealed, Hosea sends her away, as the law requires: a husband may not go on living with a wife who has committed adultery. "But God's way is higher than the legal way,"[206] Heschel writes, so He instructs Hosea to "bring Gomer back to your home, renew your love for her, even as the Lord loves the people of Israel, though they turn to other gods" (Hosea 3:1). After rejecting an array of scholarly interpretations of this story, Heschel offers his own: Hosea's marriage to the treacherous Gomer is a mirror of God's relationship with Israel. "As time went by," Heschel writes, "Hosea became aware of the fact that his personal fate was a mirror of the divine pathos, that his sorrow echoed the sorrow of God." The prophet's suffering, in other words, is an act of sympathy and "fellow suffering" with God.[207] Sympathy with the divine pathos becomes the governing experience in Hosea's life.

But the prophet goes even further, and it is this point that I wish to emphasize here. Hosea's central lament is that Israel does not know God, that it lacks "*daath elohim*" (knowledge of God). Heschel is quick to point out that in Biblical Hebrew, "*yada*" does not simply mean "to know" or "to be acquainted with." "*Yada*" means much more: it "compasses inner appropriation, feeling, a reception into the soul. It involves both an intellectual and an emotional act."[208] According to Heschel, when Hosea complains about Israel's lack of *daath*, he is lamenting its lack of sympathy with God. Boldly, Heschel declares, "In the light of his own complete emotional solidarity with God, Hosea seems to have seized upon the idea of sympathy as the essential religious requirement." Note what has happened here: for other prophets, such "knowledge" is the very core of what it means to be *a prophet*. For Hosea, such knowledge is the core of what it means to be *a member of the House of Israel*. We have here a radical democratization of prophetic experience (as Heschel imagines it): what was formerly the unique spiritual attainment of the prophet is now in some sense the responsibility of the whole people. "The words *daath elohim*," Heschel writes, "mean *sympathy for God*, attachment of the whole person, his love as well as his knowledge; an act of involvement, attachment or commitment to God." The Israelite is called to a relationship with God which is characterized not just by compassion for one another (sympathy *for*, in Scheler's terms), but also by a "suffering together, ... [by a] sharing [of] an inner experience" (or sympathy *with*). Although the prophet's sympathy differs in kind from the non-prophet's, there is still a requirement they both share: "Unlike the prophetic sympathy which arises in response to a revelation and the pathos it discloses, the general sympathy which Hosea requires of man is a constant solidarity, an emotional identification with God." The lack of such sympathy, Heschel and Hosea declare, "is the cause of man's undoing."[209] Although Heschel does not express or emphasize this clearly enough, Heschel's Hosea treats every Israelite as a "paraprophetic" figure of sorts, a person who can and must feel with God.[210]

Now note how Heschel interprets Akiva and his followers. "If the Holy and Blessed One shares in the pain of mortals, how much more so is it incumbent upon us to take our share in the pains of the Holy and Blessed One."[211] Consider the following rabbinic discussion of God's response to Israel's exile from the Land:

> According to some Sages, the Holy and Blessed One uttered lamentation and said, "Alas! Lonely sits the city!" Rabbi Johanan said: "When the ten tribes were exiled, the Divine Presence participated in their anguish, but when Judah and Benjamin were exiled, the Holy and Blessed One assumed personal responsibility, as it were, for their sins." Rabbi Simeon ben Lakish said, "When the ten tribes were exiled He lamented; when Judah and Benjamin were exiled, He said, 'I have no more strength to lament.' Whereupon He called for the professional keeners to join Him in His sorrow."[212]

Heschel is quick to point out that R. Simeon, an Amora, goes much further than the Tannaim who preceded him, "for they taught that the Holy and Blessed One participates in the suffering of Israel, but he taught that the Holy and Blessed One invites Israel to share in *His* suffering."[213] Heschel champions R. Simeon's idea (or at least his expansive interpretation of it—it hardly seems self-evident that "professional keeners" can be interchanged with all Israel)[214] and seeks to place it at the very heart of rabbinic theology—and, we could infer without much of a stretch, at the heart of his own theology as well. Heschel returns to this idea repeatedly: he begins this major chapter on the sufferings of the Shekhinah by suggesting that "this concept of the divine pathos, as expressed by the prophets of Israel, bestirred hearts to participate in the pain of the Holy and Blessed One,"[215] and ends one of its major sub-sections by describing how some sages shared in God's sufferings instead of bearing their own.[216] Now, we should take careful note of what has happened again here: Heschel has taken the central characteristic of the prophet—sympathy with the divine pathos—and radically democratized it. What was once the aspiration and responsibility of a chosen few is now available to, and indeed incumbent upon, the many.[217] What I am suggesting, in other words, is that, theologically and spiritually speaking, Rabbi Akiva is the logical heir to the prophet Hosea. Both solicit Israel's sympathy with God,[218] though each in a different tone: for Hosea, as we have seen, sympathy is portrayed as an obligation to be borne, and its absence comes with dire consequences. For Akiva, in contrast, sympathy is understood less as an obligation to be borne than as a possibility to be (seemingly voluntarily) embraced; the hope of comfort is attendant to it. But Akiva, too, ultimately sets out an enormous challenge—to make room for God's suffering by displacing ones own.

This aspect of Heschel's portrayal of Akiva and his followers represents a radicalization of his ongoing preoccupation with the ideal of self-transcendence, with the challenge of replacing self-centeredness with God-centeredness. If the prophet manifests transitive concern by caring for God, Akiva (or at least this strain in his thought) goes one step further—he willingly substitutes God's pain for his own. We should note that there is an obvious tension here: at times, Heschel seems to suggest that Israel should suffer God's burdens *in addition to* its own, but at others, he makes the much more demanding claim that Israel should feel God's pain *instead of* its own. Thus, a theology that begins by talking about a comforting divine presence ends up rendering an enormous challenge—not merely to live through one's pain, but also to recenter one's focus from one's own experience to God's.

Suffering the devastations of exile and destruction, the Jewish people were confident that "just as there is weeping on earth so is there weeping for God above."[219] This theology of divine suffering, Heschel writes, is a paradoxical "alloy of sorrow and triumph; it both burdens and comforts";[220] it is a doctrine of "lament and woe, but it is a lament that contains great comfort."[221] The suffering God is a comfort, because human beings discover that they are not alone in their pain; a burden, because human beings now bear the added responsibility of caring for God— indeed, they are faced with the spiritual task of transcending their own pain in order to focus more exclusively on God's. We might note that such a theology adds to the sum total of pain in the universe even as it attempts to ameliorate it.

All of this, of course, raises the question of divine omnipotence. If we take seriously the notion that God is vulnerable, that He, too, is in need of redemption, indeed, that He needs Israel to give him strength, what remains of God's power? "If there is mercy, there surely is no power; and if there is power, there surely is no mercy!" Heschel insists that for the rabbis, this was no mere abstract philosophical question—not "the problem of evil" to be addressed in the comforts of a seminar room, but rather, the agonized cry of a people overcome with suffering:

> The true nature of this standpoint cannot in truth be grasped by a person who can calmly look in from the outside. The Rabbis in the generation we are considering experienced things that others have not seen: the sacking of Jerusalem, the humiliation of the House of Israel, and the profanation of the Holy Name in the sight of the whole world. Stormy eras filled with human agony also harbor troubling thoughts; even the pillars of heaven shudder. And a nation which has been belittled by the nations of the world is likely to verge on belittling the great presumptions: that God is merciful and compassionate[,] and that God is the great and the powerful.[222]

As I understand it, the point Heschel is making here is an important one: for Akiva and Ishmael, questions about God's justice, mercy, and power were not abstract philosophical problems, but real-life dilemmas forged in the fires of intense national suffering. These questions had very real implications for the ongoing covenantal life of God and the Jewish people. It does not take much of a stretch to suggest that Heschel is discussing his own generation as much as Akiva's. It, too, had lived through unbearable brutality and bloodshed, and it, too, had many unanswered theological questions.

Faced with the enormity of evil in their time, Heschel writes, "Akiva and his cohorts believed that it is better to limit belief in God's power than to dampen faith in God's mercy."[223] God's mercy abounds, but God, too, is in need of redemption. Now, on the face of it, it seems that Heschel's Akiva has gone one crucial step further than Heschel's prophets. Recall that for the latter, the sufferings of the divine were those of an omnipotent God; indeed, Heschel explicitly rejected the idea that God's suffering was a function of His weakness. But here, in describing Akiva, Heschel seems to say precisely that. To borrow Heschel's own terms from *The Prophets:* perhaps Akiva speaks of passion rather than pathos?

At this point, one could be forgiven the impression that in general, *Torah min ha-shamayim* is a more radical book than *The Prophets*. The former, as we have seen, teaches a more profound notion of divine suffering than the latter; the former goes so far as to suggest that suffering penetrates even to God's very essence, a theological position the latter is careful to reject; and, as we have seen, at first glance, the former seems willing to surrender divine omnipotence in favor of divine mercy, something the latter is also explicitly unwilling to do.

But on the question of omnipotence, at least, Heschel seems to pull back:

> Don't we still have an unresolved question? For there is an obvious contradiction between the belief in God's omnipotence and the belief that He, too, is in need of salvation. Perhaps the resolution is this: just as the Creator, whose glory fills the universe, contracted (*tzimtzem*) his Shekhinah between the two staves of the Ark in order to reveal His words to Moses, so did God compress (*tzimtzem*) His Shekhinah into the history of Israel so that He might be revealed to His chosen nation as they went into exile together.[224]

Heschel's meaning in this last sentence is not entirely transparent, but the main point of the broader passage seems clear: the language of *tzimtzum* (self-contraction) suggests God's *voluntary* self-limitation. With that in mind, we can interpret the last sentence: God chooses to compress His presence so that He might be revealed to (or with) Israel in exile—this means, I think, that God chooses to be known through His compassionate presence rather than through His power. More starkly, and paradoxically: God chooses to surrender His power in order that His merciful presence may be manifest more clearly. It is almost as if God has a choice between exercising His omnipotence, thereby being revealed in glory rather than mercy; and surrendering His omnipotence, thereby potentially being revealed in His vulnerable and merciful presence. The key point here, at any rate, is that Heschel has once again returned to the notion of *self-imposed* limits on God: "Out of His participation in the sufferings of the nation, God, as it were, takes her afflictions upon Himself."[225] A God who "takes Israel's afflictions upon Himself" has made a choice to do so. Again we are confronted with pathos rather than passion, with the travails of an omnipotent God.[226]

Akiva's theology led him in a radical direction: in contrast to Ishmael, who sought to be liberated from his afflictions, Akiva embraced his and insisted that "it is advantageous for a person to be plagued by afflictions."[227] Afflictions, he taught, are the most powerful path to intimacy with God, and therefore they "can be a reward and not merely a punishment."[228] To be sure, there were other, more conventional means to achieve intimacy with God—no one was more dedicated to the study of Torah than Akiva, whose commitment did not wane even in the face of persecution and martyrdom—but none of them were as effective as afflictions: "The virtue of Torah is exceedingly great, but there are times when a person cannot draw near to the Holy and Blessed One except through afflictions."[229] Akiva cherished the love of God even unto death, and Heschel suggests that perhaps "Akiva sensed that it was impossible to achieve perfect love of God except through suffering, for a person cannot truly taste of the love of God until he is prepared to mock death itself for the glory of God's great name."[230] In light of all this, it is no surprise that Akiva could instruct his generation "to rejoice more in affliction than in fortune."[231]

Heschel wants to be careful here: Akiva's position is not masochistic, and it does not celebrate suffering for its own sake. The love of afflictions grows forth, rather, from a passionate love of God, and therefore from an unconditional acceptance of His will. "The love of affliction taught by Rabbi Akiva is not an unconditional love," Heschel writes, "as if suffering were a good *per se*. Love of affliction flows from love of the Holy and Blessed One, a love that brings with it both fortune and adversity. Both come from God, from whom no evil emerges."[232] Heschel takes a classical rabbinic term, "*yissurin shel ahavah*" (afflictions of love), and turns its conventional meaning one hundred eighty degrees: although the phrase is traditionally taken to refer to afflictions that befall a person out of God's love for him or her,[233] Heschel reads it differently, with human beings as the subject and God as the recipient—that is, as "afflictions associated with a person's love for God."[234] This approach renders theodicy irrelevant, since the sufferer seeks not explanation but only connection. In a worldview that treasures acceptance of whatever comes, the question of why seems oddly misplaced. As Heschel himself puts it: "In [Akiva's] view, there was no basis for the question, Why does evil befall the righteous? Afflictions are precious, and the righteous do not rebel against them—to them whatever God does is precious and beloved."[235]

"There is no doubt," Heschel tells us, "that the principle, 'whatever God does is for the best,' is as appropriate for the group as for the individual." Thus, implicitly, the Jewish people as a whole should embrace Akiva's practice of welcoming, even loving, its afflictions. But Heschel worries lest the individual come too willingly to accept the sufferings of the many, sufferings which the collective itself has not yet chosen to accept. Heschel's concern, it seems, is lest acceptance turn to a kind of indifference: "Who," he asks, "can accept other people's affliction with love?"[236] God, Akiva famously taught, grants pardon (or, more exactly, "remits punishment"—Naqqeh) in matters between human beings and Him, but God does not grant pardon in matters between one human being and another.[237] "Now," says Heschel, "if the Holy and Blessed One cannot grant pardon for the injury or affliction that one person brings upon another, surely we mortals cannot grant it. 'When a community is in agony, the individual is obligated to share in that agony.'" This is a somewhat opaque passage, but I think what Heschel is saying is this: the individual can accept her sufferings with love, and the community can similarly accept its, but the individual must be extremely careful when she seeks—individually—to accept the sufferings of the community as a whole (of which she is, critically, but a single part). What seems implicit here is that true acceptance of sufferings includes forgiveness of those who inflict them (thus the Jews forgive the Romans because ultimately they are mere vessels in God's hands—a claim, seemingly, more Heschel's than Akiva's), but an individual cannot forgive sins done to others. Thus, communal solidarity trumps the individual's potential for spiritual virtuosity; the individual is called to participate in the afflictions of the community, rather than to cultivate equanimity in their face. No individual can transcend the nation's suffering until the nation as a whole is ready to do so.

The key line in Heschel's discussion is perhaps this one: "The greatness of afflictions is not only because they cleanse a person's sins, but because within them there is human participation in the afflictions of heaven."[238] Akiva's loving embrace of afflictions, then, gives new depth to the ideal of covenantal mutuality: God shares in Israel's sufferings, and Israel shares in His. What we find in Akiva, then, is both an audacious mode of theologizing and an ambitious model of spiritual living: Akiva's theology affirms the sufferings of God, and his spirituality actively seeks to embrace them—indeed, to transcend one's own suffering in embracing God's.

* * *

Heschel's vision of God and his interpretation of the prophet ultimately share the same animating principle—positively, the valorization of self-transcendence and concern for the other; negatively, the impassioned rejection of "indifference" in all its forms. At the heart of prophetic theology, as we have seen, is the fact of God's care for humanity, and especially for the victims of injustice and oppression. The moral, theological, and metaphysical problem with the God of philosophy, in contrast, is precisely His indifference and self-enclosure. Recall Heschel's lament: "The God of the philosophers is all indifference, too sublime to possess a heart or to cast a glance at our world."[239] Indeed, we have seen Heschel legitimate biblical descriptions of God's anger as signifying, in his words, "the end of indifference!"[240] More soberly, Heschel writes, "Life is a *partnership* of God and man; God is not detached from or indifferent to our joys and griefs."[241] On the human side, Heschel speaks of "the scandal of indifference to God,"[242] and, as we have seen in chapter 1, he describes "indifference to the sublime wonder of living [as] the root of sin."[243] For Heschel, as I show there, indifference to wonder, indifference to God, and indifference to others are all inextricably intertwined. To become a human being, as we further saw in chapter 1, is to cultivate concern and overcome indifference. The human being, Heschel writes, "is not made for neutrality, for being aloof and indifferent."[244] In his famed speech "On Religion and Race," Heschel spoke fiercely: "There is an evil," he said, "which most of us condone and are even guilty of: *indifference to evil.* We remain neutral, impartial, and not easily moved by the wrongs done to other people. . . . The prophets' great contribution to humanity was the discovery of *the evil of indifference*." Heschel perceives full well that one's understanding of God cannot but have repercussions for one's vision of human good. Thus, as we have seen, Heschel thinks that the human correlate to the indifferent God of philosophy is the apathetic person; both are sadly indifferent to human tears. The human correlate to the pathos-filled God of the prophets, in contrast, is the prophet, who feels every injustice to the core of his being. "The prophet is a person," Heschel tells us, "who suffers the harm done to others. Wherever a crime is committed, it is as if the prophet were the victim and the prey."[245] Taking the prophet as a kind of human paradigm, we can discern an implicit mandate to *imitatio dei:* in the idiom of the rabbis, just as God self-transcends, so should you. Just as God manifests transitive concern, so should you. More concretely, just as God hears the shouts of the widows and the orphans, so should you. And again, just as God is free of all indifference, so should you be.

FIVE

"AWAKE, WHY SLEEPEST THOU, O LORD?": DIVINE SILENCE AND HUMAN PROTEST IN HESCHEL'S WRITINGS

Auschwitz is in our veins. It abides in the throbbing of our hearts. It burns in our imagination. It trembles in our conscience.
—*IEE*, 206.

The ultimate meaning of God's ways is not invalidated because of man's incapacity to comprehend it; nor is our anguish silenced because of the certainty that somewhere in the recesses of God an answer abides.
—*PT*, 293.

Sometimes rain drips like a tear.
It's God's confession in the world—
But I feel: God is sad-embarrassed,
for His sake, and for ours.

But our distress demands: Have mercy!
Instead of tears, give deeds;
Help, not remorse.
—Heschel, "Repentance," 201.

In his posthumously published *A Passion for Truth*, Heschel speaks of the Kotzker Rebbe's anger at God. Enraged by hypocrisy and deceit, Menahem Mendl railed at humanity. But the Kotzker's anger extended further, beyond human beings and toward their Creator. "Under [the Rebbe's] reverence," Heschel writes, "was dissent and contentiousness, a sense of outrage at the depth of falsehood afflicting the world as well as silent animadversion. . . . Was only man to blame? The Kotzker uncompromisingly castigated his fellow men. But did not castigation itself cast reproach upon their Maker?"[1] In addition to his anger, the Kotzker was plagued by "serious doubts." If mendacity enraged him, uncertainty tortured him. "If only I could be certain that there is punishment in the world to come," he told one of his students, "I would go out into the streets and dance for joy. If only I could be certain . . ."[2]

It does not require much of a stretch to suggest that at moments in this, his final work, Heschel allowed the Kotzker to speak on his behalf, to give voice to some of his own most deeply felt but only haltingly spoken ambivalences. Heschel had discovered the Kotzker as a young child, he wrote, and since then the latter had "remained a steady companion and a haunting challenge." The Kotzker, he told us, had "urged me to confront perplexities that I might have preferred to evade." From the warm and compassionate Hasidism of the Baal Shem Tov, Heschel had learned to live in a world suffused with meaning and the presence of God; from the dark and tension-laden Hasidism of the Kotzker, in contrast, he had learned to face the "immense mountains of absurdity" that stood before him. If the Baal Shem Tov represented the sustaining faith to which Heschel held so tenaciously, the Kotzker represented the monstrous possibility of ultimate disappointment lurking beneath the surface. In allowing himself to be guided by both men, Heschel confessed: "I had allowed two forces to carry on a struggle within me." For Heschel, I want to suggest, the Kotzker served at least partly as a vehicle for expressing his own post-Holocaust anger and doubt. Heschel essentially admits as much when he begins his chapter on "the Kotzker and Job" by noting: "This chapter is not an exposition of the Kotzker's views, but, rather, an essay on a major problem of faith which is guided by his sayings."[3] To be sure, Heschel's struggles and the Kotzker's were played out in very different keys, but they parallel each other nonetheless. To live with both the Besht and the Kotzker, Heschel wrote, was to live "both in awe and consternation, in fervor and horror, with my conscience on mercy and my eyes on Auschwitz, wavering between exaltation and dismay."[4] Note that whereas the Baal Shem stands for awe, fervor, and exaltation, Menahem Mendl stands for consternation, horror, and dismay. More important for our purposes—it seems that Heschel wants to be sure that the link is unmistakable—whereas the Baal Shem represents mercy, the Kotzker stands for Auschwitz and the enormous theological challenge it represents.[5]

Although Heschel's discussion of "the Kotzker and Job"[6] is the least linear chapter of one of his least linear books, I think we can nevertheless identify several recurring motifs in the chapter's response to the problems of anger and doubt. The first is the Kotzker's "refusal to accept the harshness of God's ways in the name of His love" and his willingness to confront and argue with God, as if to say, "Thy will be changed."[7] There was, for Menahem Mendl, "only one way to survive: to be Holy in challenging God, to pray militantly, to worship heroically."[8] His approach was "to protest, to contradict, to reject in the name of higher visions."[9] Heschel embraces the Kotzker's defiance, pointing out that it continues a venerable tradition dating back to Abraham, and insisting that in our own time, "the outcry of anguish certainly adds more to [God's] glory than callousness or even flattery of the God of pathos."[10]

If the Kotzker's anger moved him to challenge God, three countervailing forces drove him toward silence. In the first place, Reb Mendl worried about effrontery. Although he refused to "capitulate . . . even to the Lord,"[11] he understood that there had to be limits. "Temerity" could easily spill over into "impudence": "To put into words what the soul could hardly bear would have been blasphemous. The precarious dividing line between righteousness and presumption was better couched in silence."[12] Thus, although the Kotzker "reasoned with audacity . . . [he] walked in awe."[13]

The Kotzker also accepted humanity's epistemological limits. When all was said and done, there were boundaries beyond which human comprehension could not go. "No matter how painfully palpable the perplexity, any possible solution to it was hidden. A man of flesh and blood was simply not meant to comprehend the divine response to the deepest of human problems. Divine secrets were not compatible with the human intellect."[14] To worship a transcendent God, the Kotzker insisted, was "to accept the risk of not understanding Him. The incompatibility of God's ways with human understanding was, according to the Kotzker, the very essence of our being."[15] All this meant that "Reb Mendl knew full well how the most fiery accusations could sound like gibberish when articulated."[16] No wonder, then, that he tended to maintain his agonized silence.

But even beyond fear of impudence and acceptance of divine mystery, there was an additional, more tragic reason for silence. Heschel's Kotzker insisted that although God does deserve to be interrogated, human beings simply lack the moral credibility to carry out the questioning. Could human beings really accuse God over their own appalling behavior? "In a world where God is denied," Heschel writes, "where His will is defied, Torah flouted, compassion sloughed, violence applauded; in a world where God is left without allies—is it meaningful for us to court-martial Him?"[17] I do not think Heschel is suggesting that humanity's guilt somehow implies God's innocence. The situation is far more complex, and tragic, than that: humanity's guilt means not that God is innocent, but that man has no leg to stand on in accosting the divine. Reflecting on the Kotzker's complex weave of awe and audacity, Heschel points to an interesting difference between Job and the Hasidic master: "Whereas Job thought aloud, Reb Mendl's thoughts mostly remained in his heart. . . . He was a man of few words, realizing that man could make a fool of himself by questioning, challenging, or criticizing the Creator. The phrases that a man thrust against Heaven could easily boomerang." It is the last word here, "boomerang," that is critical—any challenge that man could direct at Heaven could be quickly turned back against him. Thus humanity is left mute, silenced by its own callousness. This, then, was Heschel's excruciating dilemma, one that he did not purport to solve: on the one hand, he was moved by a profound sense that Heaven, too, was implicated by human cruelty and injustice. But on the other hand, he felt paralyzed by a pervasive sense of humanity's own unspeakable guilt, and by the attendant obscenity of its presuming to serve as judge or jury for the divine. *Who are you to accuse Me?* Heschel could have imagined God saying. *It is true that I permitted gas chambers; but you actually built them.* In Kotzk, then, as in Heschel's study, "they cultivated the eloquence of silence."[18]

Heschel goes further, questioning whether theological reflection can ever "obviate the terrible agony the world is writhing in."[19] The concern here is not so much that speech would represent impertinence, but rather that words are ultimately futile. In the face of human suffering,

Heschel suggests, what is called for is not speculation but response. "The cardinal issue, Why does the God of justice and compassion permit evil to persist? is bound up with the problem of how man should aid God so that His justice and compassion prevail."[20] Heschel's approach here is to move the discussion away from theology and toward action, toward a focus on what I would call the covenantal response to human suffering. In this vein, Heschel suggests, what God needs are "partners, silent warriors."[21] It is important to emphasize that Heschel is not articulating a Pollyanna liberalism according to which human goodness will redeem the world, but rather a sense of covenantal mission whereby human beings are called to God's side in an ongoing struggle with evil. The central point here seems to be to prioritize overcoming evil rather than understanding or explaining it.[22] "The Kotzker's concern"—and, indeed, Heschel's as well—"was not theological, an intelligible answer to the problem of theodicy, but messianic, the defeat of falsehood."[23]

Heschel's final move in this chapter is to shift the focus from humanity's suffering to God's. Heschel reminds his readers that God, too, is in need of compassion. "All pain is shared anguish,"[24] he writes, and God needs human concern. Heschel ends his discussion of "the Kotzker and Job" with the story of a Jewish functionary who meets an "emaciated, poorly clad Jew" on a train in post-Holocaust Poland. The latter is so devastated and filled with rage that he at first refuses to pray. Eventually, however, he pulls out his tallit and tefillin and begins to pray after all. Asked to explain his apparent change of heart, the Jew declares: "It suddenly dawned upon me to think how lonely God must be; look with whom he is left. I felt sorry for Him."[25]

Ultimately, Heschel argues, God asks not just for compassion, but also for heroic levels of human faithfulness. Thus, what suffering calls for is not the abandonment of faith, but its impassioned re-affirmation; what God wants from humanity is the courage to affirm faith, even, and perhaps especially, amidst desolation. "In the brightness of the morning we sing praise; in the loneliness of the night we should have faith. This means being faithful to Him even in extreme misery. When we have every reason in the world to grieve, to lament, we should be able to lean on faith."[26] Heschel is no doubt speaking to his own generation when he writes: "God does not need those who praise Him in a state of euphoria.

He needs those who are in love with Him when in distress, both He and ourselves. This is the task: in the darkest night to be certain of the dawn . . . to go through Hell and to continue to trust in the goodness of God—this is the challenge and the way."[27]

None of this should be taken to suggest that Heschel thinks he has somehow "solved" the problem of evil and suffering. His protestations against human brutality and indifference on the one hand, and his declarations of compassionate faithfulness to God on the other, surely serve to soften evil's horrible sting, perhaps even to mitigate the severity of Heschel's charge against God. But on my reading they do not resolve the problem, do not exonerate God from ultimate responsibility. In his penetrating study of post-Holocaust Jewish theology, Zachary Braiterman has correctly argued that Heschel "could not sustain [his] antitheodic line of thought," but he goes too far, I think, in suggesting that "upon comparing the Kotzker with Job, [Heschel] immediately retracted his own religious protest." Heschel's work does contain the broad contours of a theodicy, and, as we have seen, one of the central thrusts of "The Kotzker and Job" is the multi-faceted impulse toward silence in the former's life and thought. But I do not think that this internal movement within Heschel's writing constitutes a "retraction" of the initial protest. In any case, it is surely an exaggeration to suggest that "the initial voice of anger directed toward God represented nothing more significant than an effective strategic device. . . . Heschel rhetorically challenged God in order to answer more forcefully the charge in God's defense against the culture of modernity."[28] Heschel's writing here seems to me to be neither as neat nor as potentially disingenuous as Braiterman implies; surely there is a middle ground between protest as the final word and protest as mere "strategic device." There is simply too much pathos in the Kotzker's argument with God for it to be interpreted solely as a rhetorical technique. In a book that begins with a confession of the author's feeling pulled in divergent directions by contrasting voices, I think it is a mistake to interpret his ultimate position on the religious question that troubles him most as fully resolved and clear-cut. As a man of deep faith, Heschel was inclined toward defense and affirmation of the divine; as a man who unblinkingly witnessed the extent of human callousness and suffering, he knew all too well the inadequacy of his own theology.

Above all, I think, as a man of enormous complexity, he eschewed an ultimate solution to the problem of evil.

That Heschel did not think he had fully "answered the charge in God's defense" becomes clear from a close reading of *Man Is Not Alone,* a work published two decades earlier than the studies of Kotzker. Chapter 16 of that book, a treatment of "the Hiding God," begins with a spirited defense of God, and then culminates—rather abruptly, without coherent transition—in an explosion of anger toward Him. Heschel begins as God's defender, dismissing the notion that contemporary times call forward the vexed question of theodicy with particular urgency; after all, it is not God but human beings who have committed history's most egregious crimes. "The major folly" of pressing the issue of theodicy, Heschel writes, "seems to lie in its shifting the responsibility for man's plight from man to God, in accusing the Invisible though the iniquity is ours. Rather than admit our own guilt, we seek, like Adam, to shift the blame upon someone else. . . . He is now thought of as the ultimate Scapegoat."[29] Put simply (and in language he might well have found altogether too sober and detached): Heschel here argues for a free-will theodicy, according to which human beings, rather than God, are accountable for the evil that pervades and degrades human life. "God is not silent," he writes; rather, "He has been silenced."[30]

Religion itself is implicated in human evil. Mired in hypocrisy, religion has at one and the same time "preached and eluded [God], praised and defied Him." It has led humanity astray with false promises and infantile theology: "Instead of being taught to answer the direct commands of God with a conscience open to His will," human beings have been "fed on the sweetness of mythology, on promises of salvation and immortality as a dessert to the pleasant repast on earth."[31] Mature theology recognizes that God is not some "watchman hired to prevent us from using our loaded guns," and it thus makes no sense to cast God as the "ultimate Scapegoat" for *our* murderous behavior.

All of this, of course, opens up the question of providence, and Heschel's response is innovative and audacious:

> We have witnessed in history how often a man, a group or a nation, lost from the sight of God, acts and succeeds, strives and achieves, but is given up on by Him. They may stride from one victory to another and yet they are done with and

abandoned, renounced and cast aside. They may possess all glory and might, but their life will be dismal. God has withdrawn from their life, even while they are heaping wickedness upon cruelty and malice upon evil. The dismissal of man, the abrogation of Providence, inaugurates eventual calamity.[32]

The process at play here is complex: a people abandon God, thereby leading to the abrogation of providence. The evil nation is "left alone. . . . The divine does not interfere with their actions nor intervene in their conscience."[33] God's turning away from the Germans, for example, means that there is no one to restrain their most murderous impulses. They turn into godless beasts of prey, even as they seem to achieve worldly success.[34] They will, Heschel is confident, ultimately be undone by their own evil, but in the meantime, it seems, providence allows them free rein over their enemies. Eventual calamity will befall the evil nation, but immense suffering will first be the fate of its victims. Heschel states all this in such a matter-of-fact way that it is easy to miss the bold originality of his argument: it is not the Jews who are the object of divine abandonment, but the Germans. But both, in very different ways, suffer the consequences of the divine turning away. Since God works to dissuade the perpetrator rather than intervening to save the victim, those who utterly quash their consciences effectively (if ultimately only temporarily) neutralize providence; they lack any sort of limit or brake upon their behavior. Put differently, implicit in God's hiding His face from the perpetrator is God's abandonment of the victim as well.[35] Tragic and horrific as this is, it is simply the way that providence works: since God manifests His providential concern primarily in attempts to stir the conscience rather than through dramatic interventions in historical events,[36] evildoers will sometimes (often) have their barbaric way with innocent victims.

Heschel describes a dialectical process of *hester panim*,[37] the hiding of the divine face. Human beings first turn away from God, and He, in turn, turns away from them.[38] Divine hiding results from prior acts of human defiance. "The will of God is to be here," Heschel writes, "manifest and near," but when God's will is thwarted, He leaves the world as if against His own will. Heschel is ambiguous about the dynamics of divine hiding. On the one hand, it seems as if God makes an active decision to depart: "When the doors of this world are slammed on Him, His truth betrayed, His will defied, He withdraws, leaving man to himself." Yet on the other, it seems that God has been displaced, that *hester panim* is not so much a description of what God does, but rather of what humanity has done to God: "God did not depart of His own volition. He was expelled. *God is in exile.*" (Note that the two passages I have just quoted follow immediately upon one another. They sit together rather uneasily in the very same paragraph.) At times, divine exile seems like a form of ontological rupture; at others, it seems that God's hiding is more an epistemological state than an ontological one—if human beings turn toward God, they discover that God is in fact present after all: "It is man who hides, who feels, who has an alibi. God is less rare than we think; when we long for Him, His distance crumbles away."[39] "A hiding God," Heschel emphasizes, "not a hidden God. He is waiting to be disclosed, to be admitted into our lives."[40]

* * *

Let us take stock for a moment of where we have come so far. The real question of our time, Heschel begins by suggesting, is not about God, but about humanity; it is the latter's cruelty, rather than the former's alleged indifference, that ought most to trouble us. Ours is an age of divine hiding, a hiding that follows upon and results from the human hiding that precedes it. But it is not a time of utter despair, since God still waits to be disclosed, to be let into human souls and deeds. Divine self-transcendence, in other words, is emphatically not equivalent to desertion of humanity. God hides Himself and curtails His power in the hopes of being discovered and responded to. These actions are thus paradoxical gestures of relational vulnerability, the very antithesis of abandonment.[41] Heschel now turns to themes familiar to us from our study of Kotzk, emphasizing that faith and faithfulness are crucial in dark times. "There are times," he writes, "when defeat is all we face, when horror is all that faith must bear. And yet, in spite of terror we are never overcome with ultimate dismay."[42]

But next, Heschel cites a passage from the book of Job: "Even that it would please God to destroy me; that He would let loose His hand and cut me off, then should I yet have comfort, yea, I would exult in even in my pain; let Him not spare me, for I have not denied the words of the Holy One" (Job 6:9–10).[43] Heschel offers no explanation or elaboration of this characteristically difficult passage from Job, no indication of how he wishes Job to be understood. At first glance, perhaps, the text would seem to offer an example of the faithfulness amidst adversity that Heschel so admires: no matter what happens, Job says, he has not and will not deny God. But look a little bit closer and the citation of this text becomes puzzling, its message starkly discontinuous with what Heschel has been saying until now. In the first place, the evil which befalls Job is not the work of human hands, and thus cannot be attributed to human freedom.[44] But even more centrally, Job may be faithful (although his friends manifestly think otherwise), but he is also furious, and his declaration of faith is suffused with anger and defiance. Now, the precise meaning of Job's words here (as elsewhere) is not entirely clear, but the tone of his remarks is unmistakable: Job is (a) raging over (b) what God has done to him. In what we have seen of Heschel so far, (a) there would appear to be no grounds for anger, since (b) after all, it is not God who is the author of our suffering. Reading closely, then, we catch an intimation that Heschel does not think that his own arguments about divine exile and human responsibility are ultimately satisfactory; indeed, there is a great deal more room for anger and confusion in his worldview than would appear from a surface reading.

Heschel next quotes the Kotzker. Paraphrasing Psalm 37:3, the Kotzker advises his students to "lie in the dust and gorge on faith" (*Lig in der Erd, un pashe dikh mit Emune*). Like so many of the Kotzker's statements, this one is epigrammatic and somewhat enigmatic. But its essential meaning, especially in this context, seems clear: no matter how low one has fallen, one should always nourish oneself with faith.[45] Back, it would seem, to faith in dark times. And yet there is, I think, a subtle hint of anger in the Kotzker's comment as well. In Yiddish, "*pashe*" is a verb that can be used only with reference to animals. Could there be some implicit protest here, some sense of indignation that human beings are reduced to an animal-like state? Faith may nurture one, but being forced to "graze" on anything is hardly a dignified way for a human being to live. Now look at what follows: Heschel cites Psalm 44, in full and without so much as an explanatory word of his own. The Psalm is perhaps the most audacious in the Psalter, and with its bold combination of profound faith and bitter, blistering lament, it merits citation in full:[46]

> *1:* We have heard with our ears, O God, our fathers have told us, what work thou didst in their days, in the times of old. *2:* How thou didst drive out the heathen with thy hand, and plantedst them; how thou didst afflict the people, and cast them out. *3:* For they got not the land in possession by their own sword, neither did their own arm save them: but thy right hand, and thine arm, and the light of thy countenance, because thou hadst a favour unto them. *4:* Thou art my King, O God: command deliverances for Jacob. *5:* Through thee will we push down our enemies: through thy name will we tread them under that rise up against us. *6:* For I will not trust in my bow, neither shall my sword save me. *7:* But thou hast saved us from our enemies, and hast put them to shame that hated us. *8:* In God we boast all the day long, and praise thy name for ever. Selah. *9:* But thou hast cast off, and put us to shame; and goest not forth with our armies. *10:* Thou makest us to turn back from the enemy: and they which hate us spoil for themselves. *11:* Thou hast given us like sheep appointed for meat; and hast scattered us among the heathen. *12:* Thou sellest thy people for nought, and dost not increase thy wealth by their price. *13:* Thou makest us a reproach to our neighbours, a scorn and a derision to them that are round about us. *14:* Thou makest us a byword among the heathen, a shaking of the head among the people. *15:* My confusion is continually before me, and the shame of my face hath covered me, *16:* For the voice of him that reproacheth and blasphemeth; by reason of the enemy and avenger. *17:* All this is come upon us; yet have we not forgotten thee, neither have we dealt falsely in thy covenant. *18:* Our heart is not turned back, neither have our steps declined from thy way; *19:* Though thou hast sore broken us in the place of dragons, and covered us with the shadow of death. *20:* If we have forgotten the name of our God, or stretched out our hands to a strange god; *21:* Shall not God search this out? for he knoweth the secrets of the heart. *22:* Yea, for thy sake are we killed all the day long; we are counted as sheep for the slaughter. *23:* Awake, why sleepest thou, O Lord? arise, cast us not off for ever. *24:* Wherefore hidest thou thy face, and forgettest our affliction and our oppression? *25:* For our soul is bowed down to the dust: our belly cleaveth unto the earth. *26:* Arise for our help, and redeem us for thy mercies' sake.

The Psalm is endlessly rich and repays careful study. For our purposes, however, a broad outline will suffice.[47] The psalmist begins by recounting Israel's salvation history (vv. 1–3), and proceeds to a confession of faith (v. 4) and a declaration of trust (vv. 5–8). Past glories are then sharply and abruptly contrasted with present defeat (vv. 9–12) and humiliation (vv. 13–16). An insistent statement of Israel's covenantal faithfulness (vv. 17–22) is followed by a weave of petitions for divine assistance (vv. 23,

26) and vehement complaints about God's failure to protect His people (vv. 24–25).

What is this psalm doing here? What does it do for Heschel's argument? On the one hand, it does contain another declaration of faith amidst dark crisis: despite finding itself in humiliating circumstances, Israel refuses to abandon its faith. Indeed, the psalmist continues to invoke God's mercies in Israel's downtrodden situation. The psalm is thus "a prayer of faith in the face of the inexplicable."[48] But on the other hand, like Job, the psalmist is angry and indignant;[49] his affirmation of faith is coupled with tortured lament. Psalm 44 audaciously contrasts Israel's heroic faithfulness (v. 17–22) with God's horrific abandonment of it; the protest of faith "expresses bewilderment rather than understanding."[50] The psalmist does not doubt that God is in control of history, but as James Luther Mays has put it, he complains that "[God's] work is strange."[51]

None of this can be easily integrated with Heschel's theology as expressed in this chapter. Until the citation from Job, we had heard about God's being in exile, about the ways in which human freedom rather than divine agency was ultimately responsible for human cruelty and degradation. But the psalmist, obviously, will have none of this: God is still the God of history, and He is obligated to be faithful to the covenant. To return again to the language we have been using (which, no doubt, would have been foreign to the psalmist himself): surely there ought to be limits to divine self-limitation? Are there not moments when self-transcendence is in fact indistinguishable from abandonment? The psalmist laments not the unbearable results of human freedom, but the tragic incomprehensibility of divine silence. As I have already mentioned, Heschel does not add so much as a single word of commentary to the psalm, so we are left to imagine the role he intends it to play. I would suggest that bringing the psalm enables Heschel to express in a traditionally rooted way what he might otherwise have found inexpressible, or even blasphemous—namely, his simmering anger at God's ultimately inexplicable silence at Auschwitz.[52] At the very least, the citation of Psalm 44 serves as a way of admitting—though without being forced to say so in so many words[53]—that all theodicy falls short of explaining (let alone justifying) Israel's horrible fate, whether in the psalmist's time or in Heschel's.

To make this point even sharper: earlier in the chapter, we explored Heschel's theology of *hester panim*. God turns away only because human beings do; some suffer because of others' brazen rebelliousness. But now consider verse 24 of our psalm: "Wherefore hidest thou thy face, and forgettest our affliction and our oppression?" If at first Heschel seemed to offer an explanation of God's hiding that he found satisfactory, now we hear the psalmist express anger and confusion over the same. How can it possibly be, he shouts, that you, God, turn away from the immensity of our suffering? Were Braiterman correct that the voice of anger expressed in Heschel is ultimately nothing more than a "strategic device," then chapter 16 would be structured quite differently: first we would encounter the psalmist's question, and then discover Heschel's answer. But instead, we find the exact opposite: first we hear Heschel's answer, and only then, after the purported answer has been fully articulated, do we encounter the question in all its emotional and theological intensity. Heschel finds himself in a double-bind: on the one hand, he cannot bring himself to pretend that he has neatly solved the problem of human suffering; but on the other hand, neither can he allow himself to express the extent of his anger and doubt. So the psalmist functions in the early Heschel as the Kotzker does in the later—as a vehicle for expressing the writer's own most conflicted religious thoughts and passions.[54] In his own, somewhat awkward way, then, Heschel offers both the broad contours of a theodicy, and an inchoate admission of its inadequacy. "Job had many successors," Heschel wrote, and "the Kotzker was one of them."[55] In a much lower key, I am suggesting, so, too, was Heschel. Far from being resolved, the problem of evil persists as a source of terrible agony in his writings.

I should note additionally that by quoting the psalm the way it does, the chapter itself in a sense imitates it. The psalm builds to a deeper and deeper tension between God and Israel, and though the reader might expect or hope for some resolution, there is none on offer. The psalm ends with an angry call to a sleeping God and a plea for divine mercy; in quoting the psalm without commentary, Heschel's chapter ends in precisely the same way—with an attempt to rouse God and an entreaty for divine intervention.[56] The fundamental dissonance, the coupling of deep faith with profound anger and no small shred of doubt, remains.

* * *

But we ought to be careful about associating the themes of anger and protest in Heschel's writings exclusively with the Holocaust. As we have seen, protest does play a key role in Heschel's response to the Nazi catastrophe, both in *Man Is Not Alone* and in *A Passion for Truth*. But it is crucial to note how early in Heschel's writings these motifs appear. In 1933, the young Abraham Heschel published his first book, a collection of Yiddish poems he had written over the previous seven years.[57] However one assesses their literary merit, the poems surely represent a treasure trove of the young Heschel's religious ideas; what is perhaps most striking about them is how many of Heschel's mature theological ideas are already telegraphed in these youthful outpourings.[58]

Although the phrase will appear only decades later, it is clear from at least some of the poems that God is "in search of man." Lamenting a suicide whose cries went unattended, the poet discerns "a [divine] cry that frightens, wakens, demands: / I ceaselessly stretched / thousands of imploring hands to you; / You, millions, why don't you help?"[59] And indeed, the poet seeks to respond to God's need. Repeatedly, he volunteers to "quench all suffering with my help; / to help each stone, each flower, / to serve each man, each worm"; with great passion, he implores God: "Help me to help!"[60] Turning to the world as a whole, he seeks to ameliorate its suffering: "Send me to exiled brothers, /prisoners in jails. / Send me with good news / and consolation to mourners. / With help to the poor, / with rescue to the sick. / Take me for a friend! / Take me for a slave!"[61]

But the poems as a whole are far less conventionally pious than might at first appear—the poet is moved less by God's search for humanity than by humanity's often desperate search for God. The young Heschel's writing is marked by a persistent sense of perplexity at God's silence, and of indignation at His inaction. At the beginning of the collection, the poet complains: "The desolate call to You, and You don't come . . . Human hands in peril / reach for the emergency brakes of Your world / which You have forgotten to set up! . . . You are meant to help here, Oh

God! / But you are silent, while needs shriek."[62] And at the end, he asks: "Haven't the prayers of generations, then, / achieved some mercy from You, God? Our devotion, ardor, / our lust for You—none of these considered?" "God, You greatest mute!" Heschel laments, "You answer screams with riddles / . . . You never say to hatred—'Out! Stop!'"[63] Even when the poet asks to serve in God's stead, he does not retract his expressions of disappointment with God; he will go, he seems to say, but his willingness does not excuse God's silence.[64]

At moments, to be sure, Heschel's compassion for God shines through: "God's tears," he writes, "Let me wipe away His lament."[65] Tenderly, the poet can lament that "Our brother God" is "fettered in jail," and attest that "You are not only Lord and Almighty, no! / You can also be poor and sorrowful. / Sometimes You behave like a child, as if I were the bigger boy."[66] In "Intimate Hymn," Heschel takes it upon himself "to unveil God—Who has disguised Himself in the world."[67] But compassion for God does not mitigate the poet's anger: "I am responsible for You too, / and demand of You—feel! / Like us, like me. / If not, I'll wander all around and scream / that God has forgotten his heart with me."[68] Bursting with indignation in the face of what can only seem like divine indifference, the poet demands of God: "Why don't you help—You, You!"[69]

Heschel's anger and ambivalence come through in full force in the closing pages of the collection. In an untitled piece, God is movingly pictured as "rend[ing] His clothes in mourning for the world."[70] But for the poet, God's suffering does not make His silence more tolerable: "Somewhere a prophet roars: Lord, accept reproof! / A youth screams disappointment: You powerless one, You, God!"[71] In "Petition," Heschel pleads with God, "God, answer us—we long for You! / Overcome Your silence, Lord of all words! / The downcast of a thousand years beg you:— reveal Yourself! / . . . Why do You tease our trust in You? / Mock our pride in You? / . . . Your silence—*gehinnom*, hell on earth."[72] In "*Tikkun Hatzot*—Midnight's Mourning Prayer," the poet goes so far as to suggest that as human hands reach out and are met with deafening silence, "[God] Himself seems a blasphemer."[73] What seems to anger Heschel most is his sense that divine feeling is not enough. It is not enough for God to be distressed at the state of the world. What is called for is action, divine intervention; less than that will not suffice.[74] "Sometimes rain drips like a tear. / It's God's confession in the world—/ But I feel: God is sad-embarrassed, / for His sake, and for ours. But our distress demands: Have mercy! / Instead of tears, give deeds; / Help, not remorse."[75]

It is worth lingering upon these last lines for a moment—"Instead of tears, give deeds; / Help, not remorse!"—because they reveal what Heschel quite possibly saw as the Achilles' heel of his theology, the ultimate weakness in his religious worldview. On the one hand, Heschel was to mature into Judaism's most eloquent advocate of the theology of divine pathos; not content with mere theologizing, he went so far as to cast himself in the prophetic mode, pleading for humanity to rediscover its own divine image and behave accordingly. And yet, as we have seen, the shortcomings of this approach seemed at times to overwhelm him: what good, he wondered, was divine *feeling* when human beings were being sent to gas chambers? Are there not moments when divine *action* would constitute a far more appropriate response than (mere) divine pathos?[76] How could a God who feels so deeply seemingly do so little? At a certain point, does inaction not suggest indifference? This is, I think, a core anxiety underlying Heschel's theology. Sometimes God's curtailing His omnipotence seems more like a crime than a virtue. And so Heschel expresses anger, frustration, and disappointment with God. With the psalmist, he thunders, "Awake, why sleepest thou, O Lord?"

We have seen that the theme of protest emerges only rarely in Heschel's mature writings; as a rule, Heschel does not allow himself to express anger and protest. When he does, he does so in the voice of others: Job, the psalmist, and the Kotzker, I have suggested, are all made to speak on his behalf. What is so striking about the poems is how different they are—here, protest is pervasive, and the poet does not shy away from his own raging voice. Interestingly, in other words, theological protest is more prevalent in the early Heschel than the late, more present in the pre-Holocaust writings than in the post-. The extent of the young Heschel's protest suggests, first, that he was far angrier at God than is usually understood; and second, perhaps surprisingly, that over time his anger became more muted—either because he had become less angry, or because he had grown more hesitant about speaking in the register of theological protest. It may be possible, in other words, that as Heschel's theology of God's search crystallized, his anger abated somewhat. Or it may be that as Heschel adopted the prophetic persona of the later writings, he came to view expressions of anger as somehow incongruous with, or even dangerous to, his theological mission—to defend Israel's faith, and to speak on behalf of its beckoning, suffering God.[77] As both "the Hiding God" and the evocations of the Kotzker indicate, Heschel did remain angry (how, after all, could a man angry at God's inaction before Auschwitz not be angry after it?). But he was also keenly aware that in contemporary times faith in God and awareness of the sacred were under profound threat, and humanity, he was convinced, could not survive the ravages of full-blown secularization. Addressing a group of Quaker leaders in Frankfurt-am-Main in 1938, Heschel writes: "The greatest task of our time is to take the souls of men out of the pit.... Let us forever remember that the sense for the sacred is as vital to us as the light of the sun. There can be no nature without spirit, no world without the Torah, no brotherhood without a father, no humanity without attachment to God."[78] Faced with the potentially disastrous consequences of the collapse of faith, Heschel may well have discovered another reason for silence, above and beyond those he adduced for the Kotzker: perhaps too robust an expression of anger at God would foment the very secularity that Heschel so passionately sought to combat. Juggling his own anger in one hand, and his sense of tremendous anxiety about the collapse of humanity's faith in the other, Heschel may well have decided that true spiritual heroism required both eloquence and reticence—the eloquence to speak and plead on God's behalf, and the reticence to contain his own simmering anger. The desperate needs of the hour, it seems, demanded another level of self-transcendence—the muting of intensely felt feelings of protest. Except for those rare moments, then, when anger seemed almost to escape from his pen, Heschel followed the Kotzker and "cultivated the eloquence of silence."[79]

All of this leads to one final, critical point: with very rare exceptions, Heschel's expressions of anger always emerge from within a position of faith. In other words, Heschel's protests are precisely that—protests from within a relationship rather than articulations of metaphysical doubt from outside it. "For Heschel there is no question that God exists."[80] From a theological perspective, then, the problem posed by the Holocaust is one of anger rather than doubt. God's ways may be frustratingly mysterious, but this does not, as a rule, give rise to the fear (let alone the conviction) that ultimately there is "no one out there." Heschel expresses anger in addresses *to God* rather than discourses *about Him*. Thus, in the poems, we find abundant expressions of outrage, but they are always articulated in the second person rather than the third ("Haven't the prayers of generations, then, /achieved some mercy from you, God?");[81] similarly, in *Man Is Not Alone,* the turn from theodicy to protest is articulated by the psalmist and his direct address of God ("Wherefore hidest thou thy face, and forgettest our affliction and our oppression?"). In his presentation to the Quakers, Heschel weaves together his disillusionment with humanity and his disappointment with God. Speaking of humanity's failure, he writes that "there has never been more reason for man to be ashamed than now. . . . Where were we when men learned to hate in the days of starvation?" Speaking of God's inaction, he begins with the third person—"The day of the Lord is a day without the Lord. Where is God?" and then, characteristically, shifts immediately to the second: "Why didst Thou not halt the trains loaded with Jews being led to the slaughter? It is so hard to rear a child, to nourish and to educate. Why dost Thou make it so easy to kill?"[82]

It is only at the end of Heschel's life, when he turns his attention to Kotzk, that glimmers of doubt, and perhaps even relational rupture, emerge. Recall that according to Heschel, the Kotzker was "tormented by serious doubts" and lamented: "If only I could be certain that there is punishment in the world to come . . . I would go out into the streets and dance for joy. If only I could be certain."[83] This doubt, as we have seen, perplexed and preoccupied the Rebbe: "Time and again, the Kotzker returned to this issue: was it conceivable that the entire world, Heaven and earth, was a palace without a master? . . . This problem tormented Reb Mendl."[84] I would suggest that between the thunderous protests of the young poet ("God, answer us—we long for You! / Overcome Your silence, Lord of all words"),[85] and the almost tragic doubt of the older theologian ("Something had gone awry in Heaven"),[86] a vast distance has been crossed. Relational distance has begun to make way for metaphysical doubt. But where protest is concerned, the overwhelming thrust of Heschel's writings remains staunchly, even stubbornly relational: "Why don't You help—You, You!"[87]

* * *

Introducing the two main characters in his monumental *Torah min ha-shamayim,* Heschel writes, "Everything cycles in the world; and just as the intellectual problems remain with us, so does the tension."[88] In every generation, then, there are Akibans, who "incline toward a mutual empathy with God,"[89] and who embrace suffering as an opportunity to fulfill the mandate of unconditional love. And there are also Ishmaelians, who are "discomfited" by Akiva's approach, and who "see in it no adequate answer to the plaintive question[s]: Why does the way of the wicked prosper? Why are there righteous people who suffer?"[90] But Heschel goes on:

> The divergences and dissensions between the two "fathers of the world" continued on their way throughout the generations. It is just that sometimes we find discrete methodologies, each internally consistent, and sometimes we find the two intellectual subsets included side by side, or intertwined, within a single method. Sometimes one approach appears to have been subsumed by the other, and sometimes they have been synthesized, so that it seems that two rival ways of grasping the world coexist within the same mind.[91]

Or, again, Heschel explains:

> The thought systems of Rabbis Ishmael and Akiva are contiguous, and at the same time, opposing forces; and the opposition [between them] lived on in the history of Jewish thought. Each approach served as a paradigm for a whole line of beliefs and perspectives, and every Sage, consciously or unconsciously, got hooked into one of the two modes of thought. Sometimes [Heschel adds], the two worldviews are commingled.[92]

Thus, in other words, although in the development of Jewish thought, there are "pure Akibans" and "pure Ishmaelians," there is also a third category, made up of those who hold a more or less uneasy alloy of both positions. I want to suggest that consciously or otherwise, in these passages Heschel was speaking about himself, and his own struggle with the reality of evil and suffering. Heschel's own theological work represents just such an admixture of Akiva and Ishmael.[93] We saw in the previous chapter that when Heschel describes the two paradigmatic approaches to suffering in rabbinic literature, he seems clearly to embrace Akiva's way. But in this chapter, we have been examining at length a Heschel who was "discomfited" by Akibanism (including his own version thereof), and who felt the need to cry out to God in protest. Put somewhat crudely, if Akiva played himself in Heschel's theological drama, the Kotzker in turn was cast as Ishmael.

Crucially, Akiva and Ishmael do not represent distinct stages in the development of Heschel's thought. On the contrary, both are consistently present over the course of his lengthy career as Jewish poet, scholar, and theologian. Heschel's Akivan side emerges most clearly in (part I of) *Torah min ha-shamayim* (1962), though a theodicy justifying God is also implicit in *Man Is Not Alone* (1951) and *God in Search of Man* (1955); his Ishmaelian side, in turn, comes through in the early poems (1933), in chapter 16 of *Man Is Not Alone* (1951), and in the later writings on the Rebbe from Kotzk (1973). Put differently, we might say that rather than representing stages in his theological trajectory, Akiva and Ishmael represent dialectical aspects of Heschel's religious personality. There is theodicy and even, at times, the embrace of suffering. But there is also a haunting sense of the inadequacy of theodicy, and a willingness to express the disappointment with God that ensues.

* * *

Over the course of his long theological career, the German Catholic political theologian Johann Baptist Metz has come to see the Holocaust as "the central and devastating challenge to Christianity and Christian theology" in the contemporary world.[94] "Everything," Metz writes, "is to be measured by Auschwitz."[95] Metz's struggles with Auschwitz have led him to develop what he calls a "mysticism of suffering unto God,"[96] an approach to theology and theodicy that seeks not to excuse God or console humanity, but rather insistently to requestion God in the face of history's horrors.[97] Metz presents a radical revision of the project of theodicy—instead of attempting, as the word itself might suggest, "a tardy and somewhat defiant justification of God in the face of evil, of suffering and wickedness of the world,"[98] he opts instead for "an incessant requestioning of God" (*Rückfragen an Gott*).[99] Metz refuses those aspects of theology that merely "manage contingencies" or "accept life's circumstances," choosing instead to draw upon and valorize biblical "articulations of dissent, of accusation, of crying out."[100] For Metz, Israel's genius lies in its "incapacity to be consoled by myths of ideas that are far removed from history"; Israel remains, unapologetically, and in contrast to early Christianity, a "landscape of cries."[101]

Metz takes particular aim at the free will defense, traditionally associated with Augustine, according to which human freedom is ultimately
to blame for evil and suffering. "Augustine's strong doctrine of freedom," Metz writes, "really arises from an apologetic intent: an apology
for the creator God. Astonishingly, this apology misled Augustine into
positing—in a way that has become commonplace among us really only
in our modern, secular age—a human freedom that is independent of
God, a virtually godless autonomy."[102] Such an approach, Metz insists,
is irreconcilable with

> the principles of the theological doctrine of freedom. Since human freedom
> simply is not autonomous but theonomous, that is, made possible by God, pos-
> ited by and received from God, then it cannot ultimately be responsible for the
> history of suffering in the world. To a certain degree this question rebounds
> back again upon God and God's foreordaining.[103]

In other words, an appeal to human freedom cannot "solve" the problem
of evil and suffering, because actions cannot be attributed to human
beings *rather than* to God—in attributing an action to a human being,
one is always already inculpating God, who is the source of human freedom. In implicating human beings in the problem of evil, then, one un-
avoidably implicates God as well. Thus, far from solving the problem
of evil, the appeal to human freedom only exacerbates it. "So we must
say," writes Metz, "that the history of suffering raises not only a question for human guilt, but also—looking through it, as it were—a question directed back at God."[104] Recall now Heschel's descriptions of the
Kotzker, and note the obvious parallels between Metz's critique of the
free-will defense, on the one hand, and Heschel's evocative portrayal
of Menahem Mendl's anxieties, on the other. As we have seen, Heschel
writes, "Under [the Rebbe's] reverence was dissent and contentiousness,
a sense of outrage at the depth of falsehood afflicting the world as well
as silent animadversion. . . . Was only man to blame? *The Kotzker uncompromisingly castigated his fellow men. But did not castigation itself cast
reproach upon their Maker?*"[105] The same point thus torments both Metz
and Heschel: blaming humanity for all cruelty and brutality, and thereby
for the extent of suffering in human history, does not, in fact, let God off
the hook. On the contrary, it only reels God further in.

One of the primary tasks of "theology as theodicy," for Metz, is to
"deconstruct . . . the various 'answers' that have been produced by theo-

dicies, traditionally conceived."[106] More important, theodicy as Metz understands it serves to "point . . . the intellectual work of theology beyond itself to the more fundamental work of prayer, of spirituality."[107] Here Metz's explicit argument converges with what we have already found implicit in Heschel: the process of theologizing must give way to—or perhaps better, must culminate in—a liturgical gesture. In Metz's words, "Directing one's questioning back toward God is the piety of theology."[108] James Matthew Ashley's description of Metz could just as easily apply to (at least one pole in) Heschel: "Theodicy does not finally issue in an argument that speaks *for* God, but presses those who ask it, in all its depth, into a stance of speaking *with* God: to prayer."[109] To state this a bit differently: when theology in general and theodicy in particular reach their limits, they are confronted with the same intractable, tormenting question: Why? Or, in the agonized words of the psalmist, "Why sleepest thou, O Lord?" When attempts to explain, justify, or exonerate God fail in the face of human suffering, no option remains but to pray, lament, and protest, to cease asking questions *about* God, and to begin instead to present questions *to* Him.[110]

For the believer who seeks tidy and definitive answers to the hoariest questions of religious faith, Metz's position will no doubt prove disappointing, for his approach to theodicy is precisely a refusal of easy answers.[111] It is, rather, an impassioned insistence upon asking and re-asking the most difficult and painful of questions of God. As we have seen, according to Metz, the theologian does not set about "reconcil[ing] God's goodness with the existence of massive empirical evil in creation . . . [but rather] enquir[es] of God concerning the temporal delay of God's restorative justice for the broken and the dead."[112] Instead of supplying the believer with explanations, then, theodicy beckons him forward to address his questions and challenges directly toward God. In this pre-eschatological era, solidarity with the victims of history means that theodicy culminates not in neat solutions but in liturgical confrontation with the divine.

There are important correlations between Heschel's approach to the problem of evil and Metz's. Most important, as we have seen, the combination of unspeakable human suffering, on the one hand, and of inexplicable divine silence, on the other, brings both men to the point of protest and lament. Indeed, both turn to traditional texts to interrogate God and summon Him forward to redeem the suffering of history's victims. But there are crucial differences between Heschel and Metz as well. Metz, as we have seen, systematically rejects traditional theodicies as theologically untenable and morally intolerable. Authentic theodicy, for Metz, is actually the *refusal* to exonerate God rather than the *attempt* to do so, and thus what Metz calls "theodicy" actually constitutes a significant example of what Zachary Braiterman labels "anti-theodicy"—that is, of the unwillingness to "justify, explain, or accept . . . the relationship that subsists between God[,] . . . evil, and suffering."[113] Heschel's approach, in contrast, is much more ambivalent and dialectical: on my interpretation, he moves uneasily between defending God, on the one hand, and being brought up short by the inadequacy of his own defense, on the other. In other words, Heschel nowhere rejects the project of theodicy in principle (as Metz does repeatedly and consistently). What he does is much more complex: he offers the broad contours of a theodicy (God is in search of man, but man turns away), but then challenges God when the depth of human suffering overwhelms his best attempts on God's behalf. Whereas Metz repudiates traditional defenses of God altogether, Heschel passionately engages them—up until the point when they seem to break, and then he turns to prayers of protest. Moreover, whereas Metz develops a full-blown theology of protest and challenge according to which the courageous believer is urged to direct her questions about God's silence and inaction *to* God, Heschel nowhere actively prescribes prayers of protest. To be sure, as I have been at pains to show, he does engage in liturgical protest—but critically, he does not explicitly encourage his readers to do the same.

Metz is more consistent and thus, in a sense, more radical than Heschel. He simply refuses the project of theodicy as conventionally defined, and places questioning and requestioning God at the very center of his theology. Heschel, in contrast, engages in a much more complex and elusive dance between conflicting impulses in his theology. On the one hand, implicit in his entire worldview is a systematic theodicy: history is a scene in which God's voice beckons even as God's will is thwarted. Human freedom generates both appalling horrors and divine disappointment. But underneath all this lies a profound anxiety, an excruciating sense that the cries of the victims remain just as loud, and the incomprehension of the faithful just as total, after Heschel's strenuous and impassioned attempts at theodicy as they were before. The depth of the theological problem, Heschel realizes, has not been solved. Heschel can perhaps defend God's self-limitation in principle, but surely there are times when divine love and concern require action rather than contraction, and manifestations of power rather than (mere) pathos. And so, as we have seen, in his portrayal of the Kotzker, in his somewhat abrupt explosion in *Man Is Not Alone*, and even already in his adolescent poems, Heschel gives voice to another dimension of his piety: the urge to cry out against God's silence, to protest His inaction, and to plead for His redemptive intervention.

There is another significant dimension to Heschel's ambivalence. On the one hand, as we have seen, he contends with God, refusing to simply accept the fate of history and its victims. But on the other hand, and in crucial contrast to Metz, he is either unwilling or unable to advocate actively for such remonstration, let alone to turn it into a cornerstone of his theology. Heschel's reticence, though, is obviously not absolute: In *Man Is Not Alone* especially, he models—and quite dramatically at that—that which he does not allow himself explicitly to endorse. This, then, is the power and the tragedy of Heschel's writing on evil: in the face of enormous devastation, one aspect of his faith will not allow him to reproach God, but another aspect will not allow him *not to*. What emerges from all this, in the end, is not resolution but relationship, not theology but liturgy—liturgy not as evasion of theology, but as culmination thereto. Jon Levenson's words about the Psalms of Lament apply, ultimately, to Heschel's own invocation of them as well: "The *cri de coeur* of the complainants is unsurpassable testimony not only to the pain of their external circumstances, but also to the pain of their internal dissonance, which only the creator God of old can heal."[114]

SIX

THE SELF THAT TRANSCENDS
ITSELF: HESCHEL ON PRAYER

Heschel's final work, *A Passion for Truth* (1973), is a vivid portrayal of the Hasidic master Reb Menahem Mendl of Kotzk (1787–1859), known above all for his zealous pursuit of truth and integrity in the religious life. One of the central preoccupations of both the Kotzker and his biographer is their insistence that falsehood and self-centeredness are inextricably linked, and that so, too, are truth and self-transcendence.[1] For Menahem Mendl, there is no greater spiritual and theological problem than humanity's obstinate self-concern. "The 'I'," Heschel writes, "becomes the central problem in the Kotzker's thinking; it is the primary counterpart to God in the world. The sin of presumptuous selfhood is the challenge and defiance that God faces in the world."[2] The Kotzker had "contempt for the self-centeredness of man," and he demanded "the abandonment of all self-interest."[3] He insisted, in fact, that an authentic quest for truth is predicated on a "total abandonment of self."[4] To strive to be a Jew, the Kotzker taught, is "to disentangle the self from enslavement to the self" and to struggle against "the inexhaustible intransigence of self-interest." Indeed, "for the Kotzker, one became an authentic Jew only when he moved out of the prison of self-interest, responding with abandon to Heaven's call." To have faith, the Kotzker taught, "meant to forget the self, to be exclusively intent on God,"[5] and to "disregard self-regard."[6]

All too often, human beings succumb to the temptation to worship themselves, "to act as if [their] own ego[s] were the hub of the world, the source and purpose of existence. What a shameless affront to deny that God is that source and purpose, the sap and the meaning."[7] Extreme self-love is inherently tied to idolatry: "In its depths," Heschel writes, "egocentricity amounts to a demonic attempt to depose God and remake the world in the image of man."[8] The goal of the spiritual life, then, is not just to transcend the self, but to move God to the center of consciousness, to place God where previously there was only self. Faith, then, is "the beginning of the end of egocentricity."[9]

If spiritual life requires us "to transcend self-interest for the sake of God," then it makes sense that Judaism would "disparage [even] religious acts motivated by self-interest." Indeed, Heschel notes, "Spiritual existence dominated by striving for a reward is easily degraded to opportunism."[10] The pursuits of internal purity or of "personal salvation" are also problematic, since the danger of idolatry—that is, of "do[ing] the Holy in order to please oneself"—is ever-present.[11] "A striking feature of the Kotzker's thinking," Heschel tells us, "is that while he strongly emphasized the importance of the individual's spiritual striving, he was averse to his concentrating on his own salvation, for this would constitute surrender to self-centeredness."[12] One who wants to serve God truly must remain vigilant, lest spiritual pursuits themselves become merely more subtle opportunities for self-seeking.

Toward the end of the book, Heschel is careful to distance himself from what he perceives as the Kotzker's extremism. The either/or position according to which "every man's pursuit ha[s] either God or the ego as its focus and goal—this dilemma [Heschel points out] is based upon the assumption that God and the ego are mutually exclusive."[13] But such stark dichotomization, Heschel insists, is not necessary. In fact, it is foreign to the biblical worldview, according to which "the satisfaction of man's legitimate needs is a blessing. There is no reason to maintain, then, that in all circumstances disregarding the self should be the norm."[14] While one must strive to overcome self-centeredness, this quest for self-transcendence need not—indeed, must not—give way to self-hatred. On the contrary, says Heschel—the self is important enough to be called to the service of God: "The Divine and the human are not by nature conceived to be at odds or in constant tension. Man is capable of acting in accord with God; he is able to be His partner in redemption, to imitate Him in acts of love and compassion."[15] Although Heschel does not develop this insight, he is making a crucial point about self-transcendence and covenant—namely, that the quest for the former must always keep the latter in mind. Although the spiritual seeker is obligated to transcend selfishness, she must pay heed not to develop a concomitant sense of derision or disdain for the very fact of her selfhood. The self, after all, has a covenantal role to play in furthering God's plans—namely, as we have seen, "to be His partner in redemption [and] to imitate Him in acts of love and compassion." According to Heschel, under no circumstances should an attempt be made to jettison or annihilate the self altogether.[16] Menahem Mendl's war on selfishness is thus a model for Heschel, but only up to a point; the Kotzker, Heschel worries, is so busy battling self-centeredness that he risks losing the all-important reality of the covenanted self. Ever the covenantal theologian, Heschel himself is wary of that risk.

We see this theme pursued elsewhere in Heschel's writing: the self-transcending self must nevertheless remain just that—an individual self, ready to respond to God's call. Consider Heschel's discussion of "The Self and the non-Self" in *GSM*.[17] On the one hand, Heschel emphasizes the centrality of self-transcendence to the very project of being human. Thus, he writes that "the essence of man, his uniqueness, is in his power to surpass the self, to rise above his needs and selfish motives,"[18] and adds further that "in order to be a man, man must be more than a man." Along the same lines, he defines "spiritual dignity" as "the attachment of the soul to a goal that lies beyond the self, a goal not within but beyond the self."[19] But Heschel simultaneously issues an impassioned warning against excess in self-effacement. "In dealing with the problem of the self," he asserts, "one must abstain from any overstatement. Regard for the self is not evil. It is when arrogating to the self what is not its due, enhancing one's interests at the expense of others or setting up the self as an ultimate goal that evil comes into being."[20] While the self should not be worshiped, in other words, neither should it be abhorred. "Elimination of the self," Heschel writes, "is in itself no virtue. To give up life or the right to satisfaction is not a moral requirement. If self-effacement were virtuous in itself, suicide would be the climax of moral living."[21]

Below, we shall see that Heschel's concern with the covenanted self, which renders him leery of the potential for self-loathing inherent in an exaggerated preoccupation with self-overcoming, similarly prevents him from speaking of mystical union with God, for union, too, potentially imperils the independence and individuality of the human self. To put the point somewhat more starkly: on the one hand, a penchant for self-castigation and relentless self-doubt has the potential to yield a limp, paralyzed self, unable to enter into relationship with God. Conversely, an overconfidence that assumes that the self can merge with the divine obliterates the very separateness upon which relationship depends. Since Heschel is so concerned with the classical Jewish idea of human beings as God's "partners" (that is, in other words, with covenant), both of these extremes must be avoided. In their stead, Heschel embraces a notion of self that is self-surpassing even as it unambiguously remains a self, neither empty of worth at one extreme, nor identical with the divine at the other.

* * *

Two decades before his investigations of the Kotzker, Heschel had published a book-length study of the meaning of prayer in Jewish life and thought. Anticipating themes later accentuated in his evocation of Menahem Mendl, Heschel argues in *Man's Quest for God* that prayer is a crucial weapon in humanity's struggle with its own unbending selfishness. If religion in general seeks to reorient humanity away from its own concerns and toward God's, the discipline of prayer in particular represents an attempt to overcome egocentrism, and thus to mold a different kind of human self.[22]

"Genuine self-expression," Heschel writes, "is an answer to an ultimate question."[23] The real goal of human life is thus not to find answers to *my* questions, but to offer myself as a response to *God's*. Self-expression is achieved, paradoxically, by paying less rather than more attention to myself, by shifting the center of my consciousness toward God and away from myself. But, as we have seen at length in chapter 1, modern civilization reinforces the worst of human self-centeredness, and thus poses an enormous spiritual challenge. Humanity has come to see the world as a mere collection of "instruments" and "tools"; "expediency" has become the rule of the day. Even God, the ultimate Subject, has been reduced to just another object to be exploited for human gains: "The standard of action is expediency, and God, too, is for the sake of our satisfaction." The disaster of modern life is a function of man having too much power rather than too little: "Others may suffer from degradation by poverty," Heschel remarks, but "we are threatened by degradation through power."[24] Although Heschel does not develop this point clearly, a tragic irony underlies his perspective on modernity: the more human beings assert themselves, the further away they move from true self-expression, since, paradoxically, it is only through self-transcendence that true self-expression can be achieved. "To be sensitive to the ultimate question one must have the ability to surpass the self; the ability to know that the self is more than the self," but in our own times, human beings are tragically "forfeiting [that very] power to transcend the self."[25] Thus, for all its purported celebration of the human, modernity in fact bankrupts humanity of its most precious commodity—its capacity to surpass and transcend itself.

Hovering in the background of Heschel's writing are inchoate notions of a true and false self. On the surface, there is the self that aggressively pursues its own pleasures and goals. But underneath lies another, deeper self, ready for the service of God, aware that here, and here alone, is the meaning of human life. "Man," Heschel laments, "has become a forgotten thing. We know his desires, his whims, his failings; we do not know his ultimate commitment. We understand what he does; we do not understand what he means. We stand in awe of many things; we do not know what we stand for."[26] In some crucial sense, then, human beings are alienated from themselves, unaware of their own "ultimate commitment[s]" and "supreme concern[s]." It is here, according to Heschel, that religion in general, and the life of prayer in particular, becomes such an important antidote to modernity's ills.

True religion, Heschel insists, "*is not expediency*"; it is not a toolbox for the fulfillment of our hungers and needs. Prayer, in fact, is "the least expedient, the least worldly, the least practical" thing we do.[27] Religion is an alternative to the "hating, hunting, and hurting" which ordinarily dominate our lives; prayer offers us an opportunity for self-purification, for remembering the "gratefulness . . . [that] makes the soul great."[28] If modern civilization is characterized by relentless self-assertion, prayer does its work, ultimately, by enabling us to "forget the self" and to stand for something greater than ourselves;[29] "the function of prayer," Heschel writes, is to overcome our "ego-centric predicament. . . . The essence of prayer lies in man's self-transcending."[30] In tandem with the notion of self-transcendence, Heschel speaks of the de-centered self.[31] Prayer reminds us to place God, rather than ourselves, at the center of our lives and consciousness:

> We do not step out of the world when we pray; we merely see the world in a different setting. The self is not the hub, but the spoke of the revolving wheel. In prayer we shift the center of living from self-consciousness to self-surrender. God is the center toward which all forces tend. He is the source, and we are the flowing of His force, the ebb and flow of His tides.[32]

Such a shift in perspective allows human beings to see with different eyes. Prayer, Heschel says, "takes the mind out of the narrowness of self-interest, and enables us to see the world in the mirror of the holy. For when we betake ourselves to the extreme opposite of the ego, we can behold a situation from the aspect of God."[33] The act of prayer thus means that human beings can "dream in league with God [and] envision His holy visions."[34]

Although he does not seem conscious of the problem, Heschel is caught in a kind of double bind here. On the one hand, as we have seen, humanity needs prayer to help undo its obsessive self-focus. But on the other hand, according to Heschel, the modern person's seemingly intractable difficulties with prayer stem, not surprisingly, from selfishness and self-preoccupation. We abstain from prayer, Heschel insists, because instead "we ring the hollow bell of selfishness"; we are distracted from our spiritual purposed by "futile self-indulgence." Unable or unwilling to refrain from "self-assertion," we erect a "thick screen of self between Him and us."[35] The bind, then, is that what modern people most need to help them overcome their selfishness is a life of prayer, but their very selfishness prevents them from being able to pray.[36] It is perhaps partly in order to solve this problem that Heschel reminds us that the very possibility of prayer is ultimately a function of divine grace. "Contact with [God]," Heschel writes, "is not our achievement. It is a gift, coming down to us from on high like a meteor, rather than rising up like a rocket."[37]

Heschel makes an important distinction between what he calls "prayer as an act of expression" and what he terms "prayer as an act of empathy."[38] In the former, the person comes to prayer with "the urge to set forth a personal concern"; the feeling or need comes before the act of prayer. In the latter, the liturgy comes first—the person does not approach the liturgy in a "prayerful mood," but instead allows the words to direct him, to elicit a set of reactions from him.[39] If, in the former case, human passions precede the act of prayer, in the latter case they follow upon them.[40] Heschel is quick to point out that it is "inaccurate to assume, as most people do, that prayer occurs primarily as an act of expression. The fact is that the more common type of prayer is an act of empathy."[41] He goes on to explain that an excessive focus on expression violates the essential ethos of prayer as he conceives it: "It is either short-sighted or vainglorious to assume that self-expression as such is the supreme goal of prayer. . . . What is the self that we should idolize it? What is the self that He be mindful of it?" A preoccupation with self-expression, in other words, defeats the very project of prayer—namely, to transcend the self and focus on what is greater than it. Indeed, Heschel continues, "The self gains when absorbed in the contemplation of the non-self, in the contemplation of God, for example. Our goal is *self-attachment* to what is greater than the self rather than *self-expression*. . . . The supreme goal of prayer is to express God, to discover the self in relation to God."[42] Liturgy helps release our thoughts from "the pitiful prison of the platitudes of the self"; an excessive focus on our own subjectivity, in contrast, makes it hard for us "to find a way out of the narrowness of the self."[43]

Since, for Heschel, "genuine prayer is an act in which man surpasses himself,"[44] it makes sense that he would offer a spirited defense of fixed liturgy—again, not just because it aids the inarticulate, but also because it forces us to hold up our concerns to the mirror of God's will, and thus to purify our aspirations. In other words, prayer teaches human beings what to value, what to care and strive for.[45] Liturgy, Heschel suggests at one point, is "a higher form of silence," in that the individual does not speak her own words, but rather allows the consecrated words of tradition to speak on her behalf.[46] This, Heschel tells us, is a form of "inner silence" which is characterized by "stillness" and the "absence of self-concern."[47] Prayer of empathy, then, is the prayer of the de-centered, self-transcending self.

Recall now what I have suggested about Heschel's inchoate sense of a true and false self. "Most of us," he writes, "do not know the answer to the one of the most important questions, namely, What is our ultimate concern? We do not know what to pray for. It is the liturgy that teaches us what to pray for. It is through the words of the liturgy that we discover *what moves us unawares,* what is urgent in our lives, what in us is related to the ultimate."[48] Reading closely, we discern two crucial notions—first, that, as a rule, we do not know ourselves; we are ignorant of what concerns us most deeply. And second, that in our innermost depths, we are already connected to God, that the ultimate does stir something within us. Prayer in general, then, and liturgy in particular, remind us of our true selves, and help to elicit our hunger for and attachment to God. That deeper, more authentic self is, of course, inherently self-transcending.[49]

Let us look carefully at a brief passage from *MQ.* For our purposes, it is important to pay close attention both to what Heschel says, and to what he does not say: "Prayer comes to pass," Heschel writes, "in a complete turning of the heart toward God, toward His goodness and power. It is the momentary disregard of our personal concerns, the absence of self-centered thoughts, which constitute the art of prayer."[50] First, note that Heschel describes self-transcendence in prayer as a "momentary" phenomenon; nowhere does he suggest that one can overcome selfishness and self-centeredness once and for all.[51] Second, notice that Heschel speaks of "the absence of self-centered *thoughts,*" not of the absence of a self; nowhere does he speak of the transformation of human consciousness and perspective leading to the dissolution or obliteration of selfhood. Self-centeredness is overcome (and this only momentarily); the self itself is not. Strikingly absent from Heschel's writing is any talk of mystical union or identification with God. Prayer always remains the act of a human being separate *from* God, beckoned forward *by* God, called to relationship *with* God; there is no mergence with the divine in Heschel.[52] This point will be crucial to keep in mind as we proceed.

* * *

Heschel's "soft" version of self-transcendence stands in stark contrast to those of two twentieth-century Christian mystics, Evelyn Underhill (1875–1941) and Thomas Merton (1915–1968). Whereas, as we have seen, Heschel insists on transcending the self without dissolving it, Underhill (at least in her early phase) and Merton consistently couple self-transcendence with mystical union. A juxtaposition of Heschel's approach and theirs will bring his understanding of what I have been calling the "covenanted self" into sharper relief, thus enabling us to see just how important it is to him that the self-transcending self remain, crucially, a self.

No modern thinker spoke of self-transcendence with greater passion or eloquence than the British spiritual writer Evelyn Underhill.[53] Although, as we shall see, Underhill's point of spiritual emphasis shifted over time from mystical union to worshipful adoration, her concern with self-overcoming persisted throughout her career as a theologian, writer, and spiritual director. But the nature and implications of that self-overcoming evolved along with her theological orientation: as Underhill developed a progressively deeper appreciation for God's transcendence, she spoke less of the self's mergence with the divine and more of its adoring, worshipful posture toward it. For the later Underhill, the gap between God and humanity had been opened wide enough to render union impossible. In terms of both theological sensibility and spiritual aspiration, then, the late Underhill had far more in common with Heschel than the early.

The mystic's "business," Underhill writes in *Mysticism* (1911), "is transcendence: a mounting up, an attainment of a higher order of reality";[54] the "end and purpose of all [the soul's] self-knowledge," she reports in the name of Catherine of Siena, is "to rise above herself."[55] Speaking three years later to "normal people," Underhill points out that to "'purify' the senses is to release them, so far as human beings may, from the tyranny of egocentric judgments";[56] in order to unite with higher levels of reality, human beings must overcome the temptation to see from "the usual angle of self-interest."[57] The true mystic learns to "look with the eyes of love"; to do this, is to "surrender your I-hood, see things . . . for their sake not for your own."[58] As the "practical man" begins to see the world differently, he begins to taste of the experience of the mystics, and their ability to "defeat the tyranny of 'the I, the Me, the Mine.'"[59]

Up to this point, Underhill sounds remarkably like Heschel, committed to the spiritual battle against self-centeredness and egocentricity. But Underhill goes much further, consistently tying the project of self-transcendence to the broader, more fundamental goal of self-obliteration.

Indeed, for Underhill, it seems that the very point of the former is to lead on to the latter. Having awakened from her spiritual slumber, Underhill tells us, the mystic feels "a passionate longing to escape from . . . the hatefulness of selfhood"[60] and to escape its constricting "bonds."[61] To progress on what Underhill calls "the Mystic Way," the mystic must engage in "the abnegation of selfhood," which leads to total "self-abandonment."[62] Indeed, the "progressive abolition of selfhood," Underhill tells us, is "of the essence of mystical development."[63]

If self-transcendence, for Underhill, leads on to self-abandonment, the latter, in turn, leads to union with the divine. The quest for union requires, at minimum, a loosening of the boundaries of self; at moments, though, Underhill goes so far as to speak of the utter dissolution of the self in God. The seeker, she writes, engages in a "perpetually renewed casting down of the hard barriers of individuality."[64] At a certain stage, in order to achieve "perfect self-abandonment . . . the last fragments of selfhood . . . must be *sought out and killed*";[65] the very "last traces of self-interest even of the most spiritual kind" must be "*eradicate[d].*"[66] "You must," Underhill advises the reader, "give yourself up to, 'die into,' melt into the Whole."[67] "Utter self-abandonment," Underhill has Eckhart remind us, is followed by "*self-loss* in the incomprehensible Being of God";[68] indeed, the "barriers of individuality . . . must be *done away with*" if one is to achieve "some share in the boundless life of the One."[69] More forcefully still, Underhill writes that "the self, deprived of 'perception, knowledge, will, work, self-seeking'—the I, the Me, the Mine—loses itself, denies itself, unforms itself, drawing 'ever nearer' to the One, till 'nothing is to be seen but a ground which rests upon itself'—the ground of the soul, in which it has union with God."[70]

As Underhill's career progressed, she focused increasingly on God's transcendence,[71] and her attention shifted from mysticism (the preoccupation of the early Underhill) to worship (the central preoccupation of the late).[72] If, as we have seen, the former revolves around the aspiration toward union with God, the latter, in contrast, focuses on "reverent adoring delight in God." Broadly speaking, worship refers to "that whole element in our life which is directed towards God the Transcendent, and done solely for God the Transcendent."[73] Note the marriage here of adoration and self-transcendence: we engage in worship "not because of its usefulness, not because we want something, not because it does us any good; but solely *for Him*."[74] Indeed:

> If the first point of worship is the creature's adoration of God, the second is that same little creature's total self-offering—total willing capitulation—to that God: in other words his *Sacrifice*. Adoration and sacrifice, in one form or another, are ... the essential notes of the worship man is called and privileged to pay.[75]

All of this can be summed up in one sentence: "To feel self-oblivious gladness in the reality and beauty of God for His own sake . . . [is to] beg[i]n to know something about worship."[76]

The inextricable link, for Underhill, between adoration of God on the one hand, and the transcendence of self-interest on the other, is most powerfully expressed in her *Worship* (1936). There, Underhill writes that "the pure act of adoration ... is the consummation of worship,"[77] and that "disinterested delight" in God is the very "perfection of worship."[78] As "genuine religious impulse becomes dominant," Underhill assures her readers, "adoration more and more takes charge";[79] indeed, "even the deep religious mood of dependence and of gratitude must give priority to *the fundamental religious mood of adoration*."[80] As one advances in prayer, selfishness ineluctably falls away; as worship rises toward ever-greater levels of purity, it "leaves egotistic piety behind."[81] Ultimately, prayer only becomes worship when it moves completely beyond self-interest;[82] genuine worship is animated by a "transcendental, self-oblivious un-demanding temper."[83] According to Underhill, self-transcendence is a necessary and constitutive piece of genuine worship, and therefore the "tendency of all worship to decline from adoration to demand," to give in to "the anthropocentric trend of the human mind,"[84] must be stead-fastly resisted. Reading Underhill's second classic closely, then, we can conclude that adoration and self-transcendence function in a kind of a dialectical spiral: worship both requires and further cultivates the over-coming of "petty subjectivism."[85] Worship is, crucially for Underhill, "an avenue which leads the creature out from his inveterate self-occupation."

For Underhill, there simply is no more effective way to purify the self than through adoration. As she writes in another place, "Adoring

remembrance of the reality of God" is the surest "method of evicting pet-
tiness, self-occupation, and unrest, those deadly enemies of the spiritual
self. . . . Adoration, as it more deeply possesses us, inevitably leads on to
self-offering."[86] Indeed, the value of worship can ultimately be measured
by the extent to which it is coupled with self-transcendence: "Devotion
by itself has little value, may even by itself be a form of self-indulgence,
unless it issues in some costly and self-giving action" which transforms
at least "some bit of life."[87]

To repeat: although Underhill's theological orientation undergoes a
none-too-subtle shift over time, her commitment to self-transcendence
as the fundamental spiritual virtue remains front and center. One can
scarcely turn a page in her work without hearing, for example, about
the need for "self-forgetfulness,"[88] or for "self-oblivious faithfulness,"[89]
or for "self-giving action."[90] Underhill is insistent that the life of prayer
in particular be animated by a concern to overcome our preoccupation
with self—our relentless self-seeking on the one hand, but also our excessive self-consciousness on the other.[91] But note just how profoundly
the meaning and context of self-transcendence have changed from the
early Underhill to the late. According to the former, the mystic sought to
forget herself so that, ultimately, she could lose herself in God; according
to the latter, in contrast, the worshipper seeks to forget herself so that her
attention can be more fully rapt on the transcendent God. Thus, while
the mystical Underhill longed for union with God, the worshipful Underhill remained keenly aware that true divine transcendence renders
union impossible. Hence, as we have seen, adoration replaces union as
the core project of the spiritual life.

* * *

It is perhaps not surprising that thinkers who focus on the necessity
of self-transcendence in the spiritual life tend to be less than enthusiastic
about the merits of petitionary prayer, which is, after all—on the surface
at least—self-interested prayer. Although impetratory prayer may give
voice to a deep sense of dependence on God, may even serve to remind
human beings of their profound neediness and vulnerability before God,
it is nevertheless *their own* neediness and vulnerability of which they

are made conscious through such prayer. In other words, whatever vir-
tues it may possess, petitionary prayer is not yet "self-forgetful" prayer.
Although it may puncture idolatrous illusions of self-sufficiency, in its
ordinary forms impetratory prayer does not fully refocus human attention on God rather than—in Underhillian terms, we might say, to the
exclusion of—humanity. There must, therefore, be more elevated forms
of prayer than petition.

Indeed, both Heschel and Underhill seek to direct our attention
elsewhere. According to Underhill, petitionary prayer is inherently selfish, and is thus, in her eyes, something to be overcome as the soul grows
in purity. Like any form of self-preoccupation, it must be transcended
in what she alternatively calls "self-giving," "self-donation," or "self-
abandonment." For Underhill petitionary prayer is at once an affront to
God and an abasement of human beings:

> What ought to be the central character of our prayers? Are they to consist chiefly
> in asking for what we want, and giving thanks for benefits received? Doesn't such
> a notion of the life of prayer involve rather a mean, ungenerous, self-interested
> outlook? An attitude towards God which we should be ashamed to take up to-
> wards anybody whom we really loved?[92]

Real prayer, Underhill insists, is self-transcending in that it focuses on
God, rather than on what God might (or ought) do for me. "Adoration,"
she writes, "and not repentance, nor petition, nor even intercession, ought
to be the governing characteristic, the attitude towards God in which
we approach prayer."[93] Spiritual love, Underhill reminds us, is the "least
self-seeking type . . . of human love."[94]

Whereas Underhill asserts that petition lies on a low rung of the
spiritual ladder, Heschel employs a different approach, insisting that,
at heart, petitionary prayer is not what it seems—that is, it is not really
petition at all, but rather a subtle form of praise.

> The focus of prayer is not the self. . . . Prayer comes to pass in a complete turning
> of the heart toward God, toward His goodness and power. It is the momentary
> disregard of our personal concerns, the absence of self-centered thoughts, which
> constitute the act of prayer. Feeling becomes prayer in the moment in which we
> forget ourselves and become aware of God. When we analyze the consciousness
> of a supplicant, we discover that it is not concentrated upon his own interests,
> but on something beyond the self. The thought of personal need is absent, and

the thought of divine grace alone is present in his mind. Thus, in beseeching Him for bread, there is one instant, at least, in which our mind is directed neither to our hunger nor to food, but to His mercy. This instant is prayer.[95]

Heir of a tradition that places the Amidah prayer, with its manifold petitions, at the heart of the worship service, Heschel cannot simply reject petition as something to be outgrown or overcome. Instead, he redirects the reader's attention away from liturgy and toward phenomenology; away from the words, that is, and toward the deeper experiences of the person at prayer. Even in reciting words of request, Heschel insists, the supplicant transcends himself and focuses his attention entirely on God. Seen from this perspective, then, what appears at first glance to be self-centeredness is, in fact, a subtle form of God-centeredness.

All of this said, however, Heschel is still clear that there are higher forms of Jewish prayer than petition: "In Jewish liturgy praise rather than petition ranks foremost. It is the more profound form, for it involves not so much the sense of one's own dependence and privation as the sense of God's majesty and glory."[96] As we have already seen, even consciousness of the self's smallness is still, problematically, consciousness of the self.[97] It is praise, therefore, rather than petition, which holds out the possibility of true self-transcendence, of a self fully oriented to God rather than to itself.[98]

As we have seen, just as there are deep and fundamental differences between Heschel the covenant theologian and Underhill the impassioned young mystic, there are also significant similarities between Heschel and the more mature Underhill. Beyond their shared preoccupation with self-transcendence as precondition for divine worship, both maintain a robust sense of the majesty and otherness of God, and of the resultant impossibility of mergence with Him. Nevertheless, however, divergences persist: Heschel consistently places greater weight upon the independent dignity and responsibility of the human self than does Underhill, and is conversely much more focused on divine relationality than she.[99] The human being, in Heschel's ideal, is God's partner rather than His mere vessel, as he often becomes for Underhill.[100] Put otherwise: Heschel's thinking is crucially covenantal in a way that Underhill's is not. (It should be obvious by now that a shared preoccupation with self-transcendence does not necessarily yield a fully shared sense of the spiritual life and its aspirations.) We shall return to these themes later. First, however, we turn to the Trappist monk Thomas Merton.[101]

* * *

One of the central motifs in Merton's enormous body of writing is the necessity for the human being to overcome his "false self" and discover his "true."[102] According to Merton, "Each one of us is shadowed by an illusory person: a false self ... [driven by] egocentric desires ... [and] ambitions." This false self "wants to exist outside the reach of God's will and God's love."[103] The true self, in contrast, is, in William Shannon's words, "the self that sleeps silently in my depths, waiting to be awakened by the power of the Spirit. It is the openness in us to the call of God to become one with God (or rather to discover that we are and always have been one with God)."[104] The spiritual life, for Merton, consists of allowing the false or imaginary self to fall away and letting the creative, inmost self emerge.[105] "In order to become oneself," Merton writes, "one must die. That is to say, in order to become one's true self, the false self must die. In order for the inner self to appear, the outer self must disappear: or at least become secondary, unimportant."[106]

We become our true selves, for Merton, by transcending our false ones; the "new being" of the Christian, he tells us, is "the effect of an inner revolution which ... implies complete self-transcendence."[107] Through the process of continual rebirth, the deepest freedom of the true self emerges; hidden in the innermost self is an "ability to love something, someone besides ourselves, and for the sake, not of ourselves, but of the one we love. . . . [Within us lies a] power which transcends and escapes the inevitability of self-love." This capacity for self-transcendence, for "loving another for his own sake," is one of the aspects of human life that makes us most like God.[108] Self-realization is achieved, paradoxically, through self-transcendence.[109]

Here Merton has developed more fully what we found inchoate in Heschel—the insistence that the spiritual life represents a struggle between a false, surface self, committed to its own illusions and selfish concerns, and a true, inner self, hungry for connection to God and capable of transcending self-concern. But Merton ultimately goes farther: he speaks not merely of self-transcendence, but of "self-annihilation" and "self-destruction" as well. "Contemplation," he writes in *The New Man*, "is the highest and most paradoxical form of self-realization, attained by apparent self-annihilation."[110] Similarly, in *The Climate of Monastic Prayer*, Merton declares:

> The unitive knowledge of God in love is not a knowledge of an object by a subject, but a far different and transcendent kind of knowledge in which the created 'self' which we are seems to disappear in God and to know him alone. . . . The self undergoes a kind of emptying and an apparent destruction until, reduced to emptiness, it no longer knows itself apart from God.[111]

In addition, there is a crucial difference between Heschel's notion of the true self and Merton's: whereas for the former, the true self seeks relationship with God, for the latter, the true self *is already, in some sense, God.* When Merton famously writes that "we must withdraw ourselves . . . from exterior things, and pass through the center of our souls to find God,"[112] Elena Malits comments that "God himself is that very center."[113] In a similar vein, Shannon notes that "contemplation is possible only by going beyond the external self to *the real self that is identified with God.*"[114]

Merton does stop short of suggesting that the self actually undergoes complete ontological dissolution (whatever that might mean)—note that he describes these processes as merely "apparent."[115] In other words, Merton is here describing the radical experience of the mystic rather than making bolder claims about her ontological status. Nevertheless, the thrust of Merton's writing is clear: the Christian so transcends herself that it seems to her as if she has no perduring human self. The mystic has so emptied herself—spiritual life as a kind of kenosis—that she has been dissolved as a separate entity and united-identified fully with God.

Merton is also careful to insist that although the mystic is in perfect union with God, she nevertheless maintains her individual identity:

> Even when the soul is mystically united with God there remains, according to Christian theology, a distinction between the nature of the soul and the nature of God. Their perfect unity is not then a fusion of natures, but a unity of love and experience. The distinction between the soul and God is no longer experienced as a separation into subject and object when the soul is united to God.[116]

Moreover, even amidst his focus on union and immanence, Merton does maintain some sense of God's otherness and transcendence.[117] Although at times he does speak of the mystic's ontological union with God— sanctity, he says, is constituted "first of all by ontological union with God 'in Christ'"[118]—the thrust of much of his writings is the union of the mystic's will with God's.[119] Sanctity, he writes, "does not consist merely in *doing* the will of God. It consists in willing the will of God. For sanctity is union with God."[120]

The function of prayer, according to Merton, is to awaken in the human being "a consciousness of our union with God."[121] This union is not fundamentally the attainment of something new, but the realization of something that is always already present. Spiritual life, in other words, brings one to "a conscious realization of the union that is already truly effected between souls and God by grace."[122] Merton speaks not only of union, but also of "identification": the path to becoming one's true self, he writes, is "to become identified with Him in Whom is hidden the reason and fulfillment of my existence."[123] According to William Shannon, for Merton, "if we are to truly know God, we must in some way be transformed into God."[124] The caveats we have seen in Merton notwithstanding, it is clear that Heschel would reject this kind of language, whether interpreted ontologically or not. Both the transcendence of God and the covenantal responsibility of humanity are dangerously compromised, he would insist, by such overbold talk of union and identification. To imagine that a human being could *in any way* be "transformed into God" is, for Heschel, to traverse the border into "blasphemy."[125]

Note how different Heschel's language is from Merton's: a genuine "understanding for man's supreme concern," Heschel writes, "is found not through self-inspection but through self-attachment to Him who is concerned with man." For Heschel, in other words, authentic self-transcendence is always tied to connection with a transcendent other. This other always remains precisely that, and the notion of union or identification with Him is thus inconceivable. I discover God most fundamentally not within but beyond me, as the voice that calls me, beckons me, and summons me forward. "Self-attachment to Him who is concerned with man" is a far cry indeed from "consciousness of one's union with God"; whereas in the latter case there is ultimately only one entity, in the former case there are always and irreducibly two. In essence, then where for Merton the goal of the spiritual life is union, for Heschel it is covenantal responsiveness. Thus, despite their shared commitment to self-transcendence, Heschel and Merton imagine the destination of the spiritual path in ultimately incommensurable ways.

Heschel's rejection of mystical union comes through most clearly in his discussion of theories both ancient and modern that view biblical prophecy as a form of ecstatic experience.[126] Heschel rejects such theories with an almost fiery passion, insisting that they misread the biblical evidence and "distort the essence of prophecy."[127] Returning to the purported irreconcilability of Greek and biblical thinking, Heschel characterizes mysticism as an example of the former, and prophetic "confrontation" as the paradigmatic instance of the latter.[128] And never the twain shall meet.

It is perfectly understandable, Heschel writes, that the Greeks aspired to "become one with a god." Such union was conceivable precisely because "god and man were not contrasted as being totally different from each other."[129] Since the gods were physically and morally similar to human beings, the boundaries between divinity and humanity were permeable. But to the biblical mind, in contrast, God remains, always, other, and thus the aspiration toward union with Him is "alien." Indeed, to suggest that the divine-human border can be crossed is nothing short of "blasphemy."[130] Thus, whereas the ecstatic merges with God, the prophet "encounter[s]" Him.[131] Prophecy is characterized always by an intense relationship between two parties, and never by a mergence into one:

> Prophecy is a confrontation. God is God, and man is man; the two may meet, but never merge. There is a fellowship, but never a fusion. . . . Prophetic consciousness is marked by a shuddering sense of the unapproachable holiness of God. The prophet knows there is a chasm that cannot be bridged, a distance that cannot be conquered.[132]

Indeed, Heschel notes simply, "The culmination of prophetic fellowship with God is insight and unanimity—not union."[133] In mysticism, according to Heschel, the human personality is dissolved, fully absorbed into God. But the "prophetic personality," by contrast, "is intensely present and fervently involved in what he perceives. The prophet is responsive, not only perceptive. The act is often a dialogue. . . . God as a person confronts the prophet as a person."[134] So, far from being dissolved, the personal identity of the prophet is actually strengthened through the prophetic encounter: "In his visions the prophet's personal identity does not melt away," Heschel writes, "but, on the contrary, gains power under the overwhelming impact of the event."[135] Put differently, we can say that according to Heschel, in blurring the line between God and the human being, mysticism does a disservice to both: it compromises God's transcendence even as it gives short shrift to humanity's role as partner and counterpart to the divine. Prophecy, in contrast, is covenantal-dialogical, and it therefore requires communion, but precludes full-blown union.[136]

* * *

So, was Heschel a mystic or, given his strenuous opposition to notions of mystical union, was he perhaps an anti-mystic? The answer to this question depends, of course, on the vexed issue of defining mysticism. The *New Catholic Encyclopedia* begins its entry on mysticism by noting, appropriately, that the term has been "used to cover a literally bewildering variety of states of mind";[137] indeed, there seem to be as many definitions of mysticism as there are scholars doing the defining. Be that as it may, one thing is clear: if we understand mysticism as Heschel himself does in *The Prophets*—that is, as the pursuit of union with the divine—then Heschel can only be described as a kind of anti-mystic.[138] As we have seen, he considers union with God impossible, and regards the suggestion thereof as theologically unacceptable.[139] Not surprisingly, then, the reader will search in vain for passages in Heschel's writings that would parallel Underhill or Merton's celebration of the human capacity for mergence with the divine.

But we do well to remember Bernard McGinn's warning that "a broad and flexible understanding of mysticism need not take the language of union with God as the defining characteristic." If, following McGinn, we take mysticism to refer more broadly to "those elements of Christian belief and practice that concern the preparation for, the consciousness of, and the effects attendant upon a heightened awareness of God's immediate and transformative presence,"[140] then, *mutatis mutandis*, Heschel can undoubtedly be classified as a Jewish mystic.[141] Indeed, on these terms, Heschel is nothing if not a mystical teacher, seeking to elicit from his readers a deeper awareness of God's presence and a heightened willingness to respond to His call. On his own terms, then, Heschel can be described as antagonistic toward mysticism,[142] but on the more expansive terms put forward by McGinn, Heschel himself is one of the giants of modern Jewish mystical writing.

To recapitulate a wide-ranging discussion: what we have seen in this chapter, and in the book as a whole, is that Heschel is one of modern Jewish theology's most ardent advocates of self-transcendence in the religious life.[143] I would suggest that for Heschel, prayer is the religious practice *par excellence* precisely because it is the activity in which human beings work directly to transcend and decenter themselves, transforming our consciousness so that concern for God lies at its very center. Indeed, we have seen Heschel deemphasize petition in prayer in favor of praise, since the former, he fears, still keeps us preoccupied with ourselves. But as I have been at pains to emphasize, in Heschel, the commitment to surpassing the self is coupled with a robust conception of indissoluble covenantal selfhood. Thus, in contrast to Merton and (the early) Underhill, Heschel steers clear of all talk of mystical union, which, from his perspective, would compromise both the transcendence of God and the integrity of the self.

There is another recurrent theme in Heschel's writing on prayer that we need to explore carefully in order fully to understand the dynamics of covenant and self-transcendence in his thought—the venture of praying in a time of divine hiddenness. It is to this spiritual project, vexed, for Heschel, both emotionally and theologically, that we turn in the following chapter.[144]

SEVEN

ENABLING IMMANENCE:
PRAYER IN A TIME OF
DIVINE HIDDENNESS

In his essay "On Prayer," published in 1970, Heschel speaks again of the centrality of self-transcendence to the act of prayer. He writes that in prayer, "I leave the world behind as well as all interests of the self. Divested of all concerns, I am overwhelmed by only one desire: to place my heart upon the altar of God."[1] Prayer, Heschel insists, "must never be a citadel for selfish concerns but rather a place for deepening concern over other people's plight."[2] And in one of his more poignant formulations, he avers that "in order to be human, one must be more than human."[3] But in this essay, Heschel's deepest concerns lie elsewhere. At its heart, "On Prayer" is a meditation on the dynamics and significance of prayer in an age of divine hiddenness.[4]

"The fundamental statement about God in Judaism," Heschel writes elsewhere, is that "God is in search of man"; this bold statement, he insists, can be said to "summarize all of human history as seen in the Bible."[5] And yet, as we have seen, human beings consistently ignore and defy God's call. God's interaction with Adam and Eve in the garden is paradigmatic for much of human history: human beings hide from the God who seeks them. But God finds this situation intolerable, and He turns away from humanity even as we turn away from Him. Thus, humanity's stubborn defiance has led to a calamitous cosmic predicament: the world is plagued by a kind of double-concealment in which humanity's hiding leads God to hide in turn. Heschel laments that "God is hiding and man is defying. At every moment God is creating and self-concealing."[6]

As we have seen at length in chapter 5, at times Heschel protests vigorously against God's self-concealment and inaction. But here, as often, he exonerates God. God has indeed chosen to hide Himself, but the burden of guilt lies elsewhere: "Is God to be blamed for all this? Is it not man who has driven Him out of our heart and minds?"[7] It is crucial to remember, Heschel says in *MNA*, that the hiding of God's face began with the hiding of humanity's: "Man was the first to hide himself from God," Heschel writes, "and [he] is still hiding. The will of God is to be here, manifest and near; but when the doors of this world are slammed on Him, His truths betrayed, His will defied, He withdraws, leaving man to Himself."[8]

Heschel's writing on God's hiddenness can be quite elusive; he moves (often uneasily, and often within a single sentence) between suggesting, on the one hand, that the divine hiddenness is a function of God's decision, and indicating, on the other, that it is a kind of exile, ostensibly forced upon God against His will. Thus, in chapter 16 of *MNA* (discussed at length in chapter 5), Heschel states that the "mist" that separates God and man "is man-made. God is not silent. He has been silenced."[9] Or he contends, as we have seen, that "the doors of the world are slammed on him.... God did not depart of His own volition; He was expelled. *God is in exile*."[10] But, at the same time, Heschel writes that as nations go astray and numb their consciences, God "gradually withdraws, abandoning one people after another, departing from their souls."[11] Heschel insists that "the prophets do not speak of the *hidden God*, but of the *hiding God*. His hiding is . . . an act, not a permanent state."[12] In "On Prayer," Heschel emphasizes again, on the one hand, the ostensibly involuntary dimension of God's hiddenness. God is "so far away," he writes, "an outcast, a refugee in His own world."[13] God is "not at home in our world"; He is "held in captivity."[14] All of us, it seems, are implicated in God's hiddenness: "We all conspire to blur all signs of His presence in the present or in the past."[15] But at the same time, Heschel writes that "God is hiding," that "at every moment, God is . . . self-concealing."[16] Note the latter pair of verbs: God is "hiding" and "self-concealing"—these are actions, conscious decisions on God's part. God is not just an "outcast" or a "refugee," but also an agent who has chosen to conceal Himself.

As we have had occasion to notice in chapter 5, Heschel moves (not necessarily consciously) between epistemological and ontological metaphors for God's present state. Thus, he speaks both of divine hiddenness (epistemology) and of divine homelessness (ontology). Prayer is an attempt to overcome one or both of these disastrous situations. If God is hidden, then prayer is an attempt to rend the veil, to penetrate the wall that separates God from humanity. "God is ensconced in mystery," Heschel writes, "hidden in the depths. Prayer is pleading with God to come out of the depths."[17] If God is homeless, then prayer is an attempt to create a space for His presence, to overcome the divine exile by inviting God back into the world: "To pray is to open a door, where both God and soul may enter. Prayer is arrival, for Him and for us."[18] In the face of God's homelessness, "our task is . . . to enable Him to enter our moments, to be at home in our time."[19] To pray, in either case, is "to overcome distance, to shatter screens . . . to heal the break between God and the world."[20]

But God's is not the only homelessness. In the midst of a world in which expediency is the only currency, human beings, too, find themselves adrift and without a home. "A dreadful oblivion prevails in the world. The world has forgotten what it means to be human. . . . The abyss is within the self."[21] Forced to "roam . . . through a world festered with aimlessness, falsehoods, and absurdities," the soul yearns "to divest itself of enforced pretensions and camouflage."[22] To pray is to be brought back into focus, to be reminded of ultimate meaning, to find a dwelling place for the soul.[23] Plagued by a sense of life's meaninglessness, the soul's "only cure is to discover [through prayer] that, over and above the anonymous stillness in the world, there is a name and a waiting."[24] "At home"—that is, in prayer—Heschel writes, "I have a Father who judges and cares, who has regard for me, and when I fail and go astray, misses me."[25] In prayer, in other words, the soul finds its home by being reminded of the truth, at once haunting and comforting, that God is perpetually in search of relationship with human beings.

There is a complexity here that Heschel nowhere explicitly names, let alone fully explores: on the one hand, he insists that God is in constant search of man, that "the Voice [of Sinai] goes on forever, and we are being pursued by it."[26] But at the same time, he argues that God is hidden—or even, as he emphasizes at certain moments, that He is actively hiding. Now, the question, of course, is whether one can affirm that God is at one and the same time pursuing humanity and hiding His face; whether it makes sense, in other words, to speak of God as simultaneously both hiding and seeking. Though he seems less than fully conscious of it, I think that Heschel is articulating a profound paradox here: God is always seeking humanity, but that fact is not always self-evident, and it becomes less and less evident the more humanity turns its face from God (and thus causes God to turn His own from us). To know that God is in search of man therefore requires both an act of discernment and a gesture of faithfulness—to perceive the presence even in the midst of apparent absence, and to engage in prayer as a means of opening a door to the divine presence. It is our turning back to God in prayer that moves God to turn back to us. Consciously or not, what I have termed Heschel's elusiveness serves to convey the inextricable mutuality of both God's exile and His return—just as God's hiddenness is a result of both human callousness and divine withdrawal, so, too, is God's reappearance consequent upon a mysterious convergence of human effort and divine decision. In an age of divine hiding, a revelation of God requires both grace and discernment, a reciprocal pair of gestures on the part of God and humanity.

At bottom, I think, we are forced to say that God's seeking is ultimately deeper and more fundamental than His hiding. The searching, in other words, is truer to who God is than the hiding; God always longs to be brought back from exile, to be re-revealed to humanity, but He awaits a human gesture to make that revelation possible. Authentic prayer is the prime example of that human gesture, a human gesture toward disclosing the divine presence.

Godlessness can lead to intense spiritual distress, Heschel writes, and "such anguish, when converted into prayer . . . may evoke the dawn of God." If human callousness and indifference lead to God's departure from the world, genuine human anguish over God's absence can bring Him back. If divine exile results from the dulling of our conscience, divine return can be accomplished through conscience's re-awakening. To pray, according to Heschel, is thus to restore our sensitivity to God, and thereby to open a portal for His return. But Heschel goes a step further and writes that "our agony over God's concealment is sharing in redeeming God's agony over man's concealment."[27] This is a kind of mysticism of pain, reminiscent of Akiva's approach as portrayed in TMHS.[28] In sharing in God's pain, human beings help to ameliorate it: if God's lament is that humanity is indifferent to His presence, then authentic human concern over that indifference is already a partial overcoming of the divine-human separation. In sharing in God's concern over the hiddenness of man, the prayerful make themselves present to God and thus mitigate the extent of divine exile.

The dynamics of God's return are as ambiguous as those of His departure. At moments, it seems that the very act of attending to God's sorrows elicits His reemergence. At other times, however, Heschel maintains that humanity must petition God to return from the depths. Again, the question of how much active divine agency is involved remains elusive. But the broader picture is clear: if humanity's turning away led to divine concealment, its re-turning toward can lead to God's redemptive reappearance. In the act of prayer, human beings disclose themselves to God and implore Him to do the same. Prayer is thus an attempt to overcome both dimensions of the double-concealment we have discussed— to make God present to humanity even as it renders humanity present to God. In the act of prayer, then, we seek simultaneously to overcome God's homelessness and our own.[29]

* * *

Heschel's reflections on God's hiddenness readily call to mind Martin Buber's.[30] "Eclipse of the light of heaven, eclipse of God," Buber writes, "—such indeed is the character of the historic hour through which the world is passing."[31] Yet when Buber speaks of this eclipse in his now-classic lectures by that title, there is a pervasive and over-arching ambiguity: who is responsible for the silence? Is the eclipse of God a function of human failure (i.e., God is available, but humanity is not), or is it the result of something God, too, has enacted? At moments, Buber describes the eclipse of God as the result (seemingly purely) of human shortcoming. "'God is dead,' he writes, "that is, realistically speaking, since the image-making power of the human heart has been in decline so that the spiritual pupil can no longer catch a glimpse of the appearance of the absolute."[32] Overriding human self-consciousness and self-reference undermine our capacity for genuine spontaneity and presence, and "he who is not present," Buber laments, "perceives no presence."[33] Human beings have so privileged the I-It relation over the I-Thou, that God, the

Eternal Thou (who is always only a Thou, and thus can never be rendered an It), has been obscured from view. "This [human] selfhood that has become omnipotent, with all the It around it, can naturally acknowledge neither God nor any genuine absolute which manifests itself to men as of non-human origin. It steps in between and shuts off from us the light of heaven."[34] In these passages, it is not so much that God is hiding, as that humanity has blinded itself, and thus obscured Him from view. God, Buber, writes, "lives in the light of His eternity. But we, 'the slayers,' remain dwellers in darkness, consigned to death."[35]

And yet, at other times, Buber speaks of God's role in the eclipse. In general, as the prophet Isaiah teaches, "the living God is not only a self-revealing but also a self-concealing God."[36] Now, upon first reading, one could be forgiven for asking: which one is it? Has God been eclipsed by human failing, or by His own decision to conceal Himself? Indeed, if one looks for a fully consistent, systematic approach to this question in Buber, one will be disappointed.[37] But before we dismiss Buber's presentation as hopelessly inconsistent, we would do well to pay attention to a third strand in his writing. "Something is taking place *between heaven and earth*," Buber writes, and it "is not a process which can be adequately accounted for by instancing the changes that have taken place in man's spirit. An eclipse of the sun is something that takes place *between the sun and our eyes*, not internally in the eye."[38] Indeed, "Something has taken place," Buber insists, "not in human subjectivity but *in Being itself*." Buber's point, I think, is that neither God alone nor humanity alone is fully to blame for God's hiddenness and inaccessibility. The eclipse of God takes place, in other words, not *within* God or *within* humanity, but in the relational space *between* them.[39] Ultimately, Buber's claim is similar to Heschel's (and in these passages, at least, more clearly made): the hiddenness of God results from the relational dynamics of the two parties, and not (or not merely) from decisions made by either one alone.[40] In a similar vein, God's return will be made possible by what will yet take place between God and man.[41]

Despite the strong parallels between Buber's and Heschel's approaches to divine hiddenness, there are also crucial differences between them. In general, I think, Buber's notion of divine eclipse is more strongly woven with a sense of divine mystery than is Heschel's. In *Eclipse*, for example, Buber speaks frequently of God's self-concealment, but he does not attempt to psychologize God or interpret His motivations.[42] Heschel, in contrast, speaks of God's disappointment, and of His decision to abandon humanity as it has abandoned Him. In other words, whereas Buber maintains more of the air of a negative theologian, who is genuinely limited in what he can say about God's motivations and decision-making, Heschel, despite his ostensible commitment to divine mystery, presumes (at least at moments) to interpret God's otherwise inexplicable actions. (One additional consequence of all this is that Heschel's discussion of divine hiding seems more unabashedly mythological than Buber's.) Put differently, we might say that Heschel is more pulled by the task of theodicy than Buber, and is thus forced, as it were, to say more than Buber about God's motivations. Whether Heschel does his theology a service by going further in the direction of theodicy than Buber is, of course, open to question.

Emil Fackenheim rightly points out that Buber's response to the Shoah emerges from a "stance of faith,"[43] and Steven Kepnes astutely notes that this is why Buber uses the metaphor of eclipse: "An eclipse suggests only that God's image is hidden; He still exists and can be trusted to reappear."[44] Differences between Buber and Heschel aside, Fackenheim's and Kepnes's insights into the former can readily be applied to the latter as well: in speaking of God as hiding, Heschel affirms not only that God exists, but also (and much more important) that He still cares about humanity and longs to reappear—and, indeed, could do so at any moment. Heschel's talk of divine hiddenness thus serves both to give voice to the pain of living in a world that appears godless, and to affirm that such godlessness is, in ultimate terms, only that—an appearance, and one which will be overcome in the fullness of time.

The point I am making is perhaps best captured in a tale Buber recounts of the Hasidic master Rabbi Pinhas of Koretz. A student complains to the Rebbe that "in adversity it is very difficult to retain perfect faith in the belief that God provides for every human being. It actually seems as if God were hiding his face from such an unhappy being. What shall he do to strengthen his faith?" And Rabbi Pinhas responds: "It ceases to be a hiding, if you know it is hiding."[45] In other words, I am suggesting, both Buber and Heschel paradoxically seek to disclose God by speaking explicitly and forcefully of His concealment.

* * *

As we have already noted, Heschel moves without self-consciousness between ontological and epistemological metaphors for God's present state—according to the former, God is somehow "exiled" from the world; according to the latter, God is merely hidden from view. If God's distance is an ontological reality, then humanity's task is to restore the divine presence to the world; if an epistemological one, then humanity's task is to reveal that which is currently (but, again, only temporarily) concealed. Thus, speaking ontologically, Heschel writes:

> God is in exile; the world is corrupt. The universe itself is not at home. To pray means to bring God back into the world, to establish His kingship for a second at least. To pray means to expand His presence. . . . To worship, therefore, means to make God immanent, to make Him present. His being immanent in the world depends upon us. When we say, "Blessed be He," we extend His glory, we bestow His spirit upon this world.[46]

In contrast, speaking epistemologically, Heschel writes, "It is the task of man to reveal what is concealed; to be the voice of the glory, to sing its silence, to utter, so to speak, what is in the heart of all things. The glory is here—invisible and silent. Man is the voice; his task is to be the song. . . . In singing we perceive what it otherwise beyond perceiving."[47] Ultimately, of course, the ontological claim is bolder and more daring, and it is this that renders the paradox more profound and pronounced. "To pray," Heschel writes, "means to bring God back into the world, to establish his kingship, to let His glory prevail."[48] Once again, the Creator is not only transcendent, but also vulnerable and dependent. The majestic God depends for His very majesty on an act of man.

* * *

Although I am not sure that Heschel was conscious of this, there is an important series of parallels between his evocations of prophecy, on the one hand, and his descriptions of prayer, on the other. First, one of the defining aspects of the prophet's experience, Heschel writes, is his ability to view the world from God's perspective; the prophets, we are told, "see the world from the point of view of God."[49] Similarly, self-transcending human beings at prayer partake of the divine perspective: "When we betake ourselves to the extreme opposite of the ego," Heschel writes, "we can behold a situation from the aspect of God."[50] Second, the prophet is concerned, Heschel asserts, less with knowing God than with being known by God. Prophetic experience, he says, is "living in the perpetual awareness of being perceived, apprehended, noted by God, of being an object of the divine Subject. . . . The Prophet does not find God in his mind as object, but finds himself an object in God's mind."[51] Likewise, according to Heschel, prayer is "an endeavor to become the object of His thought. . . . The purpose of prayer is to be brought to His attention . . . not to know Him, but to *be known* to Him." To pray, Heschel tells us, is "to strive to make our life a divine concern. For the ultimate aspiration of man is not to be a master, but an object of His knowledge. . . . To become a thought of God—this is the true career of man."[52] Third, the prophet, as we have seen at length in chapter 4, is a man who feels with God; the governing characteristic of prophetic experience is what Heschel calls "sympathy" with the divine pathos. Recall, now, what Heschel says about prayer in a time of divine concealment—namely, that "our agony over God's concealment is sharing in redeeming God's agony over man's concealment."[53]

Turning to the central theme of this work: authentic humanity is defined, we have seen, by the capacity to transcend and surpass the self. According to Heschel, no one embodies the human aspiration to self-transcendence more profoundly than the prophet himself, who "disregards the self"[54] in responding to God's call. Rather than seeking "its own fulfillment," Heschel tells us, prophecy always "points beyond itself."[55] In like manner, as we have been at pains to show in this chapter and the last, prayer constitutes the very pith of the religious life precisely because it epitomizes the human quest for self-transcendence. Finally, Heschel suggests that upon encountering divine hiddenness, the prophet ventures forward to uncover God: although "God is invisible, distant, dwelling in darkness . . . [and] His ways in history are shrouded and perplexing . . . prophecy is a moment of unshrouding, an opening of the eyes, a lifting of the curtain."[56] Prayer, as we have just seen, aspires to the same goal—it is an attempt "to open a door . . . to overcome distance, to shatter screens,"[57] and thus to break down the wall dividing God and humanity.

The parallels are both plentiful and striking: just as the prophet transcends and decenters himself, so, too, does the human being at prayer; just as the prophet sees the world from the divine perspective, so, too, does the human being at prayer; just as the prophet strives to become an object of God's concern, so, too, does the human being at prayer. Just as the prophet shares in God's pain, so also does the human being at prayer. And, finally, just as the prophet shatters the screens that divide God from humanity, so, too, does the human being at prayer. In light of all this, we are brought to a fascinating conclusion—namely, that, according to Heschel, in the act of prayer, each of us is enabled to participate in the ethos of prophecy. In prayer, then, we strive to emulate the spiritual ideal represented by the prophet, to engage in an act of *imitatio propheti.* To pray, then, is to be a worthy "descendant of the prophets."[58]

In this context, it is worth noting one final passage about self-transcendence in Heschel. As we saw in chapter 4, Heschel writes in *The Prophets* that "the outstanding feature of a person is his ability to transcend himself, his attentiveness to the nonself. To be a person is to have a concern for the nonself. It is in this limited sense that we speak of God as a personal Being: He has concern for nondivine being."[59] We can bracket the question of whether it is accurate for Heschel to say that it is only in this very limited sense that he speaks of a personal God. What is important to note is that Heschel's argument leads to an intriguing conclusion—namely, that in making self-transcendence possible, prayer becomes an act of *imitatio dei,* of "walking in God's ways." To turn fully *to* God is thus also to become crucially *like* God.

* * *

We ought to ask, in concluding, how this chapter and the one before it are connected. What intrinsic connection is there, in other words, between self-transcendence and the aspiration to bring God back into the world? For Heschel, I would suggest, human selfishness and divine immanence are at eternal loggerheads: an excess of self, the kind of self-centeredness that values only expediency and utilization, closes off one's capacity to hear and respond to the call of the other (as well as of the Other).[60] This is true both of individual lives, and of the collective life of humanity: the more focused we are on ourselves, the less porous we are, and thus the less able to be penetrated by the word, will, and presence of God we render ourselves. Self-transcendence, in contrast, is a kind of *tzimtzum*, a self-contraction that allows the other (and the Other) to make a claim upon us. In the act of overcoming myself (in prayer or elsewhere), then, I create an empty space, as it were, in which the word of God can be heard and the presence of God can dwell. Thus, in transcending the self, the human being invites God's return into his own life, and into the life of humanity as a whole.[61] *Mutatis mutandis*, the words of contemporary Christian philosopher James Mensch seem apt: "To encounter [God], we must also empty ourselves. Through such kenosis, we provide a space in which he can appear. Self-emptying is, in other words, a form of receptivity."[62] Overcoming oneself, then, is a form of opening oneself. God dwells, the Kotzker famously taught, wherever we let God in.[63]

CONCLUSION

In what ways does our investigation advance our understanding of the unity and direction of Abraham Joshua Heschel's overall project? How have we uncovered the animating core of his ostensibly diverse and even contradictory claims? We can begin to answer this by noting a dimension of his thought that is too often overlooked: Heschel sought to present traditional Judaism (as he understood it) as an antidote to the manifold ills of modernity. A refugee much of whose world had been destroyed in the genocidal fires of Nazi Europe, Heschel never tired of pointing to the moral and spiritual obtuseness of modern man, and of insisting that the barbarisms of modernity could be brought to an end only by a process of radical moral and spiritual reawakening.[1] As we have seen, Heschel sought not merely to argue for such an awakening, but more fundamentally to educe it, to remind his readers that buried deep within them was the possibility of a wholly different orientation to the world, one rooted in wonder and amazement rather than callousness and indifference.

Modernity, according to Heschel, is characterized above all by an ethos of self-assertion. The tragedy of modern times is that "we do not know any more how to justify any value except in terms of expediency."[2] Our sense of "appreciation" has been all but obliterated by an obsession with "manipulation": instead of seeing the world around us consisting of "things to be acknowledged, understood, valued or admired," we imagine it comprised merely of "things to be handled, forces to be managed, objects to be put to use."[3] This results in a horrific distortion of the world, and in an elimination of any transcendent horizon to our lives. Nature is an object to be used, and so, eventually, is man. One consequence of this is a profound indifference to the dignity of the other and, ultimately, a creeping sense of doubt about our own. The culture of expediency does not rest until it consumes all of us; "the complete manipulation of the world results in the complete instrumentalization of the self." In Heschel's mind both the malaise and the depravity of the modern world result from this relentless insistence on treating the world as "a thing I own" rather than "a mystery I face."[4]

The ethos of expediency and self-assertion cannot but breed a process of isolation and self-enclosure. Nothing outside me makes a claim upon me; manipulation, Heschel writes, "is the cause of alienation: objects and I apart, things stand dead, and I am alone."[5] This culture of self-assertion and self-enclosure, of indifference and insensitivity, is, Heschel contends, a particularly perverse and pernicious form of idolatry. Its consequences have been unprecedented bloodshed and unspeakable suffering, cruelty, and barbarism. One of Heschel's fundamental projects is thus to shake humanity loose from this delusional self-perception: we are not sovereigns of the universe, and the world is not mere material for endless consumption.

Coupled with all this self-assertion that Heschel deplores is an insidious nihilism, a sense that we do not ultimately matter, that human beings are in the end nothing more than particularly intelligent and destructive beasts. Heschel's project is to show us that we are, in fact, significant, but not in the ways in which modernity has trained us to think: we are important not because we have a bottomless capacity for self-assertion (which, tragically, we do), but rather because we have an all-too-rarely realized capacity for self-transcendence. We matter not because of how much we can acquire, but because of how deeply we are able to give. Our dignity lies not in our raw power, but in our capacity for commitment, for responsiveness and reciprocity, for gratitude and indebtedness. At some level, human beings are cognizant of all this; the pressing question is how to reawaken our now disastrously dormant awareness.

For Heschel, what I have called the existential posture of wonder is the starting point of all spirituality—and, crucially, of ethics as well. It is critical to understand why: according to Heschel, wonder is not—or, at the very least, is not primarily—about being amazed by this fact or that, by this event or that, but rather about being awake to the "unexpectedness of being as such";[6] wonder is, as Heschel repeatedly points out, the very antithesis of "taking things for granted." A sense of perpetual surprise yields the realization that the world as a whole, and my life within it, did not have to be. They are not brute facts but rather gifts bestowed. To cultivate a sense of wonder, then, is to instill in myself the knowledge, at once cognitive and experiential, that I am not the author of my own life or of the world that I inhabit. I am, most fundamentally, not a creator of life, but a recipient thereof. In Heschel's memorable formulation, "I am what is not mine."[7]

What this orientation toward wonder means, according to Heschel, is that I will have a sense of "indebtedness" and "requiredness." Something—or better, Someone—has given me life, and that Someone has the right to make a claim upon me. To state this differently, we might say that wonder means that "I" is not the first word that I speak, but the second—something (someone) else is prior to me, both chronologically and axiologically.[8] The consequence of all this is that my bearing will be focused on response rather than (self-) assertion, on reciprocity rather than expediency.

As this necessarily oversimplified phenomenological portrait suggests, wonder is the opening, the portal within us that makes us receptive and potentially responsive to the call and the need of the other—whether God or our neighbor. The posture of wonder generates a dramatic reorientation and a total reversal of consciousness. No longer subjects in search of meaning, we discover that meaning is objective, and that it envelops us. At a certain climactic moment, we cease to ask questions about God, and realize instead that God is always asking questions of us: "The more deeply we meditate, the more clearly we realize that the question we ask is a question we are asked; that man's question about God is God's question of man."[9] In Heschel's vision, then, Cartesian philosophy is flipped on its head. The subject is no longer the subject, but as it were the object of God's knowledge. I no longer ask, but am asked; no longer strive to know, but to be known; no longer assert, but respond. As I have shown in chapter 2, all of this is especially important to keep in mind when considering Heschel's method: Heschel does begin with human experience, and in that sense he is heir to the liberal tradition of theology that begins with the subject. But the priority of human experience, for Heschel, is methodological, not metaphysical. In other words, Heschel begins with human consciousness not so that he can reflect it, but precisely so that he can reorient and transform it. Heschel turns to the subject only to elicit its capacity for self-transcendence; the sovereignty of the self is systematically subverted with the realization that long before I decide to search for God, God has been in search of me.

　　To respond to God is, quite simply, to bring an end to callousness and indifference. It is in this context that Heschel's polemic against what he considers the Hellenization of Jewish theology should be understood. As we have seen in chapter 4, Heschel deems the God of Aristotle, Philo, and Maimonides to be so transcendent and self-contained as to be altogether heartless and aloof. In a world of genocide and atomic devastation, a world in which human beings are heedless and uncaring, what good is such a God? In a world in which man is impervious to the suffering of his fellow, what could be more otiose than a God who is an Unmoved Mover? In what we might imagine as a perverse form of *imitatio dei*, according to Heschel an indifferent God can only yield an indifferent humanity. But the God of the prophets is entirely different, profoundly affected by the cries of the oppressed and downtrodden. The God of Israel is a God of pathos and concern, and to worship this God—*really* to worship this God—is to have our indifference shattered, and our stubborn selfishness torn to shreds. Heschel would no doubt want us to get his logic straight, to understand the metaphysical order of priority he imagines: a return to the God of Israel is an urgent necessity not because He has the potential to bring an end to our detachment and self-enclosure. Such a God would still be a mere notion, another instrument meant to serve *our* needs, no matter how desperate. No, our detachment and self-enclosure are a function of our deafness to the God of Israel. In returning to God, we realize that He is the ultimate reality and that our detachment is a crime, that our indifference is a scandal equal in severity to any of the many outrages the prophets so vehemently condemned. The God Heschel believes in "has to be understood in terms of a transcendence, and that transcendence is not a passive thing; it is a challenging transcendence. Man is always being challenged; a question is always being asked of him."[10]

To state all of this simply: Heschel's project is a call to self-transcendence, an attempt to move humanity beyond the self-enclosed prison of purely reflexive concern, and to help us develop (or, perhaps better, to recover) our capacity for transitive concern. It is this capacity, Heschel avers, that constitutes the very core of our humanity. Put differently, the idea of self-transcendence is the foundation, for Heschel, both of who God *is* and of who man *could be*. More, it is the dynamic principle that makes covenant possible: a God who transcends egocentricity summons man, who has the potential to transcend egocentricity, in order to be His partner, to be "in travail with God's dreams and designs, with God's dream of a world redeemed, of reconciliation of heaven and earth, of a mankind which is truly His image, reflecting His wisdom, justice, and compassion."[11]

The burden of this book has been to demonstrate that self-transcendence is the axis around which all of Heschel's theology revolves. The God who, according to Heschel, is "absolute selflessness," summons humanity to moments of selflessness and "concern for the unregarded."[12] Moreover, the God who limits His power in order to make space for humanity beckons humanity to restrain its own power in turn. Thus covenant becomes a process of mutual and reciprocal self-transcendence: the God of transitive concern seeks covenantal partners who will cultivate transitive concern; the God who engages in *tzimtzum* seeks partners who will engage in *tzimtzum*.

God's self-limitation means that God is vulnerable to the decisions human beings make, so much so that God's immanence depends on human self-transcendence. Human beings have the terrifying power to drive God into exile, and to cause God to hide His face, but we also have the awesome potential to solicit and enable God's return. As we have seen in chapters 6 and 7, this is, for Heschel, the heart of prayer: to overcome the ego so as to make space for God to reenter the world. Since a mitzvah, as we have seen, is "a prayer in the form of a deed," all acts of worship are, at bottom, attempts to reestablish God's immanence. This is the most fundamental meaning of covenant: God seeks partners who will make it possible for Him to dwell within the world, and not just beyond it.

One final reorientation: one of the grievous illusions of modern man is the purported synonymy of freedom and self-assertion. This is, on Heschel's account, a calamitous error, and keeps modern man perpetually incarcerated in a prison of his own making. Heschel writes: "The slave will always ask: What will serve my interests? It is the free man who is able to transcend the causality of interest and deed, of act and the desire for personal reward. It is the free man who asks: Why should I be interested in my interests? What are the values I ought to feel in need of serving?" Real freedom is found, in other words, not in the power of self-assertion, but precisely in the power to rise above it.[13] "Inner freedom," Heschel declares, "is spiritual ecstasy, the state of being beyond all interests and selfishness."[14] Quietly but forcefully, Heschel repudiates both the modern obsession with shallow conceptions of autonomy, and, we should add, the (pseudo-) religious preoccupation with dramatic experiences: freedom is not impulsiveness, and ecstasy is not about euphoric states of trance. Freedom is found in the ability to transcend impulse, and ecstasy may be achieved in the frequently understated exercise of that very freedom. Freedom, Heschel writes, is "the state of going out of the self, an act of spiritual ecstasy, in the original sense of the term."[15]

But Heschel is under no illusions: freedom is not a state that can be achieved once and for all. Since the most that can be hoped for (or better: striven for) is *moments* of self-transcendence, the most that can be striven for is *moments* of freedom. Freedom, Heschel tells us, is not a process but an event: "It *is* not, it happens."[16] In a sentence that could be said to encapsulate the core of his message to the modern world, Heschel writes, "It is for us to decide whether freedom is self-assertion or response to a demand."[17] Our humanity, as we have seen, is constituted by our capacity to rise above the selfish ego. So, Heschel reminds us, is our freedom.[18]

NOTES

INTRODUCTION

1. For the now standard two-volume biography of Heschel, cf. Kaplan and Dresner, *Abraham Joshua Heschel,* and Kaplan, *Spiritual Radical.* The first volume studies Heschel's life in Europe through 1940, and the second his years in America, from 1940 until his death in 1972. These works are the fruit of a great deal of impressive archival research and fill in many previously obscure details about Heschel's life. The first volume is marred by a certain hagiographical tinge; the second, written by Kaplan alone, is much stronger. In general, the volumes are rich in biographical detail but less useful in terms of analysis of thought.

2. Some of the most important studies of Heschel include Rothschild, "Introduction"; Merkle, *The Genesis of Faith;* Eisen, "Re-Reading Heschel on the Commandments"; Green, "Three Warsaw Mystics"; Even-Chen, *Kol min ha-ʾarafel;* Levenson, "Religious Affirmation"; Bondi, *Ayekah?;* Erlewine, "Reclaiming the Prophets"; and Erlewine, "Rediscovering Heschel." An extremely useful survey of the scholarly literature on Heschel may be found in Marmur, "In Search of Heschel."

3. Rothschild's most significant essay by far is "Introduction"; Merkle's, *The Genesis of Faith.*In general terms, I agree with Rothschild that Heschel articulates the contours of a coherent worldview, but I am less convinced that Heschel's work can be organized into quite as orderly and systematic a package as Rothschild thinks. As will become clear in the chapters that follow, Heschel's use of language is frequently inexact and inconsistent. Merkle's is a remarkable study, and a model of the riches that can be yielded from a systematic mind applying a hermeneutics of generosity to a thinker such as Heschel. Aside from the lack of critical engagement with Heschel's writings, my one additional reservation about Merkle's work is the seemingly unselfconsciously Christian lens it applies to Heschel. The very title suggests a Christian preoccupation, since Heschel himself remarks that "awe rather than faith is the cardinal attitude of the religious Jew" (*GSM,* 77). In a similar vein, Arnold Eisen notes that Merkle's is "an intelligent Christian reading of Heschel, the emphasis squarely upon faith rather than 'works.'" Eisen, "Re-Reading Heschel," 28n4.

4. Even-Chen, *Kol min ha-ʿarafel.* Kaufman, *Contemporary Jewish Philosophies,* 171.

5. Berkovits, "Dr. A. J. Heschel's Theology of Pathos," 67–104.

6. I return to this in chapter 2.

7. Petuchowski, "Faith as the Leap of Action," 397.

8. *GSM,* 404.

9. This is expressed most clearly and succinctly in *MNA,* 137–138.

10. *MNA,* 136–137.

11. *MNA,* 137, 138.

12. *MNA,* 138. Emphasis mine. In the course of this work, all emphases in citations from Heschel are his unless otherwise noted.

13. *MNA,* 138.

14. *PT,* 98.

15. *PT,* 189.

16. *MNA,* 143. Cf.: "God does not have Himself in mind." *KGE,* 169. It is worth noting that Heschel's characterization of the God of the Bible as utterly devoid of reflexive concern is questionable, to say the least. Consider, for example, Moses' appeal to God's reputation as a reason to grant pardon to Israel after the sin of the golden calf (Exodus 32:12). In dramatic contrast to Heschel, biblical theologian Walter Brueggemann speaks of YHWH flying into a rage as a result of His "passionate, perhaps out-of-control self-regard" (309). Indeed, Brueggemann contends, YHWH "takes with savage seriousness [His] right to be worshiped, honored, and obeyed" (272); He manifests "a recurring streak of self-regard that may express itself in vigorous and negative ways" (274). At times downright "self-indulgent" (276), YHWH's self-regard is totally "uncompromising" (298). References are to Brueggemann, *Theology of the Old Testament.* For a useful study of Heschel's interpretation of the divine pathos in comparison with the approaches of Brueggemann and Terence Fretheim, see Schlimm, "Different Perspectives on Divine Pathos," 673–694. In a similar vein, Baruch Schwartz has recently argued that according to the prophet Ezekiel, what motivates God to restore Israel is His fear of "bad publicity" and His desire "to end the dishonor that his reputation has suffered" (306, 307). God is, Schwartz writes, "obsessed with the need to rehabilitate his

honor" (307); indeed, He has manifold "emotional needs and frustrations" (309). Schwartz, "The Ultimate Aim of Israel's Restoration in Ezekiel," 305–319.

17. *GSM,* 412.

18. *Prophets,* II, 262.

19. *Prophets,* II, 5.

20. *MNA,* 244.

21. Cf. Christopher Insole's provocative suggestion that some contemporary apophatic thought runs the risk of projecting our own narcissistic self-satisfaction onto God. Insole, "Anthropomorphism and the Apophatic God," 475–483, esp. 481–483.

22. *Prophets,* II, 266.

23. *Prophets,* I, 216.

24. *Prophets,* I, 219.

25. *Prophets,* II, 264. Cf. II, 10.

26. *Prophets,* II, 51.

27. *MNA,* 71–72.

28. *MNA,* 138.

29. See, e.g., *GSM,* 369, and *Prophets,* I, xiv.

30. *Prophets,* I, xiv–xv.

31. *Prophets,* II, 14.

32. *Prophets,* II, 32.

33. *Prophets,* II, 38.

34. *Prophets,* II, 39.

35. *Prophets,* II, 64.

36. *Prophets,* II, 76.

37. Heschel, "Jewish Theology," in *MGSA,* 159. A difficult question arises here: Does the fact that God has needs not suggest that God does have reflexive concern after all? Aren't needs, to some degree at least, inherently reflexive? Heschel nowhere addresses this question, but I suspect that he would have argued that since God's primary needs are that others (the widow, the orphan, the stranger) be regarded and attended to, God's needs do not really constitute reflexive concern. But matters become more nettlesome once we take worship into account: Does God's insistence that He be worshipped not imply reflexive concern? A great deal depends on what

one imagines are the purposes of worship. Here, I think, Heschel would have had two broad strategies available to him. The first would have been to insist that worship is for humanity's good rather than God's—but such an approach would seem to undercut the depth and passion of his insistence on God's needs. Cf. Arthur Green's comments, cited below at note 109. The second would have been to argue that the primary purpose of worship is to awaken humanity to the task of fulfilling its divinely assigned task, which, again, is primarily about responsibility to other (human) selves. I am not sure that this strategy would have been fully effective either, since despite the utter centrality of the ethical in Heschel's vision of the theological, the latter emphatically cannot simply be reduced to the former. In my view, Heschel might have been better off insisting that in contrast to human, divine concern is overwhelmingly transitive, even if not exclusively so. In any case, the matter requires further investigation. I am grateful to David Shatz for our exchange on these issues.

38. *GSM*, 156.

39. Heschel, "Divine Pathos," in *Between God and Man*, 119.

40. *MNA*, 248.

41. *GSM*, 413.

42. Heschel, "The Individual Jew and His Obligations," in *IF*, 201.

43. *MNA*, 241. Cf. also, for example, *WM*, 75.

44. *MNA*, 242.

45. *MNA*, 242.

46. *GSM*, 156–157. As discussed in chapters 5 and 7, and as this passage already makes clear, Heschel moves (seemingly without self-consciousness) between the idea that God is present in the world but hidden from human perception (epistemology), and the much more radical view that God is in exile, somehow actually absent from the world (ontology).

47. *GSM*, 358.

48. *MQ*, 62.

49. *MNA*, 243.

50. *WM*, 119.

51. *MNA*, 243.

52. I am in agreement with Christian theologian Marcel Sarot that it does not make sense to speak of God's voluntarily limiting His omnipotence. Accordingly, Sarot has argued that theologians should speak of God's "self-restraint" rather than of His "self-limitation." I think the latter term is acceptable, provided that one does not take it to suggest that God can literally limit or surrender His omnipotence; in speaking here of God's self-limitation in Heschel's theology, I refer to God's decision to limit the *exercise* of His power, not of His (at any rate impossible) decision to limit that power itself. Sarot, "Omnipotence and Self-Limitation," 172–185.

53. Heschel's affirmation both of God's omnipotence and of His self-restraint enables him (among other things) to explain God's current silence in the face of evil (but cf. the discussion of this point in chapter 5) while still insisting that God maintains the power ultimately to redeem the world.

54. Even-Chen, "God's Omnipotence," 54. Shoshana Ronen's "Absolute Goodness or Omnipotence" is animated by a similar misapprehension. Ronen goes so far as to insist that hester panim, the hiding of God's face, is incompatible with Heschel's thinking (141); she seems unaware that Heschel himself invokes hester panim and makes it central to his post-Holocaust reflections. Cf. *MNA*, chapter 16, 151–157, which we explore at length in chapter 5.

55. Even-Chen, "God's Omnipotence," 63.

56. *Prophets*, II, 100. Note also Heschel's claim that "pathos is both a disclosure of [God's] concern and a concealment of His power" (II, 12)—a concealment, but not a negation or denial.

57. In contemporary theological terms, we might say that on the question

of divine power, Heschel is much closer to Open Theism than to Process Theology. In a sentence that could have been written by Heschel, open theist William Hasker writes that "a universe containing genuinely free creatures is one in which God has generously decided that there shall be certain events that are not positively controlled by him: namely, the free choice of the creatures." In other words, according to Hasker, God is essentially omnipotent but has chosen to exercise (or, as the case may be, not to exercise) His omnipotence in a particular way. Hasker, "God Takes Risks," 221. Richard Rice contrasts this approach with that of Process Theology, insisting that "for the open view of God . . . the ultimate metaphysical fact is not God-and-world [as it is for process thought], but God, period. God could exist without the creatures, but he chooses not to. Thus the world owes its existence to God's free choice, not to metaphysical necessity" (185). Similarly, Rice writes, divine restraint in the face of human freedom is a matter of "divine policy" rather than "metaphysical necessity" (189). Rice, "Process Theism," 163–200.

58. Even-Chen, "God's Omnipotence," 56.

59. *GSM*, 358.

60. *GSM*, 171.

61. *GSM*, 241.

62. Heschel, "The Patient as a Person," in *IF*, 33.

63. Heschel, "Carl Stern's Interview with Dr. Heschel," in *MGSA*, 397.

64. Perhaps not surprisingly, Even-Chen adopts the standard view that according to Heschel, "the burden of the Holocaust rests [seemingly exclusively] with man" (54). As I show in chapter 5, this view depends on what I believe is a misreading of the explosive pages on "The Hiding God" in *MNA*, 154–157.

65. "Jewish Theology," *MGSA*, 159, 160.

66. "Jewish Theology," *MGSA*, 159.

67. *Prophets*, II, 21.

68. Ward, *Religion and Creation*, 22. Ward notes that there is a vast difference between "a God who wills to relate to the world affectively, and a God who, out of weakness, is hurt by the world."

69. Fretheim, "Prayer in the Old Testament," 57.

70. *GSM*, 84.

71. Heschel, "What We Might Do Together," in *MGSA*, 300.

72. *GSM*, 157.

73. *WM*, 90.

74. Heschel, "A Preface to an Understanding of Revelation," in *MGSA*, 186.

75. *GSM*, 312.

76. *GSM*, 313. Cf. the following: "It is the task of man to reveal what is concealed; to be the voice of the glory, to sing its silence. . . . The glory is here—invisible and silent. Man is the voice; his task is to be the song." "The Vocation of the Cantor," *IF*, 244–245.

77. Heschel, "Sacred Image of Man," in *IF*, 162, and "Pikuach Neshama: To Save a Soul," in *MGSA*, 66.

78. *GSM*, 286.

79. *GSM*, 36.

80. Heschel, "Children and Youth," in *IF*, 40. Cf.: "Man . . . undertook to build a Paradise by his own might, and he is driving God from his Paradise. . . . But now we have discovered that our Paradise is built on top of a volcano. The Paradise we have built may turn out to be a vast camp for the extermination of man." "Sacred Image of Man," *IF*, 165.

81. Heschel, "Children and Youth," in *IF*, 41.

82. Heschel, "A Preface to an Understanding of Revelation," in *MGSA*, 188.

83. Heschel, "Israel and Diaspora," in *IF*, 218.

84. *GSM*, 171. Cf. Heschel, "A Preface to an Understanding of Revelation," in *MGSA*, 189. Cf.: "There is a passion and drive for cruel deeds which only the awe

and fear of God can soothe; there is a suf-focating selfishness in man which only holiness can ventilate" (*GSM*, 169). In my view, Heschel never fully confronts the reality that the awe and fear of God can stir the human passion and drive for cruel deeds as much as it soothes them, that humanity's "suffocating selfishness" can be nurtured, rather than "ventilated," by religious passion. One wonders whether time would have tempered Heschel's vast confidence in religion's ameliora-tive effects. In a similar vein, see Magid, "The Role of the Secular," 138–160, esp. 138–140, 144. Magid labels Heschel a Cold War theologian and asks what revisions in his theology are rendered necessary by a time when "the problem with our world may arguably be not the lack of God but too much God" (144).

To be fair, Heschel is keenly aware of the potentially insidious sides of reli-gion. As he puts it, "Even more frustrat-ing than the fact that evil is real, mighty and tempting is the fact that it thrives so well in the disguise of the good. In this world, it seems, the holy and the unholy do not exist apart, but are mixed, interre-lated and confounded. It is a world where idols may be rich in beauty, and where the worship of God may be tinged with wickedness. . . . Piety is at times evil in disguise, an instrument in the pursuit of power" (*GSM*, 369–370). And yet even in the face of all this, Heschel never seems to doubt that religion, and religion alone, can rein in humanity's impulse for cru-elty. Immediately after acknowledging just how much damage religion can do, he goes on to assert that "religion . . . with its demands and visions, is not a luxury but a matter of life and death" (*GSM*, 372).

Martin Kavka expresses grave concerns that Heschel (or the early Heschel, at any rate) can sound downright "theocratic," as when he famously calls on Americans "to let [God] in—into our banks and fac-tories, into our Congress and clubs, into our courts and investigating committees, into our homes and theatres. For God is everywhere or nowhere . . . concerned with everything or nothing" (*MQ*, 150). In general, I take the thrust of Heschel's remarks to be about weakening the bar-riers between religion and society rather than church and state, but Heschel's in-vocation of Congress and the courts does open the door to Kavka's worries, even if the reader sympathizes with the con-crete instances Heschel likely has in mind (Joseph McCarthy's demagoguery and the Supreme Court's decision in *Brown v. Board of Education*). Heschel would likely also have insisted that the question for so-ciety is not only religion or secularity, but also what kind of religion—and here the anti-fundamentalist strains in Heschel's writings are clear and consistent (as I show in chapter 3). Kavka, "The Meaning of That Hour," 108–136. In any event, I am in agreement with Robert Erlewine that "Heschel's theocentrism hardly promotes a theocracy or religious violence. All theo-centrisms are not the same and should not be treated as such." Erlewine, "Rediscov-ering Heschel," 188.

Both Kavka and Magid make persua-sive cases that Heschel's political think-ing changed over time to make more space for the secular. This domain would thus constitute an important exception to the remarkable consistency Heschel's writing tends to show over time (cf. be-low, pp. 25–26).

85. *GSM*, 153.

86. Heschel, "The Meaning of This Hour," in *MQ*, 150–151.

87. *WM*, 48.

88. *MNA*, 48.

89. *MNA*, 128.

90. *MNA*, 48–49.

91. *MNA*, 128–129.

92. *GSM*, 133, 132.

93. See, for example, *WM*, 106–111.

94. *WM,* 111.

95. Morgan, "Religion, History and Moral Discourse," 63.

96. *MQ,* 144.

97. *GSM,* 260.

98. *Prophets,* I, xii.

99. *GSM,* 275.

100. *Prophets,* I, 209.

101. *Prophets,* I, 207.

102. *MNA,* 154–157, citing Psalm 44.

103. *MQ,* 7.

104. *MQ,* 15.

105. Heschel, "Prayer as Discipline," in *IF,* 258.

106. *MQ,* 69. For the idea that a mitzvah is "a prayer in the form of a deed," cf. also, for example, *GSM,* 375, and "The God of Israel and Christian Renewal," *MGSA,* 278.

107. *MQ,* 8.

108. See, for the *locus classicus* of this idea, the commentary of Nachmanides to Exodus 29:46.

109. Green, "Abraham Joshua Heschel," 2–76. Green adds: "Heschel has subtly turned around the order of priorities [of the kabbalists]. Yes, the *mitzvoth* are indeed divine need, he says, but it is in the first case these commandments—the life of goodness and justice—that God needs of us. In doing this, of course, Heschel is restoring the link between the Hasidic masters he knew and the prophets of ancient Israel" (75–76). Cf. also Kaufman, "Abraham Joshua Heschel and Hasidic Thought," 137–155.

110. On this last point, see Erlewine, "Reclaiming the Prophets," esp. 204–206.

111. Horwitz, "Abraham Joshua Heschel," 297.

112. In a similar vein, I find Arnold Eisen's contention, that for Heschel "mitzvot are less a way to transformation of the world than a means of transforming the self," to be quite problematic—that is a distinction I am not sure Heschel could recognize or even fully make sense of. The urgent challenge facing human be-ings at all times is, according to Heschel, to effect world-transformation through self-transformation. Eisen, "Re-Thinking Heschel," 22.

113. *GSM,* 138. Emphasis mine. Interestingly, neither Eliezer Schweid nor Arnold Eisen (see following note) seems to notice this passage.

114. Schweid, *Prophets to Their People and to Humanity,"* 235, 236. I am grateful to Lenny Levin for our discussion of this point in Schweid. Arnold Eisen goes one step further and conjectures that Heschel "did believe that he had attained the status of prophecy, at least to some extent." Eisen, "Prophecy as 'Vocation,'" 843. More convincing in my view is Eisen's suggestion that as part of his "pedagogy of return" for the Jews of America, Heschel "crafted a larger-than-life image of himself to assist in the observation of piety from afar. If that is the case, we should perhaps read Heschel's life, as well as his work, as a way or providing instruction to his audience." Eisen, "Re-Thinking Heschel," 27. Alexander Even-Chen and Ephraim Meir go even farther, suggesting that Heschel attributed a "quasi-messianic" status to himself and believed that his divinely-given task was "to be the savior of an entire generation." Even-Chen and Meir, Between Heschel and Buber, 58. It is difficult to know what was in Heschel's heart, but these are very bold claims to make, and the evidence on offer (a single poem published when he was twenty-six years old and a stray remark reported by a student, neither of which is all that convincing on its own terms) is rather flimsy. To believe that one has unique spiritual gifts and attendant responsibilities is one thing; to suspect that one has attained prophetic status is another; to imagine that one is a "quasi-messianic" figure and a "savior" is, needless to say, still another. Regarding Heschel, the first claim seems relatively uncontroversial, the second speculative, and the third wildly so.

115. Worth noting in this context is Steven Katz's astute analysis of *PT*, in which he suggests that Heschel's primary goal in writing the book was to edify, challenge, and uplift his readers:

> Truth is something to be lived. Kierkegaard and the Kotzker intend to teach not by doctrine but by example, and Heschel likewise. We are introduced to the Kotzker not primarily in order to study his life but to change our own. Heschel intends, through the medium of an investigation of Kierkegaard and Reb Mendl, to evoke *subjective* response from his readers. He is concerned to do what his two mentors were concerned to do: to throw the reader back on himself. The ultimate aim is not to teach us about Kotzk or Copenhagen but about each of us here and now.... In the interpretation of this book what is ideally revealed is the interpreter.... [The book] is a mirror through which we are able to see ourselves.

Indeed, Katz suggests, the use of Kierkegaard and the Kotzker as "intermediaries" allows Heschel to offer some stinging assessments of his generation without too quickly alienating his readers by using the first person. Katz, "Abraham Joshua Heschel," 95–96.

116. The classic discussion of the evolution in Buber's thought is Mendes-Flohr, *From Mysticism to Dialogue*. More recently, see Koren, *The Mystery of the Earth*.

117. Even-Chen, *Kol min ha-ʾarafel*, 13.

118. Marmur, "In Search of Heschel," 31.

119. Y. Rosh Hashanah, 3:5, 58d.

120. Kaplan, *Holiness in Words*, 33.

1. WONDER, INTUITION, AND THE PATH TO GOD

1. *GSM*, 43.

2. For the term "religiosity," Buber is indebted to the German sociologist Georg Simmel. For a brief discussion of how Buber transforms "religiosity" from a sociological to a metaphysical category, see Mendes-Flohr, *From Mysticism to Dialogue*, 78–79.

3. Buber, "Jewish Religiosity," in *On Judaism*, 80 (originally published in *Vom Geist des Judentums*).

4. Mendes-Flohr, *From Mysticism to Dialogue*, 79. He continues: "With its superstructure of dogma and ritual prescription, religion tends to pinion religiosity to a conditional universe, and thereby undermines its very essence."

5. Buber, "Jewish Religiosity," in *On Judaism*, 80.

6. Buber, "Jewish Religiosity," in *On Judaism*, 80.

7. *MQ*, 50.

8. See, at length, both *PT* and *KGE*. For example: "If a man offered prayers today because he did so yesterday," the Kotzker taught, "he was worse off than a scoundrel." *PT*, 10–11.

9. *MQ*, vi.

10. *MNA*, 58.

11. *GSM*, 45.

12. *GSM*, 43.

13. *GSM*, 85.

14. *GSM*, 45.

15. "Wonder is a state of mind in which we do not look at reality through the latticework of our memorized knowledge; in which nothing is taken for granted. We can never draw the truth out of borrowed or inherited knowledge" (*MNA*, 12).

16. *GSM*, 48–49.

17. *GSM*, 63.

18. *GSM*, 310. Cf. 137. It would be interesting to compare Heschel's approach to ritual here with Max Kadushin's conception of Rabbinic Judaism as "normal mysticism," wherein "the ordinary, familiar everyday things and occurrences ... constitute occasions for the experience of God." Kadushin focused especially on the spiritual impact of *berakhot*, or Jewish ritual blessings. Kadushin, *The Rabbinic Mind*, 203. Moreover, Kadushin empha-

sized the democratic nature of normal mysticism—that is, the fact that "it was the experience of every member of the nation, not alone of such as had special training or temperamental aptitudes." Kadushin, *Organic Thinking*, 238.

19. Heschel, "On Prayer," in *MGSA*, 266. Wonder, Heschel says there, is "reverence and awe, openness to the mystery that surrounds us," whereas radical amazement is the sense of being "overwhelmed by the awareness of eternity in daily living."

20. I am grateful to my former student Ilana Kurshan for this formulation.

21. *GSM*, 41. The same passage appears in *MNA*, 13. As a careful reading of this passage makes clear, Heschel moves between describing the source of amazement as ontological ("all of reality") and describing it as epistemological ("amazed at the ability to see"). Compare further the characterization of amazement in *MNA*, 12 (ontology) with the one in *MNA*, 14 (epistemology). I think it is fair to say that for Heschel, the ontological version is primary. In any case, the two are so intertwined for him that he is likely unconscious of the linguistic slippage.

22. *GSM*, 107. Cf. the following: "What fills us with radical amazement is . . . the fact that even the minimum of perception is a maximum of enigma. The most incomprehensible fact is the fact that we comprehend at all" (47).

23. And yet cf.: "Doubts may be resolved, radical amazement can never be erased" (*MNA*, 13). In this passage again, Heschel seems to use radical amazement as a synonym for wonder.

24. *GSM*, 45. Although Heschel writes "approximate cause," he clearly intends "proximate cause." An interesting partial parallel: Martin Buber describes "the concept of miracle which is permissible from the historical approach" as an "abiding astonishment." Both the philosopher

and the religious person begin with a sense of "wonder at the phenomenon," but whereas the former "neutralizes his wonder" through explanation, the latter "abides in that wonder; no knowledge, no cognition, can weaken his astonishment. Any causal explanation only deepens the wonder for him." See Buber, *Moses*, 75. Of course, Buber's focus is on events in history, whereas Heschel's here is on "the fact that there are facts at all." But the centrality of abiding wonder to religious thought and experience is a shared emphasis of both thinkers.

25. *GSM*, 46. Cf.: "Wonder lasts forever" (*MNA*, 12).

26. *MNA*, 30. And cf. *MNA*, 72. Heschel would no doubt have been appalled by Richard Dawkins's insistence that while "the mystic is content to bask in the wonder and revel in a mystery that we were not meant to understand[,] the scientist feels the same wonder but is restless, not content; recognizes the mystery as profound, then adds, 'But we're working on it.'" Cf. Dawkins, *Unweaving the Rainbow*, 17. Dawkins at once caricatures the mystic—as if the endurance of wonder depended on ignorance—and unself-consciously portrays the scientist as hopelessly self-satisfied. Cf. Heschel's rather tart comments about "writers of popular science books" and "interpreters of science to the laymen," in *GSM*, 43.

27. *GSM*, 51.

28. Such theologies, it hardly needs mentioning, offer fool's gold. Over time, as the gaps in scientific understanding are closed, the plausibility of belief in God fades accordingly. This, of course, often sends believers in search of new gaps in scientific understanding, real or imagined. As Denys Turner puts it, "If you think you have to find a place for God somewhere in the universe, then you are going to have to expel a usurping occupant somewhere from it." See Turner, *Faith Seeking*, 8.

29. *GSM*, 92. Cf., for example, *MNA*, 107.

30. "Why are there essents rather than nothing at all?" It is with this question that Heidegger famously opens *An Introduction to Metaphysics*. Of course, for Heidegger, this question does not necessarily lead to God, much less already contain an awareness of God within it.

31. *MNA*, 12. Cf. also *MNA*, 30, 58. In a similar vein, Nicholas Lash writes: "The world does not tell us that it was created. But the world does leave us with a question: how come *anything*? What is this all *about*? It is a question which we seek to formulate when we are moved to wonder by the sheer fact of the world's existence." Lash's formulation is more cognitive-conceptual than Heschel's more immediate intuitive sense, but the thrust of their positions is the same. See Lash, *Holiness, Speech, and Silence*, 87.

Denys Turner interestingly contends that the real debate between the (sophisticated) theist and the (sophisticated) atheist is about the very legitimacy of this "why" question (*Faith Seeking*, 19). In the face of Bertrand Russell's well-known insistence that the world is "just there, that's all," Turner maintains: "I do not see why . . . you cannot ask not alone of this or that, or of this or that kind of thing, why it exists, but why anything at all should exist rather than nothing" (13). The theist, then, is one who is willing to ask why "once too often," even as he realizes that "there is no intellectual possibility of understanding an answer" (20).

For a recent non-theistic treatment of the question and its philosophical status, see Rundle, *Why There Is Something Rather Than Nothing*.

32. Turner, *Faith Seeking*, 15. I should clarify that I am appealing to Turner to help draw out Heschel's approach to wonder; I make no claim that their positions are completely overlapping. In general, Heschel is more focused than Turner on immediate awareness and intuition,

and is also more open to the possibility that the sense of wonder already contains within it, as we shall see, a great deal of (purportedly pre-conceptual) content.

33. Turner, *Faith Seeking*, 21. It will be fruitful to keep this in mind when we explore the connection in Heschel between wonder, on the one hand, and gratitude and indebtedness, on the other, later in the chapter.

34. *MNA*, 70. Cf. *GSM*, 99.

35. *GSM*, 39. Cf.: "The reaction to sublime objects . . . [is] wonder and amazement" (41).

36. *GSM*, 39. In other words, for Heschel, the sublime is not so much an esthetic category as a theological (or pre-theological) one.

37. The world is, according to Heschel, "replete with indicativeness" of that which surpasses it; indeed, the universe is itself "an immense allusion." *MNA*, 107.

38. *GSM*, 40.

39. *GSM*, 41.

40. *GSM*, 46.

41. "The beginning of awe is wonder" (*GSM*, 74).

42. *GSM*, 74.

43. At times Heschel speaks as if wonder and awe are synonyms: "Awe," he writes on one occasion, "is the sense of wonder and humility inspired by the sublime or felt in the presence of mystery" (*GSM*, 77). More consistently, he could have stated that awe is the maturation or ripening of the sense of wonder and humility inspired by the sublime or felt in the presence of mystery.

44. *GSM*, 75. Cf. 106.

45. *GSM*, 54.

46. *GSM*, 56.

47. *GSM*, 57. Cf. *MNA*, 27.

48. *MNA*, 64. Similarly, Heschel writes, "The ineffable is something with which we are confronted everywhere and at all times" (*MNA*, 14).

49. *MNA*, 20. We shall return to Heschel's response to subjectivist inter-

pretations of religious language at length below.

50. *GSM*, 60.

51. *GSM*, 62.

52. *GSM*, 61.

53. See, most eloquently, *MNA*, 130.

54. *GSM*, 66.

55. *GSM*, 66.

56. *GSM*, 66. Cf. the following: "Israel was taught how to accost Him who is beyond the mystery.... Out of the darkness comes a voice disclosing that the ultimate mystery is not an enigma but the God of mercy; that the Creator of all is the 'Father in Heaven'" (353).

57. As we shall see, Heschel's protestations notwithstanding, his intuition may in fact be *derived* from biblical thinking, rather than merely *reflecting* it.

58. *GSM*, 91.

59. *GSM*, 91.

60. *GSM*, 90.

61. *GSM*, 91.

62. At one point, Heschel writes simply that "one must not confound biblical theology with the mystical view that God is all, and all is God." *Prophets*, I, 168. Cf. also Heschel's insistence that the Baal Shem Tov, too, was far from pantheistic. *KGE*, 22–23. And yet there are a few scattered passages in Heschel's writings in which he can sound panentheistic, as when he writes, for example, that God is "not a being, but being in and beyond all beings" (*MNA*, 78), or when he asserts that "God means: *Togetherness of all beings in holy otherness*" (*MNA*, 109). Cf. also *Prophets*, II, 267. And, indeed, some scholars have categorized Heschel's thought as a form of panentheism. Cf., for example, Rothschild, "Introduction,"17; Friedman, "Divine Need and Human Wonder," 69; Jaeger, "Abraham Heschel and the Theology of Jürgen Moltmann," 173; and, most recently, Even-Chen and Meir, *Between Heschel and Buber*, 88. But as John Merkle has convincingly demon-

strated, such interpretations of Heschel are based on misreadings of the passages in question, and they cut against the overwhelming thrust of Heschel's entire theological oeuvre. The world is, according to Heschel, not an emanation but a creation, and thus *created being is not a part of God*. Perhaps the most definitive statement in Heschel is this one: "The Torah and the world are God's possessions. The world is His, but He is not His world." "God, Torah, and Israel," in *MGSA*, 199. Or again: "God is not all in all. He is in all beings but He is *not* all beings" (*MNA*, 148). To be fair, all Rothschild seems to mean by his use of the term is that in Heschel's thought, God's glory is "ubiquitously sensed in and behind all things" (16). But as Merkle rightly notes, although this is an accurate description of Heschel's view, it is not what panentheism means—a panentheist would not simply see God's presence everywhere, but would see all things as a part of God; affirming the immanence of God is not panentheism, and it is thus a "misleading" term to apply to Heschel's thought. Merkle, "Heschel's Monotheism vis-à-vis Pantheism and Panentheism," 26–33. For Merkle's comments about Rothschild, cf. 30.

63. *GSM*, 94. In personal correspondence, Paul Capetz expresses surprise at Heschel's contention that God is only "accidentally immanent"; would it not be more in line with traditional Jewish theology to claim that God is "both perfectly transcendent and perfectly immanent" (9/26/10)? I suspect that the polemical context is determinative here: in arguing against pantheism, Heschel dilates upon God's transcendence—which is precisely what pantheism loses sight of. In another context, one in which Heschel was focused on God's pathos and His perpetual pursuit of man, for example, it is unlikely that he would have spoken of God's immanence as only "accidental."

Perhaps anticipating (and rejecting) some later neo-pagan and eco-theological trends, Heschel writes: "To the Greeks as to many other peoples, the earth is generally known as Mother Earth.... Such a concept is alien to the Biblical man. He recognizes only one parent: God as his father. The earth is his sister rather than his mother. Man and earth are equally the creations of God" (*MNA*, 92). For this reason, Heschel tells us, biblical theology insists that human beings stand together with all things in a "fellowship of praise" (91). To Judaism, then, the desanctification of nature need not entail alienation from it. On the contrary, "the adoration of nature is as absurd as the alienation from nature is unnecessary" (90).

64. *GSM*, 97. According to Heschel, pantheism is not just a false metaphysical doctrine, but also a worldview that can only lead to despair: "He who accepts this world as the ultimate reality will, if his mind is realistic and his heart sensitive to suffering, tend to doubt that the good is either the origin or the ultimate goal of history" (376). And cf. the discussions in *MNA*, 106, 113, 115–117, 148.

65. *GSM*, 97, 98, 99. For a brief analysis of how this verse serves as a "refrain" in these pages of *GSM*, see Marmur, "Heschel's Rhetoric of Citation," 57–58.

66. In light of all this, it is difficult to make sense of Alexander Even-Chen's suggestion that "[Paul] Tillich emphasizes the transcendent nature of God, whereas Heschel focuses upon God's immanence." Even-Chen, "Faith and the Courage to Be," 341. It is problematic, to say the least, to characterize a thinker who speaks on countless occasions of the world as a vast allusion to the transcendent God, and who contends, as we have just seen, that God is "essentially transcendent and only accidentally immanent," as focused on divine immanence. Compare also Heschel's simple declaration that God's

"essence is transcendent" (*MNA*, 150). Even-Chen's reading of Tillich also needs a great deal of nuancing (strangely, he draws his conclusion based on only one line in Tillich). The latter's idea of God is notoriously elusive, so much so that while one critic can argue that Tillich's "overall picture" is of a "remote, transcendent God," others can speak of the "nearly total immanence" of Tillich's God. Compare Feinberg, *No One Like Him: The Doctrine of God*, 120, with Grenz and Olsen, *20th-Century Theology: God and the World in a Transitional Age*, 125. It is perhaps worth noting, in this context, that some have gone so far as to peg Tillich unequivocally as a pantheist. Cf. Hook, "The Atheism of Paul Tillich," 60. For Hook, this is tantamount to atheism (which, from his perspective, is a compliment). Of Tillich's definition of God as being-itself, Hook wryly notes, "In this sense Tillich's God is like the God of Spinoza and the God of Hegel. Both Spinoza and Hegel were denounced for their atheism by the theologians of the past, because their God was not a Being or an Entity. Tillich, however, is one of the foremost theologians of our time" (62).

67. *GSM*, 82. Heschel suggests that the "glory" (*kavod*) in biblical thinking is equivalent to the *Shechinah* (or indwelling presence) in rabbinic.

68. *GSM*, 84.

69. Habakuk 2:14 and *GSM*, 84.

70. *GSM*, 84.

71. *GSM*, 85.

72. *GSM*, 112.

73. *GSM*, 112. Cf. *GSM*, 162: "Religion begins with a consciousness that something is asked of us." Cf. also, for example, *MNA*, 68–69, 76, 98, 215.

74. *MNA*, 72.

75. *GSM*, 112, 162.

76. *GSM*, 112. Cf., for example, *MNA*, 68. Cf. also *MNA*, 175, 223.

77. *GSM*, 112. Cf. also *MNA*, 69.

78. *MNA*, 69. Heschel adds, "To a noble person it is a holy joy to remember, an overwhelming thrill to be grateful; while to a person whose character is neither rich nor strong, gratitude is a most painful sensation" (*MNA*, 162).

79. *GSM*, 112.

80. *MNA*, 39. The inextricability of wonder and indebtedness, for Heschel, is also evident in the following: "Perhaps this is the essence of human misery: to forget that life is a gift as well as a trust. 'How can I repay unto the Lord all His bountiful dealings toward me?' How to answer the mystery that surrounds us, the ineffable that calls on our souls? This is, indeed, the universal theme of religion. The world is full of wonder. Who will answer?" (*GSM*, 352).

In exploring the meaning of piety, Heschel beautifully distinguishes between a "possession" and a "gift." Whereas the former suggests "self-excommunication and loneliness," the latter suggests connection and relatedness: "In receiving a gift the recipient obtains, besides the present, also the love of the giver. A gift is thus the vessel that contains the affection, which is destroyed as soon as the recipient begins to look on it as a possession" (*MNA*, 291).

81. *WM*, 108.

82. *WM*, 118, 108.

83. *WM*, 108.

84. *MNA*, 36, and throughout Heschel's writings. Cf. esp. *GSM*, 105.

85. *MNA*, 39.

86. *MNA*, 38.

87. *MNA*, 39.

88. *MNA*, 65. Heschel here evokes a kind of mysticism wherein human beings attain communion with the universe and what is in it; together, humanity and nature praise God (cf. *MNA*, 74). It should be emphasized here that for Heschel, union with nature (and with humanity, for that matter) is decidedly not union with God. On the contrary, according to

Heschel, we unite with nature in order to praise our mutual creator. As I show at length in chapter 6, Heschel unambiguously rejects the notion of full mystical union with God.

89. *GSM*, 397.

90. *MNA*, 146. Cf. 224.

91. Indeed, according to Heschel, there is an innate urge in human beings to serve that which is greater than they: "As surely as we are driven to live, we are driven to serve spiritual ends that surpass our own interests" (*GSM*, 291).

92. *GSM*, 107, 409. It is worth emphasizing that Heschel's belief in humanity's capacity for self-transcendence does not lead him to paint a roseate picture of human nature. Far from it: he expressly repudiates Schopenhauer's contention that the Hebrew spirit is optimistic, going so far as to suggest that "there is one line that expresses the mood of the Jewish man throughout the ages: 'The Earth is given into the hand of the wicked.'" See Heschel, "The Concept of Man in Jewish Thought," 130–132 and 144n57. Heschel argues further there that "the tragic tension in the life of piety" is rooted in the realization that despite "the demand to serve God in purity, selflessly . . . the regard for the ego permeates all our thinking. Is it ever possible to disentangle oneself from the intricate plexus of self-interests?" (136).

93. *GSM*, 107.

94. *GSM*, 98, 162. Fritz Rothschild writes that for Heschel the experience of the ineffable "shatters man's solipsistic pretensions and [thereby] opens his soul to an attitude in which the question of God can be raised." Rothschild, "Introduction," 14.

95. *GSM*, 153.

96. *GSM*, 111.

97. *GSM*, 43.

98. Notice also how Heschel links indifference and self-assertion as contrasts to awe in *GSM*, 111.

99. *GSM*, 111.

100. *MNA,* 138.

101. *MNA,* 211.

102. *MNA,* 137.

103. *MNA,* 138. Emphasis mine.

104. *GSM,* 399.

105. *MNA,* 142.

106. *MNA,* 226.

107. *MNA,* 213. Compare this last image with Heschel's discussion of self-transcendence in prayer, in *MQ,* 7. "Eliminating self-regard" is uncharacteristically strong language for Heschel; we might expect him to speak of subduing self-regard rather than eliminating it.

108. *MNA,* 46–47. Cf. *WM,* 30.

109. *MNA,* 47. Cf. 70.

110. *MNA,* 47. Here Heschel sounds like the Jesuit theologian Karl Rahner. Cf. the discussion of Heschel and Rahner below, in chapter 2.

111. *MNA,* 48.

112. *MNA,* 47.

113. *MNA,* 48. Cf. *WM,* 48.

114. *MNA,* 48.

115. *MNA,* 48–49.

116. *MNA,* 128. Cf.: "The primary topic . . . of Biblical thinking is not man's knowledge of God but rather man's being known by God, man's being an object of Divine knowledge and concern" (Heschel, "Concept of Man," 110–111). Cf. *GSM,* 84. In reviewing Heschel's study of *The Prophets* when it was first published, Maurice Friedman rightly noted that there was an unresolved tension in Heschel's thought (Friedman labeled it an "unworked-through unclarity") between one mode in which "the primary factor [in the divine-human encounter] is our being seen and known by Him" (*Prophets,* II, 268), and another mode in which what is primary is the "dialogical structure of the prophetic relationship." Friedman, "The Prophetic Experience," 121. Compare Heschel's assertion, on the one hand, that the prophetic experience is characterized by a "subject-subject structure" (*Prophets,* II, 146), with his insistence, on the other,

that prayer is not a dialogue with God: "We do not communicate with God. We only make ourselves communicable to Him" (*MQ,* 10).

117. *MNA,* 128–129. In a similar vein, Merold Westphal writes (with obvious Levinasian inflection): "In prayer, it is the voice of the One whose face we do not see that 'shatters' my cogito, and thereby my I doubt, I understand, I affirm, I deny, I will, I refuse, I imagine, and I feel. These are no longer the origin of either me or my world; and, since they are not its Alpha, they have no right to be its Omega either." Westphal, "Prayer as the Posture of the Decentered Self," 19.

118. *GSM,* 160.

119. *GSM,* 133, 132.

120. *MNA,* 85.

121. Bondi, *Ayekah?,* 6.

122. *GSM,* 98.

123. *GSM,* 36.

124. *GSM,* 34.

125. *MNA,* 77. Cf. 126. In a recent essay, philosopher David Owens speaks of this cultural change in almost breathless terms: "Weber speaks of a tension," he writes, "but for many, science's disenchantment of the world is instead a liberation. Science empowers us; *it gets us what we want.* . . . The scientific picture of the world leaves out much that used to prevent us from doing what we want. It excludes from reality all sorts of imaginary beings, forces, and powers that used to constrain us. Once these mind-forged manacles are broken, we can take advantage of the technology science provides." Given that we now know that our bodies are mere machines, he writes, "we can treat [them] just as we would our car or our house." Perhaps tellingly, he begins to express some ambivalence when he turns to consider the disenchantment of the human mind. Owens, "Disenchantment," 165, 170.

126. *GSM,* 36.

127. *GSM,* 78.

128. *MNA*, 183.

129. *GSM*, 369. "A civilization that is devoted exclusively to the utilitarian," Heschel writes, "is at bottom not different from barbarism" (*EL*, 55).

130. *GSM*, 46. Interesting parallels can be drawn between Heschel's worries about modern man and his self-enclosure, and Buber's concerns about the growth of what he famously called "the it-world." "However the history of the individual and that of the human race may diverge in other respects," Buber writes, "they agree in this at least: both signify a progressive increase of the It-world" (87). Indeed, according to Buber, the more human beings learn to "experience and use," the weaker becomes their capacity to "relate," and thus to "live in the spirit" (89). A human being who focuses on experience and use, Buber terms an "ego"—("Egos appear by setting themselves apart from other egos")—whereas one who lives in relation, he calls a "person" ("Persons appear by entering into relation with other persons") (111–112ff.). For Buber, then, the problem of modernity is that human beings are increasingly "dominated by the ego," perilously preoccupied with use rather than relation. Page numbers are from Buber, *I and Thou*.

131. *WM*, 101.

132. *WM*, 110.

133. See, for example, "The Meaning of This Hour," in *MQ*, 150. In *The Sabbath*, Heschel argues that the seventh day is about "surpassing civilization" by stepping back from our imprisonment to technology. The Sabbath is, he writes, "a day on which we stop worshipping the idols of technical civilization. . . . We live, as it were, *independent of technical civilization*" (28). Heschel associates technology with space, and the Sabbath, of course, with time. Thus, the latter can serve as a corrective to the excesses of a culture that glorifies the former (3, and elsewhere). Heschel

is, to be clear, no Luddite: "The solution of mankind's most vexing problem will not be found in renouncing technical civilization, but in attaining some degree of independence of it" (28).

134. *MNA*, 189. Cf. 285. "Selling himself into slavery to things, man becomes a utensil that is broken at the fountain [of profit]" (*The Sabbath*, 3).

135. *WM*, 88.

136. *GSM*, 349. The same sentence appears in *MQ*, 104.

137. *MNA*, 77.

138. *MNA*, 83.

139. *MNA*, 92.

140. *GSM*, 350. Cf. *MNA*, 233–234. For an important Christian critique of attempts to put God and religion in the service of human needs, cf. Gustafson, *Ethics from a Theocentric Perspective*, 16–25. I am grateful to Paul Capetz for the reference.

141. *GSM*, 36.

142. *GSM*, 372.

143. *MNA*, 211.

144. *MNA*, 185.

145. *GSM*, 111. "Religion," Heschel writes, "consists of God's question and man's answer" (137).

146. *EL*, 107.

147. *GSM*, 369. Cf., more expansively, 369–372. At one point, Heschel goes so far as to query God: "Why dost Thou permit faith to blend so easily with bigotry, arrogance, cruelty, folly and superstition?" (*GSM*, 155).

148. *MNA*, 160.

149. Heschel, "On Prayer," *MGSA*, 262.

150. As noted in the Introduction (note 84), one can be permitted to wonder whether the passage of time would have chastened Heschel in his insistence on religion's unique capacity to "ventilate" and "soothe" what is darkest in humanity. At a time when America's primary enemy was "godless Communism," such faith and rhetoric made sense; at a time when its primary enemy is radical Islam, one can

speculate whether Heschel would have paid more sustained attention to religion's capacity to stoke the embers of man's cruelty rather than extinguish them.

151. Or, perhaps less clumsily, "resource"—the German is *Bestand*. Heidegger, "The Question Concerning Technology," 322.

152. Polt, *Heidegger: An Introduction*, 171.

153. Heidegger, *Discourse on Thinking*, 50.

154. Heidegger, "Technology," 321.

155. Heidegger, "Technology," 322.

156. Heidegger, "Technology," 333.

157. Cf., for example, the discussion in Rubenstein, *Strange Wonder*, 17ff.

158. Dreyfus, "Heidegger on the Connection Between Nihilism, Art, Technology, and Politics," 36off.

159. Heidegger, *Discourse on Thinking*, 56.

160. Heidegger, "Technology," 332–333.

161. Pattison, *Routledge Philosophy Guidebook to the Later Heidegger*, 56.

162. Heidegger, "Technology," 332.

163. With Heidegger obviously in his sights, Heschel writes, "A major difference between ontological and biblical thinking is that the first seeks to relate the human being to a transcendence called being as such, whereas the second, realizing that human being is more than being, that human being is living being, seeks to relate man to divine living, to a transcendence called the living God" (*WM*, 69). Moreover, he avers that "whereas ontology asks about *being as being*, theology asks about *being as creation*, about being as a divine act" (71). Accordingly, humanity's search for meaning leads it not to being as such, but rather to "what is beyond, over, and above being" (71–72). The ultimate human problem, Heschel tells us, is "not being but living.... Human living is being-challenged-in-the-world, not simply

being-in-the-world" (68, 105). In general, as Shaul Magid has pointed out in private conversation, a comprehensive study of *WM* as a Heschelian response to Heideggerian ontology is a desideratum. Cf. his very brief comments in Magid, "The Role of the Secular in Abraham Joshua Heschel's Theology," 151. In a similar vein, Heschel contrasts pagan and prophetic experience, arguing that for the former, "existence is experiencing being," whereas for the latter, it is "experiencing concern. It is living in perpetual awareness of being perceived, apprehended, noted by God, of being an object of the divine subject" (*Prophets*, II, 263).

164. Connell, "Against Idolatry," 154.

165. Caputo, "People of God, People of Being," 99.

166. Macquarrie, *Heidegger and Christianity*, 70.

167. Westphal, "Onto-theology, Metanarrative," 145.

168. Heidegger, *Identity and Difference*, 56.

169. Westphal, "Onto-theology, Metanarrative," 147.

170. Heidegger, *Identity and Difference*, 72.

171. Compare Heschel's observation that "God cannot be sensed as a second thought, as an explanation of the origin of the universe. He is either the first and the last, or just another concept" (*GSM*, 120).

172. Westphal, "Overcoming Onto-Theology," 148.

173. Westphal, "Overcoming Onto-Theology," 148.

174. Westphal, "Onto-Theology, Metanarrative," 146.

175. Westphal, "Overcoming Onto-Theology," 152.

176. George Connell convincingly argues, borrowing language from Nietzsche's *Beyond Good and Evil*, that although Heidegger encourages the "religious instinct" in the realms of both thought

and emotion, he nevertheless consistently refuses "theistic satisfaction" ("Against Idolatry," 144). He "stimulate[s] a religious itch," Connell writes, but "forbid[s] one to scratch it" (152). This refusal of theistic satisfaction is rooted in Heidegger's insistence that the question of Being remains precisely that—a question. To posit an answer is effectively to liquidate the question. And it is precisely in the anxiety provoked by the question that Being shows itself (162). Thus, while Westphal (like Heschel) rejects onto-theology in the name of non-idolatrous worship of the biblical God, Heidegger rejects onto-theology in the name of an awareness of Being.

177. Although, again, Heidegger's broader worldview might well necessitate exactly that. See previous note. In other words, no matter how consistently Westphal (and Heschel) highlights the sense of mystery that is constitutive of biblical faith, Heidegger would likely insist that any theism—even faith in the God of Israel—ends up occluding, or diluting, the fullness of the mystery of being. But neither Westphal nor Heschel, I suspect, would be particularly exercised by Heidegger's demurral from their broader worldview; they would be more interested in how his dismissal of onto-theology can be employed to ground an abandonment of the metaphysical god and a return to what they see as authentic biblical monotheism.

178. See the extended discussion in chapter 4 below.

179. MNA, 152,

180. Nussbaum, Upheavals of Thought, 54.

181. Nussbaum, Upheavals of Thought, 55, 53.

182. Fuller, From Wonder, 12. Wonder, Fuller writes, "gives us a vision of our relatedness to the world, to other human beings, and to the ultimate source from which existence emerges."

183. Fuller, From Wonder, 15.

184. Fuller, From Wonder, 99.

185. Fuller, From Wonder, 106.

186. See, e.g., Fuller, From Wonder, 101, 157. And compare Nussbaum's insistence that the young child is prepared by "early wonder" to "have concern about people outside of herself," and thus to avoid the "pathological narcissism" that refuses "to ascribe reality to others," let alone to encounter them with compassion and empathy (Nussbaum, Upheavals of Thought, 427). And cf. 321.

187. Fuller, From Wonder, 106

188. Fuller, From Wonder, 133.

189. Fuller, From Wonder, 15. Cf. 133, where Fuller suggests that wonder tends to "produce belief in the presence and causal relevance of some reality that lies beyond profane reality."

190. Fuller, From Wonder, viii.

191. MNA, 41.

192. MNA, 61.

193. GSM, 74.

194. MNA, 73, and GSM, 153. For an introductory survey of Western philosophy on the question of whether faith can be willed, see Pojman, Religious Belief and the Will.

195. GSM, 120, and MNA, 74. Cf. also GSM, 153, where Heschel tells us that "faith is preceded by awe, by acts of amazement at things that we apprehend but cannot comprehend" (emphasis mine).

196. GSM, 46.

197. A genealogical note: Moshe Waldoks and Arthur Green have rightly noted that some of the central themes of part I of GSM are found in germinal form in the works of the poet and mystic Hillel Zeitlin, whom Heschel knew in Warsaw, particularly in Zeitlin's Be-Hevyon HaNeshamah (1913). There, Zeitlin offers the outlines of a phenomenology of religion, focused on the experiences of wonder (Pele) and amazement (Hishtommemut). Waldoks writes that "Heschel's academic training allowed him to de-

velop in a more systematic fashion, many themes begun by Zeitlin. While Heschel never acknowledged his debt to Zeitlin, their shared emphasis on the centrality of wonder and amazement as religious categories is remarkable." See Waldoks, *Hillel Zeitlin*, 282n195. Cf. 313n89, and 209–251, and especially 241–243. Green, in turn, characterizes Zeitlin's work as "the *Vorlage* of Heschel's grand introduction to *God in Search of Man*," and he astutely notes that for Zeitlin, as for Heschel, "amazement is the human emotion that allows us to be open to the divine presence or revelation." Now, to be sure, Green recognizes that Heschel's treatment of these themes is far more developed than Zeitlin's, but he nevertheless argues that "the thrust of Heschel's presentation remains an expansion of Zeitlin's: it is only by cultivating an openness to the human emotions associated with wonder, awe, and amazement that we will be able to comprehend and appreciate the religious claim for revelation." See Green, "Three Warsaw Mystics," 33.

Waldoks's and Green's broader point about Zeitlin's impact on Heschel is well taken, but I think crucial differences between the two should be noted as well. Zeitlin's work, for example, does not really explore the question of how wonder and amazement serve to open the human being to the possibility of revelation. But more important, I would argue that Zeitlin's notion of amazement differs in fundamental ways from Heschel's: whereas the former's is tied to a sense of despair—the innermost core of religion is born, for Zeitlin *de profundis*—the latter's is connected much more to a sense of seemingly delighted surprise, and to a sense of indebtedness to the Author of life. In other words, although there are moments when Heschel describes religion as emerging from loneliness and even desperation, the overall thrust of part I of *GSM* is far more positive and optimistic

than that of Zeitlin's essay; the latter's religious sense is much more closely associated with a sense of terror, and a kind of existential anguish, than anything we find in Heschel. I would also suggest, incidentally, that Heschel's notion of amazement is, in fact, *less* complex and developed than Zeitlin's. For Heschel, as we have seen, amazement is a form of intensified wonder; for Zeitlin, in contrast, it is a multi-dimensional emotion comprised of "wonder . . . fright . . . trembling . . . humility . . . self-abnegation . . . [and] vast love" (Zeitlin, *Be-Hevyon HaNeshamah*, 25). It is also worth noting, in anticipation of our discussion in chapter 6 below, that Heschel does not share—indeed, I will suggest that he actively rejects—the monistic temptation that so drew Zeitlin throughout his career, and to which he makes explicit, if only passing, reference in the essay in question. In awe (*yirʾah*), Zeitlin writes, "the drop is absorbed in the sea, the ray is gathered into the sun, the person is extinguished—and is no longer" (39).

198. *GSM*, 108. Cf.: "The categories of religious thinking . . . are unique and represent a way of thinking on a level that is deeper than the level of concepts, utterances, symbols. It is immediate, ineffable, metasymbolic" (103).

199. *MNA*, 62.

200. *GSM*, 131, 138.

201. *GSM*, 115.

202. See, similarly, Even-Chen, *Kol min ha-ʾarafel*, 17.

203. *GSM*, 106. The same sentence appears in *MNA*, 22.

204. *GSM*, 115.

205. Arthur Cohen dismisses this phrase as "perplexing" and as an example of "purposeful obscurity," since "certainty presumes the presence of some form of knowledge. The knowledge may not be discursive or even translatable from non-discursive into rational language, but it is knowledge, whatever its

privacy and incommunicability." See Cohen, *The Natural and Supernatural Jew*, 240n11. Whether or not it is a successful formulation, I think what Heschel intends by "certainty without knowledge" is the affirmation that one is confident that something is true, all the while knowing that it cannot be justified in conventional epistemological terms. As he writes in *MNA*, "The issue that emerges before us is not whether there is a God, but whether we know that there is a God; not whether He exists, but whether we are intelligent enough to advance adequate reasons for affirming it. The problem is: How do we tell it to our minds?" (71). What is at question, in other words, is not our certainty, but our epistemological standing.

206. Heschel writes: "Silence is preferable to speech. *Words are not indispensable to cognition.* They are only necessary when we wish to communicate our ideas to others or to prove to them that we have attained cognition" (*GSM*, 123; emphasis mine). Or again: "Intuition and expression must not be equated. Thought contains elements that cannot be reduced to verbal expression and are beyond the level of verbalization" (124n1).

207. *MNA*, 133.

208. *Prophets*, II, 1–2. Likewise, in articulating his critique of the medieval philosophical project of integrating faith and reason, Heschel notes that faith's "certainty is intuitive, not speculative," and adds, "Not all that is evident is capable of being demonstrated." Heschel, "Reason and Revelation," 407, 408.

209. In general, it appears that Heschel uses the terms "insight" and "intuition" more or less interchangeably.

In considering Heschel's idea of intuitive knowledge, Gordon Tucker makes the suggestive association to "Spinoza's tantalizing notion of a third kind of knowledge, which he called *scientia intuitiva,* and which he described as being

superior to that of both sense perception and reason." See Tucker, "A. J. Heschel and the Problem of Religious Certainty," 128.

210. *GSM*, 120–121. The third paragraph also appears in *MNA*, 84–85. Cf. *GSM*, 131. And cf. also *MNA*, 19, 43, 62–63, 67–68, 72, 73, 75, 83, 84–85, 98, 133, 171. Cf. also *Prophets*, II, 3.

211. *GSM*, 148.

212. *GSM*, 121.

213. Arthur Cohen rightly notes that Heschel's argument here seems to presuppose that "certainty is given with experience, [that] truth is correlative to the depth, intensity, and inexpressible mystery of experience" (Cohen, *The Natural and Supernatural Jew*, 246).

214. Carl Jung helpfully expresses both the epistemological anxiety and the subjective confidence of many believers thus: "That religious experiences exist no longer needs proof. But it will always remain doubtful whether what metaphysics and theology call God and the gods is the real ground of these experiences. The question is idle, actually, and answers itself by reason of the subjectively overwhelming numinosity of the experience. Anyone who has had it is *seized* by it and therefore not in a position to indulge in fruitless metaphysical or epistemological speculations. Absolute certainty brings its own evidence and has no need of anthropomorphic proofs." Jung, "The Undiscovered Self (Present and Future)," 392.

215. *MNA*, 27. Throwing all epistemological caution to the wind, Heschel writes: "The reality of the ineffable is, as we have shown [!], beyond dispute. The imperative of awe is its certificate of evidence, a universal certificate which we all witness" (*MNA*, 63). Of course, whether an experience can ever constitute "evidence" for its own veracity is, to say the least, open to question. It will not do simply to assert that it can, and does.

216. *MQ,* 95.

217. *GSM,* 116.

218. *MNA,* 19.

219. *MNA,* 62.

220. *MNA,* 21.

221. *MNA,* 98.

222. *MNA,* 165.

223. *MNA,* 78–79.

224. *MNA,* 81.

225. *GSM,* 119.

226. Fackenheim, review of *Man Is Not Alone,* 86.

227. Cohen, *The Natural and The Supernatural Jew,* 252.

228. "The Biblical View of Reality," in *MGSA,* 365.

229. "On Prayer," MGSA, 267.

230. Fogelin, *Figuratively Speaking,* 17.

231. *MNA.* 107.

232. *GSM,* 39.

233. Erlewine, "Rediscovering Heschel," 174–194, esp. 181–189.

234. Taylor, *A Secular Age,* 36.

235. Taylor, *A Secular Age,* 38.

236. Erlewine, "Rediscovering Heschel," 183.

237. Erlewine, "Rediscovering Heschel," 184, 185. Though I agree with Erlewine's contention that Heschel ultimately wants to subvert the assumptions of the buffered, sovereign self, I am not sure he takes Heschel's own ambivalences seriously enough. What makes *MNA,* for example, so complicated to interpret is that Heschel does not just simply reject modern epistemology and its pretensions out of hand, but instead gestures toward it again and again (and again), only to become irritated by it each time. The reader can thus quite reasonably be left puzzled by just what Heschel is up to in the text: is he repudiating the assumptions of modern philosophy or attempting to engage them?

238. *GSM,* 170.

239. *PT,* 300.

240. *IEE,* 112.

241. *IF,* 218.

242. *PT,* 228. Heschel attributes this diagnosis of society to Menahem Mendl of Kotzk, but, given many similar formulations in his own name, it requires no great leap to assume that this one represents his own view as well.

243. Nietzsche, *Human, All Too Human,* #448, 214–215. Italics are mine.

244. Webb, *Re-Figuring Theology,* 97.

245. This is Stephen Webb's formulation, describing Louis Wirth Marvick's discussion of hyperbole in *Mallarmé and the Sublime,* 85–86.

246. Arthur Cohen misfires, I think, when he writes that the goal of Heschel's "rhetoric of belief" is "to shame disbelief into faith." Heschel's prose can indeed come across that way, but I suspect that his intention is less to shame the reader than to startle him, to convince him to consider the possibility, first, that he has had religious experiences and, second, that these experiences may point to a reality beyond him, and beyond the world. To the extent that Heschel's dramatic declarations merely shame the reader as opposed to eliciting greater openness in him, they fail to meet what I think were his own objectives. Cohen also asserts that Heschel's approach is "neither meaningful nor effective"; as a result of Heschel's overheated prose, he contends, "the faithless are confirmed in disbelief." I would guess that this is true for many readers, for the reasons I have indicated above (readers need to share some assumptions with the writer in order for hyperbole to move rather than alienate them), but it seems extreme to assume that such formulations are never effective and always serve only to push readers further away. I suspect that Heschel's most immoderate statements are rarely effective in achieving his goals, but I doubt that they are never effective. Cohen, *The Natural and The Supernatural Jew,* 253.

247. Webb, *Re-Figuring Theology*, 92.

248. *MNA*, 282.

249. "The Biblical View of Reality," *MGSA*, 365.

250. Emil Fackenheim observes trenchantly that "to confuse religious immediacy and theological argument is to fall easy prey to the illusion that the unbeliever lacks faith only because of his own spiritual lethargy." Fackenheim, review of *Man Is Not Alone*, 86.

251. Heschel, "Quest for Certainty," 265.

252. Heschel, "Quest for Certainty," 265-266.

253. Heschel, "Quest for Certainty," 266.

254. Heschel "Reason and Revelation," 404-408.

255. See Dawkins, *Unweaving the Rainbow*, 17.

256. Alexander Even-Chen argues that Heschel readily acknowledges that religious experience is always already culturally conditioned. Where prophecy and revelation are concerned, I suspect Even-Chen is right; as we see in chapter 3, according to Heschel the prophet's personality plays a constitutive role in revelation. But crucially, Even-Chen fails to distinguish between instances of prophecy and revelation, where his claims make sense, and the kind of pre-revelational intuitions being discussed here, where they do not. As I have been at pains to show, Heschel is deeply invested in the possibility of pre-cultural—and therefore universal—religious intuitions. Even-Chen, "Mysticism and Prophecy," 359-370; and Even-Chen, *Akedat Yitshak*, 210-211.

257. Heschel's own persistent contrasting of biblical and Greek thought only buttresses—again, against his own intentions—the suggestion that fundamental perceptions of the world are deeply impacted by cultural location.

258. James, *Varieties*, 422, 424.

259. James, *Varieties*, 422.

260. James, *Varieties*, 427.

261. Tucker, "A. J. Heschel," 129.

262. *MNA*, 81.

263. James, *Varieties*, 379.

264. Tucker, "A. J. Heschel," 133.

265. William Kaufman writes simply: "The problem of a philosophy of Judaism such as Heschel's, which relies so heavily on intuition ... is that there are those who have had contrasting and contradictory intuitions." See Kaufman, *Contemporary Jewish Philosophies*, 171. Although Heschel never explicitly grapples with this important challenge, a plausible case can be made that it is always on his mind. In fact, the insistence—convincing or not—that his intuitions are universal is an attempt precisely to respond to—or override—the objection Kaufman legitimately raises.

266. Fiorenza, "Systematic Theology," 42-43.

267. Fiorenza, "Systematic Theology," 43.

268. Fiorenza, "Systematic Theology," 44. In his enormously influential study of religious experience, Wayne Proudfoot writes: "There is no uninterpreted experience. Our experience is already informed and constituted by our conceptions and tacit theories about ourselves and our world. All observation is theory-laden." Proudfoot, *Religious Experience*, 43.

269. Grenz and Franke, *Beyond Foundationalism*, 48.

270. Grenz and Franke, *Beyond Foundationalism*, 49.

271. A preoccupation with certainty, coupled with an attempt to ground it in a purportedly universal, pre-cultural religious experience, is often associated with what has come to be called liberal religious foundationalism. According to the standard narrative, a variety of modern religious thinkers went searching for an unshakeable foundation for religious

knowledge. While conservatives found it in a supposedly inerrant Bible, liberals found it in universal religious experience. The father of liberal foundationalism, on these accounts, was Friedrich Schleiermacher, who—so the story is usually told—affirmed the reality of just such an experience (or "intuition," or "feeling") and insisted that "all legitimate doctrines were derivable from this foundational experience." Murphy, *Beyond Liberalism and Fundamentalism,* 22. Cf., more broadly, 11–25. And cf. Grenz and Franke, *Beyond Foundationalism.* Given this description, does it make sense to label Heschel a foundationalist of the liberal stripe? If a focus on certainty, combined with an insistence upon universally available pre-cultural experience, is enough to constitute foundationalism, then presumably Heschel could be fit into this conceptual box. But I am not sure how much light this would actually shed on Heschel's project as a thinker. In my estimation, it is less than clear that importing the term foundationalism from the realm of epistemology to the world of theology is all that helpful for understanding the latter. Epistemologists who are called foundationalists—or at least classical foundationalists—attempt to ground all of human knowledge on a bedrock of invincible certainty, insisting that our justified beliefs are structured like a building, with upper stories resting on that firm, certain, indubitable foundation. The trouble is that, as far as I can tell, very few modern theologians actually view religious knowledge that way. (Many Schleiermacher scholars insist that, contrary to the standard picture, even Schleiermacher himself did not hold the view commonly attributed to him.) Heschel, to take the case at hand, does devote a great deal of energy to securing certainty of the reality of God using what are usually considered pages from the foundationalist playbook (viz., universal, pre-conceptual, pre-cultural experience). But he emphatically does not suggest that all Jewish doctrines are "derivable from this foundation." On the contrary, as I will be at paints to show in what follows, he believes that core Jewish ideas about God (divine pathos, most prominently) derive from revelation, not intuition (and not inference from intuition). To state this another way: a variety of religious thinkers who are frequently "accused" of foundationalism (in theological circles, the word foundationalism is most often used as a term of opprobrium by those who consider themselves non- or post-foundationalists) may not in fact be as committed to grounding belief in pre-cultural experience as critics have thought (Schleiermacher and Rahner are crucial examples). And even those who are (like Heschel) simply do not have the kind of systematic epistemological ambitions that the term suggests, let alone a desire to insist that all their key theological ideas are somehow derivable from that initial experience. Conceptually, perhaps, it is important to point out that although a concern with certainty intertwined with an affirmation of pre-cultural experience is often associated with foundationalism, there is no *necessary* link between them. For a particularly influential version of the argument that Schleiermacher was a foundationalist, see Lindbeck, *The Nature of Doctrine.* For an influential rejoinder, see Gerrish, "The Nature of Doctrine," 87–92. For non-foundationalist interpretations of Rahner, see esp. Kilby, *Karl Rahner: Philosophy and Theology,* and Craigo-Snell, *Silence, Love, and Death,* 14–19. In questioning foundationalist readings of Rahner, Kilby and Craigo-Snell had been anticipated, among others, by Kress, *A Rahner Handbook,* 84–85. For fruitful exchanges on foundationalism and theology, I am grateful to Wayne

Proudfoot, John Franke, John Thiel, and Yonatan Brafman.

272. My point, needless to say, is not to blame Heschel for failing to anticipate a philosophical consensus that emerged only after his death. My point is, rather, to ask how Heschel can be interpreted in order for his to remain a viable and compelling voice in contemporary Jewish theology.

273. A note on Heschel's phenomenology: Alexander Even-Chen rightly notes that although Heschel makes use of phenomenological methods, he is decidedly not content to limit himself to phenomenology. After all, Heschel "wants to enable the modern person to re-create the connection between God and humanity," and this means that he cannot ultimately bracket questions about what is or is not objectively real. See Even-Chen, *Kol min ha-ʾarafel*, 10. Cf. 14–17. In a similar vein, John Merkle observes that although Heschel's approach begins in phenomenology, he also moves unabashedly beyond it. See Merkle, *The Genesis of Faith*, 32. I would state this even more starkly: the mature Heschel is, first and last, a religious thinker with normative commitments. Phenomenology is part of his toolkit, but in no way is it his primary commitment. In the introduction to his English-language study of the prophets, Heschel notes that when he first undertook to study the prophets, like a good phenomenologist he had no intention "to pass judgment on the truth of their claim to have received revelation"; his intention, he writes, was "to illumine the prophets' claim; not to explain their consciousness, but to understand it" (*Prophets*, I, xi). But by the time of the English reworking, he writes that "while I still maintain the soundness of the [earlier] method . . . I have long since become wary of impartiality, which is itself a way of being partial. The prophet's existence is either ir-

relevant or relevant. If irrelevant, I cannot truly be involved in it; if relevant, then my impartiality is but a pretense" (xii). Since Heschel is concerned not just with what phenomena "are," but also with what they "mean," he has no choice but "to suspend indifference and be involved" (xii–xiii). Thus, "reflection about the prophets gives way to communion with the prophets."

In the first chapter of *GSM*, Heschel had already spoken of striving for "the depth of insight . . . [made available] in the communion of the self with reality" (*GSM*, 6). He had insisted that "only those will apprehend religion who can probe its depth, who can combine intuition and love with the rigor of method. . . . It is not enough to describe the given content of religious consciousness," and had expressed the confidence that "by penetrating the consciousness of the pious man, we may conceive the reality behind it" (*GSM*, 8). Similarly, in *MNA*, Heschel had urged that "it is not enough to describe the given content of the consciousness of the ineffable." This first task was not ambitious enough. Again, Heschel had been more confident: "While penetrating the consciousness of the ineffable," he had averred, "we may conceive the reality behind it" (*MNA*, 60–61). This confidence may bear the influence of the early Husserl, whose first works had seemed to offer a way beyond Kant's *Critique of Pure Reason* and to restore human access to the divine. Samuel Moyn captures this moment of confidence well when he writes that phenomenology "permitted a sophisticated return to the analysis of religious experience, now not the last stop (and subjectivistic refuge) of theology, but, thanks to the bridge of intentionality that Husserl had thrown from consciousness to reality, as a way station to the objectivity of the divine." Crucially, according to Moyn, "Husserl's phenomenology, far from initially being understood as a stifling prison of consciousness, seemed to unlock the door to the fresh air of the world of objects. . . . Intentionality, from this point of view, undermined the hegemony of the knowing subject and represented an important step toward the acknowledgment of the authority of objects in constituting human experience." Moyn, *Origins of the Other*, 40, 46. Moyn's last sentence is particularly important since, as I have been arguing, Heschel's larger project involves a commitment to self-transcendence and responsiveness. The possibility of responsiveness, of course, depends on escaping from the prison of consciousness; it emerges only in encounter with something real beyond us. Undermining the hegemony of the knowing subject is, as we have seen, part and parcel of Heschel's larger project, in which, as he puts it, our focus moves from knowing to being known. This interpretation of phenomenology is of a piece, then, with Heschel's ethical and theological commitment to privileging "response to a demand" over "self-assertion" (*Prophets*, I, xv).

To recap my analysis: (A) Heschel's commitment to phenomenology is far from absolute—for him, it is a tool, not an encompassing worldview; (B) In light of the ways the early Husserl had been understood, it may be that Heschel thought that his commitment to "communion with the prophets" and his desire to "conceive the reality behind" religious consciousness represented a less-than-absolute rupture with what he believed Husserl himself had made possible. To my mind, B does not lessen the force of A. My interpretation is closer to Even-Chen, *Kol min ha-ʾarafel*,16–17, than to Perlman, *Abraham Heschel's Idea of Revelation*, 45–46, who argues, counterintuitively, for Heschel's debt to the later Husserl, who had taken a neo-Kantian turn and, as it were, reentered the subjectivist prison.

Dror Bondi moves in a similar direction, arguing, intriguingly, that Heschel developed his own unique approach to phenomenology based on attempting to overcome the absolute subject-object dichotomy altogether (*Ayekah?*, 65–79).

274. *GSM*, 140, 132.

275. *GSM*, 138.

276. *GSM*, 132, and *MNA*, 165. At one point Heschel writes that "we cannot be in rapport with the reality of the divine except for rare, fugitive moments" (*MNA*, 169). I would suggest that the only way to make sense of this seemingly uncharacteristic statement is to understand it as referring to these rare moments of illumination and "radical insight," when God's presence and greatness are unambiguously manifest and overwhelming. It should not be taken as contradicting Heschel's pervasive insistence that the more basic, intuitive sense for God remains eternally available.

At one point in *MNA*, Heschel offers a startling portrayal of a shattering, high-voltage experience of God: "A tremor seizes our limbs; our nerves are struck, quiver like strings; our whole being bursts into shudders. But then a cry, wrested from our very core, fills the world around us, as if a mountain were suddenly about to place itself in front of us. It is one word: GOD" (78). But its obvious power notwithstanding, we should be careful not to overemphasize this passage in interpreting Heschel's writings: the description presented here is discontinuous with Heschel's central concern, namely, the more pervasive ("lower-voltage") experience of wonder and its attendant intuitions.

277. *GSM*, 164.

278. *GSM*, 147. Cf. 152: "All Abraham could achieve by his own power was wonder and amazement; the knowledge that there is a living God was given him by God." Cf. Genesis Rabbah 39:1, and

compare Midrash HaGadol to Gen. 11:28, and cf. Maimonides, *Mishneh Torah*, Laws of Idol Worship, 1:3.

279. *GSM*, 128. Cf. 146: "Without God's aid, man cannot find Him. Without man's seeking, His aid is not granted."

280. At one point, Heschel writes: "The sense of wonder, awe, and mystery does not give us a knowledge of God. It only leads to a plane where the question about God becomes an inescapable concern" (*GSM*, 118–119). This formulation is too strong to be consistent with much of what we have seen Heschel say regarding the pre-conceptual knowledge supposedly available through insight and intuition.

281. *GSM*,108. The same sentence appears in *MNA*, 179, with one minor alteration: instead of "the sense of wonder, awe, and mystery" Heschel speaks of "the sense of the ineffable." But the point is very much the same. Cf. also *MNA*, 99–100.

282. "There is . . . no alternative for prophecy, no surrogate for tradition" (*GSM*, 152).

283. *GSM*, 163–164. And cf. *MNA*, 133.

2. THEOLOGICAL METHOD AND RELIGIOUS ANTHROPOLOGY

1. *MNA*, 129. See, similarly: "The Bible is a book about man. It is not a theology from the point of view of man but rather an anthropology from the point of view of God." Heschel, "The Concept of Man in Jewish Thought," 102. Again, contrasting his way of thinking with that of his professors in Berlin, Heschel notes that "to them, religion was a feeling. To me, religion included the insights of the Torah which is a vision of man from the point of view of God" (*MQ*, 95).

2. Barth, *The Word of God and the Word of Man*, 43.

3. This description of the "dominant mode of modern theology" is taken from John Webster, *Barth*, 51.

4. My decision to examine these questions through dialogue with Christian figures as opposed to Jewish ones is at least partly a function of the fact that the former tend to be much more focused on methodology than the latter.

5. Barth, "No!," in Brunner and Barth, *Natural Theology*, 75, 76.

6. Barth, "No!," in Brunner and Barth, *Natural Theology*, 80.

7. Barth, "No!," in Brunner and Barth, *Natural Theology*, 81.

8. John Baillie rightly notes that Barth follows a "tradition of Lutheran christocentrism which made Christ the Mediator no less of knowledge than of salvation." Baillie, *Our Knowledge of God*, 17.

9. Barth, "No!," in Brunner and Barth, *Natural Theology*, 89.

10. Brunner, "Nature and Grace," in Brunner and Barth, *Natural Theology*, 22.

11. Brunner, "Nature and Grace," in Brunner and Barth, *Natural Theology*, 24.

12. Brunner, "Nature and Grace," in Brunner and Barth, *Natural Theology*, 32.

13. Thus, when Brunner says that "the original image of God in man has been destroyed" ("Nature and Grace," in Brunner and Barth, *Natural Theology*, 22), he is referring to the material image. Speaking of the formal image, on the very next page, he writes, "This *function* or calling as a bearer of the image is not only not abolished by sin; rather it is the presupposition of the ability to sin and continues within the state of sin" (23).

14. Brunner, "Nature and Grace," in Brunner and Barth, *Natural Theology*, 31.

15. Brunner, "Nature and Grace," in Brunner and Barth, *Natural Theology*, 31.

16. Brunner, "Nature and Grace," in Brunner and Barth, *Natural Theology*, 32–33.

17. Hart, "A Capacity for Ambiguity?," 298, 304.

18. In understanding Barth's vehemence in responding to Brunner, it is

important to keep in mind the historical context of their exchange. Nineteen
thirty-four was the year of the Barmen
Declaration, an impassioned protest
on the part of the "Confessing Church"
against those Christians who had taken
an accommodationist—or worse, an
actively enthusiastic—stance toward the
Nazis. Barth felt that any compromise at
all between nature and grace, or between
church and state, threatened to devolve
into a legitimation of compromise between Christianity and Nazism. According to Barth, Christianity could not be
integrated with any humanly devised ideology or worldview; it must rather stand
in absolute judgment over them. This was
true for all human philosophies, but all
the more so for Germany's rapidly metastasizing Nazi ideology. Still, the disagreement between Barth and Brunner should
not be reduced *merely* to its context. As
Trevor Hart has pointed out, "It is easy
to see how this specific context served to
exaggerate the issues: but the issues were
already there to be exaggerated." Cf. Hart,
"A Capacity for Ambiguity?," 291.

One additional and perhaps ironic
note about context: James Barr has argued quite interestingly that Nazism in
many ways looks more like a revealed
theology than like a natural one: "It
may be more correct," he writes, "to say
that the average theology of those who
supported National Socialism was a revelational theology, in which new 'events'
and the 'crisis' of modern experience
formed an extension—or even in effect a
replacement—of ancient revelation, than
to see it as a form of natural theology."
Barr, *Biblical Faith and Natural Theology*,
112. As Barth himself says, the Evangelical
Church in Germany was "confronted by
the demand to recognize in the political
events of the year 1933, and especially in
the form of the God-sent Adolf Hitler,
a source of specific new revelation from

God, which demanding obedience and
trust, took its place beside the revelation
attested in Holy Scripture, claiming that
it should be acknowledged by Christian
proclamation and theology as equally
binding and obligatory." See Barth,
Church Dogmatics, 173. And cf. the discussion in Grant, "Why Should Theology Be
Unnatural?," 95ff.

19. *GSM*, 99.

20. Hart, "A Capacity for Ambiguity?," 293.

21. *MNA*, 100.

22. In dismissing Brunner's notion
of an *Anknüpfungspunkt*, Barth insists
that "the Holy Ghost . . . does not stand
in need of any point of contact but that
which he himself creates. Only retrospectively is it possible to reflect on the way in
which he 'makes contact' with man, and
this retrospect will ever be a retrospect
upon a *miracle*." Barth, "No!," in Brunner
and Barth, *Natural Theology*, 121.

23. *MNA*, 100.

24. It would of course be interesting
to know whether and how well Heschel
knew Barth's writings by the time he
wrote *MNA* (1951) and *GSM* (1955). While
to the best of my knowledge, there is
no literary evidence to help answer this
question, it is worth noting that in their
biography of Heschel, Edward Kaplan
and Samuel Dresner claim that sometime
around September 1938 Heschel engaged in debate with a group of Barth's
students about the role of the churches
during the rise of Hitler. Interestingly
(if also somewhat laconically), they
mention that part of the disagreement
hinged on Barth's students' emphasis on
"the intrinsic evil of humankind," and
Heschel's rejection of such an approach.
(At stake was the question of in what way
Christianity must respond to "current
catastrophic events.") Assuming that the
facts that Kaplan and Dresner report are
correct, we can surmise that Heschel was

not just anti-Barthian in his approach, but self-consciously so. See Kaplan and Dresner, *Abraham Joshua Heschel*, 272. For literary evidence that Heschel was acquainted with the Church Dogmatics at the very latest by 1970, see Heschel, "God, Torah, and Israel," in *MGSA*, 419n70. Perhaps worth mentioning in this context is Edward Kaplan's report that when Heschel discovered during Vatican II that the Catholic Church's Declaration on the Jews would be severely "watered down" and perhaps even abandoned altogether, he appealed to (the Protestant) Barth to intervene. Barth, Kaplan tells us, "was supportive but finally decided not to act." Kaplan, *Spiritual Radical*, 441n48. In terms of Barth's awareness of Heschel: shortly after the latter's death, J. A. Sanders speculated that "Karl Barth's most penetrating single essay, *The Humanity of God,* which appeared in 1956, was influenced by Heschel's *God in Search of Man,* which appeared the year before." J. A. Sanders, "Apostle to the Gentiles," 61.

25. Brunner, "Nature and Grace," in Brunner and Barth, *Natural Theology,* 25.

26. Hart, "A Capacity for Ambiguity?," 295. Colin Grant has recently suggested another path Brunner could have taken in challenging Barth's insistence on the total eradication of the divine image through sin. Brunner should have asked, Grant says, "whether sin can really be so total. Does humanity really have the capacity to displace God completely? Can humanity really obliterate all sense of divine claim and reality?" In his attempt to place so much emphasis on divine sovereignty and human weakness, has not Barth ironically ended up granting human beings an inordinate amount of power to sever their link with God? See Grant, "Why Should Theology Be Unnatural?," 94. Cf. 102. Needless to say, Heschel would undoubtedly embrace this challenge to Barth. For He-

schel, I suspect, a crucial aspect of God's power is located precisely in the fact that the voice of God pursuing man can be ignored but never totally silenced.

27. Brunner, "Nature and Grace," in Brunner and Barth, *Natural Theology,* 27.

28. See, similarly, Moody, "An Introduction to Emil Brunner," 321.

29. In *GSM,* Heschel himself suggests that the relative weight of sin-consciousness is a key point of division between Judaism and Christianity. "To the mind of the Jew," he writes, "mitsvah bears more reality and is a term more frequently and more prominently used than *averah* [sin]. In the Christian vocabulary the frequency and importance of the two terms is just the reverse.... Life revolves around the right and the wrong deed, but we have been trained to be more mitsvah-conscious than *averah* or sin-conscious" (363). Of course, some Jewish sources do in fact talk about original sin. For an important discussion of the notion of original sin in kabbalistic sources, and of its especial presence as a "prominent, even a dominant trope" in Lurianic Kabbalah, see Magid, *From Metaphysics to Midrash,* 10, 34–74.

30. *MNA,* 264.

31. Brunner, "Nature and Grace," in Brunner and Barth, *Natural Theology,* 22.

32. *MNA,* 73. Cf.: "Judaism, in stressing the fundamental importance of the *mitsvah,* assumes that man is endowed with the ability to fulfill what God demands, at least to some degree. This may, indeed, be an article of prophetic faith: the belief in our ability to do His will" (Heschel, "Concept of Man," in *MNA,* 140).

33. Brunner, "Die andere Aufgabe der Theologie," 255–276.

34. Letters from Barth to Thurneysen, January 30–31, 1933, and February 10, 1933, 361, cited in Sauter, "Argue Theologically," 36. Barth, of course, rejected

all attempts to do theology "from below": "Aside from the path from above to below, there is no other way at all" (Barth, "Die dogmatische Prinzipienlehre bei Wihelm Hermann," 595). Sauter comments that for Barth, "the pattern from above/from below becomes the Shibboleth which divides the spirits. 'Natural theology' is every attempt to think theologically 'from below.' Whoever avoids this decision, who interposes other tasks, who seeks a 'both-and' instead of an 'either/or' with all its consequences, can only be a traitor to the task of theology" (Sauter, "Argue Theo-logically," 41).

35. Actually, one could argue that modernity's secularizing assumptions were themselves paradoxically rooted in Reformation attempts to preserve God's absolute sovereignty by pushing God, as it were, further and further upward into Heaven, thus leaving the world itself empty of the divine presence. For a classic statement of this argument, see Berger, *The Sacred Canopy*, 105–125, esp. 111–113.

36. Grant, "Why Should Theology Be Unnatural?," 97.

37. This claim is pervasive in Heschel's writings, but in this context, see especially *MNA*, 149–150, where he says that "the ineffable cries out of all things" and emphatically insists that there is "a divine presence hidden within the order of nature."

38. *MNA*, 179. Cf.: "The relation to the lasting is at the root of all existence" (204).

39. *MNA*, 211.

40. *GSM*, 137.

41. *GSM*, 143. Heschel attributes this last line (which interprets Psalm 36:10) to the Hasidic master Rabbi Aaron of Karlin (but provides no reference). Cf.: "There is in us more kinship with the divine than we are able to believe. The souls of men are candles of the Lord, lit on the cosmic way, rather than fireworks produced by

the combustion of nature's explosive compositions" (*MNA*, 215).

42. *MNA*, 251.

43. *GSM*, 141.

44. *GSM*, 138.

45. "Man's secret lies in openness to transcendence. Existence is interspersed with suggestions of transcendence, and openness to transcendence is a constitutive element of being human" (*WM*, 66).

46. *GSM*, 141–142.

47. *MNA*, 130–131.

48. *MNA*, 109. William Kaufman rightly contrasts Heschel's approach with Barth's, noting that for the former, in dramatic contrast to the latter, "truth is accessible to human religious sensibilities," which must be awakened "to an openness to God's revelation." But Kaufman's interpretation goes off the rails when he nevertheless insists that "in the final analysis, Heschel and Barth share the same emphasis: God's quest for man" (170). No doubt, there is a great deal of truth to this last statement, but as should be obvious to the reader by now, it occludes far more than it reveals, and it loses sight of the vast anthropological and methodological gulf between the two thinkers. As I have been at pains to show, neither Heschel nor Barth would have looked kindly upon being identified as members of the same camp. Kaufman goes on to accuse Heschel of a "studied indifference to inconsistency" and maintains that "on reading Heschel, one gets the impression that inconsistency is not only tolerated but is made a virtue" (171). For all its hostility, this last charge, I fear, reveals less about Heschel's work than about Kaufman's incomplete understanding thereof. As we shall shortly see, it is precisely because of Heschel's method of correlation that he begins with human experience and intuition, and then moves to a robust affirmation of the content of revelation (and the attendant emphasis on God's quest

for man). This ostensible inconsistency is only the playing out of Heschel's methodological project. To be clear: I am not suggesting that there are no inconsistencies in Heschel's writings. That would be no less fatuous than insisting that he raises inconsistency to the level of virtue. Page references are to Kaufman, *Contemporary Jewish Philosophies*.

49. Livingston and Fiorenza, *Modern Christian Thought*, 203.

50. Cited in Milbank, "Henri de Lubac," 76.

51. Kerr, "French Theology," 108.

52. Kerr, "French Theology," 113.

53. Kerr, "French Theology," 115.

54. Rahner, "Order," 297.

55. Dych, *Karl Rahner*, 35.

56. Rahner, "Concerning the Relationship between Nature and Grace," 302. The consequence of this, for Rahner, is that "pure nature is a 'remainder concept,' what-would-have-been had God not intended, in a prior way, Christ and grace as the ultimate meaning of man." Carr, "Theology and Experience," 363.

57. Cf. the discussion in Craigo-Snell, *Silence, Love, and Death*, 29.

58. Weger, *Karl Rahner*, 86.

59. Rahner, "Teresa of Avila," 125.

60. Kilby, "Rahner," 97. The *Vorgriff*, then, is a pre-apprehension of God; the supernatural existential is "the universal experience of grace, or at least of grace offered" (97–98, and cf. 104n3 for a brief comment on how the precise meaning of this term changes over time).

61. Kilby, "Rahner," 97.

62. Carr, "Theology and Experience," 359.

63. Carr, "Theology and Experience," 360.

64. Carr, "Theology and Experience," 371.

65. Carr, "Theology and Experience," 371. And cf. Carr's discussion, 375–376.

66. For Rahner's hesitations about de Lubac's formulations on this point, see Rahner, "Concerning the Relationship between Nature and Grace," 303.

67. Tillich, *Systematic Theology*, 4 (henceforth *ST*).

68. *ST*, 6.

69. *ST*, 31.

70. *ST*, 5.

71. *ST*, 8. Of course, many have accused Tillich of succumbing to the lures of the philosophical "situation" in which he found himself, such that the unique message of the Bible is ultimately "obliterated." Tillich's attempts to correlate Christian theology with his speculative ontology amount, in the eyes of many, to a reduction of the former to the latter. Thus God, for Tillich, is best understood as "Being-itself," sin is difficult to distinguish from finitude, etc. If Tillich's critics are right—and Heschel would no doubt have thought that they were—then his work stands as testimony to just how difficult a task it is to achieve the "mutual interdependence" he sought.

72. *ST*, 60.

73. *ST*, 8.

74. *ST*, 6.

75. *ST*, 7.

76. *ST*, 65.

77. *ST*, 61.

78. *ST*, 7.

79. *ST*, 52.

80. Fritz Rothschild contends that although Heschel's "method of correlation [is] similar to Paul Tillich's, [it was] independently conceived." Unfortunately, he does share the basis for this judgment. Rothschild, "Architect and Herald of a New Theology," 211. Dror Bondi has sensitively and astutely explored Heschel's approach to theological questions and answers, but he seems unaware of the connection to Tillich. See Bondi, *Ayekah?*, 140–182, and, in more abbreviated form, Bondi, "Heschel's 'Dialogue of Questions,'" 132–136. Alexander Even-Chen, in contrast, has attempted to draw links between Heschel and Tillich, but misses the method of questions and answers entirely

as a point of connection. Even-Chen, "Faith and the Courage to Be," 337–356.

Let me emphasize that acknowledgment of Heschel's possible methodological debt to Tillich should not be taken to imply substantive agreement between them. On the contrary, Heschel strongly demurred, for example, from Tillich's conception of "the God who is Being itself, the ground and abyss of every being." Tillich, *Biblical Religion*, 182–183. In an interview with Carl Stern, Heschel declared: "There are a great many who read the word of God and don't believe in Him. Let me give you an example. One of the most popular definitions of God common in America today was developed by a great Protestant theologian: God is the ground of being. So everybody is ready to accept it. Why not? Ground of being causes me no harm. Let there be a ground of being, doesn't cause me any harm, and I'm ready to accept it. It's meaningless. Isn't there a God who is above the ground?" Heschel, "Interview with Carl Stern," MGSA, 408. Correlation as Tillich executed it, Heschel would have charged, amounts to little more than the liquidation of authentic biblical thinking. He would no doubt have endorsed philosopher (and rabbi) Bernard Martin's assertion that notwithstanding Tillich's insistence that his theology is based on what he learns from revelation, his "theoretical interpretation of the divine life is very far removed from the existential knowledge of the God given in the biblical revelation. One may doubt, indeed, that Tillich and the Bible are even talking about the same God. The God who is described by Tillich seems to have very little in common with the God of Abraham, Isaac, and Jacob or the God of Jesus and Paul. One wonders even whether Tillich is not guilty of a gross abuse of language in calling his 'being-itself' God." Thus, Martin concludes, "It seems certain that Tillich's

description of the divine life is largely dependent upon his ontology, and that with a different ontology he would have a different conception of God." Cf. Martin, *The Existentialist Theology of Paul Tillich*, 174–175. Note also Heschel's insistence that "the insights and demands of religion cannot be completely synchronized with the conclusions of any particular system of philosophy" (*GSM*, 17).

In this context, it is also worth noting that Heschel famously rails against the interpretation of religious language as symbolic. In an extended polemic, he insists that if religious language is only symbolically true, then God and religion are themselves simply "fiction[s]" (*MQ*, 128, 144). When human beings worship symbols, he contends, they are simply worshipping their own inventions, and this is little more than "solipsism" (129). "The will of God," Heschel declares, "is neither a metaphor nor a euphemism but more powerful and more real than our own experience" (131). In the end, what is important to Heschel is that from his perspective, authentic religion has to be rooted in divine revelation (129). If everything theology says is symbolic, then it is nothing more than a projectionist discourse—which is to say, a purely human contrivance. Needless to say, in such a worldview, divine commandments are relegated to the status of mere "ceremonies." Heschel encapsulates his opposition thus: "The primary function of symbols . . . is to express *what we think;* the primary function of the mitzvot is to express *what God wills.* Religious symbolism is a *search for God,* Jewish observance, *a response to God*" (136). In other words, whereas, for Heschel, authentic religion is focused on self-transcendence, symbolic religion is concerned only with "self-expression" (135).

It is not entirely obvious whom Heschel has in his sights here. Edward

Kaplan suggests that Heschel is arguing against Buber, whose understanding of prophecy as fundamentally symbolic, Heschel thinks (and Kaplan seems to agree), "imperils the acknowledgment of God as on objective reality—let alone as the primary source of prophetic authority." See Kaplan, "Sacred versus Symbolic Religion," 213–231 (the passage cited is on 216–217), and, much more briefly, Kaplan, *Holiness in Words*, 82–84. In the latter presentation, Kaplan modifies his critical presentation of Buber somewhat (182n26). It should be noted in this context that Franz Rosenzweig similarly accused the early Buber of not taking the reality of revelation seriously enough. See Rosenzweig, "Atheistic Theology," 10–24, and cf. Mendes-Flohr, *From Mysticism to Dialogue*, 180n247. Mendes-Flohr contends that the early Buber was "definitely not theistic; there is even evidence that he was a nonbeliever." Mendes-Flohr, *From Mysticism to Dialogue*, 165–166n321. Aaron Mackler, in contrast, argues that Heschel's polemic against symbols is a response to Tillich. Mackler, "Symbols, Reality, and God," 290–300. And see similarly Even-Chen, "Heschel and Tillich," 349. Given Heschel's reticence to criticize his opponents by name, it is difficult to decide the issue. In any case, if the object of Heschel's ire is Tillich, a strong case could be made (as Mackler rightly notes) that Heschel offers a less-than-nuanced presentation of Tillich's view. The latter, after all, insists that symbols are more than mere human constructions—as he puts it, symbols "participate in that to which they point." Mackler argues (correctly, in my view) that what motivates Heschel to read Tillich so flatly is his conviction that no matter what Tillich says about symbols per se, the latter's notion of God is still static rather than active, and hence his theology cannot make adequate space for the reality of biblical revelation,

in which God makes His will known to humanity. In other words, according to Heschel, any theology that fails to acknowledge the fact of God's revelation of His will in the end amounts to theological projectionism. Thus, in my view, the issue Heschel has with Tillich and/or the early Buber is not so much their notions of symbolism, but rather that which he thinks underlies them: an inadequate sense of the reality of God. Norman Solomon seems unaware of Heschel's impassioned argument against understanding religious language symbolically when he writes, bafflingly, that "Tillich's contention that all spiritual and theological knowledge cannot be other than a symbol ... is indeed very close to Heschel's own outlook, and draws on much the same religious and philosophical language." See Solomon, "Heschel in the Context of Modern Jewish Religious Thought," 14.

Quite possibly also at play in Heschel's attack on symbolism, as Moshe Idel proposes, is a twentieth-century refraction of a disputed point in the history of Jewish mysticism. Following the theosophical-theurgical, Zoharic, and Lurianic schools of Kabbalah, Gershom Scholem insisted that the mystic's "essential mode of thinking is ... symbolical in the strictest sense." Deeply influenced by his Hasidic forebears, who were much more focused on divine immediacy (and thus attributed a much diminished role to symbols in Jewish religious experience), Heschel's rejected symbolism in the strongest possible terms: "What we need is immediacy," he wrote; "this will not be found through introducing a set of symbols." "Symbolism and Jewish Faith," in *MGSA*, 99. Idel, "Abraham J. Heschel on Mysticism and Hasidism," 80–105, esp. 88–95. For Scholem's comments, see *Major Trends*, 26.

81. *GSM*, 3.
82. *GSM*, 130.

83. *GSM*, 3.

84. *GSM*, 168.

85. *GSM*, 169.

86. Heschel, "Interview at Notre Dame," in *MGSA*, 389–390. Elsewhere, Heschel writes that religion must direct its attention not just to theology but also, crucially, to "the pre-theological situation": "We must recover the situations which both precede and correspond to the theological formulations; we must recall the questions which religious doctrines are trying to answer." Heschel, "What We Might Do Together," in *MGSA*, 295.

87. *GSM*, 112.

88. *WM*, 74.

89. *GSM*, 117.

90. Duffy, *The Graced Horizon*, 222–223.

91. *MNA*, 193. *MNA*, 193–197 are reproduced, more or less verbatim, in *WM*, 57–60. This particular passage is repeated in *WM*, 57.

92. *MNA*, 194–195. The passage is repeated in *WM*, 58.

93. *MNA*, 198.

94. *MNA*, 213.

95. *MNA*, 215.

96. *MNA*, 241.

97. *MNA*, 212.

98. *MNA*, 214. Repeated in *WM*, 60.

99. *MNA*, 194. Repeated in *WM*, 57.

100. *WM*, 74. Heschel does not explicitly explore whether and why self-transcendence requires religion: cannot one be focused on responsiveness to the other without also invoking a transcendent Other? I suspect Heschel would insist that only religion has the power to enact the kind of fundamental reorientation self-transcendence requires (even if there are any number of individuals who constitute exceptions). Whether or not this is a convincing claim remains open to question, to say the very least. The question of why combatting egocentrism requires God (and a revealed

law) is raised by Eliezer Berkovits, who oddly offers something of a non-sequitur in response: he suggests that since God desires non-egocentric behavior from us, it makes sense that God would reveal a law to help us live accordingly. Needless to say, this is not an answer to the question Berkovits initially poses—not why God would want to help along the process, but whether and why the struggle with egocentrism would require God in the first place. Berkovits, *God, Man, and History*, 119–122. I am grateful to David Shatz for our exchange on this point. On the question of self-transcendence with or without God, an interesting dialogue could be constructed between Heschel and his contemporary, psychologist Viktor Frankl, who—without being a theologian or advocating for theism—famously insists that "being human always points, and is directed, to something or someone, other than oneself—be it a meaning to fulfill or another human being to encounter. The more one forgets himself . . . the more human he is." This "constitutive characteristic" Frankl terms "the self-transcendence of human existence." Frankl, *Man's Search for Meaning*, 110–111.

101. Fiorenza, "Systematic Theology," 61.

102. "Dissent," *AJHEW*, 106–107.

103. "Dissent," *AJHEW*, 106–107.

104. Tracy, *Blessed Rage*, 32. Cf. 34.

105. Tracy, *Blessed Rage*, 7.

106. See, for example, *GSM*, 268–270, 273–275. I will discuss these passages and their implications at length in the next chapter. For an elaboration of this theme, see Hartman, "Judaism as an Interpretive Tradition," esp. 11–23. And cf. my remarks in "The Promise and Peril of Jewish Barthianism," 318–319.

107. It is perhaps tempting to connect all this with the fact that, whereas for Tillich, human questions are correlated with theological answers, for Heschel the fundamental question is answered not

primarily with theology, but rather with commandments. But as the Jewish experience of modernity unequivocally teaches, commandments, too, can be subject to challenge and critique. This distinction between Heschel and Tillich is a real one, but I do not think it is pertinent to our discussion here.

108. I borrow this term from the title of James Bacik's important study, *Apologetics and the Eclipse of Mystery.*

109. For a sampling of mystagogical passages in Rahner, see the references in Bacik, *Apologetics and the Eclipse of Mystery,* 129n17.

110. Bacik, *Apologetics and the Eclipse of Mystery,* 17

111. Bacik, *Apologetics and the Eclipse of Mystery,* 40.

112. Otto, *The Idea of the Holy,* 7.

113. Rahner, "Theology and the Arts," 25.

114. Rahner, "Theology and the Arts," 26.

115. If Rahner was the more reflective theorist of mystagogy, Heschel was surely the more poetically and rhetorically gifted practitioner.

116. Thus, for example, Yehudah Mirsky writes of his "nagging suspicion that Heschel is presenting poetry rather than theology." My contention is that Heschel would have rejected this "rather than" as rooted in a failure to understand the project, and therefore the method, of depth theology. See Mirsky, "The Rhapsodist," 41. When William Kaufman writes that "surely, Heschel, as a philosopher, would not have wished that people read his works as poetry" (Kaufman, *Contemporary Jewish Philosophies,* 167), he is indubitably right, in that Heschel would not have wished his works to be read as *mere* poetry, in contradistinction to theology. But the insistent contrast between theology and poetry, Heschel would likely assert, reveals both a misunderstanding of theology and an impoverished conception of the poetic. In other words, I do not

think that Heschel would have objected at all to being read as a poetic theologian in a Rahnerian mode. On the contrary, for a depth theologian seeking to re-awaken dormant human sensibilities and insights, the poetic, evocative mode is perhaps the most potent tool available.

117. David Novak, a student and ardent defender of Heschel's, writes that in a postmodern age, when logical positivism is long gone and "all canons of meaning are open to critical reappraisal . . . we are now in a better position to appreciate that a poet is not someone who senses less than we do; he or she senses something more than we do. Poets stand at the very frontier of language, not at its back door. . . . Without the continual infusion of poetry into any language, our language itself becomes but our tool for the manipulation of the world, that which carries our world to its imminent dissolution rather than what celebrates its transcendent source." Novak, "Heschel on Revelation," 44.

3. REVELATION AND CO-REVELATION

1. *GSM,* 168. As we have seen, one of Heschel's central goals as a writer is to re-awaken the now dormant question inside of us. Adam Lipszyc observes intriguingly that Heschel made use of an "interesting modification" of the maieutic method: "If in the original Socratic form," he writes, "the method assumed the autonomy of the mind and by means of a series of questions tried to lead pupil's mind [*sic*] toward *the answer* already present in his mind, in Heschel's variation the method is meant to lead the pupil (or the reader!) towards the question already present in the depths of his or her soul." Lipszyc, "The Mark of the Question," 62.

2. I cite from an early draft of an introductory essay Morgan has prepared on the religious worldviews of Heschel

and Joseph Soloveitchik (February 2009). My only quibble with Morgan's formulation is that I am not sure that Heschel would have been content to offer therapy to modern Jews alone; his goal was, I think, to transform the way humanity more broadly experienced, thought about, and responded to the world. Jacob Y. Teshima reports on a conversation in which Heschel was very explicit about his broad, universalist spiritual concerns. See Teshima, "My Teacher," 65.

3. GSM, 169.

4. GSM, 170. Robert Gordis, Heschel's colleague at the Jewish Theological Seminary, offers a novel response to the rejection of revelation on account of human insignificance. "To adopt this position," Gordis writes, "really means to be guilty of anthropomorphism, for we would be conceiving God in human terms, as being bound by human limitations." Of course, this argument represents a brilliant inversion of the accusation that in describing a God who cares for each individual, theology is guilty of anthropomorphizing. On the contrary, Gordis insists, to suggest that God is somehow beyond caring for lowly individuals is to attribute human weakness and inability to Him. Cf. Gordis, A Faith for Moderns, 138.

5. GSM, 170–171.

6. GSM, 169. As I have noted repeatedly above (Introduction, note 84; and chapter 1, note 150), Heschel nowhere adequately deals with the sobering fact that religion can induce violence as easily as it can restrain it.

7. GSM, 171.

8. GSM, 171.

9. GSM, 171. Given his points of emphasis, the reader can come away with the impression—mistaken, I think—that for Heschel, the Bible's contemporary role is mainly (or even exclusively) negative, serving only as a cosmic "no!" in the face of humanity's seemingly unquenchable thirst for blood. It is important also to keep in mind the flipside of that "no"—for Heschel, as we shall see, the Bible also functions to remind humanity of God's love and concern, to convey to us "the assurance that beyond all evil is the compassion of God" (GSM, 238).

10. GSM, 173.

11. GSM, 173. Cf. 126–127.

12. GSM, 173.

13. GSM, 174.

14. GSM, 174.

15. GSM, 174.

16. GSM, 175.

17. The move between the notion that "each of us is a potential recipient of a kind of proto-revelation," on the one hand, and my invocation of "the subtle experience of the sensitive person," on the other, is conscious on my part. I am suggesting—though I cannot prove this point, and I am not wedded to it—that Heschel thinks that God reaches out to all of us, although only some of us are attentive enough to hear the muted divine voice. One could also plausibly offer a very different interpretation, according to which just as God only chooses some people to be prophets, so also God only chooses some people to speak to in fragments and syllables. Heschel simply does not say enough about "proto-revelation" to enable us to resolve this ambiguity definitively.

18. And yet we should note that Heschel also articulates a kind of counterpoint to this theology of continuity. At one point, he writes that "the authenticity of revelation is shown in its being different from all other events and experiences. Its truth is in its uniqueness. Only as something incomparable can it be trusted" (GSM, 221). Whether and precisely how these passages sit together is a matter worthy of further exploration.

19. Buber, "The Man of Today," 8.

20. Buber, "The Man of Today," 9–10.

21. *GSM,* 174.

22. Actually, Buber says that such experiences are not just *one* approach to the realities of creation, revelation, and redemption, but *the* approach to them (Buber, "Man of Today," 8). I am not sure Heschel would go quite this far.

23. Buber, "The Man of Today," 13. Buber speaks of "a beginning" in the context of anticipatory experiences of redemption, but the point is very much the same.

24. Mitchell and Wiles, "Does Christianity Need a Revelation?," 103.

25. Placher, *The Domestication of Transcendence,* 186.

26. Cf. Mitchell and Wiles, "Does Christianity Need a Revelation?," 103–114.

27. *GSM,* 198.

28. *GSM,* 197.

29. *GSM,* 198.

30. *GSM,* 196.

31. *GSM,* 131.

32. *GSM,* 66.

33. *GSM,* 245, 247.

34. *GSM,* 108.

35. Thus, Neil Gillman is mistaken, I think, in suggesting that "when we view the world through the eyes of radical amazement, what we perceive is a world infused with the presence of God, a God who . . . cries for attention—not only in history but even in nature as well—a God who pursues us, a God who is perpetually in search of human acknowledgment." Gillman, "The Dynamics of Prophecy," in *Doing Jewish Theology,* 27. Contra Gillman, radical amazement alone does not yield the sense that God "cries out" for us; as we have seen, such pathos-laden images depend on revelation.

36. *GSM,* 163–164.

37. *GSM,* 238.

38. *GSM,* 168.

39. *GSM,* 261.

40. As we shall see in chapter 4, there may be more of Maimonides in Heschel than he is prepared to admit.

41. *GSM,* 178–179. In a similar vein, Jacob Petuchowski insists that biblical descriptions of the scene at Sinai constitute

> an attempt to put into human words something which transcends the language of men. When infinite God speaks to finite man, only the language of poetry may try to capture what has transpired. The thunders and lightnings at Sinai, as they appear in the biblical narrative, are an echo sounding through the ages of what happened there. They testify to the fact of revelation, to the impact it had on the people. But it is only the man of a prosaic mind, the man lacking in imagination, who would read this biblical account as if it were a news bulletin reporting in every detail what actually happened. (Petuchowski, *Ever Since Sinai,* 67)

42. *GSM,* 181.

43. *GSM,* 183

44. *GSM,* 180.

45. Heschel would likely suggest that a theological literalist is not a realist at all, but rather an idolater.

46. Soskice, "Theological Realism," 108.

47. *GSM,* 184.

48. *GSM,* 185.

49. *GSM,* 185.

50. *GSM,* 185.

51. See, for example, Gillman, "Toward a Theology for Conservative Judaism," 6, and Gillman, "Authority and Parameters in Jewish Decision Making," in *Doing Jewish Theology,* 106.

52. *GSM,* 185.

53. *GSM,* 186–187. One should not be tripped up or misled by Heschel's invocation of the way of negation. His aim here is to point to radical limits on our knowing (either God or revelation), not to espouse a particular form of negative theology. As we shall discuss in the next chapter, Heschel explicitly rejects nega-

tive theology in its more extreme (i.e., Maimonidean) versions.

54. *GSM*, 186.

55. *GSM*, 189.

56. See, similarly, Gillman, "Toward a Theology for Conservative Judaism," 21n24. Note also Heschel's comment that "*mitzvoth* are expressions and interpretations of the will of God" (*MQ*, 134). Arnold Eisen rightly notes that "the ambiguity of that formulation is intended." Eisen, "Re-Reading Heschel on the Commandments," 17.

57. *GSM*, 181.

58. *GSM*, 219.

59. *GSM*, 241.

60. *GSM*, 222.

61. *GSM*, 245.

62. *GSM*, 244.

63. *GSM*, 184.

64. *GSM*, 186.

65. *GSM*, 187.

66. *GSM*, 265.

67. Dorff, *Conservative Judaism*, 1st ed., 121.

68. Dorff, *Conservative Judaism*, 1st ed., 118–119.

69. Dorff, *Conservative Judaism*, 2nd, rev. ed., 123.

70. Dorff, *For the Love of God and People*, 33. And yet, strangely, Dorff also says, *in the very next sentence*, "Heschel maintains that God revealed His will at Mount Sinai, but we do not have it in hand. All we have is our ancestors' and our own understanding of its contents."

71. *GSM*, 265.

72. *GSM*, 186.

73. *Prophets*, II, 3. Emphasis mine.

74. Cf. also Heschel's contention that revelation conveys "insights"—again, not necessarily in words (*GSM*, 207).

75. Novak, "Revelation," 286. Cf. also Novak, "Heschel on Revelation," 37–45, esp. 42.

76. Buber, *I and Thou*, 158–160. In an interview given more than a decade after the publication of *GSM*, Heschel insists

that for Buber, revelation is merely a "vague encounter," and judges this view "untenable": "A Jew cannot live by such a conception of revelation. Buber does not do justice to the claims of the prophets. So I have to choose between him and the Bible itself." "Interview at Notre Dame," in *MGSA*, 385.

77. Rosenzweig, "The Content of Revelation," 285.

78. For a more nuanced view of Buber and Rosenzweig's approaches to revelation, suggesting that they move between understanding revelation as speechless encounter and understanding it as conveying speech, see Horwitz, "Revelation and the Bible," 355–364, esp. 357–358. I have chosen to simplify matters in the text because Heschel seems to respond, as we shall see, to the more common interpretation of Buber and Rosenzweig, according to which they present revelation as conveying no content beyond the divine presence itself.

79. *GSM*, 261.

80. Lamm, in *The Condition of Jewish Belief: A Symposium*, 124.

81. Kaplan, *Know How to Answer*, 78–79. In a similar vein, Kaplan's disciple (and son-in-law) Ira Eisenstein writes, "I can understand why our ancestors believed the Torah (and its authoritative interpretations) to have been 'divine revelation.' For me, however, those concepts and values explicitly conveyed or implied in it which I can accept represent *discovery*, partial and tentative glimpses into the true nature of human life." Cf. Eisenstein, in *The Condition of Jewish Belief*, 46. For Eisenstein, more clearly even than for Kaplan (who still speaks, however metaphorically, of "an activity of God"), we can see that divine revelation simply *is* human discovery, without remainder. Cf. also Kohn, *The Moral Life of Man*, 224–225.

82. Astley, "Revelation Revisited," 340.

83. Gillman, "Toward a Theology for Conservative Judaism," 8. Cf. Gillman,

"Authority and Parameters," in *Doing Jewish Theology*, 105.

84. Gillman, "Toward a Theology for Conservative Judaism," 10. Cf. Gillman, "Authority and Parameters," in *Doing Jewish Theology*, 106–107.

85. Petuchowski, "The Concept of Revelation in Modern Judaism," 50.

86. Petuchowski, "Reflections on Revelation," 4–5.

87. Petuchowski, "The Concept of Revelation in Modern Judaism," 52. Of course, there is a great deal to say about, and much to question in, Petuchowski's confidence that in the post-Holocaust world—he is writing in the late 1950s and early 1960s—talk of a personal God had become less rather than more difficult. It is one thing to assume that overconfident descriptions of the immanent God of progress have grown obsolete; it is quite another to assume that talk of a radically other, transcendent God could be easily restored in their place. A full exploration of this issue is obviously far beyond the scope of the present work. For more on Jewish religious thought in America in that period, and on the rise of an existential Jewish theology (of which both Heschel and Petuchowski were important representatives), see Goldy, *The Emergence of Jewish Theology in America*, and Morgan, *Beyond Auschwitz*.

88. Petuchowski, "Revelation and the Modern Jew," 123. Of course, Petuchowski's comments, too, have the potential to becloud certain issues: in classifying thinkers like Rosenzweig and Heschel together, Petuchowski ignores important disagreements over what is actually revealed by God. In other words, Heschel would be quick to point out that, unlike Rosenzweig—and Petuchowski himself, a committed Rosenzweigian—he believes in a God who reveals more than just "Himself." All of this should perhaps serve as a reminder that insistent

dichotomizing in the face of real multiplicity and diversity is often less than helpful. For Petuchowski's Rosenzweigianism, see, for example, "Revelation and the Modern Jew," 125–129; *Ever Since Sinai*, 71–74; and *The Condition of Jewish Belief*, 158.

89. *GSM*, 272.

90. *GSM*, 257–258.

91. *GSM*, 258.

92. *GSM*, 220.

93. *GSM*, 257. Or again, Heschel writes: "The essence of our faith in the sanctity of the Bible is that its words contain that which God wants us to know and to fulfill. How these words were written down is not the fundamental problem. This is why the theme of Biblical criticism is not the theme of faith" (258).

94. Neil Gillman puts this well when he writes that:

> The overwhelming conclusions of [*Torah min ha-shamayim*] are first, that rabbinic literature subjected the issue of revelation to an intricate and subtle nuanced inquiry in comparison to which most contemporary efforts appear positively simplistic; second, that the contemporary traditionalist view far from exhausts the range of options reflected in that literature; and third, that we contemporaries are not the first to question, on theological grounds, the dogma of verbal revelation. In retrospect, Heschel's critique of the literalist position in *God in Search of Man* clearly nurses from the material that he was to study in this later work. ("Toward a Theology for Conservative Judaism," 12)

95. Petuchowski, "The Supposed Dogma," 359.

96. Petuchowski, "The Supposed Dogma," 360. Or again: "Literary history cannot solve the questions asked by Theology, and the question as to the *fact* of Revelation is a *theological* question."

Petuchowski, "The Concept of Revelation in Reform Judaism," 110.

97. Petuchowski, "The Concept of Revelation in Reform Judaism," 107.

98. Petuchowski, "The Supposed Dogma," 359.

99. Petuchowski, *Ever Since Sinai*, 83.

100. The similarities between Heschel's approach and Petuchowski's have been noted in passing by Rosenberg in "Biblical Criticism in Modern Jewish Thought," 90.

101. Grant, *An Introduction to New Testament Thought*, 30.

102. *GSM*, 220. In this context, note Jon Levenson's observation that in Heschel's writings, "the thinking and experience of all the prophets tend to run together in a blur." Levenson, "Religious Affirmation," 43.

103. This fundamental problem is missed, for example, by Alexander Even-Chen, in his essay "The Torah, Revelation, and Scientific Critique in the Teachings of Abraham Joshua Heschel," 67–76.

In light of the important similarities we have seen between Heschel and Petuchowski's respective approaches to the problem of revelation and historical criticism, it is easy to lose sight of an important distinction between them. Whereas, as I have argued, Heschel affirms that revelation conveys positive content, Petuchowski argues in Rosenzweigian terms that what God reveals is His love (*Ever Since Sinai*, 72). This difference means, I would suggest, that Petuchowski would have a somewhat less complicated task in incorporating the findings of historical criticism into his theology than would Heschel. After all, the former readily admits that the content of scripture is a human response (or a series of human responses) to the initial revelation of divine love. Thus, the fact of multiple responses with diverse agendas is not necessarily problematic. The latter, on the other hand, in insisting that revela-

tion does convey positive content, leaves himself open to the challenge that he has evaded the deeper challenges posed by historical criticism and its insistence upon multiple authors with divergent—nay, contradictory—ideologies.

104. *GSM*, 258. Cf.: "Our problem . . . is how to share the certainty of Israel that the Bible contains that which God wants us to know and to hearken to" (246).

105. *GSM*, 260.

106. *GSM*, 260. Cf. *Prophets*, II, 146.

107. As we discuss below, the fact that God reveals His will to human partners He knows are limited and therefore liable to distort (and even abuse) it could well be described as an aspect of divine self-transcendence.

108. *GSM*, 264.

109. Compare the words of Scottish theologian John Baillie:

> The witness itself is a human activity and as such is fallible. Nevertheless we cannot believe that God, having performed His mighty acts and having illumined the minds of prophet and apostle to understand their true import, left the prophetic and apostolic *testimony* to take care of itself. It were indeed a strange conception of the divine providential activity which would deny that the Biblical writers were divinely assisted in their attempt to communicate to the world the illumination which, for the world's sake, they had themselves received. The same Holy Spirit who had enlightened them unto their own salvation must also have aided their efforts, whether spoken or written, to convey the message of salvation to those whom their words would reach. This is what is meant by the inspiration of Holy Scripture. (Baillie, *The Idea of Revelation in Recent Thought*, 111)

110. "They asked *Wisdom*: What should be the punishment of a sinner?

And Wisdom said: *Misfortune pursues sinners* (Proverbs 13:21). They asked *prophecy:* What should be the punishment of a sinner? And prophecy said: *The soul that sins shall die* (Ezekiel 18:4, 20). They asked *the Holy One,* Blessed Be He: What should be the punishment of the sinner? And He said: *Let him repent and he will be atoned for"* (Y. Makkot II, 31d). Heschel's translation, *GSM,* 261–262.

111. *GSM,* 261.

112. *GSM,* 262. Cf., in a different register, Heschel's reminder that God and the Torah are emphatically not the same thing. *KGE,* 50–52, 643–646; *PT,* 58–60. It is sometimes difficult to discern precisely which statements attributed to the Hasidic masters cited there Heschel himself endorses, but the general thrust—a warning not conflate Torah and God—does seem to be Heschel's own position.

113. *GSM,* 268.

114. *GSM,* 268.

115. *GSM,* 269. Heschel here anticipates David Hartman's important essay on "Judaism as an Interpretive Tradition," 3–36, especially 10–20.

116. *GSM,* 270. All of that said, Heschel is quick to warn lest we assume too much haste in condemning biblical texts as primitive or barbaric. Anticipating a theme we will discuss in the following chapter, Heschel gives the example of divine anger:

> We must always remember that the Bible is not a book composed for one age, and its significance cannot be assessed by the particular moral and literary standards of one generation. Passages that were considered outdated by one generation have been a fountain of comfort to the next. Many of us once considered Jeremiah's outcry: "Pour out Thy wrath upon the nations that know Thee not, and upon families that call not on Thy name; for they have devoured Jacob, yea they

have devoured him, consumed him, and have laid waste his habitation" (10:25), to be primitive. But what other words could there be to recite when mothers saw how their infants were sent to the gas chambers of Nazi extermination camps? Shall we presume to sit in judgment in the name of morality over those who taught the world what justice means? (*GSM,* 270–271)

117. *GSM,* 272–273. Note the democratizing impulse in Heschel: it is not just the rabbinic scholar but "every man" who is called to "responsible experience."

118. *GSM,* 273.

119. *GSM,* 274.

120. *GSM,* 274.

121. *MNA,* 164.

122. *KGE,* 80–82, 398–399.

123. *MNA,* 164–165.

124. *GSM,* 3.

125. "Dissent," unpublished manuscript appearing in *AJHEW,* 106.

126. *GSM,* 3. These are the words Heschel famously uses to assess religion's story state in the modern world.

127. "Customs and ceremonies" is how Heschel describes what is left of religion when the fire and vitality have been drained out of it. See, for example, *IF,* 217; *MGSA,* 145, 147, 149, 155.

128. "Dissent," *AJHEW,* 106.

129. "Dissent," *AJHEW,* 107.

130. Cf. Levenson, "Religious Affirmation and Historical Criticism," 30.

131. *GSM,* 222.

132. *GSM,* 236. And yet the implication that a failure to see the truth of prophecy is *necessarily* the result of callousness and self-assertion, I think, invites precisely the kind of criticisms we will see Arthur Cohen make below, namely that Heschel displays "deficient sympathy and compassion for those who are trapped in their unknowing and disbelief." Cohen, *The Natural and the Supernatural Jew,* 252.

133. Levenson, "Religious Affirmation and Historical Criticism," 30.

134. *GSM*, 240, 247.

135. *GSM*, 240. Levenson rightly notes that "the tension between this argument that the Jewish scriptures are self-evidently the most excellent and Heschel's commitment to religious pluralism and interfaith dialogue is painful. The tension is not one that he succeeded in resolving, probing, or interpreting" (Levenson, "Religious Affirmation and Historical Criticism," 33n27).

136. *GSM*, 241. Again, a few pages later, Heschel writes, "If God is alive, then the Bible is His voice. No other work is as worthy of being considered a manifestation of His will. There is no other mirror in the world where His will and spiritual guidance is as unmistakably reflected" (*GSM*, 245). Christians and Muslims would no doubt be surprised to hear this.

137. Levenson, "Religious Affirmation and Historical Criticism," 33.

138. *GSM*, 241.

139. Levenson, "Religious Affirmation and Historical Criticism," 34.

140. *GSM*, 232.

141. *GSM*, 233.

142. *GSM*, 242.

143. Cohen, *The Natural and the Supernatural Jew*, 252. And yet, as I argued, in chapter 1, I think Cohen is probably mistaken in assuming that Heschel's goal is to shame his readers into belief (246n25, 253). More likely, Heschel wants to shake them so violently that he chips away at the barrier that, in his view, keeps them walled off from the transcendent.

144. Erlewine, "Reclaiming the Prophets," 195.

145. Without openness to wonder, in other words, there is no possibility of openness to God's self-disclosure. Cohen captures this well: for Heschel, "to be without that natural wonder which discloses the reality of God is to remain closed to that supernatural wonder which is God's revelation in Scripture." *The Natural and the Supernatural Jew,* 247–248.

146. *GSM*, 241, 250.

147. This is Stephen Webb's formulation, describing Louis Wirth Marvick's discussion of hyperbole in *Mallarmé and the Sublime*, 85–86.

148. *GSM*, 235.

149. *GSM*, 236.

150. *GSM*, 238.

151. *GSM*, 236. The implicit confession here is quite moving: during a time of divine hiddenness (on which see chapter 7, below), without revelation we would be utterly lost.

152. *GSM*, 233–234.

153. In a related vein, Heschel writes at one point that "more decisive than *the origin of the Bible in God* is *the presence of God in the Bible*. It is the sense for the presence that leads us to a belief in its origin" (*GSM*, 250). Or, in one of his most beautiful formulations, Heschel declares: "The way to faith in the 'Torah from Heaven' (*Torah min ha-shamayim*) is the preparation of the heart to perceive the heavenly in the Torah (*shamayim min ha-Torah*). Such a perception [Heschel admits] may be momentary; it may happen in a mere blink of an eye. But all of life is scarcely worth that momentary gift of heaven" (*TMHS*, III, 30; *HT*, 667). (This same inversion (*Torah min ha-shamayim—shamayim min ha-Torah*) is put to somewhat different use in *GSM*, 256. And compare Avery Dulles's comments: "The revelatory power of Scripture depends on the continued presence and activity of God in the situation in which the Scripture is read and proclaimed. . . . The Bible's proved capacity to enlarge and stabilize the vision of those who submit to its power is one of the reasons why it has come to be accepted as inspired." See Dulles, *Models of Revelation*, 208–209.

154. As we have already seen William Kaufman protest: "The problem of a philosophy of Judaism such as Heschel's, which relies so heavily on intuition . . . is that there are those who have had contrasting and contradictory intuitions." Kaufman, *Contemporary Jewish Philosophies*, 171. Heschel never really confronts this crucial challenge.

155. *GSM*, 197.

156. *The Sabbath*, 96.

157. *GSM*, 201.

158. *GSM*, 202.

159. *GSM*, 201.

160. *GSM*, 202.

161. *GSM*, 201.

162. *GSM*, 202. Heschel's emphatic focus on singular events and distinctive moments as bearers of divine truth represents, among other things, a rejection of the type of Enlightenment thinking that assumes "the character of the divine lives in its universality, which excludes all limitation by, and confinement to, the individual." Prophetic visions are ruled out by Spinoza, for example, precisely because "they seek God in the particular and accidental instead of in the universal and necessary." Of course, as we shall see in the following chapter, Heschel utterly rejects the metaphysical assumptions underlying Spinoza's worldview, not least the latter's insistence that "the ultimate source of all certainty lies not in becoming but in pure being . . . in the immutable grounds of being and in the self-contained unity of the nature of things." For Heschel, as we shall see, this is Greek thinking at its worst and must be repudiated. Cassirer, *The Philosophy of the Enlightenment*, 189, 185. Heschel, not surprisingly, had no love lost for Spinoza, the man who, he said, "attempted to destroy Jewish theology." "Jewish Theology," in *MGSA*, 155. (The crime of which Heschel accuses Spinoza there is the latter's disastrously influential contention that "the Bible was not theology but only law.")

163. *GSM*, 203.

164. Norman Solomon thus rather dramatically mischaracterizes Heschel's approach when he describes the latter's position on revelation as "Forget all that stuff about Moses on Mount Sinai and thunder and lightning and a voice proclaiming the Ten Commandments. It doesn't matter. What matters is whether, in your moments of profound mystical experience, you are stirred to turn towards God." Solomon, "Heschel in the Context of Modern Jewish Religious Thought," 10. Heschel's point in the passage cited by Solomon (9–10; *GSM*, 168) is not that the historicity of Sinai is irrelevant, but that historicity alone would be inadequate to sustain the ongoing relevance of what happened at that moment. Solomon simply elides Heschel's repeated emphasis on (a) particular moments of revelation (b) that God initiates. Solomon is obviously even further from the mark when he interprets Heschel's position as "reducing revelation to moments of profound mystery that anyone might experience, and that the Hebrew prophets experienced to a high degree" (Solomon, "Heschel in the Context of Modern Jewish Religious Thought," 10).

165. *GSM*, 205. Cf. *The Sabbath*, 96.

166. *GSM*, 209.

167. *GSM*, 210. Jewish faith, for Heschel, consists not of "a comprehension of abstract principles" but rather of "an inner attachment to sacred events. . . . Revelation lasts a moment," Heschel adds, "acceptance continues" (*GSM*, 213).

168. The position Heschel here rejects is articulately espoused by Robert Gordis, who writes: "Now, God is eternal and unchanging, but man is perpetually in flux, varying in his capacity to receive the Revelation of his Maker. Hence the idea of progressive and growing revelation is not merely compatible with faith in its divine origin, but is the only view that reckons with the nature of the human

participant in the process" (Gordis, *A Faith for Moderns*, 150). Now, contradicting Heschel explicitly, Gordis continues: revelation "is not an event, but a process. The theophany at Sinai marked the commencement, not the conclusion, of Revelation.... The revelation of God's will was not limited to the Biblical period. The era of the prophets was the Golden Age of Revelation, but it did not exhaust the process" (153, 152). Or again: "Revelation parallels creation. The great creative act that brought the universe into existence began in the dim past, yet the process is never-ending. Similarly, the classic events in Revelation took part in the past, and have been recorded in the words of the Prophets, sages, and saints. But God's communication with man, we may firmly believe, has not ended in time any more than it is limited in space" (154).

169. *GSM,* 128.

170. *GSM,* 129.

171. *GSM,* 215.

172. *GSM,* 215. See, most famously, Rashi to Exodus 19:1, and the sources cited by Heschel, *GSM,* 217n2.

173. Compare also the following: "Sacred history may be described as an attempt to overcome the dividing line of past and present, as an attempt *to see the past in the present tense*" (*GSM,* 211–212). Jewish living represents an attempt to bring the past into the present, and it thus depends on the recognition that "there are events which never become past" (211). Although Sinai happened only once, at a particular moment in history, its reverberations in human consciousness and experience persist. According to this formulation, there is no continuous revelation, but there is what I would term continuous reverberation.

174. *GSM,* 146, citing *Zohar,* 1:90a.

175. *GSM,* 205.

176. *GSM,* 129.

177. See Avot 6:2 and *GSM,* 145. Of course, this passage suggests that contem-

porary divine communication is in some sense connected to, and rooted in, the Sinai experience (some biblical texts call Sinai "Horeb"). In general, see the various sources marshaled in *GSM,* 145–146.

178. *GSM,* 171. Cf. 254.

179. *GSM,* 174–175.

180. *GSM,* 138. The insistence that, according to Heschel, God continues to speak even though the age of prophecy has ended is a recurrent theme in the work of Alexander Even-Chen. See Even-Chen, *Kol min ha-ʿArafel.*

181. *GSM,* 260.

182. Lamm, in *The Condition of Jewish Belief,* 124.

183. Heschel, "Toward an Understanding of Halakha," 144.

184. *MQ,* 133.

185. *GSM,* 275. In his subtle and learned Christian "bibliology," Telford Work "put[s] the Christological analogy to use in developing a doctrine of Scripture," drawing astute parallels between Christ's divinity-humanity and scripture's. For our purposes here, it is worth taking note of the ways Work builds upon Hans Urs von Balthasar's notion of "linguistic kenosis." Work writes: "God's investment in the words of Scripture means that in the shorter term, in their sojourn in the world, the divine words are subject to a ... similar surrender to sinful speakers, hearers, and readers. Following Balthasar, we may call the treatment they endure a kind of linguistic *kenosis.*" Or again, Work states that "the Bible is part of our voyage home, a point of departure for idolaters and a means of sustenance for weary pilgrims. And that must mean that in delivering it to the world, God makes His words vulnerable, for a time, to abuse." Now, it goes without saying that the differences between a Christologically rooted interpretation of scripture and a covenantal Jewish one are bound to be fundamental and in crucial respects irreconcilable, but the parallels between the

two approaches are nevertheless striking. See Work, *Living and Active*, 19, 65–66, 64. For the germ of Work's theory, cf. von Balthasar, *Explorations in Theology I*, 80. Cf. also Pinnock, *The Scripture Principle*, 97–98.

186. *GSM*, 275.

4. THE PATHOS OF THE SELF-TRANSCENDENT GOD

1. Heschel, "Jewish Theology," in *MGSA*, 155.

2. Heschel, "Jewish Theology," 156.

3. Heschel, "Jewish Theology," 156. Cf. *KGE*, 15.

4. Heschel, "Jewish Theology," 158.

5. Heschel, "Jewish Theology," 159.

6. Heschel, "Jewish Theology," 158.

7. It should go without saying, I hope, that I cannot possibly do justice to the complexity of Maimonides' thinking on this (or any other) matter in a few short paragraphs; my intention here is merely to sketch some of the broad contours of Maimonides' approach to the question of God in order to better understand what Heschel is rejecting, and why. The critical literature on Maimonides is almost literally endless. For a useful and highly sympathetic discussion of Maimonides' understanding of what a philosophically rigorous monotheism entails, a good place to begin is Seeskin, *Searching for a Distant God*, 3–65.

8. Cf., for example: "There is absolutely no likeness in any respect whatever between Him and the things created by Him." Maimonides, *The Guide of the Perplexed*, I: 35 (80).

9. Psalm 65:2, cited in Maimonides, *Guide*, I: 59 (139).

10. Maimonides, *Guide*, I:52 (117–118). Emphasis mine.

11. It is worth noting that the stark dichotomization of Hebraic and Hellenic thought was widespread during the 1940s and 1950s, especially among proponents of Christian neo-Orthodoxy and the Biblical Theology Movement. For a classic statement of this position, see Boman, *Hebrew Thought Compared with Greek*. Boman, among others, contended that the differences between Greek and biblical ways of thinking were rooted in the divergent patterns of thought generated by the Greek and Hebrew languages. "Not only are the [Hebrew and Greek] languages essentially different," he insisted, "but so too are the kinds of images and thinking involved in them. This distinction goes very deeply into the psychic life" (17). In light of this, Boman's own goal was to "present the peculiarity of Hebrew thinking in comparison with the Greek" (25). The argument for a linguistic basis of the purported Hebraic-Hellenic distinction has been thoroughly discredited by James Barr in *The Semantics of Biblical Language*, 34–64. Heschel's version of the distinction, it should be noted, does not seem to be based on any specious claims about language. But it is important to remember that one of the dangers of constructing an encompassing typology is that one loses the shades of color within the respective types. In Heschel's case, this means that as a result of the relentless dichotomization of biblical and Hellenistic thinking, the complexity and diversity of Greek thought and culture are all but completely effaced—whether consciously or not, it is difficult to say. What is true of the antitype (Greece) is arguably also the case for the ideal type (the prophets). Thus Jon Levenson contends that in Heschel's hands, "the thinking and experience of all the prophets tend to run together in a blur." Levenson, "Religious Affirmation," 43. For a significant recent critique of what he calls "the theory of theology's fall into Hellenistic philosophy," see Gavrilyuk, *The Suffering of the Impassible God*. A comprehensive study of this motif in twentieth-century theology is a

desideratum. In a Christian context, such an investigation would have to address, among many others, Adolf von Harnack and Anders Nygren. In a Jewish context, it would have to explore the radically disparate uses of the Athens-Jerusalem duality in figures such as Lev Shestov, Leo Strauss, Emmanuel Levinas, Will Herberg, and, of course, Abraham Joshua Heschel.

12. Heschel, "The God of Israel and Christian Renewal," in *MGSA*, 268. Speaking to Jewish educators, Heschel remarks, "I do not approve of the term 'the notion of God.' The God of Israel is a name, not a notion. There is a difference between a 'name' and a 'notion.' I am suggesting to you: don't teach notions of God, teach the name of God" ("Jewish Theology," 162).

13. Heschel, "The God of Israel," 268. Cf. Heschel, "Jewish Theology," 161–162.

14. Heschel, "The God of Israel," 269. Cf. *GSM*, 5–6, where Heschel contrasts "conceptual" and "situational" thinking. Whereas the former is "an act of reasoning," the latter "involves an inner experience." While the conceptual thinker adopts a posture of detachment, the situational thinker adopts a position of "concern," open not merely to judging, but also to being himself placed "under judgment."

15. Heschel, "The God of Israel," 271.

16. *MNA*, 54.

17. *MNA*, 54–55.

18. *MNA*, 55.

19. *MNA*, 244.

20. *GSM*, 125–126.

21. *GSM*, 126.

22. *MNA*, 244.

23. *MNA*, 138.

24. *MNA*, 143. I have questioned this claim about the God of the Hebrew Bible above, in the Introduction.

25. *MNA*, 143.

26. *GSM*, 13.

27. *GSM*, 14.

28. *GSM*, 15.

29. *GSM*, 15.

30. *GSM*, 15.

31. *GSM*, 13–14.

32. In *GSM*, for example, Heschel refers to Maimonides as one of "the leading exponents of Jewish thought" (187), and as "one of the greatest scholars of the law of all times" (340).

33. *GSM*, 21. In a similar vein, Heschel faults Maimonides for his overly abstract approach to law. In his great legal code the *Mishneh Torah*, Heschel writes that Maimonides

> took in the theoretical opinions [of the talmudic teachers], but left out the concrete circumstances, the promptings and processes of forming judgments, and the names of the disputants and the pronouncers of decisions. Here lies the inherent defect of his codification: instead of the process, the concept; instead of the case, the law; instead of the people, the matter; instead of history, theory; instead of the living atmosphere, the anonymous authorship; *instead of the situation, the abstraction.*" (Heschel, *Maimonides*, 96) (emphasis mine)

34. *GSM*, 21.

35. *GSM*, 22.

36. Heschel, "Jewish Theology," 156.

37. It should be pointed out that Heschel's overall relationship to Maimonides is far more complex than this analysis taken alone would suggest. On the one hand, as I have shown, Heschel strongly rejects Maimonides' attempted synthesis of Greek and biblical thinking, precisely because, he contends, the biblical is essentially erased by the Greek. Thus, it is no exaggeration to label Heschel's project thoroughly anti-Maimonidean in this regard. On the other hand, however, there are other aspects of Maimonides' life and thought that Hes-

chel admired, and arguably even sought to emulate, most prominently the former's purported turn, toward the end of his life, to a more active engagement with real people and their problems. Heschel speaks of

> Maimonides' last metamorphosis: From metaphysics to medicine, from contemplation to practice, from specu- lation to the imitation of God. God is not only the object of knowledge; He is the example one is to follow. Human beings whom He seeks to guide ... take the place of abstract concepts which constitute the means of the intellectual perception of God. Pre- occupation with the concrete man and the effort to aid him in his suffering is now the form of religious devotion. (Heschel, "The Last Days of Mai- monides," in *IF,* 289–290)

It is worth noting that Maimonides' own life thus seems to serve as an exception (or as a counterexample) to Heschel's insistence that worshipping a detached, indifferent God leads to a life of detach- ment and indifference. Heschel, of course, might retort that Maimonides was a better man (and a better Jew) than his theology.

Commenting on this passage, Michael Marmur astutely notes:

> The decision to place the figure of Mai- monides at the very peak of Heschel's social agenda, as the finale of the *Inse- curity of Freedom,* is no coincidence. He clearly found this example of progres- sion from the seclusion of study and reflection to engagement with people in society a potent source of personal inspiration. (Marmur, "Heschel's Two Maimonides," 242)

In the rich and insightful study just cited, Marmur demonstrates at length the complexity and ambivalence of Heschel's approach to Maimonides. He speaks of

Heschel's "two Maimonides," the first as the problematic "epitome of ... hyper- rationalism" (237), and the second as a man "imbued with radical prophetic passion" (239). Marmur rightly notes that the second Maimonides is a hero for Heschel, the first a kind of anti-hero. For our project here, which is an analysis of ways of thinking and talking about God, Maimonides as Heschelian anti-hero is what is critical.

38. Merkle, "Heschel's Theology of Di- vine Pathos," in *Abraham Joshua Heschel: Exploring His Life and Thought,* 72.

39. Michael Chester eloquently ob- serves that for Heschel, the Greek celebra- tion of "the power and ability of human reason" and of an "analytical approach to the questions of humanity and God ... re- sulted in the dehumanization of man and the depersonalization of God." Chester, *Divine Pathos and Human Being,* 119.

Interestingly, one contemporary scholar insists that for Maimonides, the highest human ideal is total emotionness: just as God has no emotional states, so should we aspire to have none. But it is not at all clear that this is Maimonides' view, and I have been careful not to attribute it to him here. Daniel Frank, "Anger as a Vice." And cf., for a brief rejoinder, David Shatz, "Maimonides' Moral Theory," 177. Needless to say, Heschel would have been horrified by the notion that anyone could consider emotionlessness a Jewish ideal (or a human ideal of any kind).

40. *Prophets,* II, 37.

41. *Prophets,* II, 37–38.

42. *Prophets,* II. 38.

43. *Prophets,* II, 40.

44. Cf., for example, "It is easy to see how on the basis of the ontological view of the Eleatics there emerged a static conception of God. According to Greek thinking, impassivity and immobility are characteristic of the divine. ... The ontological basis of this system of thought

may, of course, be challenged by another ontological system which sees in changeability the very sign of real being. Such a system will lead to a dynamic rather than a static idea of God." Heschel, "Divine Pathos," 121. Cf., for a somewhat more opaque formulation, *Prophets* II, 42.

45. Cf. Held, "The Promise and Peril of Jewish Barthianism," 317.

46. *MNA*, 101.

47. *Prophets*, II, 39.

48. *Prophets*, II, 4. In light of what we have seen, Fritz Rothschild famously contrasts Aristotle's Unmoved Mover with what he terms Heschel's "Most Moved Mover." Rothschild, "Introduction," 25.

49. Heschel, "Jewish Theology," 160. Heschel's emphasis on the divine pathos as the central element in prophetic teaching has influenced a variety of biblical theologians, most prominent among them Terence Fretheim and Walter Brueggemann. For an interesting exploration of Fretheim and Brueggemann's debt to Heschel, as well as of their significant divergences from him, see Schlimm, "Different Perspectives on Divine Pathos," 673–694.

50. *Prophets*, II, 15.

51. *Prophets*, I, 156. Cf. *IEE*, 129.

52. *IEE*, 159.

53. *Prophets*, I, 109.

54. *Prophets*, I, 100.

55. *Prophets*, I, 110.

56. *Prophets*, I, 32.

57. *Prophets*, I, 109–110.

58. *Prophets*, II, 4.

59. *Prophets*, I, 112.

60. *Prophets*, I, 151.

61. *Prophets*, I, 111.

62. *Prophets*, I, 113.

63. *Prophets*, I, 151.

64. It bears emphasizing that for Heschel, in contrast to so much of liberal theology, humanity alone is incapable of bringing redemption. If one can say, according to Heschel, that God seeks

humanity's participation in the work of redemption, it nevertheless remains true—and in some crucial sense, even more fundamental—that humanity alone cannot accomplish the goal. Human effort is necessary, but it is far from sufficient to the task; redemption is ultimately the work of God. Heschel writes:

> Had the prophets relied on human resources for justice and righteousness, on man's ability to fulfill all of God's demands, on man's power to achieve redemption, they would not have insisted upon the premise of messianic redemption, for messianism implies that any course of living, even the supreme efforts of man by himself, must fail in redeeming the world. In other words, human history is not sufficient unto itself. (*Prophets*, I, 184)

65. *Prophets*, II, 100. As I have noted in the introduction, Alexander Even-Chen misses this passage entirely in his discussion of divine omnipotence in Heschel, which enables him to fit *The Prophets* into his broader (and mistaken, in my view) claim that for Heschel, at least after World War II, "God is not almighty." Even-Chen, "God's Omnipotence," 41–71 (the phrase cited is on 52). I have discussed this issue in detail in the Introduction.

66. *Prophets*, II, 101.

67. *Prophets*, II, 4.

68. *Prophets*, II, 51.

69. *Prophets*, I, 48.

70. *Prophets*, I, 44.

71. *Prophets*, I, 47.

72. *Prophets*, I, 48. "Hosea is able to express as no other prophet the love of God for Israel in its most varied forms—as compassion (11:8), as a mother's tenderness (1:6–8; 2:3, 6, 21, 25; 11:1), as love between husband and wife (3:1ff.)" (49).

73. *Prophets*, I, 107.

74. For Heschel, Maurice Friedman writes, "God's anger and his mercy are

not opposites but correlatives." Maurice Friedman, "Abraham Heschel among Contemporary Philosophers," 296.

75. *Prophets*, I, 5–6. Cf.: "To man, the anger of God incites the fear of pain; to God, the anger *is* pain. Again and again the prophet refers to what anger means *sub specie dei*, the sorrow, the disillusionment caused by the people's disloyalty" (*Prophets*, II, 93).

76. *Prophets*, I, 142.

77. *Prophets*, II, 73.

78. *Prophets*, II, 68.

79. *Prophets*, II, 73.

80. *Prophets*, II, 63. "Pathos includes love, but goes beyond it. God's relation to man is not an indiscriminate outpouring of goodness, oblivious to the condition and merit of the recipient, but an intimate accessibility, manifesting itself in His sensitive and manifold reactions."

81. *Prophets*, II, 68, 62.

82. *Prophets*, II, 62.

83. *Prophets*, II, 78.

84. *Prophets*, II, 66.

85. *Prophets*, II, 62, 69.

86. *Prophets* I, 218; II, 266.

87. *Prophets*, II, 78.

88. *Prophets*, II, 77.

89. *Prophets*, II, 65.

90. *Prophets*, II, 70, 69.

91. *Prophets*, II, 74.

92. *Prophets*, II, 75.

93. Otto, *The Idea of the Holy*, 24.

94. *Prophets*, II, 77.

95. *Prophets*, II, 63.

96. *Prophets*, II, 68. Cf. II, 63, 72.

97. *Prophets*, II, 64. "The exploitation of the poor is to us a misdemeanor; to God it is a disaster. Our reaction is disapproval; God's reaction is something no language can convey" (64–65).

98. *Prophets*, II, 64.

99. *Prophets*, II, 64.

100. *Prophets*, II, 61.

101. Glick, *The Reality of Christianity*, 118.

102. Wilken, "Marcion," 8:5700–5702.

103. Micka, *The Problem of Divine Anger*, 21. Cf. *Prophets*, II, 80.

104. Micka, *The Problem of Divine Anger*, 23.

105. Tertullian, *Adversus Marcionem*, I, 6, cited in Heschel, *Prophets*, II, 80.

106. *Prophets*, II, 83. Although some scholars have insisted that any "Marcionism" in Christian theology "necessarily leads to anti-Judaism" (Mussner, "Kommende Schwerpunkte Biblischer Theologie," 237–251), others have recently attempted to complicate that narrative. While Marcion had a great deal of harsh things to say about the creator god of the Old Testament, they point out, he had far less to say about the Jews themselves than did many of his more orthodox opponents. Contrast Marcion with Tertullian, for example. Whereas the latter blames the Jews for killing Christ, the former does not—blame for that crime lies with the creator god rather than with his people. More important, whereas Marcion's opponents attempted to wrench the Old Testament away from the Jews and to appropriate its covenantal symbols, Marcion himself did not. Consider Stephen Wilson's remarks:

> It is clear that both the Marcionite and the Catholic positions involve a denigration of Judaism. Putting it simply, it is as if the Marcionite said to the Jew: "Keep your God, your Scriptures, and some of your law; we consider them to be inferior, superseded in every way by the gospel." The Catholic said: "We'll take your God, your Messiah, your Scriptures, and some of your law; as for you, you are disinherited, cast into a limbo, and your survival serves only as a warning of the consequences of obdurate wickedness." I would not like to be found defending either view of Judaism. However, it might be argued that the one which more obviously belittles Jewish symbols was, ironically, in practice the lesser of two evils.

All of this has led various scholars to wonder whether the Jews would have been better off historically had Marcion won and the Church effectively left the Jews alone. See, *inter alia*, Efromysen, "The Patristic Connection," 98–117; Wilson, "Marcion and the Jews," 45–58 (comment above is at 58); and Räisänen, "Marcion and the Origins of Christian Anti-Judaism," 121–135. Heschel's remarks obviously the reflect the older, more traditional perspective on Marcion and the perniciousness of his influence on Christian-Jewish relations.

107. Muller, *The Uses of the Past*, 83, cited in *Prophets*, II, 83.

108. Volz, *Das Dämonische in YHWH*, 9, cited in *Prophets*, II, 83.

109. Pauck, *Harnack and Troeltsch*, 37.

110. von Harnack, *Marcion*, 134.

111. Heschel is also concerned to fend off the charge that the "Old Testament" valorizes justice to the exclusion of love. "The logic of justice may seem impersonal," he writes, "yet the concern for justice is an act of love." *Prophets*, I, 201. And against the accusation that Judaism is concerned with actions to the exclusion of inwardness, Heschel points out that for the prophets, the people are held accountable for their "hearts" and not just their "deeds." *Prophets*, I, 208.

112. *Prophets*, II, 76.

113. *Prophets*, II, 77.

114. *Prophets*, II, 7.

115. *Prophets*, II, 9.

116. *Prophets*, II, 9.

117. *Prophets*, II, 7. Cf. also II, 52.

118. *Prophets*, II, 61. Emphasis mine.

119. *Prophets*, II, 74.

120. Gavrilyuk, *The Suffering of the Impassible God*.

121. Gavrilyuk, *The Suffering of the Impassible God*, 53. Cf. Micka, *The Problem of Divine Anger*, 39–77.

122. Gavrilyuk, *The Suffering of the Impassible God*, 53.

123. Gavrilyuk, *The Suffering of the Impassible God*, 58, 59.

124. Gavrilyuk, *The Suffering of the Impassible God*, 60.

125. I would suggest that the key distinction for Heschel, the one that renders divine and human anger so vastly different, is most clearly articulated in a pair of rabbinic texts cited in a footnote to Heschel's discussion of "The Meaning and Mystery of Wrath." Heschel first quotes the Mekhilta's comment on the following biblical verse: "For I the Lord am a jealous God" (Exodus 20:5). The Midrash interprets God as saying, "I am a God above jealousy. I am the master of jealousy and jealousy is not master of me." In a similar vein, Genesis Rabbah contains the comment that "man's anger controls him, but God controls His anger" (Genesis Rabbah 49:8). God is unique, in other words, in maintaining genuine freedom even amidst His anger. *Prophets*, II, 63n6. And yet compare Walter Brueggeman's evocation of YHWH's "rage," rooted in "passionate, perhaps out-of-control self-regard." Brueggemann, *Theology of the Old Testament*, 309. And cf. my brief discussion of God's self-regard, above, in the Introduction, note 16.

126. *Prophets*, II, 4.

127. *Prophets*, II, 39.

128. *TMHS*, I, 65; *HT*, 105.

129. *Prophets*, II, 11.

130. *Prophets*, II, 50.

131. *Prophets*, II, 51.

132. *Prophets*, II, 56.

133. *Prophets*, II, 50. "The error in regarding the divine pathos as anthropomorphism consisted in regarding a unique theological category as a common psychological concept. This was due to the complex nature of prophetic language, which of necessity combines otherness and likeness, uniqueness and comparability, in speaking about God. One is more easily cognizant of the aspects of pathos resembling human emotions than of aspects which set pathos apart as superhuman. Regarded as a form of humaniza-

tion of God, the profound significance of this fundamental category is lost."

134. *Prophets*, II, 56.

135. *Prophets*, II, 51.

136. *Prophets*, II, 52.

137. *Prophets*, II, 51–52. Cf. II, 40, 99.

138. *Prophets*, II, 11. In light of comments such as these, which are integral to his understanding of prophetic theology, Heschel would likely have felt a fair bit of ambivalence about the central role *The Prophets* has played in the recent Christian theological turn to divine passibility. For examples of the latter, see Moltmann, *The Crucified God*, 270–272; Bauckham, "'Only the Suffering God Can Help,'" 9–10; and the sources cited in Weinandy, *Does God Suffer?*, 8n23. Weinandy, himself a staunch opponent of passibilism, is closer to the mark, I think, in forcefully emphasizing the simultaneity of divine pathos and divine otherness in Heschel (64–68). For a study of Heschel's influence on Moltmann, see Jaeger, "Abraham Heschel and the Theology of Jürgen Moltmann," 167–179. For the distinction between them regarding whether pathos characterizes essence, cf. esp. 178.

139. *Prophets*, II, 263–264. Emphasis mine.

140. *Prophets*, II, 265. Cf. II, 215.

141. *Prophets*, II, 265. Terence Fretheim offers an interesting challenge to Heschel on this point, insisting that "there is not evidence in the OT that there is a God in himself who is invulnerable to [His] interaction with the world. There is no duality between God in himself and God in his relation to the world; whoever says God, says the God who reveals and acts. There is no other God behind the God who participates in the history of the world." Fretheim, "The Repentance of God," 69n30.

142. Berkovits, "Dr. A. J. Heschel's Theology of Pathos," 70. For an incisive response to Berkovits's critique of

Heschel, see Merkle, "Heschel's Theology of Divine Pathos," 75–81. Cf. Chester, *Divine Pathos and Human Being*, 57, 132–133, 146–150, 187–189. And note also Steven Katz's withering assessment of Berkovits's consistently inaccurate and ungenerous readings of other thinkers, "Eliezer Berkovits and Modern Jewish Philosophy," 94–140. For Katz's comments on Berkovits more broadly, see esp. 96–97; for his observations on the latter's treatment of Heschel, see 125–133. For another significant response to Berkovits's attack, see Tanenzapf, "Abraham Heschel and his Critics," 279–285.

There is something ironic about Fretheim's and Berkovits's critiques taken together. If, according to the one, Heschel is guilty of importing too much Maimonideanism into biblical thinking (pathos is not essence), according to the other, he is guilty of having imported too little.

143. *GSM*, 178–179.

144. Berkovits, "Theology of Pathos," 70.

145. Berkovits, "Theology of Pathos," 80, citing *Prophets*, II, 56.

146. Berkovits, "Theology of Pathos," 72.

147. Berkovits, "Theology of Pathos," 68.

148. Merkle astutely points out that Berkovits and Heschel work from irreconcilable starting points:

> Berkovits begins with the preconceived notion that God is impassible.... Heschel begins not with a preconceived notion but with an observation concerning biblical faith: "It is the greatness of God according to the Bible that man is not an abstraction to Him, nor is His judgment a generalization." Berkovits starts with the presupposition that God is absolutely different, "totally other," and hence impassible. Heschel starts with the divine-human relationship in which it is evident, according to a biblical perspective, that God is supreme but not the absolute antithesis of humanity.

(Merkle, "Heschel's Theology of Divine Pathos," 76–77, citing *Prophets*, II, 37)

Cf. also Chester, *Divine Pathos and Human Being*, 148.

149. Underneath the vehemence, this may have been the most substantive point of Berkovits's critique. In a similar vein, cf., for example, Friedman, "The Prophetic Experience," 173.

150. This is, implicitly, Fretheim's point. Cf. above, n 40.

151. The problem, of course, is that we lack criteria by which to determine when to pay heed to philosophy and when to resist it.

152. *GSM*, 12–13.

153. Lest I be misunderstood: I do not think I have resolved the question of pathos and essence in Heschel, but have instead attempted to draw out what I think is at stake in it. At any rate, I suspect that any thinker who seeks to take biblical language about divine pathos seriously, without, however, taking it literally (and thus anthropomorphically), will face some version of the same tension.

Maurice Friedman suggests that Heschel was fully aware that he had not fully solved the problem of anthropomorphism—and that he did not wish to: "'Anthropomorphic language may be preferable to abstract langue,' Heschel said to me, 'for when you use abstract language you may have the illusion of adequacy.'" "Abraham Heschel among Contemporary Philosophers," 296.

154. *Prophets*, I, 26. The thorny problem of anthropopathism emerges here again: if God's pathos is so radically different from ours, what does it mean to suggest that the prophet's life is animated by sympathy with it, indeed, that he "participates" in it? As Maurice Friedman comments, "When one talks of God's pathos and the prophet's sympathy with it, it is difficult not to attribute feelings to

God in a way very like those of man, even if infinitely greater than his." Friedman, "Prophetic Experience," 119. At any rate, what Heschel is after here is relational closeness coupled with an unbridgeable metaphysical gap.

155. *Prophets*, II, 87. See also I, 38; II, 89, 101.

156. Friedman, "Prophetic Experience," 119.

157. *Prophets*, II, 88.

158. *Prophets*, II, 89.

159. See *Prophets*, II, 93–95, and Scheler, *The Nature of Sympathy*.

160. *Prophets*, II, 94.

161. *Prophets*, I, 114. Especially striking here are the words of Jeremiah: "You enticed me, O Lord, and I was enticed; You overpowered me and You prevailed" (Jeremiah 20:7, NJPS). Heschel suggests the following translation: "O Lord, Thou hast seduced me, And I am seduced; Thou hast raped me, and I am overcome."

162. *Prophets*, II, 91. "The prophet has to be called in order to respond, he has to receive in order to reciprocate."

163. *Prophets*, II, 98. Cf. I, 114.

164. *Prophets*, II, 89.

165. *Prophets*, II, 99.

166. *Prophets*, II, 89. Nathan Rotenstreich writes that "since sympathy is, by definition, addressing itself only to the divine revelation or to the divine pathos and not to the divine essence, sympathy cannot bring about a unification of man with God, that unification which goes by the name of *unio mystica*." Rotenstreich, "On Prophetic Consciousness," 191. As I discuss at some length in chapter 6, for Heschel this is not a limitation to lament, but a crucial aspect of his theology: covenantal theology positively requires the rejection of mystical union as a possibility, let alone as an ideal.

167. *Prophets*, I, 119.

168. *Prophets*, I, 125. Cf. I: 119; II: 92. None of this, Heschel insists, should be

confused with a religion of pure senti-
mentality; sympathy, he emphasizes, "is
not an end in itself. . . . Not mere feeling, but action, will mitigate the world's
misery, society's injustice or the people's
alienation from God" (II, 89).

169. It should be clear that the priority I refer to is axiological rather than
chronological.

170. *Prophets,* I, 218.

171. *Prophets,* I, 219.

172. In fact, I see no evidence at all
in Heschel that he entertained the possibility of the religious-theological ever
conflicting with the ethical. On the
contrary, as Robert Erlewine very insightfully points out, "Heschel's theocentrism
rejects the neo-humanist conception
of God as some sort of transcendental
condition for the encounter with the
other, but it also stands in conflict with
a theocentrism that subordinates morality to one's primary obligation to God,
though on theocentric grounds, i.e., the
prophetic revelation of divine concern for
human beings." Erlewine, "Reclaiming
the Prophets," 205. Cf. the excursus on
Heschel and Yeshayahu Leibowitz, chapter 6, note 144.

173. *Prophets,* I, 218.

174. Susannah Heschel writes that
"Heschel's achievement was to bring to
the fore the centrality of prophetic critique without neglecting the religious experience underlying their passions." The
point could be made much more strongly:
Heschel brought prophetic social critique
to the fore, all the while insisting that
such critique was *thoroughly rooted in, and
inextricably intertwined with,* the religious
experience underlying prophetic passion.
Heschel, "Theological Affinities," 174. Cf.
also Hartman, *Conflicting Visions,* 177.

175. Crucially, Akiva is thus open to—
indeed, he seems to celebrate—starkly
anthropomorphic images, while Ishmael
rejects them as "not befitting the divine

dignity." See, for example, *TMHS,* li;
(omitted from *HT,* 41), and *TMHS,* 13;
HT, 56–57.

176. *TMHS,* xli; *HT,* 32: "Intellectual
debates and psychological rumblings are
the stuff of every generation. Spiritual
problems continually shed forms and take
on new ones. Before you can understand
the intellectual movements of recent
times, you must inquire into the chain of
tradition that precedes them." Gordon
Tucker rightly notes that "here Heschel is
tipping us off to what is, in many ways, his
real agenda in this work, that is, contemporary Jewish issues, such as post-Shoah
theology, attitudes to prayer, fundamen-
talisms, etc. These contemporary issues
will sometimes be dealt with overtly in
subsequent chapters, and sometimes co-
vertly, but they will always be there" (*HT,*
32n111).

177. *HT,* xxiv.

178. *TMHS,* 172–182; *HT,* 190–207.

179. *HT,* 189.

180. Tucker speaks of a "tilt" toward Ishmael in the book. *HT,* xxvi. Cf.
also Tucker, "Heschel's *Torah min ha-
shamayim,*" 55.

181. Tucker makes a similar point:
"Although Ishmael seems clearly to get
preferred in matters of autonomy of
reason, in exegesis, the conventionality of
worship, and the freedom of the prophet,
Akiva seems to get the clear nod when it
comes to God's participation in Israel's
sorrows." Tucker, "Heschel's *Torah min
ha-shamayim,*" 55.

In an early review of *TMHS,* Jacob
Levinger rightly recognized that despite
its ostensibly historical-critical packag-
ing, Heschel's study of the rabbis was
ultimately animated by a normative theological agenda. But Levinger's comments
focused exclusively on revelation and on
Heschel's desire "to liberate the average
Hebrew reader from his limited Orthodox
perspective, according to which there

is only one approach to the divinity of Torah." He missed (or ignored, perhaps because he focused on the second volume of the work rather than the first) the other central normative theological project of the book, namely, to situate a theology of divine suffering and human solidarity therewith in the very heart of the rabbinic canon. Heschel's (Akivan) approach to suffering is no less critical to *TMHS* as a whole than is his (Ishmaelian) approach to revelation. See Levinger, "Heʾarot le-Torah min ha-shamayim," 45–47.

And yet, despite their obvious affinities, there are (at least) two significant issues in Akiva's thinking (as Heschel understands it) at which I suspect Heschel would have demurred. First, as we shall see, Akiva is willing to talk about suffering reaching God's essence. From Heschel's broader body of work, including occasions when he theologizes in his own voice, it is clear that he does not believe human beings can know anything at all about God's essence. Put differently, my sense is that on this question, Heschel is ultimately more in line with Ishmael (and with the prophets as he understands them) than with Akiva, even as he sympathizes with the impulse that gave rise to the latter's view. Cf. *TMHS*, xliv; abridged (with an important sentence about Ishmael excised) in *HT*, 35. Second, as we shall again see, Akiva is willing, at least at moments, to choose between God's omnipotence and His mercy, sacrificing the former, as it were, for the sake of the latter. As I have argued in the introduction, the dominant perspective in Heschel's thought is that God's power is not limited but rather *self-limited*. This is, I have suggested, a critical aspect of God's self-transcendence.

182. Robert Eisen has stated this point forcefully. See Eisen, "A. J. Heschel's Rabbinic Theology," 218–219. I complicate this question a bit in the next chapter,

on Heschel's post-Holocaust theology of protest.

183. *AJH*, 83; *HT*, 119.

184. *TMHS*, 65; *HT*, 105.

185. We return to this claim about God's participation in Israel's woes touching "His very essence" below. Note here that in this, Rabbi Akiva goes further than any prophet (not to mention Heschel himself) would have dared.

186. *TMHS*, 65–66; *HT*, 106.

187. *TMHS*, 73; *HT*, 111.

188. Y. Sukkah 4:3 (54c); Mekhilta DeRabbi Ishmael, Pisha 14; Sifre Behaʿalotekha 84. Cited in *TMHS*, 66; *HT*, 106.

189. Exodus Rabbah 42:3, cited in *TMHS*, 66; *HT*, 106. Tucker correctly notes (*HT*, 106n1) that Akiva is playing here with the inherent ambiguity of the term *"Elohim"* in Hebrew; since it can mean "God" or "gods," and Hebrew has no capital letters, *"V'Elohav"* in the verse can be taken to mean "their God" as opposed to "their gods."

190. *TMHS*, 66; *HT*, 107: "From time immemorial the people had perceived the salvation of Israel as a human need, a national need, through which, to be sure, God's name would be magnified in the world. But now Rabbi Akiva taught that Israel's salvation is a divine need." Heschel suggests further that in contrast to classical theology, according to which "salvation was conditional upon Israel's merit," Akivan theology insists that since salvation is "the concern and need" of God, salvation will eventually come to Israel regardless of their merit.

191. *TMHS*, 67; *HT*, 108.

192. *Prophets*, I, 108.

193. See *Prophets*, I, 110ff, esp. 112.

194. How important was this divine suffering-with to Heschel himself? In a telling moment—ostensibly explaining the position of the Baal Shem Tov but no doubt also expressing his own—Heschel

writes: "All of man's sorrow is the sorrow of the Shhekhinah as well. . . . This thought, expressed by the sages of the Mishnah [Sanhedrin 6:5], became a vast spiritual reality, opening a new dimension to all experience: my grief is God's grief. If there is some consolation in the anguish that is shared by many, the anguish shared by the Divine Presence is far more than a consolation." *PT*, 32. Cf. *KGE*, 26.

195. *TMHS*, 74; *HT*, 113. Consider, for example, an early rabbinic homily: "'You neglected the Rock that begot you' [Deuteronomy 32:18]. The word *teshi* ["neglected"] can be understood in relation the word *teshishut* ["feebleness"], whence the interpretation 'You weaken the Power of the One on high'" (Sifre Ha'azinu 319).

196. *TMHS*, 74; *HT*, 113.

197. *TMHS*, 86 (omitted in the Tucker translation).

198. And he can also show, in the process, that seemingly radical kabbalistic notions are actually well grounded in the theological worldview of one of rabbinic Judaism's most important theological thinkers.

199. Both *The Prophets* and the first volume of *TMHS* were published in 1962.

200. *Prophets*, I, 47.

201. *Prophets*, I, 49.

202. *Prophets*, I, 48. Cf. also 51.

203. *Prophets*, I, 49.

204. Cf. *Prophets*, I, 50: "This is one of the boldest conceptions of religious thinking. . . . It has the aura of sublimity. It involves restraint, bringing with it duties and responsibilities, but it also endows with a nobility that is a synonym for eternity. Israel is the consort of God."

205. *Prophets*, I, 51.

206. *Prophets*, I, 53.

207. *Prophets*, I, 56.

208. *Prophets*, I, 57.

209. *Prophets*, I, 60. Cf. Hosea 4:6. Let me emphasize that I am not interested here in biblical scholarship as much as in twentieth-century theology. In other words, I am investigating Heschel's Hosea rather than Hosea himself. I leave it to others to determine whether Heschel's interpretation of "*daath elohim*" is sustainable according to the canons of contemporary biblical scholarship. Whether it is or not is ultimately beside my point.

210. Describing Akiva's position, Heschel writes, "What is the meaning of sufferings? They are both ours and His, and thus salvation is both ours and His. One who asks: 'Why is this exile come upon us?' (should be answered with) 'Upon us and not upon Him?' One who removes *God* from the community has denied the very essence of the faith" (*TMHS*, 86; *HT*, 120). Tucker rightly notes that the language used here is reminiscent of the question of and response to the wicked son in the Passover Haggadah. He then astutely adds: "In the Haggadah, the crucial ideology is the horizontal solidarity of all Israel, and the Wicked Son's transgression is removing himself from that solidarity. Here the crucial ideology is the vertical solidarity of God and Israel in the 'vale of tears,' and the ultimate transgression is to remove God from that solidarity" (*HT*, 120n38; cf. xxii–xxiii, note 2).

211. *TMHS*, 84; *HT*, 119.

212. Lamentations Rabbah, Prologue 2. *TMHS*, 85; *HT*, 120.

213. *TMHS*, 85; *HT*, 120.

214. Again, I am not interested here in the historical R. Akiva or R. Simeon, but in the theological purpose they serve in Heschel's writings. I speak here ultimately not of Akiva, but of Heschel's Akiva.

215. *TMHS*, 65; *HT*, 105.

216. *TMHS*, 86; *HT*, 121. "They [that is, Akiva and his school] dared to look, and in so doing, they found that the pains of the nation were indeed paralleled by the pains of the Creator. And thus, instead

of bearing their own afflictions, they began instead to share in the afflictions of Heaven." More dramatically, Heschel writes: "This response constitutes an elevation of human suffering. It elevates the mystery of suffering above and beyond the human realm, and seeks to nullify the afflictions of mortals before the afflictions of Heaven" (*TMHS*, 84; *HT*, 120 [adapted]).

217. Note that Heschel articulates this in both the indicative and the imperative mode—indicative, in that such a notion has already "bestirred" the hearts of Israel; imperative, in that it is "incumbent upon *us* to take *our share* in the pains of the Holy and Blessed One" (*TMHS*, 65; *HT*, 105).

218. Note again, however, that each is soliciting sympathy for a different type of divine pathos. In the case of the prophet Hosea, Israel is called to sympathize with the pathos of love and anger; in the case of the sage Akiva, it is called to sympathize with the pathos of fellow-suffering. The varying forms of pathos invoked would presumably call forth sympathy of varying texture.

219. *TMHS*, 82; *HT*, 117.

220. *TMHS*, 67; *HT*, 108.

221. *TMHS*, 86; *HT*, 121.

222. *TMHS*, 83; *HT*, 118.

223. *TMHS*, 83; *HT*, 119.

224. *TMHS*, 86; *HT*, 121. Actually, this last sentence is a bit ambiguous: Heschel speaks of God compressing His presence so that He might be revealed "*im am bechiro*," which Tucker renders as "*to* His chosen nation." More exactly, it might be translated as "*with* His chosen nation."

225. *TMHS*, 86. Omitted from *HT*.

226. On this point (as on so many others), Heschel is not entirely consistent. Several chapters later, for example, he will return to the earlier formulation: "Better to limit belief in God's power than to dampen faith in God's mercy" (*TMHS*,

172; *HT*, 210)—exactly the same sentence as earlier in our chapter (*TMHS*, 83; *HT*, 119). Here, at least, Heschel is not so much espousing a fully formed theology as he is playing with a series of images, and holding them up to the light at different angles: does Akiva hold that God is merciful, but not omnipotent (as might appear from the sentence quoted in this note), or that God is merciful and has chosen to surrender His omnipotence (as is suggested by the passage we have been discussing)? I am not sure Heschel was interested in resolving the question here, so much as in exploring its contours. At any rate, I have argued that in Heschel's own theology, the idea that God limits His own power is the dominant view—and thus forms an important part of his theology of divine self-transcendence.

In *TMHS* as in the *Prophets*, Even-Chen fails to see the complexity in Heschel's presentation. He asserts flatly that Akiva's position is that God is not omnipotent, and also that "Heschel's own opinion follows Akiva." Strangely, he makes no mention at all of the passage we have been discussing from *TMHS*, 86; *HT*, 121, and this unfortunately leads him to a one-dimensional (and to my mind, mistaken) interpretation of Heschel's views. Even-Chen, "God's Omnipotence," 67–68. For a misreading of Heschel along similar lines, see Ronen, "Absolute Goodness or Omnipotence."

227. *TMHS*, 104; *HT*, 139.

228. *TMHS*, 93; *HT*, 130. Indeed, Rabbi Eliezer ben Jacob, one of Akiva's disciples, is reported to have said: "When a person suffers afflictions, he must express gratitude to the Holy and Blessed One. Why? Because it is his afflictions that draw him to the Holy and Blessed One." Midrash Tanhuma Tetze 2, cited in *TMHS*, 95; *HT*, 132.

229. *TMHS*, 95; *HT*, 132.

230. *TMHS*, 98; *HT*, 134–135.

231. Sifre Va-athanan 32, cited in *TMHS*, 93; *HT*, 130.

232. *TMHS*, 97; *HT*, 133.

233. "The Holy and Blessed One afflicts him in this world, even if he is without transgression, so as to increase his reward in the future world even beyond his merits" (Rashi to BT Berakhot 5a).

234. *TMHS*, 98 and note 7; *HT*, 134 and note 22. Heschel does not seem conscious of the bold originality of his interpretation. At any rate, he does not call attention to it.

235. *TMHS*, 97; *HT*, 133.

236. *TMHS*, 98; *HT*, 134.

237. Sifre Zuta, p. 248, cited in Heschel, *TMHS*, 98; *HT*, 134. Cf. Heschel's remarks about the possibility of forgiveness after the Holocaust in Simon Wiesenthal, *The Sunflower*, 130–131.

238. *TMHS*, 98; *HT*, 135.

239. *MNA*, 244.

240. *Prophets*, II, 64.

241. *WM*, 75.

242. Abraham Joshua Heschel, "The Holy Dimension," in *MGSA*, 365.

243. *GSM*, 43.

244. *MNA*, 185.

245. Abraham Joshua Heschel, "Religion and Race," in *IF*, 92.

5. "AWAKE, WHY SLEEPEST THOU, O LORD?"

1. *PT*, 264. Cf. *KGE*, 595. Cf. Heschel's description of the Kotzker as "disaffected, disillusioned, [and] beset by many anxieties." One major source of the Rebbe's anxiety, he speculates, was "the thought that ultimately God Himself was responsible for the inherent falsehood of human existence" (*PT*, 233).

2. *PT*, 275. Cf. *KGE*, 605. Cf. pp. 272–273: "Time and again, the Kotzker returned to this issue: was it conceivable that the entire world, Heaven and earth, was a palace without a master? . . . This problem tormented Reb Mendl." In

referring to a palace without a master, of course, Heschel is alluding to a classical midrash about Abram's first encounter with God. The patriarch, we are told, "was traveling from place to place when he saw a palace in flames [or perhaps: lit up—*doleket*]. 'Is it possible that the palace lacks a person to look after it?' he wondered. The owner of the building looked out and said, 'I am the owner of this palace'" (Gen. R. 39:1). In other places in his writing, Heschel takes the midrash to mean that Abram saw a palace "lit up," and intuited an awareness of God from his sense of wonder. Here, however, he implicitly takes the midrash to mean that Abram saw a palace "in flames" (the more plausible rendering of the Hebrew *doleket*) and wondered whether there could be a God in such a world. Cf. *KGE*, 603. And compare Heschel's invocation of the story in *GSM*, 111–112, with his use of it in *GSM*, 367. And cf. *GSM*, 113n7. For a fascinating recent scholarly reinterpretation of the story, see Mandel, "The Call of Abraham," 267–284, and for a recent theological re-appropriation, see Held, "Wonder and Indignation."

3. *PT*, 261. Let me emphasize that I am not suggesting that the Kotzker can be read as a stand-in for Heschel in general— "Despite the awe his thoughts evoke, he cannot serve as a model. For it is surely not the will of God that man lead a tortured life" (*PT*, 205)—but only that when it comes to facing the immensity of evil, the former articulates a crucial dimension of the latter's religious world.

Interestingly, in the chapter of *KGE* that most nearly parallels "The Kotzker and Job," no suggestion is offered that what is in fact presented is an essay on faith rather than an exposition of Kotzk (and, in fact, the two chapters read quite differently, not least because Heschel's own voice is much more muted in *KGE*). At least in part for that reason, I focus here on the Kotzker of *PT* rather than *KGE*. A systematic comparison of Heschel's presentation of the Kotzker in English (*PT*) and in Yiddish (*KGE*) is a desideratum. There is obviously a great deal of overlap (as some of the notes to this chapter indicate), but the portraits are not exactly the same, and not only because the English-language work is so much shorter than the Yiddish.

4. *PT*, xiv.

5. As if to emphasize Menahem Mendl's contemporaneity, Heschel writes, "Did the Kotzker intuit the coming triumph of Satan that brought the Holocaust to his people a few generations later? 'I am not worried about hunger; what worries me is human cruelty,' he exclaimed" (*PT*, 167). Cf. 203, 210.

6. *PT*, 263–303.

7. *PT*, 265.

8. *PT*, 267.

9. *PT*, 265.

10. *PT*, 269.

11. *PT*, 269.

12. *PT*, 277. Cf. *KGE*, 607.

13. *PT*, 278.

14. *PT*, 269. Cf. *KGE*, 600.

15. *PT*, 295.

16. *PT*, 280. At one point, Heschel also describes the Kotzker as insisting (at moments?) that "though in this world it might seem at times that God's ways are unjust, ultimately all His ways would be revealed as just." Moreover, since God does not owe us anything, "there are no grounds for complaint against God." *PT*, 279. Cf. *KGE*, 608. But as we have seen, piety of this sort is decidedly not the dominant thrust of Heschel's portrayal of Menahem Mendl.

17. *PT*, 298.

18. *PT*, 280. Cf. *KGE*, 609. It may seem strange at first blush to attribute "the eloquence of silence" to a writer as prolific as Heschel. The silence I refer to is obviously not theological silence writ large,

but silence about the specific question of anger at, and disappointment with, God. On this latter point, Heschel tended to be remarkably reticent. It is with the rare exceptions to this reticence that I am mostly concerned here.

19. *PT*, 300.

20. *PT*, 298.

21. *PT*, 300. Cf. the words of post-Holocaust Jewish theologian Irving ("Yitz") Greenberg, who writes: "There is one response to such overwhelming tragedy [as the Shoah]: the reaffirmation of meaningfulness, worth, and life—through acts of love and life-giving. The act of creating a life or enhancing its dignity is the counter-testimony to Auschwitz.... To leap in and pull a child out of a pit, to clean its face and heal its body, is to make the most powerful statement—the only statement that counts." Greenberg, "Cloud of Smoke, Pillar of Fire," 41–42.

22. An interesting link could be drawn between Heschel's comments here and the Zionist writings of Rabbi Joseph Soloveitchik. Confronted in *"Kol Dodi Dofek"* with the enormity of the Holocaust, Soloveitchik speaks of Judaism's concern with "Halakhic" rather than "metaphysical" responses to evil. In other words, Judaism is concerned not with why suffering occurs, but rather with what to do in its face. In either case, of course, one could accuse Heschel or Soloveitchik of deflecting the theological (or "metaphysical") issue, but each is insistent upon Judaism's shift of emphasis away from speculation and toward response. See Soloveitchik, *Fate and Destiny*.

23. *PT*, 298.

24. *PT*, 300.

25. *PT*, 302–303. In the language of the previous chapter, we might say that in this moment, the old Jew becomes a full-blooded Akivan, focusing on God's sorrow instead of his own. Zachary Braiter-

man dismisses the story as "not a little precious." See Braiterman, (God) After Auschwitz, 68. Be that as it may, it does provide a useful window into Heschel's perspective on the religious significance of compassion for God. By attributing the sentiment to a survivor of the camps, Heschel places the words directly in Job's mouth, as it were. Cf. Eliezer Berkovits's use of the motif of Job—actual victims of the Holocaust, and "Job's brother"—people who experienced the Shoah only at second hand. See Berkovits, Faith after the Holocaust, 69.

26. PT, 190. In speaking of praise in the morning and faithfulness at night, Heschel is interpreting Psalm 92:3.

27. PT, 301.

28. Braiterman, (God) After Auschwitz, 68–69. Braiterman is followed by Chester, Divine Pathos and Human Being, 94.

29. MNA, 151–152.

30. MNA, 152.

31. MNA, 152. Given Heschel's less than consistent use of commas, this sentence can be read in two ways: either human beings have been fed on hopes of salvation and immortality (both of which occur) in the world to come, or they have been fed on hopes of salvation (presumably, in this world) and immortality in the world to come. If the latter version is what he intends, then Heschel seems to be offering a forceful critique of both Judaism and Christianity and the ways they often allow—indeed, encourage—believers to turn away from religion's primary message (human responsibility), and toward false mythologies of divine beneficence instead; if the former version is what he intends, then Heschel seems to be articulating a distinctly Jewish critique of traditional Christianity, with its focus on achieving individual immortality at the purported expense of collective human responsibility. Either way, the larger point is that theologies that are excessively

focused on divine promise undermine rather than facilitate human maturity and responsibility.

32. MNA, 152–153.

33. MNA, 153.

34. "Having all in abundance save His blessing, they find their wealth a shell in which there is curse without mercy" (MNA, 153).

35. Heschel's ideas here might fruitfully be compared with the post-Holocaust theology of Eliezer Berkovits. According to Berkovits, God's long-suffering patience with the wicked entails the hiding of God's face (hester panim) from the innocent sufferer. The nature of creation is such that some will suffer as a result of others misusing their freedom. Berkovits argues that the Bible speaks of the hiding of the face not only as a result of divine anger, but also as a consequence of the evil perpetrated by human beings. To be sure, there are crucial differences between the two approaches: whereas for Berkovits, hester panim from the righteous is the result of divine patience with the wicked, for Heschel, hester panim from the wicked is what enables them to murder the innocent without remorse or compunction. The two theologians disagree, in other words, as to whom God is primarily turning away from. But at the same time, both use the radical freedom granted to the wicked and invoke the biblical motif of hester panim to explain (at least partly) the horrific suffering of the righteous. Both Berkovits and Heschel employ versions of a free will theodicy in which the biblical notion of hester panim plays a defining (although, again, quite different) role. See Berkovits, Faith after the Holocaust, esp. 86–113.

36. Heschel nowhere develops a full-blown theory of divine providence, and his notions of providence are not fully consistent over time. But for our purposes, it is important to note that

even after Israel's surprising military victory in the Six Day War of 1967, when he does speak of a "a hidden Presence in history [that] breaks forth in rare moments," he is still careful to insist that "the presence of God in history is never conceived to mean His penetration of history. God's will does not dominate the affairs of men." *IEE*, 136, 131. If, as Arnold Eisen suggests, these passages in *IEE* evince a "weak view of providence," the discussion in *MNA* evinces an even weaker one. Eisen, "Abraham Joshua Heschel," 11.

37. David Wolpe is simply mistaken when he writes that Heschel speaks of *hester panim* "without making the link" to the Shoah. Wolpe, "Hester Panim," 45. The idea of *hester panim* is inextricably woven with the Shoah throughout chapter 16 of *MNA*, as is evidenced, for example, by the way the chapter opens: "For us, contemporaries and survivors of history's most terrible horrors, it is impossible to meditate upon the compassion of God without asking: Where is God?" (*MNA*, 151).

Shoshana Ronen declares that the notion of *hester panim* is incompatible with Heschel's theology (which, she mistakenly assumes, posits a powerless God)—an odd claim indeed, given that Heschel's discussion here in *MNA* (of which she makes no mention) is centered precisely on an exploration of the dynamics of *hester panim* as he understands it. Ronen, "Absolute Goodness or Omnipotence," 141.

38. I discuss whether and how the same theologian can insist at one and the same time both that God is in search of man and that God is hiding his face below, in chapter 7.

39. *MNA*, 153.

40. *MNA*, 154. In his later writings, Heschel attributes this formulation to the Baal Shem Tov. See *PT*, 18.

41. And yet the description we have seen, of God "giving up" on the Germans and thereby seemingly abandoning the Jews to their fate, has a dissonant and profoundly disturbing resonance.

42. *MNA*, 154–155.

43. Heschel here appears to offer a kind of synthesis of the KJ and JPS translations. Although he tends to use the KJ, he needs JPS in this case because it renders "*lo khichadti*" as "have not denied," instead of KJ's "have not concealed." It is the former meaning—Job's maintaining his faith in the face of suffering—that Heschel needs in this section. Note that NJPS interprets "*velo khichadti imre qodesh*" as having the opposite sense: "Would that God consented to crush me, loosed His hand and cut me off. Then this would be my consolation, as I writhed in unsparing pains: *That I did not suppress my words against the Holy One*." The correct translation of Job is for our purposes beside the point; what matters is how Heschel understood and utilized Job.

44. It is worth pointing out that Heschel does not seem particularly preoccupied with the problem of natural evil; a European refugee whose family was slaughtered by the Nazis, he seems understandably focused specifically on the problem of moral evil. But cf. *TMHS*, I, 90–92; *HT*, 123–126.

45. I am grateful to David Roskies, Jeremy Dauber, and especially Arthur Green for conversations about this statement of the Kotzker's.

Later, in *A Passion for Truth*, Heschel will render the statement somewhat differently—"Live in agony and survive by faith," or "Though life may all be hell, survive by faith"—and interpret it specifically as mandating faith in the face of arguments against it: "Men must live by faith despite their agonizing subjection to arguments disputing its tenets" (*PT*, 190). Or again: "Man had to live by faith despite his agony, despite his perennial subjection to disputing its validity. 'Be in a hell of a mess and survive on faith,' he taught" (PT, 295). Here in MNA, in contrast, the challenge to faith does not seem to come from arguments against it, but from experiences that render it difficult, even excruciating, to affirm. See similarly KGE, 170.

46. I quote the Psalm as Heschel cites it, in the King James translation.

47. The summary provided is basically a quotation of the one offered by James Mays in his important commentary on the Psalms. See Mays, Psalms, 176.

48. Mays, Psalms, 179.

49. Indeed, biblical scholar Franz De-litzsch has described Psalm 44 as "the national mirroring of the Book of Job." See Delitzsch, Psalms, 66.

50. Mays, Psalms, 178.

51. Mays, Psalms, 177. Cf. Isaiah 28:21.

52. Compare Wolpe's one-dimensional characterization of Heschel: "Heschel is concerned to 'get God off the hook.' Indeed he says so explicitly, arguing, 'He is now thought of as the ultimate Scapegoat'" (Wolpe, "Hester Panim," 45, citing MNA, 152). As we have seen, Heschel does in fact say this. But as I have demonstrated, he says other things as well, many of which cannot be reconciled with Wolpe's depiction of his thought.

53. Notable here are Heschel's descriptions of the Kotzker's steadfast commitment to restraint in speech: "The less spoken, the better. . . . A lock ought to hang over one's mouth. . . . 'Let your heart burst before uttering so much as a moan.' . . . 'When a man has reason to scream, and cannot though he wants to—he has achieved the greatest scream'" (PT, 281ff.). Perhaps Heschel felt that citing precedent for his anger was somehow more permissible than expressing it in his own language. Cf. Braiterman, (God) After Auschwitz, 183n37.

54. Braiterman writes, "Himself a master stylist, Heschel never challenged God in his own voice. He accused God, but only under a clumsy guise of rhetorical device and biblical citation. In fact," he insists, "no bridge eased the shift from Heschel's condemnation of humanity to his citation of Psalm 44." This "abrupt transition," he argues, "obliquely indicate[s] how Heschel shied away from the very complaint slipping into his own discourse" (Braiterman, (God) After Auschwitz, 183n37). But note, first, that Heschel does attempt to build a bridge between his condemnation of humanity and his citation of Psalm 44; that role is played by his descriptions of divine hiding on the one hand, and his evocation of faith in the face of disappointment and defeat on the other. Job and the Kotzker then serve subtly to shift the mood and tone of the text—they are men of faith, but also of anger and frustration. Though he affirms God, Job also expresses his anger with Him—and the psalmist follows suit. Note also that although he is reticent about his own place in this nexus of faith and anger, Heschel does quote Psalm 44 in full within the text of his chapter, and does not attempt to soften its challenge to God, or to mitigate its stunning effect in any way whatsoever. It is interesting that Braiterman is forced to acknowledge Heschel's citation of the psalm only in a note, since it cuts so strongly against his overarching thesis.

55. PT, 278.

56. All of this should make clear that Alexander Even-Chen's description of the God of MNA as "completely disarmed" is at best oversimplified, and at worst simply mistaken. It would make no sense at all for Heschel (via the psalmist) to attempt to rouse, and to appeal for salvation to, a "God who has only His mercy and love" but no power, and who thus "cannot offer redemption." Even-Chen, "God's

Omnipotence," 53, 54. Cf. my discussion, in the Introduction, of Heschel's conception of divine omnipotence as *voluntarily* limited.

57. *INGM*, a translation by Morton M. Leifman of *Der Shem HaMeforash: Mentsch.* An earlier "free rendition" into English was authored and privately distributed by Zalman M. Schachter-Shalomi as *Human, God's Ineffable Name* (n.d.).

58. Edward Kaplan has rightly observed that "Heschel wrote poems in Yiddish that announce the themes of his mature theology: human loneliness; God's quest for the righteous person; awe and wonder before nature; a passion for truth; and an unwavering commitment to repair the corrupted world." Kaplan also notes the young Heschel's "indignation at God's distance," but does not seem to realize that this theme, too, as I have been at pains to show, will play a critical role in the mature theology. See Edward Kaplan, introduction to *INGM*, 7.

59. Heschel, "Suicide," in *INGM*, 37.

60. Heschel, "Help," in *INGM*, 33.

61. Heschel, "My Song," in *INGM*, 203–205.

62. Heschel, "Help," in *INGM*, 33.

63. Heschel, "Repentance," in *INGM*, 201.

64. See especially Heschel, "Help," in *INGM*, 33, with its intricate weave of complaint about God and willingness to serve. One theme does not give way to the other, but the two rather form a complex back-and-forth pattern.

65. Heschel, "God's Tears," in *INGM*, 43.

66. Heschel, "Brother God," in *INGM*, 65. But even here, I wonder whether the poet's compassion is offered with a grain of irony; it may not be a compliment to God—an ostensible "adult"—to describe His "behaving like a child."

67. Heschel, "Intimate Hymn," in *INGM*, 69. Cf. the striking image in "Brother God": "God is fettered in jail, /

in labyrinths of infinity. / You escape and go through all the streets / But your divinity masks you, God" (*INGM*, 65). But note the angry lament in "Petition": "Truly, You hide from our craving for you" (*INGM*, 195).

68. Heschel, "Millions of Eyes, Clogged," in *INGM*, 35.

69. Heschel, "Cry through the Nights," in *INGM*, 51.

70. Cf. Heschel, "*Tikkun Hatzot*—Midnight's Mourning Prayer," in *INGM*, 197–199.

71. Heschel, "Untitled," in *INGM*, 193.

72. Heschel, "Petition," in *INGM*, 195.

73. Heschel, "*Tikkun Hatzot*—Midnight's Mourning Prayer," in *INGM*, 197–199.

74. Recall Heschel's assertion some four decades later that "the outcry of anguish certainly adds more to [God's] glory than … flattery of the God of pathos" (*PT*, 269, and cf. 265).

75. Heschel, "Repentance," in *INGM*, 201.

76. Cf. "Millions of Eyes, Clogged," in which the poet demands of God both that He "feel" human suffering, and that He intervene to ameliorate it (*INGM*, 35). Here, in the early Heschel, divine feeling and divine intervention seem to be inextricably linked. Over time, I would suggest, Heschel sought to uncouple these two aspects of divine response, emphasizing the former and consistently downplaying the latter.

77. Edward Kaplan has written that after World War II, Heschel "had decided that he would represent, for the post-Holocaust world, a model of observant East European Jewry and the continuing covenant." Kaplan, *Holiness in Words*, 122. Though I would place greater emphasis on Heschel's self-consciously prophetic mode of speech than Kaplan seems to in this sentence, we are in agreement that Heschel may have consciously muted the strand of protest in his later writing.

Another dimension of Heschel's relative silence may be rooted in the inspiration he clearly took from R. Akiva and his generation, who suffered terribly but "did not rebel" (*TMHS*, I, 161; *HT*, 197).

78. Heschel, "The Meaning of This Hour," in *MQ*, 150.

79. *PT*, 280.

80. Erlewine, "Rediscovering Heschel," 185.

81. Heschel, "Repentance," in *INGM*, 201.

82. Heschel, "The Meaning of This Hour," in *MQ*, 148.

83. *PT*, 275.

84. *PT*, 272–273; *KGE*, 603.

85. Heschel, "Petition," in *INGM*, 195.

86. *PT*, 264. *KGE*, 595.

87. Heschel, "Cry through the Nights," in *INGM*, 51.

88. *TMHS*, xli–xlii; *HT*, 33.

89. *TMHS*, xliv; *HT*, 35.

90. *TMHS*, xlvi; *HT*, 36.

91. *TMHS*, xli–xlii; *HT*, 33.

92. *TMHS*, ix; *HT*, 9. Strangely, the last crucial sentence is omitted from Tucker's translation. Note that the two passages cited are not quite identical in meaning. Whereas the first speaks of the two views being "synthesized" with one another (*nitztarfah zu le-zo*), the second speaks instead of co-mingling (*meshammeshot be-irbuviah*). The latter terms suggests less coherence than does the former.

93. Thus, I am obviously in disagreement with Robert Eisen, who argues that "Heschel follows Akiva in insisting that God is just and that all responsibility for evil resides with human beings." Eisen, "A. J. Heschel's Rabbinic Theology," 219. As I have been at pains to show, the definitive claim that *all* responsibility for evil falls on human shoulders is too simple and does not adequately account for the persistent complexity in Heschel's thought.

94. Ashley, *Interruptions*, 123.

95. Metz, "Christians and Jews after Auschwitz," 21.

96. "Suffering unto God" is J. Matthew Ashley's provocative English rendering of Metz's *"Leiden an Gott."* Ashley explains in a translator's note:

> In German *Leiden an* translates *suffering from*, as in 'suffering from a cold.' What cannot be rendered into English is Metz' correlation of *Leiden an Gott* with *Rückfragen an Gott* [to reinquire or ask again of God]. In the light of this wordplay, I have chosen "suffering unto God" in order to express (a) that this is a form of relationship to God and (b) that it is an active, dynamic state and not just a passive enduring. (in Metz, "Suffering unto God," 611)

97. Metz, "Suffering unto God," 621–622.

98. Metz, "Suffering unto God," 612.

99. Cf. the following:

> In taking up . . . the themes of theodicy in theology, I am not suggesting (as the word and its history might suggest) a belated and somewhat obstinate attempt to justify God in the face of evil, in the face of suffering and wickedness in the world. What is really at stake is the question of how one is to speak about God at all in the face of the abysmal histories of suffering in the world, in "his" world. In my view that is *the* question for theology; theology must not eliminate it or overrespond to it. It is *the* eschatological question, the question before which theology does not develop its answers reconciling everything, but rather directs its questioning incessantly back toward God. (Metz, "Theology as Theodicy," 55–56)

100. Metz, "Suffering unto God," 613.

101. Metz, "Suffering unto God," 614. Cf. Metz, "Theology as Theodicy," 68. The term "landscape of cries" is from the

Jewish poet and Holocaust refugee Nelly
Sachs. Cf. J. Matthew Ashley's comments
in "Theology as Theodicy," 188n6.
102. Metz, "Suffering unto God," 616–
617. Cf. Metz, "Theology as Theodicy,"
59–60.
103. Metz, "Suffering unto God," 617.
Cf. Metz, "Theology as Theodicy," 60–61.
104. Metz, "Theology as Theodicy," 61.
105. *PT,* 264. Emphasis mine. More
explicitly, Heschel attributes the following to the Kotzker: "This is how God deals
with man. First He lets him act the way
he pleases, then he appears and criticizes
him, saying, 'What have you done!'" (*PT,*
274). Cf. *KGE,* 605.
106. Ashley, *Interruptions,* 125. Traditional theodicy, Metz writes, "raised the
impression that it was trying to reconcile
itself to and collude with the almighty God
behind the back, as it were, of nameless suffering," and it thus needed to be rejected
(Metz, "Theology as Theodicy," 62).
107. Ashley, *Interruptions,* 125.
108. Metz, "Theology as Theodicy," 56.
109. Ashley, *Interruptions,* 126.
110. The "mysticism of suffering unto
God," Metz notes, "is found particularly
in Israel's prayer traditions: in the Psalms,
in Job, in Lamentations, and last but not
least in many passages in the prophetic
books. This language of prayer is itself a
language of suffering, a language of crisis,
a language of affliction and of radical
danger, a language of complaint and
grievance, a language of crying out and,
literally, of the grumbling of the children
of Israel" (Metz, "Theology as Theodicy,"
66–67).
It is to this language, not coinciden-
tally—at once canonized (and thus
presumably sanctioned) by tradition and
unabashed in its challenge to God—that
Heschel turns at the end of his discussion
of "The Hiding God" (*MNA,* chap. 16).
111. Consider Metz's searing dismissal
of pie-in-the-sky theology:

Was Israel, for example, happy with its
God? Was Jesus happy with his Father?
Does religion make one happy? Does
it make one mature? Does it give one
identity? home, [*sic*] security, peace
with oneself? Does it soothe anxieties? Does it answer questions? Does
it fulfill our wishes, at least the most
ardent? I do not think so. . . . Biblical
consolation does not remove us to a
mythical realm of tensionless reconciliation with ourselves. The Gospel
is no catalyst or automated assembly
line for human self-discovery. In my
opinion, this is where all the critics of
religion from Feuerbach to Freud have
been mistaken. (Metz, "Theology as
Theodicy," 68)

112. Simon, "'No One, Not Even
God,'" 200.
113. Braiterman, *(God) After Auschwitz,* 4.
114. Levenson, *Creation and the Persistence of Evil,* 25. Cf. the following:

[In these Psalms,] The failure of God
is openly acknowledged: no smug faith
here, no flight into an otherworldly
ideal. But God is also *reproached* for his
failure, told that it is neither inevitable
nor excusable: no limited God here,
no God stymied by invincible evil, no
faithless resignation before the relent-
lessness of circumstance. . . . In the
Hebrew Bible, it is possible . . . to fault
God himself for [human suffering] and
to dare him to act. . . . This implies that
more than just human repentance is
necessary if life is to be just and God is
really to rule. (24–25, 49–50)

6. THE SELF THAT TRANSCENDS ITSELF

1. "The twin themes of the Kotzker
—how to discard falsehood and how to
overcome self-regard—are essentially
one" (*PT,* 133). Cf.: "The greatest falsehood consists of a person constantly hav-

ing himself in mind, as if the ego were the beginning and the end, the cause and the purpose of human existence" (*KGE*, 111).

2. *PT*, 97.

3. *PT*, 88.

4. *PT*, 11.

5. *PT*, 87.

6. *PT*, 189–190. Cf. 192, 312. Cf.: "When faith comes, ego goes" (*KGE*, 169).

7. *PT*, 133.

8. *PT*, 98.

9. *PT*, 189.

10. *PT*, 102.

11. *PT*, 264. Cf. *KGE*, 107, 109, 134, 158.

12. *PT*, 313. Cf. *KGE*, 107.

13. *PT*, 307–308.

14. *PT*, 308. Cf. *KGE*, 628, regarding R. Mordkhe Yosef of Izbica's disagreements with the Kotzker. Heschel obviously has deep respect, even reverence, for Menahem Mendl, but it does not seem coincidental that he dedicates the final chapter of his monumental Yiddish study of Kotzk to an analysis of the views of the Izbicer, a former student who rebelled against the Kotzker's extremism and sought, Heschel argues, to return to the path of the Baal Shem Tov. *KGE*, 623–646.

15. *PT*, 308.

16. At one point, Heschel does use the term "self-annihilation" (somewhat opaquely) to describe the last phase of the Kotzker's vision of the spiritual struggle (*PT*, 130). But it is clear from what we have just seen that Heschel would eschew such language when speaking for himself. Precisely how Heschel intends this term to be understood here in *PT* is, at any rate, difficult to discern.

17. *GSM*, 396–400.

18. *GSM*, 397.

19. *GSM*, 399.

20. *GSM*, 400.

21. *GSM*, 398.

22. Heschel would no doubt have enthusiastically endorsed Christian philosopher Merold Westphal's insistence that "prayer is a deep, quite possibly the deepest decentering of the self, deep enough to begin dismantling, or, if you like, deconstructing . . . burning preoccupation with myself." Westphal, "Prayer as the Posture of the Decentered Self," 15.

23. *MQ*, xii.

24. *MQ*, xiii.

25. *MQ*, xii.

26. *MQ*, xii.

27. *MQ*, xiii.

28. *MQ*, 5.

29. *MQ*, xiii. Heschel expresses gratitude for the religious law, which "remind[s] my distraught mind that it is time to think of God, time to disregard my ego for at least a moment! It is such happiness to belong to an order of the divine will" (*MQ*, 68). Like self-expression, then, true joy depends on the possibility of self-transcendence.

30. *MQ*, 56–57, 15.

31. Compare Heschel's claim that "selfish interests are centripetal; freedom from selfish interests is centrifugal, a turning away from the self" (*GSM*, 397).

32. *MQ*, 7. Cf. 57. Recall *PT*, 133, cited above, at note 7. And notice Heschel's use of the same image in speaking of Jewish-Christian relations in the modern world:

> Parochialism has become untenable. There was a time when you could not pry out of a Boston man that the Boston state house is not the hub of the solar system or that one's own denomination has not the monopoly of the holy spirit. Today we know that even the solar system is not the hub of the universe. (Heschel, "No Religion Is an Island," in *MGSA*, 237)

This is obviously not the place to explore Heschel's theological approach to Jewish-Christian relations. I simply note here that the same project of decentering the self ("not the hub") applies, according to

Heschel, not just to individuals, but also to faith communities as a whole.

In a similar vein, Heschel writes about the importance of self-transcendence for the Jewish people as a whole: "What we have learned from Jewish history is that if a man is not more than human then he is less than human. Judaism is an attempt to prove that in order to be a man, you have to be more than a man, that in order to be a people we have to be more than a people" (GSM, 422; emphasis mine). Cf. "To Be a Jew: What Is It?" in MGSA, 7, 8.

33. MQ, 7. "To worship," Heschel writes, is "to see the word from the point of view of God" (MQ, xii).

34. MQ, 19.

35. MQ, 4.

36. Cf. the words of theologian Jean-Louis Chrétien: "One can be turned to God only in praying, and one can pray only by being turned to God." Chrétien, "The Wounded Word," 157.

37. MQ, 9. This passage about the centrality of divine initiative in human prayer is not explicitly offered as a resolution to the bind I have described (indeed, as I have already mentioned, I am not persuaded that Heschel was even conscious of it). But divine grace does seem to be the only way through Heschel's portrayal of humanity's tragic predicament of needing prayer to help address a human failing but being unable to access its salve as a result of that very failing.

Cf. the words of Henri Nouwen: "The paradox of prayer is that it asks for a serious effort while it can only be received as a gift." Nouwen, Reaching Out, 126.

38. MQ, 28.

39. Chrétien: "To say a prayer is to be appropriated by it." Chrétien, "The Wounded Word," 172.

40. There is an ambiguity here that I find difficult to resolve. It is clear that in speaking of prayer as an act of empathy, Heschel intends that liturgy comes first,

and human feeling comes second. And in speaking of prayer as an act of expression, the feeling comes first, and only then . . . what? It is not entirely clear whether what comes next is liturgy (one comes to the tradition's words seeking expression for one's own passions and emotions) or spontaneous improvised prayers (one finds one's own words for one's needs). Heschel's suggestion that one problem with prayer of expression is that people are not articulate enough would suggest that improvised prayers are intended. His comments about how "empathy generates expression," in contrast, point to a sense of expression as inherently liturgical. For our purposes here, it is not crucial to resolve this ambiguity. See MQ, 32.

41. MQ, 28.

42. MQ, 31.

43. MQ, 33. It is perhaps important to note here that Heschel also offers a critique of excessive focus on prayer of empathy, to the exclusion of expression. Such a focus ignores the reality of the "whole person" who comes to pray: "Every one of us bears a vast accumulation of unuttered sorrow, scruples, hopes, and yearnings, frozen in the muteness of our natures" (MQ, 32). These, too, must be given their rightful place in coming before God. But for the line I am attempting to draw through Heschel's work, his skepticism toward excessive emphasis on expression is more central. (I would add, not incidentally, that a careful reading of the text as a whole bears out this prioritization.)

44. MQ, 25.

45. Cf. Joseph Soloveitchik, who insists that human beings are "ignorant" and unaware of their true needs. Liturgical prayer, he asserts, teaches both the individual and the community what they really need (and thus what they should and should not petition God about). Soloveitchik, "Redemption, Prayer, Talmud Torah," 61–63, 65. For Soloveitchik's

298   NOTES TO PAGES 204–207

version of the idea of a true and false self and its Jewish legal implications, see pp. 63–64.

46. Cf.: "The spirit of Israel speaks, the self is silent" (MQ, 44).

47. MQ, 44.

48. MQ, 33. Emphasis mine.

49. Cf. the discussion of the self's perpetual attachment to God, and its urge to self-transcendence, in chapter 2, above. Even-Chen and Meir state nicely that "what is pivotal in Heschel's Hasidism is not the elimination of the ego, but the discovery of its deepest layer." Between Heschel and Buber, 88.

50. MQ, 15.

51. One is reminded of Louis Jacobs's insistence that for the talmudic rabbis, "the struggle against the yetzer ha-ra [evil inclination] is never-ending in this life. Nowhere in the Rabbinic literature is there the faintest suggestion that it is possible for man to destroy the yetzer ha-ra completely in this life." Jacobs, A Jewish Theology, 245.

52. At one point, Heschel's language does appear at first glance to suggest a more radical notion like the abolition or annihilation of the self—but only at first glance. In prayer, Heschel suggests, we actively "sacrifice" ourselves to God. Prayer, he tells us, "is not a substitute for sacrifice. Prayer is sacrifice.... In moments of prayer ... we do not sacrifice. We are the sacrifice" (MQ, 71). But note that Heschel also offers an explanation of what he intends by self-sacrifice: "We try to surrender our vanities, to burn our insolence, to abandon bias, cant, envy. We lay all our forces before Him." Again, then, it is selfishness and the internal forces that turn us away from God that we seek to relinquish in prayer. What is laid down, as it were, is selfishness, and not selfhood itself. In a related vein, see Hartman, "Prayer and Religious Consciousness," 117.

53. For a useful intellectual biography of Underhill, see Greene, Evelyn Underhill.

54. Underhill, Mysticism, 203.

55. Underhill, Mysticism, 398.

56. Underhill, Practical Mysticism, 33.

57. Underhill, Practical Mysticism, 37.

58. Underhill, Practical Mysticism, 71.

59. Underhill, Practical Mysticism, 73.

60. Underhill, Mysticism, 200.

61. Underhill, Mysticism, 193.

62. Underhill, Mysticism, 205. Similarly, Meister Eckhart reports that one of the stages of spiritual poverty is "utter self-abandonment" (in Underhill, Mysticism, 208). Of course, this talk of "self-abandonment" calls to mind Heschel's description of the Kotzker's commitment to "total abandonment of self" (PT, 11, cited above at note 4). But keep in mind that, as we have seen, the Kotzker does not seem to intend a complete loss of self, and that, at any rate, Heschel himself disavows the Kotzker's more extreme formulations of self-abnegation.

63. Underhill, Mysticism, 264.

64. Underhill, Practical Mysticism, 74.

65. Underhill, Practical Mysticism, 105. Emphases in this paragraph are my own.

66. Underhill, Practical Mysticism, 109.

67. Underhill, Practical Mysticism, 106.

68. Underhill, Mysticism, 208.

69. Underhill, Mysticism, 220.

70. Underhill, Mysticism, 401. Underhill is plainly ambivalent (to the point of self-contradiction) where self-annihilation is concerned. Thus, she can say, first, that "the [Muslim] doctrine of annihilation as the end of the soul's ascent ... is decisively rejected by all European mystics, though a belief in it is constantly imputed to them by their enemies" (171; cf. 419, 424). And yet she can then write that the "last and drastic purgation of the spirit ... [includes] the doing away of separateness, the annihilation of selfhood" (396), and warn that "so long as the subject still feels himself to be somewhat [separate from

the divine], he has not yet annihilated selfhood and come to that ground where his being can be united with the Being of God" (399; cf. 434).

71. Following Underhill's own lead, a variety of scholars have pointed to the crucial influence of Baron von Hügel (1852–1925), Underhill's mentor and spiritual director, on the evolution of her thinking. Crucially, von Hügel had criticized the early Underhill for ostensibly suggesting an "identity of the deepest of man's soul and God" (letter from von Hügel to Underhill, October 30, 1911, cited in Greene, *Evelyn Underhill*, 39). Over time, Underhill seemed to take this criticism very much to heart. Thus, Grace Brame can write that "there is no doubt that [Underhill's] sense of the transcendence, the perfection, and the awesomeness of God was a continuously growing thing.... This [development] was greatly fostered by her relationship with von Hügel." See Brame, introduction to *The Ways of The Spirit*, 17. For evidence of this in Underhill's own writings, see especially her essay "God and Spirit," in *Evelyn Underhill*, 181, where she writes:

This doctrine of God's penetration of the soul is not to be suspected as a disguised pantheism. No theologian of the modern world has been more consistent and emphatic than von Hugel [*sic*] in his warnings concerning the impoverishment and perversion of the religious sense which comes from opening the door to any kind of pantheistic monism. These words are the words of a teacher intensely concerned to safeguard those twin truths of the distinctness of God and the derivative being of man, without which we can never hope to construct a sane and realistic, because humble and creaturely, theology of the spirit.

She goes on to warn that just as deism can result from excessive focus on God's "ut-

ter distinctness," pantheism "ever lies in wait for the 'exclusive mystic'" (181–182)—that is, for one who fails to balance his sense of God's immanence with a healthy dose of divine transcendence. "The full and genuine Christian doctrine," she notes, "means the immanence of an Absolute Spirit who yet remains utterly transcendent—the Wholly Other" (183).

All of this said, it is important to note that the break between the first phase and the second is not absolute: even in her later, more transcendence-focused period, Underhill does at times sound the themes of mystical union so familiar from her earlier period. See, for one example, "The Possibilities of Prayer," (1927) in which she writes of "self-mergence" with God (in Underhill, *Evelyn Underhill*, 158).

On Von Hügel, see Johns, *Mysticism and Ethics*; Leonard, *Creative Tension*; and Kelly, *Baron Friedrich von Hügel's Philosophy of Religion*.

72. This focus pervades Underhill's writings from the early 1920s on, but see especially her "Worship" (1929) in Underhill, *Collected Papers*, 73–92, and Underhill, *Worship*. Cf. also "Abba: Meditations Based on the Lord's Prayer," in Underhill, *Practical Mysticism and Abba*. I am grateful to Prof. Carol Zaleski of Smith College for our exchange on this point.

73. Underhill, "Worship," in Underhill, *Collected Papers*, 75.

74. Underhill, "Worship," in Underhill, *Collected Papers*, 74. Cf.: "Solemn yet joyous adoration ... obliterates all thoughts of self" (80).

75. Underhill, "Worship," in Underhill, *Collected Papers*, 91.

76. Underhill, "Worship," in Underhill, *Collected Papers*, 81.

77. Underhill, *Worship*, xii.

78. Underhill, *Worship*, 5.

79. Underhill, *Worship*, 9.

80. Underhill, *Worship*, 8.

81. Underhill, *Worship*, 5.

82. Underhill, *Worship*, 9.

83. Underhill, *Worship*, 17.

84. Underhill, *Worship*, 17.

85. Underhill, *Worship*, 16.

86. Underhill, *The Spiritual Life*, 131–132.

87. Underhill, *The Spiritual Life*, 127–128.

88. See, for example, "Prayer," in Underhill, *Evelyn Underhill*, 140.

89. See, for example, "Spiritual Life," in Underhill, *The Essentials of Mysticism*, 129, and cf. "Life as Prayer," in Underhill, *Collected Papers*, 72.

90. See, for example, Underhill, "Spiritual Life," 128, and cf. "The Place of Will, Intellect and Feeling in Prayer," in Underhill, *The Essentials of Mysticism*, 88.

91. See, for example, Underhill's assertion that "nothing is worse than . . . always feeling our own devotional pulses." "The Degrees of Prayer," Underhill, *Collected Papers*, 40.

For Heschel, too, self-centeredness tends to appear in two variations—either as "self-seeking" or as "self-conscious[ness]." Only when both are overcome can God truly be present to the human being. Cf. *PT*, 136.

On the pernicious implications of excessive self-consciousness, compare, in a more dialogical register, the words of Martin Buber:

The single presupposition of a genuine state of prayer is . . . the readiness of the whole man for th[e divine] Presence, simple turned-towardness, unreserved spontaneity. . . . But in this our stage of subjectivized reflection not only the concentration of the one who prays, but also his spontaneity is assailed. The assailant is consciousness, the over-consciousness of this man here that he is praying, that he is *praying*, that *he* is praying. And the assailant appears to be invincible. The subjective knowledge of the one turning-towards about his turning-towards, this holding back

of an I which does not enter into the action with the rest of the person, an I to which the action is an object—all this depossesses the moment, takes away its spontaneity. The specifically modern man who has not yet let go of God knows what that means: he who is not present perceives no Presence. (Buber, *Eclipse*, 126)

92. "Prayer," in Underhill, *Evelyn Underhill*, 140.

93. Underhill, "Prayer," in Underhill, *Evelyn Underhill*, 141. In the same volume, cf. Underhill's insistence that ideal prayer is "non-utilitarian" in nature ("The Possibilities of Prayer," 151). And cf. also her contention that "adoration, and not intercession or petition, is the very heart of the life of prayer" (Underhill, *The Ways of The Spirit*, 136).

94. Underhill, "The Place of Will, Intellect and Feeling," in Underhill, *The Essentials of Mysticism*, 112.

95. *MQ*, 15.

96. *MQ*, 63–64.

Heschel's axiological prioritization of praise over petition can be fruitfully compared with Joseph Soloveitchik's opposite approach, which emphasizes petition as the very heart of Jewish prayer. Soloveitchik writes:

Prayer as a personal experience, as a creative gesture, is possible only if and when man discovers himself in crisis or in need. That is why the Jewish idea of prayer differs from the mystical idea, insofar as we have emphasized the centrality of the petition, while the mystics have stressed the relevance of the hymn. Since prayer flows from a personality which finds itself in need, despondent and hopeless, its main theme is not praise or adoration, but rather request, demand, supplication. (Soloveitchik, "The Crisis of Human Finitude," 161)

And, in a similar vein, he contends:

> The principal topic of Jewish prayer is *tehinnah* [petition or supplication]; praise and thanksgiving are merely prologues and epilogues. Most of the Psalms are petitionary. Isaac prayed for progeny. . . . Christians and mystics considered *tehinnah* an unworthy form of prayer, a cash-and-carry relationship, a form of trade or barter, a sacrifice for a recompense, a self-directed prayer. . . . This [focus on supplication] is based on our singling out of one particular emotion above all others as the central requisite for prayer, namely, dependence and helplessness. Though contradictory emotions may exist, such as joy, sadness, gratitude, submission, shyness, etc., the feeling of dependence in our state of wretchedness is paramount. (Soloveitchik, "Prayer as Dialogue," 84)

Soloveitchik forcefully repudiates approaches to prayer that denigrate petition, casting such approaches as non-Jewish, and contrary to "the Jewish idea of prayer." And he explicitly deprioritizes praise and adoration, characterizing them as mere "prologues" to the heart of Jewish prayer. According to the Soloveitchik of these essays, the goal of prayer is not to forget the self entirely, but rather to surrender illusions of self-sufficiency, to become more deeply aware of—and expressive of—our vulnerability and dependence on God. Of course, Soloveitchik might well argue that this, too, is a form of self-transcendence. As Jean-Louis Chrétien notes, "To ask is to actually acknowledge not being the origin of every good and every gift. . . . All prayer confesses God by dispossessing us of our egocentrism" (Chrétien, "The Wounded Word," 153). But Heschel and Underhill would likely demur, insisting that a concern with the self's vulnerability is still just that—a concern with the self. Be that

as it may, in both mood (delight versus "despondence") and aspiration (feeling the self's "depth crisis" versus forgetting the self altogether), the contrast between Soloveitchik's approach to prayer and Heschel's is both stark and dramatic. (Note, by the way, that even Soloveitchik tries to take the acquisitive edge off of petitionary prayer: "In praying we do not seek a response to a particular request as much as we desire fellowship with God. Prayer is not a means for wheedling some benefit from God" [Soloveitchik, "Prayer as Dialogue," 78].)

Compare also Soloveitchik's richly dialectical approach to self-discovery, on the one hand, and self-sacrifice, on the other, in "Redemption, Prayer, Talmud Torah," 55–72.

In his classic study of Prayer, Friedrich Heiler writes that "in mysticism, contemplative adoration forms the climax of all prayer and meditation; in prophetic religion, praise and thanksgiving are secondary to petition and intercession." While the early Underhill serves as a good example of the former and Soloveitchik of the latter, Heschel and the later Underhill elude such straightforward typological thinking. Heschel especially is a prophetic thinker (for Heiler, this primarily means dialogical as opposed to unitive), but with a mystical ethos—that is, he focuses on self-transcendence and praise of God, spiritual postures Heiler identifies with the mystics. See Heiler, *Prayer*, 230 and elsewhere.

97. Westphal astutely observes that even thanksgiving differs from praise in that the former is still centered on the self. "We can distinguish praise from thanksgiving," he writes, "as follows: to give thanks is to praise God for the good things I have received from God, while to praise God is to thank God for who God is, for what Luther calls God's 'bare goodness,' considered without reference to how I may

302	NOTES TO PAGES 211-212

benefit from it." Westphal, "Prayer as the Posture of the Decentered Self," 14.

98. For precisely the same reason, Westphal describes praise as "the alpha or perhaps the omega of prayer." Westphal, "Prayer as the Posture of the Decentered Self," 23. David Hartman seems to miss this crucial distinction between praise and petition in Heschel's writings. Hartman, "Prayer and Religious Consciousness," 120–121.

99. Cf. Hartman's apt observation that for Heschel, "The main thrust of prayer is not self-annihilation but, on the contrary, making ourselves the object of God's attention." Thus, prayer "elevates [the worshiper] out of insignificance." Hartman, "Prayer and Religious Consciousness," 120, 121.

100. See, for example, in Underhill, Evelyn Underhill, "The Possibilities of Prayer," 151, and "God and Spirit," 189. But compare "Prayer," in which Underhill talks about those of great spiritual attainment becoming God's "fellow-workers" (143).

101. For a comparison of Heschel's view with the very different approach of Joseph Soloveitchik, who unabashedly valorizes petitionary prayer, see above, note 96.

102. This idea pervades almost all of Merton's writings. A good place to begin an exploration of this theme is in Merton's New Seeds of Contemplation. See also the many sources collected by Shannon, Thomas Merton: An Introduction, 86–94. For studies on Merton's idea of the self and its growth, see Malits, The Solitary Explorer; Shannon, Thomas Merton's Dark Path (revised and updated as Thomas Merton's Paradise Journey); and Carr, A Search for Wisdom and Spirit. Cf. also Finley, Merton's Palace of Nowhere.

103. Merton, New Seeds of Contemplation, 34–35.

104. Shannon, Thomas Merton: An Introduction, 89.

105. For the variety of terms Merton uses to characterize the true (for example, "inner . . . hidden . . . creative, mysterious . . . inmost . . . real . . . deepest, most hidden") and false (for example, "superficial . . . empirical . . . outward . . . shadow . . . smoke . . . contingent . . . imaginary . . . private . . . illusory . . . fake . . . petty") selves, see Shannon, Thomas Merton: An Introduction, 88–89, and Malits, The Solitary Explorer, 128.

106. Merton, "Rebirth and the New Man," 196.

107. Merton, "Rebirth and the New Man," 193.

108. Unpublished material from the original manuscript of The Seven Storey Mountain, presented in Higgins, Thomas Merton on Prayer, 32–33.

109. Merton writes:

Self-realization in this true religious sense is . . . less an awareness of ourselves than an awareness of the God to whom we are drawn in the depths of our being. We become real, and experience our actuality, not when we pause to reflect upon our own self as an isolated individual entity, but rather when, transcending ourselves and passing beyond reflection, we center our whole soul upon the God Who is our life. That is to say we fully 'realize' ourselves when we cease to be conscious of ourselves in separateness and know nothing but the one God Who is above all knowledge. (Merton, The New Man, 122)

Although, as we shall see, Heschel would have been wary of Merton's notion that in self-realization "we cease to be conscious of ourselves in separateness," there is nonetheless a crucial sense in which what Merton writes here resonates deeply with what he have already seen in Heschel: the paradox that authentic self-realization can be achieved through (and presumably *only* through) self-transcendence is common to both of them. Of course, whether or not Heschel and Merton intend the same state in speaking of self-transcendence is an important and difficult question; on this, see below.

110. Merton, *The New Man*, 19.

111. Merton, *Contemplative Prayer*, 94.

112. Merton, *The New Man*, 118.

113. Malits, *A Solitary Explorer*, 125. Cf. Merton in *The New Man*: "Contemplation is a mystery in which God reveals Himself to us as the very center of our most intimate self—*intimior intimo meo* as St. Augustine said" (19).

114. Shannon, *Thomas Merton: An Introduction*, 94. Of course, one could spill a great deal of ink speculating about the precise valence of "identified" in this sentence.

115. Compare the following, from Merton's introduction to the Japanese edition of *The New Man:*

> The true Christian rebirth is a renewed transformation, a "Passover" in which man is progressively liberated from selfishness and not only grows in love, but in some sense "becomes love." The perfection of the new birth is reached when there is no more selfishness, there is only love. In the language of the mystics, there is no more ego-self, there is only Christ; self no longer acts, only the Spirit acts in pure love . . .
>
> It is not enough to remain the same "self," the same individual ego, with a new set of activities and new lot of religious practices. One must be born of the Spirit who is free, and who teaches the inmost depths of the heart by taking that heart to Himself, by making Himself one with our heart, by creating for us, invisibly, a new identity: by being Himself that identity. (reprinted in Merton, *Honorable Reader*, 134)

Here, Merton starts out with a kind of caveat—the mystic only becomes love "in some sense"—but ends with a rather robust formulation: the mystic's new identity *is* God.

116. Merton, "The Recovery of Paradise," 515n4. Cf. also Merton, *What Are These Wounds?*, 14.

117. In *The New Man*, for example, Merton writes:

> In mystical experience the spirit of man is indeed aware of the reality of God as the 'Other' immanently present within itself, but the more conscious it becomes of His reality and of His 'Otherness,' the more it also becomes conscious of the union and 'sameness' which unite Him to itself. (117)

118. Merton, *Life and Holiness*, 70.

119. In his otherwise very useful study of Merton, John Higgins seems confused about this point: he marshals quotations from Merton about the union of wills and suggests that they prove Merton's emphasis on ontological union. See Higgins, *Thomas Merton on Prayer*, 25–26na. And cf. my discussion of Dennis Tamburello below. I should perhaps mention another exasperating failure of Higgins's book (or, at least, of its editors): a great many of the references to Merton's works point to the wrong pages.

120. Merton, *No Man Is an Island*, 58.

121. Merton, *Spiritual Direction and Meditation*, 76.

122. Merton, *Spiritual Direction and Meditation*, 76.

123. Merton, *New Seeds of Contemplation*, 35–36.

124. Shannon, *Thomas Merton's Paradise Journey*, 61. Shannon reports that Merton said the following to a fellow monk: "You have to see your will and God's will dualistically for a long time. You have to experience duality for a long

time until you see it's not there" (284). In contrast, Heschel's theology maintains an important sense of duality (God and the human are always two) all the way down.

125. I use this word carefully. Cf. *Prophets*, II, 136, which I discuss below.

126. Heschel astutely notes the profound difference in motivation animating ancient and modern authors: whereas the former invoked ecstasy in order to minimize the role of the prophet and thus to "guarantee the divine authenticity of the message received," the latter "reduce the experience of the prophet to a mental aberration" and thus none-too-subtly belittle and reject the entire phenomenon. *Prophets*, II, 133.

For a fruitful discussion of Heschel's dichotomization of mysticism and prophecy, cf. Even-Chen, "Mysticism and Prophecy," 359–370, esp. 360–367.

127. *Prophets*, II, 131. "If ecstasy were essential to prophetic experience," Heschel insists, then "Moses, Amos, Hosea, Isaiah and Jeremiah would have to be disqualified as prophets, since no trace of ecstasy is found in their experiences" (132; cf. also 134).

128. Interestingly, Heschel suggests in his dissertation that ecstasy and mystical union found their way into Christianity and Islam, but seemingly not into Judaism. See Heschel, *Die Prophetie*, 13. For an important discussion of why Heschel might have argued as he did, see Green, "Three Warsaw Mystics," 45*–49*. For the classic scholarly claim that Judaism has only a very limited notion of mystical union, see Scholem, *Major Trends in Jewish Mysticism*, 122–123, and "Devekut or Communion with God," 203–204. For the most famous challenge to Scholem's position, see Idel, *Kabbalah: New Perspectives*, 35–73, and *The Mystical Experience in Abraham Abulafia*, 124–125.

129. *Prophets*, II, 135.

130. *Prophets*, II, 136.

131. *Prophets*, II, 137.

132. *Prophets*, II, 144, 137. Cf. also *Prophets* II, 99: "There is no fusion of being, *unio mystica*, but an intimate harmony in will and feeling, a state that may be called *unio sympathetica*.... One does not feel united with the divine Being, but emotionally identified with divine pathos." Cf. the discussion of prophetic sympathy above, chapter 4. For a useful discussion of Heschel's rejection of mystical union in the name of prophetic theology, see Even-Chen, "Mysticism and Prophecy," 360–367, and Even-Chen, *Akedat Yitshak*, 203–209.

133. *Prophets*, II, 3.

134. *Prophets*, II, 137–138. It is worth noting the important parallels between Heschel's polemic against mysticism and Buber's. In a crucial passage in *I and Thou*, the latter writes:

> What has to be given up [in any authentic encounter] is not the I, as most mystics suppose: the I is indispensable for any relationship, including the highest, which always presupposes an I and You. What has to be given up is not the I but that false drive for self-affirmation (*Selbstbehauptungstriebs*) which impels man to flee from the unreliable, unsolid, unlasting, unpredictable, dangerous world of relation into the having of things. (Buber, *I and Thou*, 126)

In a way that anticipates Heschel, Buber couples a commitment to self-transcendence, on the one hand, with an insistence on maintaining a robust sense of selfhood, on the other. For a discussion of Buber's move beyond an early preoccupation with mysticism to a mature concern with "dialogue," see, most famously, Mendes-Flohr, *From Mysticism to Dialogue*, esp. 93–126.

135. *Prophets*, II, 138.

136. It is important to point out that although Heschel does explicitly describe prophecy as dialogical, he resists the application of this term to prayer (and thus parts ways, at least partially, from Buber):

> Prayer is not a soliloquy. But is it a dialogue with God? Does man address Him as person to person? It is incorrect to describe prayer by analogy with human conversation; we do not communicate with God. We only make ourselves communicable to Him. Prayer is an emanation of what is most precious in us toward Him, the outpouring of the heart before Him. (*MQ*, 10)

But note well: Heschel's hesitation in describing prayer as dialogue is not about the fundamental two-ness of the encounter (which he nowhere questions), but about the false sense of symmetry that the term dialogue might suggest.

137. Corbishley, "Mysticism," 10:175. I cannot resist noting William Harmless's observation that in popular parlance, the term "mysticism" can become a "catch-all" for all sorts of "religious weirdness." See Harmless, *Mystics*, 3.

138. In describing Martin Buber's intellectual and spiritual trajectory, Nahum N. Glatzer characterizes the later Buber, who had come to reject (and deride) his earlier fascination with union, as an "antimystic." See Glatzer's comments in Buber, *The Way of Response*, 13. In a similar vein, Eugene Borowitz writes:

> If a mystic is one who wishes to transcend individuality by union with Deity, Buber is no mystic. He envisages meaning as arising from what transpires *between* two persons. . . . If either person does not steadfastly maintain individuality, there is no meeting, only merging, probably the

submerging of one in the other. Rather than surrender oneself in dialogue, Buber believes that only maintaining one's particularity while sharing it with another truly calls relationship into being. (Borowitz, *Choices in Modern Jewish Thought*, 144)

Borowitz's words could, *mutatis mutandis*, apply to Heschel as easily as they do to Buber. Like Heschel, Buber, too, understood mysticism as focused on union.

139. The term "mystical union," too, requires careful analysis (which, I should add, it does not always receive from those skeptical of mystics' claims). It is crucial to remember that in speaking of mystical union, many mystics intend to suggest a union "spiritual" rather than "essential" in nature; in other words, they speak of "conforming one's will to God" rather than of "losing one's identity and being totally absorbed in God." Or, put slightly differently, they are concerned with a "'relational' union, described in such terms as a union of wills or spirits, or as a union in love . . . [rather than] an 'essential' union, described in such terms as 'absorption' into God or 'identity' with God." (Dennis Tamburello, by the way, insists that "Christianity has tended to shun" notions of essential union with God.) Of course, these are not hard and fast rules binding mystical speech, and, not surprisingly, many mystics move easily between these two types of mystical union. See Tamburello, *Ordinary Mysticism*, 25, 104, 132n38.

An in-depth analysis of the various—and not entirely consistent—ways in which Underhill and Merton speak of unia mystica would no doubt be interesting. But for our purposes, it is also besides the point: what is most noteworthy, I think, is the way in which Heschel consistently eschews any language that is suggestive of union, for the reasons I have suggested above. Of course, he would likely have been much more comfortable with notions of spiritual union rather than essential (the ontological sting, as it were, of the latter is absent in the former). But the critical point is that Heschel refuses such language altogether.

140. McGinn, "Mysticism," 19.

141. See, for example, Heschel's most powerful evocation of God's "immediate and transformative presence," in *MNA*, 78–79. Arguing that Heschel should unquestionably be considered a mystic, Arthur Green writes, "It would seem that the only way Heschel might *not* be a mystic is if we insist on the most rigid of definitions, naming the mystic as an experiential monist, one knows that any distinction between God, world, and soul is false, and that there exists nought but the One" (Green, "Three Warsaw Mystics," 52*). Given Heschel's lack of interest in kabbalistic metaphysics, Green helpfully labels him a "post-Kabbalistic Jewish mystic" (5*).

142. All of this said, one should avoid the mistake of too facilely associating Merton, for example, with the Greek mystics Heschel derides in *The Prophets*. For one thing, as we have seen, Merton did maintain a deep sense of God's transcendence, and thus of the separateness of God and humanity, even in the midst of his robust talk of mystical union; for another, Merton was much more concerned with the mystic's mandate to ethical action than were Heschel's Greeks. I think it is clear that Heschel would reject—indeed, recoil at—much of Merton's talk of union and identification, but there is also no doubt that he would see more nuance and complexity in Merton than he found in the Greeks.

Of course, the question of whether or not Heschel's portrayal of the Greek ecstatics is fair or accurate is far beyond the scope of this discussion. In this context, needless to say, I am interested in Heschel's interpretation of the Greek mystics rather than in any historical reconstruction of them.

143. For a comparison of Heschel's approach to self-transcendence with the much more extreme version thereof advocated by Yeshayahu Leibowitz, see the excursus in the following note.

144. Undoubtedly the most extreme version of self-transcendence in twentieth-century Jewish thought has been put forward in the writings of Israeli philosopher and social critic Yeshayahu Leibowitz (1903–1994). Leibowitz's religious vision revolves around an absolute commitment to obeying the will of God as manifest in Jewish law, and to obeying it only *because* it is the will of God. For Leibowitz, to a degree unprecedented in Jewish thought, divine and human purposes represent a kind of zero-sum game—either an act serves God or it serves humanity; it cannot ultimately serve both. Whenever a believer has human benefits in mind while performing the commandments, he ineluctably dilutes the purity of his worship. Worship "for its own sake" (*li-shema*) is acting for the sake of God—that is, because, *and only because*, the act has been mandated by God's law. The introduction of human motivations of any kind, in contrast—whether psychological, sociological, political, *or even ethical*—means that the act in question loses status, and is considered worship "not for its own sake" (*she-lo li-shema*). For Leibowitz, such worship is not really worship at all, but social work at best, and idolatry at worst; it is an attempt, in other words, to place divine commands at the service of human ends.

It is important to emphasize just how radically Leibowitz develops this idea—and it is *the* central idea running through the vast corpus of his writing. Authentic Jewish prayer, for example, "is not intended to serve as an outlet for the feelings and thoughts of man. It is not the spontaneous outpouring of one's soul which necessarily varies with individuals, their moods and states of mind." On the contrary, as Leibowitz is fond of pointing out, Jewish law requires that the bridegroom and the widower recite the very same liturgical formulae—without regard for their emotional state. See especially Leibowitz, "Of Prayer," in *Judaism, Human Values, and the Jewish State*, 31–32 and elsewhere.

For Leibowitz, it is in sacrificing Isaac that Abraham learns the true meaning of the "fear of God"—Abraham puts aside all human concerns, whether parental love or moral intuition, and does as God commands. The *Aqedah* thus represents *the* paradigmatic event for all Jewish worship: all human values are set aside, nullified in the face of God's command. See especially "Abraham and Job" [Hebrew], in Leibowitz, *Yahadut, ʿAm Yehudi, u-Medinat Yisrael*, 391–394.

Obviously, such a theology represents a radical decentering of the human. As Jerome Gellman has put it, after the *Aqedah*, for Leibowitz, "No longer is Abraham to think of humanity as in the center, with God as 'functionary' providing its needs. . . . Instead, God is at the center." Indeed, morality and religion are utterly separated; they mix, writes Gellman, "only to the extent that religion becomes idolatrous, placing human beings in the center instead of God." See Gellman, "The Meaning of the Aqedah," 33. "Ethics," Leibowitz writes, "is an anthropocentric-atheistic category, which cannot be reconciled with religious consciousness or religious feeling. The latter recognize only 'the right and the good in the eyes of the Lord'—and not 'the right and the good'!" (see Leibowitz, *Torah u-mitsvot ba-zeman ha-zeh*, 172).

It is crucial for us to see just how dramatically this decentering project differs

from Heschel's. Whereas Heschel consistently emphasizes the inextricability of religion and ethics, Leibowitz just as relentlessly insists upon their total separation. For Heschel, as we have seen, the goal of the spiritual life is to overcome selfishness and self-preoccupation. Morality, we might say, is found on the divine side of the divine-human divide; in choosing the ethical life, the human being escapes the prison of selfishness and obeys God's ethical call. For Leibowitz, in contrast, the ethical falls unambiguously on the human side of the (stark and impermeable) divine-human barrier, and one who seeks to transcend the self must also transcend ethics (at least where obedience to divine command so requires). Put differently, we might say that whereas Heschel's goal is the transcendence of *the self*, Leibowitz's is, much more radically, the transcendence of *the human* altogether (though, again, Heschel would rebel at any suggestion that ethics can ever be properly categorized as merely human). It is indeed telling that whereas Leibowitz holds up the *Aqedah* as the paradigm of Jewish faith, Heschel places the prophetic encounter with God in its stead. In the former case, a stark tension is manifest between the theological and the ethical; in the latter case, a passionate marriage between the theological and the ethical is evinced. A commitment to self-transcendence, then, can entail radically different relationships to ethics—for Leibowitz, a decentering of the ethical as merely human; for Heschel, a recentering of the ethical as quintessentially divine.

In the context of our broader discussion of prayer, it is perhaps not surprising that whereas Heschel, who emphasizes the centrality of relationship and responsiveness in covenantal life, places prayer at the very heart of the spiritual life, Leibowitz, who emphasizes obedience to the will of God, insists that, in David

Hartman's words, "Prayer has no unique singular status in a Judaic way of life." It is a commandment like any other—nothing more and nothing less. See Hartman, "Prayer and Religious Consciousness," 112. It is also worth noting in this context that Leibowitz also invokes the mandate to self-transcendence to argue against contemporary Jewish calls for liturgical change. Since Jewish observance in general is about transcending human concerns and replacing them with divine ones,

> there is no point to demand that liturgical formulas be modified to fit the needs of men or the mental climate of the times. Prayer cut to fit the needs and current attitudes of men loses its religious importance and becomes one of the activities men carry on at their pleasure to satisfy their spiritual needs, much like poetry, music, or the art of cinema. (Leibowitz, "Of Prayer," 33)

The most important collections of Leibowitz's essays are Yahadut, ʿAm Yehudi, u-Medinat Yisrael, and Emunah, historyah va- ḥarakhim: maʾamarim ve-hartsaʾot. A collection of Leibowitz's essays in English translation has been published as Judaism, Human Values, and the Jewish State. Important studies of Leibowitz are collected in Sagi, Yeshayahu Leibowitz, and Ravitzky, Yeshaʾyahu Libovits. For an incisive analysis of the paradox at the heart of Leibowitz's life work—that is, of his stark dichotomization of the ethical and the religious, on the one hand, and his radical ethical critique of religious politics in Israel, on the other—see Halbertal, "Yeshayahu Leibowitz," in Sagi, Yeshayahu Leibowitz, 221–227. For an analysis of some of the purportedly detrimental effects of Leibowitz's dichotomization, see Schiffman, "The Detaching of the Ethical," in Ravitzky, Yeshayahu Leibowitz, 59–73.

7. ENABLING IMMANENCE

1. Heschel, "On Prayer," in MGSA, 259.
2. Heschel, "On Prayer," 262.
3. Heschel, "On Prayer," 266.
4. Thus, David Hartman's contention that "A. J. Heschel approaches prayer from the religious perspective of a committed Halakhic Jew driven by a vivid and gripping awareness of God" is insufficiently nuanced. As we shall see, Heschel's writings on prayer sometimes evince a vivid and gripping awareness of God's ostensible *absence*, and attempt to grapple with that excruciating reality. See Hartman, "Prayer and Religious Consciousness," 116.
5. Heschel, "Jewish Theology," in MGSA, 158.
6. Heschel, "On Prayer," 258.
7. Heschel, "On Prayer," 267.
8. MNA, 153.
9. MNA, 152.
10. MNA, 153. Or, again: "It is not God who is obscure. It is man who conceals Him" (MNA, 153–154).
11. MNA, 152.
12. MNA, 153.
13. Heschel, "On Prayer," 259.
14. Heschel, "On Prayer," 260.
15. Heschel, "On Prayer," 260.
16. Heschel, "On Prayer," 258.
17. Heschel, "On Prayer," 258. Cf. the following, attributed to the Hasidic master Reb Simcha Bunem of Peshischa (Przysucha): "'Create an opening for Me'—God says: 'Open a door for Me.' How do you open a door? You knock until the door opens up." KGE, 409.
18. Heschel, "On Prayer," 259.
19. Heschel, "On Prayer," 260.
20. Heschel, "On Prayer," 259.
21. Heschel, "On Prayer," 259.
22. Heschel, "On Prayer," 258.
23. "A soul without prayer," Heschel declares, "is a soul without a home." Heschel, "On Prayer," 258.
24. Heschel, "On Prayer," 260. With this sentence, Heschel means to suggest

that if one is able to penetrate beyond present realities, one will discover that there is, after all, a personal Other ("a name") who awaits our turning toward Him ("a waiting").

25. Heschel, "On Prayer," 258–259.

26. See, for example, Heschel, "The Vocation of the Cantor," in *IF*, 250.

27. Heschel, "On Prayer," 258.

28. Cf. the discussion above, chapter 4.

29. Heschel attributes the following striking teaching to the Kotzker Rebbe: "Prayer is not one-sided. God passes through all the heavens by breaking through a gate of mercy, from His side, while Isaac [the Kotzker is commenting on Gen. 25:21] breaks through a gate of mercy, from his. Prayer is a breakthrough on the part of both man and God." *KGE*, 546.

30. For recent scholarly literature on Buber's notion of divine eclipse (and on the problem of evil in Buber's broader corpus), see Kepnes, *The Text as Thou*, 121–143; Braiterman, *(God) After Auschwitz*, 62–67; Forman-Barzilai, "Agonism in Faith," 156–179; Wright, "Beyond the 'Eclipse of God,'" 203–225; and Adams, "The Silence of God," 51–68.

31. Buber, *Eclipse*, 23.

32. Buber, *Eclipse*, 119.

33. Buber, *Eclipse*, 126.

34. Buber, *Eclipse*, 129.

35. Buber, *Eclipse*, 24.

36. Buber, *Eclipse*, 66. Cf. Isaiah 45:15.

37. Indeed, attempts to portray a straightforward, unambiguous Buber on the question of divine eclipse fall flat. Thus, for example, Samuel Hugo Bergman misses widely (and is forced to ignore explicit counterevidence) when he insists that, according to Buber, "God never hides His face; He is never other than Thou to us; He is always present. It is we who are not always present and who do not open the channels leading from God to us. . . . We hide our faces from God by

limiting the mode, manner, place and time of God's presence." Bergman, *Faith and Reason*, 91–92. As I have just shown, Buber does say this—but he also says virtually the opposite, and we are thus forced to pursue a more complex and nuanced interpretation than Bergman's.

38. Buber, *Eclipse*, 23: "*nicht in diesem darin.*" Note the correction from the standard English translation, which reads, incorrectly, "not in the sun itself." As Robert Adams has rightly pointed out, "On grounds of both gender and word order, the reference of *diesem* cannot be to the sun (*die Sonne*)." Adams, "The Silence of God," 68n10. The emphases in this passage and in the next are mine.

39. Buber, *Eclipse*, 68. Given Buber's consistent emphasis on the primacy of "the relation," both in *I and Thou* and in everything that follows, it makes sense that rupture no less than encounter would result from something that takes place in "the between" (or in its collapse). In personal correspondence (April 6, 2008), Jon Levenson has written (of Buber) that "the Divine-human relationship cannot be adequately analyzed in terms of subject-object relations, and causality within it cannot be analyzed as if the relationship had no reality but was resolvable into attributes of the two that stand in relation."

40. In an earlier essay, Buber had made a distinction between two very different types of blockage in divine-human communication. In one type, "the obstruction/eclipse (*ikuv*) comes from below, from humanity," whereas in the other, "the terrible estrangement (*hitnakrut*) comes from God Himself, even though it comes as a response to humanity's transgression: God totally disappears (*mit'alem kalil*) from the world and pays no attention to its existence." The options available to humanity in each circumstance are different: in the first case, "humanity can struggle and through faithful service

arrive at renewed contact." But in the second case, which Buber dubs "the hiding of God's face" (*hester panim*), "humanity is incapable of overcoming" the breach. Such times, Buber writes, are agonizing for the person of faith: "For one who believes in a living God, who knows about Him, and is fated to spend his life in a time of His hiddenness, it is very difficult to live" (or, more literally: "Is his life any life at all?"). See Buber, "The Dialogue between Heaven and Earth," in *On Judaism*, 250–251. Strangely, Buber's discussion of this crucial distinction is omitted from the English translation. See Buber, "The Dialogue between Heaven and Earth," in *On Judaism*, 214–225.

41. Levenson (April 6, 2008): "The self-revealing God (God in search of man) requires a quest, a spiritual act, an opening to him on the part of man: in that the self-revealing God is hiding his face—*Deus absconditus et revelatus.*"

42. The sentence from the Hebrew original of "The Dialogue between Heaven and Earth," cited above in note 40, where divine hiding is described as a response to human wrongdoing, seems to be the proverbial exception that proves the rule.

43. Fackenheim, *God's Presence in History*, 49.

44. Kepnes, *The Text as Thou*, 136. The same logic applies to Heschel's ostensibly even stronger image of a "blackout of God" (Heschel, "On Prayer," 267).

45. Buber, *Tales of the Hasidim*, 122. Cf. Moore, *Martin Buber*, 213–214.

46. Heschel, "Prayer as Discipline," in *IF*, 258.

47. Heschel, "The Vocation of the Cantor," in *IF*, 244–245. But note how easily Heschel moves back to ontology. Heschel's next sentence: "Song, and particularly liturgical song, is . . . a way of bringing down the spirit from heaven to earth."

48. *MQ*, 62.

49. *Prophets*, I, 14.

50. *MQ*, 7. Cf. xii.

51. *Prophets*, II, 263, 265. Cf. also 267–268.

52. *MQ*, 10.

53. Heschel, "On Prayer," 258.

54. *Prophets*, II, 140.

55. *Prophets*, II, 141. Cf. also I, 207, 209.

56. *Prophets*, I, 193.

57. Heschel, "On Prayer," 259.

58. The allusion here is to Heschel's famous interview with Carl Stern, originally broadcast in February 1973. Asked by the latter whether he himself is a prophet, Heschel responds, "I won't accept this praise. . . . It is a claim almost arrogant enough to say that I'm a descendent of the prophets, what is called *B'nai Nevi'im*. So let us hope and pray that I am worthy of being a descendant of the prophets." See Heschel, "Carl Stern's Interview with Dr. Heschel," in *MGSA*, 400. For the rabbinic source with which Heschel is playing here, see BT Pesahim 66a.

59. *Prophets*, II, 266.

60. Cf., for two related Hasidic teachings, *KGE*, 107 (about the ego getting between human beings and God) and 526 (about making God king over the self as a means of making Him king over the world).

61. Heschel hints as much when he writes, in his first English-language essay, that the "purpose of sacrifice does not lie in pauperization as such but in the yielding of all aspirations to God, thus creating space for him in the heart." Cf. Heschel, "An Analysis of Piety," in *MGSA*, 316.

62. Mensch, "Prayer as Kenosis," 67.

63. Cf. *KGE*, 26.

CONCLUSION

1. It is worth noting that Heschel is—perhaps paradoxically—profoundly influenced by modernity even as he condemns some of what he considers to be its

core aspects. Most significant, the depth and passion of Heschel's universalism—his unflagging insistence on "the unity of man," and on God's love for "all men"—is itself nourished by Enlightenment universalism. Heschel would no doubt have maintained that these Enlightenment commitments are themselves grounded in Scripture, and he may even have been right, but it nevertheless took modernity to bring these values and ideals to the fore. Perhaps because of a certain lack of historical self-consciousness, and perhaps out of a desire to ground his teachings unequivocally in the sources of tradition, Heschel never really acknowledges the profundity of his debt to modern thinking and values.

For a provocative meditation on Heschel's complex relationship with modernity, see Shaul Magid, "Heretics of Modernity," in which he labels Heschel a "modern critic of modernity" (111). In my view, Magid underestimates the depth of Heschel's disillusionment with core aspects of modernity. It is simply wrong to describe Heschel's relationship to modernity as "almost celebratory"; as we have seen again and again in this work, Heschel is haunted by a vivid awareness of modernity's unique propensity for cruelty and barbarism. But Magid is nevertheless correct that Heschel aspired to heal the modern world rather than leave it behind. Heschel was profoundly *of* the modern

world, even as he "both question[ed] and deeply criticize[d] basic tenets" of it (115).

2. *GSM*, 34.

3. *WM*, 82.

4. *WM*, 88.

5. *WM*, 82.

6. *MNA*, 12.

7. *MNA*, 48.

8. Cf. Held, "Living and Dreaming with God," 18.

9. *GSM*, 132.

10. Heschel, "Choose Life!" in *MGSA*, 251.

11. *WM*, 119.

12. *MNA*, 71.

13. For Heschel, freedom is "liberation from the tyranny of the self-centered ego." "Religion in a Free Society," in *IF*, 15.

14. *MNA*, 142.

15. *GSM*, 410. Heschel elsewhere defines spiritual ecstasy as the act of "stepping out of the framework of routine reflexive concern." "Religion in a Free Society," in *IF*, 15.

16. *GSM*, 411.

17. *Prophets*, I, xv. "Freedom," Heschel insists, *"presupposes the capacity for sacrifice."* "Religion in a Free Society," in *IF*, 15.

18. For many of Heschel's most important thoughts on the meaning of freedom, see *GSM*, 409–412, and "Religion in a Free Society," in *IF*, 14–15. For a useful overview of Heschel's approach to freedom, cf. M. C. Fierman, "Some Thoughts on Freedom."

BIBLIOGRAPHY

Adams, Robert Merrihew. "The Silence of God in the Thought of Martin Buber." *Philosophia* 30 (2003): 51–68.

Ashley, James Matthew. *Interruptions: Mysticism, Politics, and Theology in the Work of Johann Baptist Metz.* Notre Dame, Ind.: University of Notre Dame Press, 1998.

Astley, Jeff. "Revelation Revisited." *Theology* 83 (1980): 339–345.

Bacik, James. *Apologetics and the Eclipse of Mystery: Mystagogy according to Karl Rahner.* Notre Dame, Ind.: University of Notre Dame Press, 1980.

Baillie, John. *The Idea of Revelation in Recent Thought.* New York: Columbia University Press, 1956.

———. *Our Knowledge of God.* New York: Scribner, 1939.

Barr, James. *Biblical Faith and Natural Theology.* Oxford: Clarendon Press, 1993.

———. *Old and New in Interpretation: A Study of the Two Testaments.* London: SCM Press, 1966.

———. *The Semantics of Biblical Language.* London: Oxford University Press, 1961.

Barth, Karl. *Church Dogmatics.* Vol. 2, *The Doctrine of God.* New York: Scribner, 1936.

———. "Die dogmatische Prinzipienlehre bei Wilhelm Hermann." In *Vortrage und kleinere Arbeiten,* edited by Hol-

ger Finze, 545–603. Vol. 1, *1922–1925.* Zürich: Theologischer Verlag, 1990.

———. *The Word of God and the Word of Man.* Translated by Douglas Horton. New York: Harper, 1957.

Bauckham, Richard. "'Only the Suffering God Can Help': Divine Passibility in Modern Theology." *Themelios* 9, no. 3 (1984): 6–12.

Berger, Peter L. *The Sacred Canopy: Elements of a Sociological Theory of Religion.* New York: Anchor Books, 1967.

Bergman, Samuel Hugo. *Faith and Reason: An Introduction to Modern Jewish Thought.* Edited and translated by Alfred Jospe. New York: Schocken Books, 1961.

Berkovits, Eliezer. "Dr. A. J. Heschel's Theology of Pathos." *Tradition: A Journal of Orthodox Thought* 6 (1964): 67–104.

———. *Faith after the Holocaust.* New York: Ktav, 1973.

———. *God, Man, and History.* Jerusalem: Shalem, 2004.

Boman, Thorlief. *Hebrew Thought Compared with Greek.* Translated by Jules L. Moreau. Philadelphia: Westminster Press, 1960.

Bondi, Dror. *Ayekah?: sheʾelato shel Elohim ve-targum ha-masoret be-haguto shel Avraham Yehoshuʿa Heschel* [Where art thou? God's question and the trans-

lation of tradition in the thought of
Abraham Joshua Heschel]. Jerusalem:
Shalem Press, 2008.
———. "Heschel's 'Dialogue of Ques-
tions' with Modern Thought." In
*Abraham Joshua Heschel: Philosophy,
Theology, and Interreligious Dialogue,*
edited by Stanislaw Krajweski and
Adam Lipszyc, 132–136. Wiesbaden:
Harrassowitz Verlag, 2009.
Borowitz, Eugene. *Choices in Modern
Jewish Thought: A Partisan Guide.* New
York: Behrman House, 1983.
Braiterman, Zachary. *(God) After Ausch-
witz: Tradition and Change in Post-
Holocaust Jewish Thought.* Princeton,
N.J.: Princeton University Press, 1998.
Brueggemann, Walter. *Theology of the Old
Testament: Testimony, Dispute, Advo-
cacy.* Minneapolis: Fortress Press, 1997.
Brunner, Emil. "Die andere Aufgabe
der Theologie." *Zwischen den Zeiten* 7
(1929): 255–276.
Brunner, Emil, and Karl Barth. *Natural
Theology: Comprising "Nature and
Grace" by Professor Dr. Emil Brunner
and the Reply "No!" by Dr. Karl Barth.*
Translated by Peter Fraenkel. London:
Centenary Press, 1946.
Buber, Martin. *Eclipse of God: Studies in
the Relation between Religion and Phi-
losophy.* New York: Harper, 1952.
———. *I and Thou.* Translated by Walter
Kaufmann. New York: Scribner, 1970.
———. "The Man of Today and the Jewish
Bible." In *On the Bible: Eighteen Studies,*
1–13. New York: Syracuse University
Press, 2000.
———. *Moses.* New York: Harper & Row,
1946.
———. *On Judaism.* Edited by Nahum N.
Glatzer. New York: Schocken Books,
1967.
———. *Tales of the Hasidim.* Translated
by Olga Marx. New York: Schocken
Books, 1947.
———. *Vom Geist des Judentums.* Leipzig:
Kurt Wolff Verlag, 1916.

———. *The Way of Response: Martin
Buber: Selections from His Writings.* Ed-
ited by Nahum N. Glatzer. New York:
Schocken Books, 1966.
Caputo, John. "People of God, People of
Being: The Theological Presupposi-
tions of Heidegger's Path of Thought."
In *Appropriating Heidegger,* edited by
James Faulconer and Mark Wrathall,
85–100. New York: Cambridge Univer-
sity Press, 2000.
Carr, Anne. *A Search for Wisdom and
Spirit: Thomas Merton's Theology of the
Self.* Notre Dame, Ind.: University of
Notre Dame Press, 1988.
———. "Theology and Experience in the
Thought of Karl Rahner." *Journal of Re-
ligion* 53, no. 3 (1973): 359–376.
Cassirer, Ernst. *The Philosophy of the En-
lightenment.* Translated by Franz C. A.
Koelln and James P. Pettegrove. Bos-
ton: Beacon, 1955.
Chester, Michael. *Divine Pathos and Hu-
man Being: The Theology of Abraham
Joshua Heschel.* London: Vallentine
Mitchell, 2005.
Chrétien, Jean-Louis. "The Wounded
Word: The Phenomenology of Prayer."
In *Phenomenology and the "Theological
Turn": The French Debate,* edited by
Dominique Janicaud et al., 147–175.
New York: Fordham University Press,
2000.
Cohen, Arthur. *The Natural and the
Supernatural Jew: An Historical and
Theological Introduction.* 2nd rev. ed.
New York: Behrman House, 1979.
*The Condition of Jewish Belief: A Sympo-
sium.* Compiled by the editors of *Com-
mentary* magazine. New York: Macmil-
lan, 1966.
Connell, George. "Against Idolatry:
Heidegger and Natural Theology." In
*Postmodern Philosophy and Christian
Thought,* edited by Merold Westphal,
144–168. Bloomington: Indiana Uni-
versity Press, 1999.
Corbishley, T. "Mysticism." In *The New*

Catholic Encyclopedia, 10: 175–179. New York: McGraw-Hill, 1967.

Craigo-Snell, Shannon. *Silence, Love, and Death: Saying 'Yes' to God in the Theology of Karl Rahner*. Milwaukee: Marquette University Press, 2008.

Dawkins, Richard. *Unweaving the Rainbow: Science, Delusion, and the Appetite for Wonder*. Boston: Houghton-Mifflin, 1998.

Delitzsch, Franz. *Psalms*. Translated by James Martin. Grand Rapids, Mich.: William B. Eerdmans, 1949.

Dorff, Elliot. *Conservative Judaism: Our Ancestors to Our Descendants*. 1st ed. New York: United Synagogue of Conservative Judaism, 1977.

———. *Conservative Judaism: Our Ancestors to Our Descendants*. 2nd rev. ed. New York: United Synagogue of Conservative Judaism, 1996.

———. *For the Love of God and People: A Philosophy of Jewish Law*. Philadelphia: Jewish Publication Society, 2007.

Dreyfus, Hubert L. "Heidegger on the Connection Between Nihilism, Art, Technology, and Politics." In *The Cambridge Companion to Heidegger*, edited by Charles B. Guignon, 289–316. 2nd ed. Cambridge: Cambridge University Press, 2006.

Duffy, Stephen. *The Graced Horizon: Nature and Grace in Modern Catholic Thought*. Collegeville, Minn.: Liturgical Press, 1992.

Dulles, Avery. *Models of Revelation*. Maryknoll, N.Y.: Orbis, 1983.

Dych, William, S.J. *Karl Rahner*. New York: Continuum, 1992.

Efromysen, Daniel. "The Patristic Connection." In *Antisemitism and the Foundations of Christianity*, edited by Alan. T. Davies, 98–117. New York: Paulist Press, 1979.

Eisen, Arnold. "Abraham Joshua Heschel and the Challenge of Religious Pluralism." *Modern Judaism* 29, no. 1 (2009): 4–15.

———. "Prophecy as 'Vocation': New Perspectives on the Thought and Activism of Rabbi Abraham Joshua Heschel" [Hebrew]. In *Derekh ha-ruah: Sefer Ha-Yovel le-Eliezer Schweid*, vol. 2, edited by Yehoyada Amir, 835–850. Jerusalem: Van Leer, 2005.

———. "Re-Reading Heschel on the Commandments." *Modern Judaism* 9, no. 1 (1989): 1–34.

Eisen, Robert. "A. J. Heschel's Rabbinic Theology as a Response to the Holocaust." *Modern Judaism* 23, no. 3 (2003): 211–225.

Erlewine, Robert. "Reclaiming the Prophets: Cohen, Heschel, and Crossing the Theocentric-Neo-Humanist Divide." *Journal of Jewish Thought and Philosophy* 17, no. 2 (2009): 177–206.

———. "Rediscovering Heschel: Theocentrism, Secularism, and Porous Thinking." *Modern Judaism* 32, no. 2 (2012): 174–194.

Even-Chen, Alexander. *Akedat Yitshak: ba-farshanut ha-mistit veha-filosofit shel ha-mikra*. Tel Aviv: Yediot Aharonot, 2006.

———. "Faith and the Courage to Be: Heschel and Tillich." In *Interaction between Judaism and Christianity in History, Religion, Art and Literature*, edited by Marcel Poorthuis, 337–356. Leiden: Brill, 2009.

———. "God's Omnipotence and Presence in Abraham Joshua Heschel's Philosophy." *Shofar* 26, no. 1 (2007): 41–71.

———. *Kol min ha-ʿarafel: Avraham Yehoshuʿa Heshel: ben fenomenologyah le-mistikah* [A voice from the darkness: Abraham Joshua Heschel—between phenomenology and mysticism]. Tel Aviv: Am Oved, 1999.

———. "Mysticism and Prophecy according to Abraham Joshua Heschel" [Hebrew]. *Kabbalah* 5 (2000): 359–370.

———. "The Torah, Revelation, and Scientific Critique in the Teachings of

Abraham Joshua Heschel." *Conservative Judaism* 50, no. 2–3 (1998): 67–76.

Even-Chen, Alexander, and Ephraim Meir. *Between Heschel and Buber: A Comparative Study*. Boston: Academic Studies Press, 2012.

Fackenheim, Emil L. *God's Presence in History: Jewish Affirmations and Philosophical Reflections*. New York: New York University Press, 1970.

———. Review of *Man Is Not Alone*. *Judaism* 1, no. 1 (1952): 85–89.

Feinberg, John S. *No One Like Him: The Doctrine of God*. Wheaton, Ill.: Crossway Books, 2001.

Fierman, M. C. "Some Thoughts on Freedom in the Theology of Abraham Joshua Heschel." *CCAR Journal* 23, no. 3 (1976): 91–100.

Finley, James. *Merton's Palace of Nowhere: A Search for God through Awareness of the True Self*. Notre Dame, Ind.: Ave Maria Press, 1978.

Fiorenza, Francis Schüssler. "Systematic Theology: Tasks and Methods." In *Systematic Theology: Roman Catholic Perspectives*, vol. 1, edited by Francis Schüssler Fiorenza and John P. Galvin, 1–88. Minneapolis: Fortress Press, 1991.

Fogelin, Robert J. *Figuratively Speaking*. Rev. ed. New York: Oxford, 2011.

Forman-Barzilai, David. "Agonism in Faith: Buber's Eternal Thou after the Holocaust." *Modern Judaism* 23, no. 2 (2003): 156–179.

Frank, Daniel. "Anger as a Vice: A Maimonidean Critique of Aristotle's Ethics." *History of Philosophy Quarterly* 7 (1990): 269–281.

Frankl, Victor E. *Man's Search for Meaning*. Boston: Beacon Press, 2006.

Fretheim, Terence E. "Prayer in the Old Testament: Creating Space in the World for God." In *A Primer on Prayer*, edited by Paul Sponheim, 51–62. Philadelphia: Fortress Press, 1988.

———. "The Repentance of God: A Key to Evaluating Old Testament God-Talk." *Horizons in Biblical Theology* 10, no. 1 (1988): 47–70.

Friedman, Maurice. "Abraham Heschel among Contemporary Philosophers: From Divine Pathos to Prophetic Action." *Philosophy Today* 18, no. 4 (Winter 1974): 293–305.

———. "Divine Need and Human Wonder: The Philosophy of Abraham J. Heschel." *Judaism* 25, no. 1 (1976): 65–78.

———. "The Prophetic Experience." *Judaism* 13, no. 1 (1964): 117–121.

Fuller, Robert C. *Wonder: From Emotion to Spirituality*. Chapel Hill: University of North Carolina Press, 2006.

Gavrilyuk, Paul L. *The Suffering of the Impassible God: The Dialectics of Patristic Thought*. Oxford: Oxford University Press, 2004.

Gellman, Jerome. "The Meaning of the Aqedah [Binding of Isaac] for Jewish Spirituality." *Studies in Jewish Civilization* 13 (2003): 31–44.

Gerrish, Brian. "The Nature of Doctrine." *Journal of Religion* 68 (1988): 87–92.

Gillman, Neil. *Doing Jewish Theology: God, Torah, and Israel in Modern Judaism*. 2008 hardcover ed. Woodstock, Vt.: Jewish Lights, 2008.

———. "Toward a Theology for Conservative Judaism." *Conservative Judaism* 37, no. 1 (1983): 4–22.

Glick, G. Wayne. *The Reality of Christianity: A Study of Adolf Von Harnack as Historian and Theologian*. New York: Harper & Row, 1967.

Goldy, Robert G. *The Emergence of Jewish Theology in America*. Bloomington: Indiana University Press, 1990.

Gordis, Robert. *A Faith for Moderns*. New York: Bloch, 1960.

Grant, Colin. "Why Should Theology Be Unnatural?" *Modern Theology* 23, no. 1 (2007): 91–106.

Grant, Frederick C. *An Introduction to New Testament Thought*. New York: Abingdon-Cokesbury Press, 1950.

Green, Arthur. "Abraham Joshua Heschel: Recasting Hasidism for Moderns." *Modern Judaism* 29, no. 1 (2009): 62–79.

———. "Three Warsaw Mystics." In *Kolot rabim: Sefer Ha-Zikaron le Rivka Shats-Ufenheimer*, edited by Rachel Elior and Joseph Dan. *Jerusalem Studies in Jewish Thought* 13 (1996): 1–58.

Greenberg, Irving. "Cloud of Smoke, Pillar of Fire: Judaism, Christianity, Modernity after the Holocaust." In *Auschwitz: Beginning of a New Era?*, edited by Eva Fleischner, 1–55. New York: Ktav, 1977.

Greene, Dana. *Evelyn Underhill: Artist of the Infinite Life*. New York: Crossroad, 1990.

Grenz, Stanley J., and John R. Franke. *Beyond Foundationalism: Shaping Theology in a Postmodern Context*. Louisville: Westminster John Knox Press, 2001.

Grenz, Stanley J., and Roger E. Olsen. *20th Century Theology: God and the World in a Transitional Age*. Downer's Grove, Ill.: InterVarsity Press, 1992.

Gustafson, James M. *Ethics from a Theocentric Perspective*. Vol. 1 of *Theology and Ethics*. Chicago: University of Chicago Press, 1981.

Halbertal, Moshe. "Yeshayahu Leibowitz: Between Religious Thought and Social Criticism" [Hebrew]. In Sagi, *Yeshayahu Leibowitz*, 221–227.

Harmless, William, S.J. *Mystics*. New York: Oxford University Press, 2008.

Hart, Trevor. "A Capacity for Ambiguity? The Barth-Brunner Debate Revisited." *Tyndale Bulletin* 44, no. 2 (1993): 289–305.

Hartman, David. *Conflicting Visions: Spiritual Possibilities of Modern Israel*. New York: Schocken Books, 1990.

———. "Judaism as an Interpretive Tradition." In *A Heart of Many Rooms: Celebrating the Many Voices within Judaism*, 3–36. Woodstock, Vt.: Jewish Lights, 1999.

———. "Prayer and Religious Consciousness: An Analysis of Jewish Prayer in the Works of Joseph B. Soloveitchik, Yeshayahu Leibowitz, and Abraham Joshua Heschel." *Modern Judaism* 23, no. 2 (2003): 105–125.

Hasker, William. "God Takes Risks." In *Contemporary Debates in the Philosophy of Religion*, edited by Michael L. Peterson and Raymond J. VanArragon, 218–227. Malden, Mass.: Blackwell, 2004.

Heidegger, Martin. *Discourse on Thinking*. Translated by John M. Anderson and E. Hans Freund. New York: Harper & Row, 1975.

———. *Identity and Difference*. Translated by Joan Stambaugh. New York: Harper & Row, 1969.

———. *An Introduction to Metaphysics*. Translated by Ralph Manheim. New Haven, Conn.: Yale University Press, 1959.

———. "The Question Concerning Technology." In *Basic Writings from Being and Time (1927) to The Task of Thinking (1964)*, edited by David F. Krell, 307–342. New York: Harper & Row, 1977.

Heiler, Freidrich. *Prayer: A Study in the History and Psychology of Religion*. Translated and edited by Samuel McComb and John Edgar Park. London: Oxford University Press, 1932.

Held, Shai. "Living and Dreaming with God." In *Jewish Theology in Our Time: A New Generation Explores the Foundations and Future of Jewish Belief*, edited by Elliot J. Cosgrove, 17–22. Woodstock, Vt.: Jewish Lights, 2010.

———. "The Promise and Peril of Jewish Barthianism: The Theology of Michael Wyschogrod." *Modern Judaism* 25, no. 3 (2005): 316–326.

———. "Wonder and Indignation: Abraham's Uneasy Faith." *Jewish Review of Books* 3, no. 4 (Winter 2013): 36–37.

Heschel, Abraham Joshua. *Between God and Man: Selections from the Writings of Abraham Joshua Heschel*. Selected, ed-

ited, and introduced by Fritz A. Roths-
child. New York: Free Press, 1959.
———. "The Concept of Man in Jewish
Thought." In *To Grow in Wisdom: An
Anthology of Abraham Joshua Heschel*,
edited by Jacob Neusner and Noam
N.M. Neusner, 97–145. Lanham, Md.:
Madison Books, 1990.
———. *Die Prophetie*. Krakow: Polish
Academy of Sciences, 1936.
———. *The Earth Is the Lord's: The Inner
Life of the Jew in Eastern Europe*. New
York: Farrar, Straus & Giroux, 1950.
———. *God in Search of Man: A Philosophy
of Judaism*. New York: Farrar, Straus &
Giroux, 1955.
———. *Heavenly Torah as Refracted
through the Generations*. Translated by
Gordon Tucker with Leonard Levin.
New York: Crossroad, 2005.
———. *The Ineffable Name of God: Man*.
Translated by Morton Leifman. New
York: Continuum, 2005. Originally
published as *Der Shem Ha-Meforash:
Mentsch*. Warsaw: Indzl Publishing
House, 1933. Also translated and
privately distributed by Zalman M.
Schachter-Shalomi as *Human, God's In-
effable Name*, n.d.
———. *The Insecurity of Freedom: Essays
on Human Existence*. Philadelphia: Jew-
ish Publication Society, 1966.
———. *Israel: An Echo of Eternity*. New
York: Farrar, Strauss & Giroux, 1967.
———. *Maimonides: A Biography*. Trans-
lated by Joachim Neugroschel. New
York: Image Books, 1991.
———. *Man Is Not Alone: A Philosophy of
Religion*. New York: Farrar, Straus &
Young, 1951.
———. *Man's Quest for God: Studies in
Prayer and Symbolism*. New York:
Scribner, 1954.
———. *Moral Grandeur and Spiritual
Audacity: Essays*. Edited by Susannah
Heschel. New York: Farrar, Straus &
Giroux, 1996.

———. *A Passion for Truth*. New York:
Farrar, Straus & Giroux, 1973.
———. *Prophetic Inspiration after the
Prophets: Maimonides and Other Me-
dieval Authorities*. Edited by Morris Fai-
erstein. Hoboken, N.J.: Ktav, 1996.
———. *The Prophets: An Introduction*. 2
vols. New York: Harper &Row, 1962.
———. "The Quest for Certainty in Saa-
dia's Philosophy." *Jewish Quarterly Re-
view* 33, no. 2–3 (1943): 265–313.
———. "Reason and Revelation in Saadia's
Philosophy." *Jewish Quarterly Review*
34, no. 4 (1944): 391–408.
———. *The Sabbath: Its Meaning for
Modern Man*. New York: Farrar, Straus
& Giroux, 1951.
———. *To Grow in Wisdom: An Anthology
of Abraham Joshua Heschel*. Lanham,
Md.: Madison Books, 1990.
———. *Torah min ha-shamayim be-
aspaklaryah shel ha-dorot* [Theology
of ancient Judaism]. 3 vols. New York:
Soncino, 1962 (vols. 1–2). New York:
Jewish Theological Seminary, 1995
(vol. 3).
———. *Who Is Man?* Stanford, Calif.:
Stanford University Press, 1965.
Heschel, Susannah. "Theological Affini-
ties in the Writings of Abraham Joshua
Heschel and Martin Luther King, Jr."
In *Black Zion: African American Reli-
gious Encounters with Judaism*, edited
by Yvonne Chireau and Nathaniel
Deutsch, 168–186. Oxford: Oxford Uni-
versity Press, 2000.
Higgins, John J. *Thomas Merton on Prayer*.
Garden City, N.Y.: Doubleday, 1973.
Hook, Sidney. "The Atheism of Paul Til-
lich." In *Religious Experience and Truth:
A Symposium*, edited by Sidney Hook,
59–64. New York: New York University
Press, 1961.
Horwitz, Rivka. "Abraham Joshua
Heschel on Prayer and His Hasidic
Sources." *Modern Judaism* 19, no. 3
(1999): 293–310.

———. "Revelation and the Bible according to Twentieth-Century Jewish Philosophy." In *Jewish Spirituality: From the Sixteenth-Century Revival to the Present*, edited by Arthur Green, 355–364. New York: Crossroad, 1986.

Idel, Moshe. "Abraham J. Heschel on Mysticism and Hasidism." *Modern Judaism* 29, no. 1 (February 2009): 80–105.

———. *Kabbalah: New Perspectives.* New Haven, Conn.: Yale University Press, 1988.

———. *The Mystical Experience in Abraham Abulafia.* Albany: State University of New York Press, 1988.

Insole, Christopher. "Anthropomorphism and the Apophatic God." *Modern Theology* 17, no. 4 (2001): 475–483.

Jacobs, Louis. *A Jewish Theology.* West Orange, N.J.: Behrman House, 1973.

Jaeger, John. "Abraham Heschel and the Theology of Jürgen Moltmann." *Perspectives in Religious Studies* 24, no. 2 (2006): 167–179.

James, William. *The Varieties of Religious Experience.* New York: Dover, 2002.

Johns, David L. *Mysticism and Ethics in Friedrich von Hügel.* Lewiston, N.Y.: Edwin Mellen Press, 2004.

Jung, Carl. "The Undiscovered Self (Present and Future)." In *The Essential Jung*, edited by Anthony Storr, 349–403. Princeton, N.J.: Princeton University Press, 1983.

Kadushin, Max. *Organic Thinking: A Study in Rabbinic Thought.* New York: Jewish Theological Seminary of America, 1938.

———. *The Rabbinic Mind.* 2nd ed. New York: Blaisdell, 1965.

Kaplan, Edward K. *Holiness in Words: Abraham Joshua Heschel's Poetics of Piety.* Albany: State University of New York Press, 1996.

———. "Introduction." In Heschel, *The Ineffable Name of God: Man*, 7–18.

———. "Sacred versus Symbolic Religion: A. J. Heschel and Martin Buber." *Modern Judaism* 14, no. 3 (1994): 213–231.

———. *Spiritual Radical: Abraham Joshua Heschel in America.* New Haven, Conn.: Yale University Press, 2007.

Kaplan, Edward K., and Samuel H. Dresner. *Abraham Joshua Heschel: Prophetic Witness.* New Haven, Conn.: Yale University Press, 1998.

Kaplan, Mordecai M. *Know How to Answer: A Guide to Reconstructionism.* New York: Jewish Reconstructionist Federation, 1951.

Katz, Steven T. "Abraham Joshua Heschel and Hasidism." *Journal of Jewish Studies* 31 (1980): 82–104.

———. "Eliezer Berkovits and Modern Jewish Philosophy." In *Post-Holocaust Dialogues: Critical Studies in Modern Jewish Thought*, 94–140. New York: New York University Press, 1985.

Kaufman, William E. *Contemporary Jewish Philosophies.* Detroit: Wayne State University Press, 1976.

Kaufman, Tzippi. "Abraham Joshua Heschel and Hasidic Thought: Worship within Corporeality as Total Ethical Demand" [Hebrew]. *Akdamut* 24 (2010): 137–155.

Kavka, Martin. "The Meaning of That Hour: Prophecy, Phenomenology, and the Public Sphere in the Early Writings of Abraham Joshua Heschel." In *Religion and Violence in a Secular World: Toward a New Political Theology*, edited by Clayton Crockett, 108–136. Charlottesville: University of Virginia Press, 2006.

Kelly, James J. *Baron Friedrich von Hügel's Philosophy of Religion.* Leuven: Leuven University Press, 1983.

Kepnes, Steven. *The Text as Thou: Martin Buber's Dialogical Hermeneutics and Narrative Theology.* Bloomington: Indiana University Press, 1992.

Kerr, Fergus, O.P. "French Theology: Yves

Congar and Henri de Lubac." In *The Modern Theologians: An Introduction to Christian Theology in the Twentieth Century*, edited by David F. Ford, 105–117. 2nd ed. Oxford: Blackwell, 1997.

Kilby, Karen. "Karl Rahner." In *The Modern Theologians: An Introduction to Christian Theology in the Twentieth Century*, edited by David F. Ford, 92–105. 1st ed. Oxford: Blackwell, 1989.

———. *Karl Rahner: Philosophy and Theology*. New York: Routledge, 2004.

Kohn, Jacob. *The Moral Life of Man: Its Philosophical Foundations*. New York: Philosophical Library, 1956.

Koren, Israel. *The Mystery of the Earth: Mysticism and Hasidism in the Thought of Martin Buber*. Leiden: Brill, 2010.

Kress, Robert. *A Rahner Handbook*. Atlanta: John Knox Press, 1982.

Lash, Nicholas. *Holiness, Speech, and Silence: Reflections on the Question of God*. Burlington, Vt.: Ashgate, 2004.

Leibowitz, Yeshayahu. *Emunah, historyah va-ʿarakhim: maʾamarim ve-hartsaʾot* [Faith, history, and values: Essays and lectures]. Jerusalem: Academon, 1982.

———. *Judaism, Human Values, and the Jewish State*. Edited by Eliezer Goldman. Cambridge, Mass.: Harvard University Press, 1992.

———. *Torah u-mitsvot ba-zeman ha-zeh: hartsaʾot u-maʾamarim* [Torah and mitzvot in our time: Lectures and essays]. Tel Aviv: Masada, 1954.

———. *Yahadut, ʿam yehudi, u-medinat yisrael* [Judaism, the Jewish people, and the State of Israel]. Jerusalem: Schocken Books, 1979.

Leonard, Ellen M. *Creative Tension: The Spiritual Legacy of Friedrich von Hügel*. Scranton, Pa.: University of Scranton Press, 1997.

Levenson, Jon D. *Creation and the Persistence of Evil: The Jewish Drama of Divine Omnipotence*. San Francisco: Harper & Row, 1988.

———. "Religious Affirmation and Historical Criticism in Heschel's Biblical Interpretation." *AJS Review* 25, no. 1 (2000/2001): 25–44.

Levinger, Jacob. "Heʾarot le-torah min ha-shamayim be-aspaklarya shel ha-dorot le-rabbi A. J. Heschel." *Deʿot* 31 (1966): 45–48.

Lindbeck, George A. *The Nature of Doctrine: Religion and Theology in a Postliberal Age*. Philadelphia: Westminster Press, 1984.

Lipszyc, Adam. "The Mark of the Question: Heschel and Jabès on Divine Presence and Absence." In *Abraham Joshua Heschel: Philosophy, Theology, and Interreligious Dialogue*, edited by Stanislaw Krajweski and Adam Lipszyc, 60–66. Wiesbaden: Harrassowitz Verlag, 2009.

Livingston, James C., and Francis Schüssler Fiorenza. *Modern Christian Thought*. With Sarah Coakley and James H. Evans Jr. Vol. 2. 2nd ed. Upper Saddle River, N.J.: Prentice-Hall, 2001.

Mackler, Aaron. "Symbols, Reality, and God: Heschel's Rejection of a Tillichian Understanding of Religious Symbols." *Judaism* 40, no. 3 (1991): 290–300.

Macquarrie, John. *Heidegger and Christianity: The Hensley Henson Lectures, 1993–94*. New York: Continuum, 1994.

Magid, Shaul. "Abraham Joshua Heschel and Thomas Merton: Heretics of Modernity." *Conservative Judaism* 50, no. 2–3 (1998): 112–125.

Magid, Shaul. *From Metaphysics to Midrash: Myth, History and the Interpretation of Scripture in Lurianic Kabbala*. Bloomington: Indiana University Press, 2008.

———. "The Role of the Secular in Abraham Joshua Heschel's Theology: (Re)Reading Heschel after 9/11." *Modern Judaism* 29, no. 1 (2009): 138–160.

Maimonides, Moses. *The Guide of the Perplexed*. Translated by Shlomo Pines. Chicago: University of Chicago Press, 1963.

Malits, Elena. *The Solitary Explorer:*

Thomas Merton's Transforming Journey. San Francisco: Harper & Row, 1980.

Mandel, Paul. "The Call of Abraham: A Midrash Revisited." *Prooftexts* 14 (1994): 267–284.

Marmur, Michael. "Heschel's Rhetoric of Citation: The Use of Sources in *God in Search of Man.*" Ph.D. diss., Hebrew University, 2005.

———. "Heschel's Two Maimonides." *Jewish Quarterly Review* 98, no. 2 (2008): 230–254.

———. "In Search of Heschel." *Shofar* 26, no. 1 (2007): 9–40.

Martin, Bernard. *The Existentialist Theology of Paul Tillich.* New York: Bookman Associates, 1963.

Marvick, Louis Wirth. *Mallarmé and the Sublime.* Albany: State University of New York Press, 1986.

Mays, James Luther. *Psalms.* Louisville: John Knox Press, 1994.

McGinn, Bernard. "Mysticism." In *The New Westminster Dictionary of Christian Spirituality,* edited by Philip Sheldrake, 19–25. 1st American ed. Louisville: Westminster John Knox Press, 2005.

Mendes-Flohr, Paul. *From Mysticism to Dialogue: Martin Buber's Transformation of German Social Thought.* Detroit: Wayne State University Press, 1989.

Mensch, James R. "Prayer as Kenosis." In *The Phenomenology of Prayer,* edited by Bruce Ellis Benson and Norman Wirzba, 63–74. New York: Fordham University Press, 2005.

Merkle, John C. *Abraham Joshua Heschel: Exploring His Life and Thought.* New York: Macmillan, 1985.

———. *The Genesis of Faith: The Depth Theology of Abraham Joshua Heschel.* New York: Macmillan, 1985.

———. "Heschel's Monotheism vis-à-vis Pantheism and Panentheism." *Studies in Jewish-Christian Relations* 2, no. 2 (2007): 26–33.

Merton, Thomas. *Contemplative Prayer.* New York: Herder and Herder, 1969.

———. *Honorable Reader: Reflections on My Work.* Edited by Robert E. Daggy. New York: Crossroad, 1989.

———. *Life and Holiness.* New York: Doubleday, 1996.

———. *The New Man.* New York: Farrar, Straus & Cudahy, 1961.

———. *New Seeds of Contemplation.* New York: New Directions, 1961.

———. *No Man Is an Island.* New York: Dell, 1957.

———. "Rebirth and the New Man in Christianity." In *Love and Living,* edited by Naomi Burton Stone and Brother Patrick Hart, 192–202. New York: Farrar, Straus, and Giroux, 1979.

———. "The Recovery of Paradise." In *A Thomas Merton Reader,* edited by Thomas P. McDonnell, 399–403. New York: Harcourt, Brace & World, 1962.

———. *Spiritual Direction and Meditation.* Collegeville, Minn.: Liturgical Press, 1960.

———. *What Are These Wounds? The Life of a Cistercian Mystic, Saint Lutgarde of Aywières.* Milwaukee: Bruce Publishing Company, 1950.

Metz, Johann Baptist. "Christians and Jews after Auschwitz." In *The Emergent Church: The Future of Christianity in a Postbourgeois World,* translated by Peter Mann, 17–33. New York: Crossroad, 1981.

———. "Suffering unto God." Translated by J. Matthew Ashley. *Critical Inquiry* 20, no. 4 (1994): 611–622.

———. "Theology as Theodicy." In *A Passion for God: The Mystical-Political Dimension of Christianity,* translated by James Matthew Ashley, 54–71. New York: Paulist Press, 1998.

Micka, Ermin F. *The Problem of Divine Anger in Arnobius and Lactantius.* Washington, D.C.: Catholic University of America Press, 1943.

Milbank, John. "Henri de Lubac." In *The Modern Theologians: An Introduction to Christian Theology since 1918,* edited by David F. Ford with Rachel Muers, 76–91. 3rd ed. Oxford: Blackwell Publishers, 2005.

Mirsky, Yehudah. "The Rhapsodist." *New Republic* 220, no. 16 (1999): 36–42.

Mitchell, Basil, and Maurice Wiles. "Does Christianity Need a Revelation? A Discussion." *Theology* 83, no. 691 (1980): 103–114.

Moltmann, Jürgen. *The Crucified God: The Cross of Christ as the Foundation and Criticism of Christian Theology.* Translated by R. A. Wilson and John Bowden. London: SCM Press, 1974.

Moody, Dale. "An Introduction to Emil Brunner." *Review and Expositor* 44, no. 3 (1947): 312–330.

Moore, Donald J. *Martin Buber: Prophet of Religious Secularism.* 2nd. ed. New York: Fordham University Press, 1996.

Morgan, Michael L. *Beyond Auschwitz: Post-Holocaust Jewish Thought in America.* Oxford: Oxford University Press, 2001.

———. "Religion, History and Moral Discourse." In *Philosophy in an Age of Pluralism: The Philosophy of Charles Taylor in Question,* edited by James Tully, 49–66. Cambridge: Cambridge University Press, 1994.

Moyn, Samuel. *Origins of the Other: Emmanuel Levinas between Revelation and Ethics.* Ithaca, N.Y.: Cornell University Press, 2005.

Muller, Herbert Joseph. *The Uses of the Past: Profiles of Former Societies.* New York: Oxford University Press, 1952.

Murphy, Nancey. *Beyond Liberalism and Fundamentalism: How Modern and Postmodern Philosophy Set the Theological Agenda.* Valley Forge, Pa.: Trinity Press International, 1996.

Mussner, Franz. "Kommende Schwerpunkte Biblischer Theologie." In *Eine Bibel—zwei Testamente: Positionen Biblischer Theologie,* edited by Christoph Dohmen and Thomas Söding, 237–251. Paderborn: Uni-Taschenbücher, 1993.

Nietzsche, Friedrich. *Human, All Too Human: A Book for Free Spirits.* Translated by Marion Faber with Stephen Lehmann. Lincoln: University of Nebraska Press, 1984.

Nouwen, Henri J. *Reaching Out: The Three Movements of the Spiritual Life.* Garden City, N.Y.: Doubleday, 1975.

Novak, David. "Heschel on Revelation." In *Tradition in the Public Square: A David Novak Reader,* edited by Randi Rashkover and Martin Kavka, 37–45. Grand Rapids, Mich.: William B. Eerdmans, 2008.

———. "Revelation." In *Modern Judaism: An Oxford Guide,* edited by Nicholas de Lange and Miri Freud-Kandel, 278–289. Oxford: Oxford University Press, 2005.

Nussbaum, Martha. *Upheavals of Thought: The Intelligence of Emotions.* Cambridge: Cambridge University Press, 2001.

Otto, Rudolf. *The Idea of the Holy: An Inquiry into the Non-Rational Factor in the Idea of the Divine and Its Relation to the Rational.* Translated by John W. Harvey. London: Oxford University Press, 1923.

Owens, David. "Disenchantment." In *Philosophers without Gods: Meditations on Atheism and the Secular Life,* edited by Louise M. Antony, 165–179. Oxford: Oxford University Press, 2007.

Pattison, George. *Routledge Philosophy Guidebook to the Later Heidegger.* London: Routledge, 2000.

Pauck, Wilhelm. *Harnack and Troeltsch: Two Historical Theologians.* New York: Oxford University Press, 1968.

Perlman, Lawrence. *Abraham Heschel's Idea of Revelation.* Atlanta: Scholars Press, 1989.

Petuchowski, Jacob J. "The Concept of Revelation in Modern Judaism." In *Three Ways to the One God: The Faith Experience in Judaism, Christianity, and Islam,* edited by Abdoldjavad Falaturi,

Jacob J. Petuchowski, and Walter
Strolz. New York: Crossroad, 1987.
———. "The Concept of Revelation
in Reform Judaism." In *Studies in
Modern Theology and Prayer,* edited by
Elizabeth R. Petuchowski and Aaron
M. Petuchowski, 101–114. Philadelphia:
Jewish Publication Society, 1998.
———. *Ever since Sinai: A Modern View of
Torah.* New York: Scribe Publications,
1961.
———. "Faith as the Leap of Action: The
Theology of Abraham Joshua Heschel."
Commentary 25, no. 5 (1958): 390–397.
———. "Reflections on Revelation."
CCAR Journal 13, no. 6 (1966): 4–11.
———. "Revelation and the Modern Jew."
In Petuchowski, *Heirs of the Pharisees,*
116–129. New York: Basic Books, 1970.
———. "The Supposed Dogma of the Mo-
saic Authorship of the Pentateuch." *Hib-
bert Journal* 57, no. 227 (1959): 356–360.
Pinnock, Clark. *The Scripture Principle.*
San Francisco: Harper & Row, 1984.
Placher, William C. *The Domestication
of Transcendence: How Modern Think-
ing about God Went Wrong.* Louisville:
Westminster/John Knox Press, 1996.
Pojman, Louis P. *Religious Belief and the
Will.* London: Routledge & Kegan
Paul, 1986.
Polt, Richard. *Heidegger: An Introduction.*
Ithaca, N.Y.: Cornell University Press,
1999.
Poorthuis, Marcel, Joshua Schwartz, and
Joseph Turner, eds. *Interaction between
Judaism and Christianity in History, Re-
ligion, Art, and Literature.* Leiden: Brill,
2009.
Proudfoot, Wayne. *Religious Experience.*
Berkeley: University of California
Press, 1985.
Rahner, Karl. "Concerning the Relation-
ship between Nature and Grace." In
Theological Investigations, vol. 1, trans-
lated by Cornelius Ernst, 297–317. Bal-
timore: Helicon Press, 1961.
———. *Foundations of the Christian Faith:*

*An Introduction to the Idea of Chris-
tianity.* Translated by William V. Dych.
New York: Seabury Press, 1978.
———. "Order." In *Sacramentum Mundi:
An Encyclopedia of Theology,* edited by
Karl Rahner with Cornelius Ernst and
Kevin Smyth. Vol. 4. New York: Herder
and Herder, 1969.
———. "Teresa of Avila: Doctor of the
Church." In *Opportunities for Faith.*
New York: Seabury Press, 1970.
———. "Theology and the Arts." *Thought*
57, no. 25 (1982): 17–29.
Räisänen, Heikki. "Marcion and the Ori-
gins of Christian Anti-Judaism: A Re-
appraisal." *Temenos* 33 (1997): 121–135.
Ravitzky, Aviezer, ed. *Yeshaʿyahu Libo-
vits: ben shamranut le-radikaliyut* [Ye-
shayahu Leibowitz: Between conser-
vatism and radicalism]. Tel Aviv: Van
Leer Institute, 2007.
Rice, Richard. "Process Theism and the
Open View of God: The Crucial Dif-
ference." In *Searching for an Adequate
God: A Dialogue between Process and
Free Will Theists,* edited by John B.
Cobb Jr. and Clark H. Pinnock, 163–
200. Grand Rapids, Mich.: William B.
Eerdmans, 2000.
Ronen, Shoshana. "Absolute Good or
Omnipotence: God after Auschwitz in
the Theology of Abraham J. Heschel
and Hans Jonas." In *Abraham Joshua
Heschel: Philosophy, Theology, and Inter-
religious Dialogue,* edited by Stanislaw
Krajweski and Adam Lipszyc, 137–144.
Wiesbaden: Harrassowitz Verlag, 2009.
Rosenberg, Shalom. "Biblical Criticism in
Modern Jewish Thought" [Hebrew]. In
Ha-mikra va-ʾanahnu, edited by Uriel
Simon. Tel Aviv: Dvir, 1979.
Rosenzweig, Franz. "Atheistic Theology."
In *Philosophical and Theological Writ-
ings,* edited by Paul W. Franks and
Michael L. Morgan, 10–24. India-
napolis: Hackett, 2000.
———. "The Content of Revelation." In
Franz Rosenzweig: His Life and Thought,

edited by Nahum N. Glatzer, 285. New
York: Schocken Books, 1953.

Rotenstreich, Nathan. "On Prophetic
Consciousness." *Journal of Religion* 54,
no. 3 (1974): 185–198.

Rothschild, Fritz A. "Architect and
Herald of a New Theology." *America*
128, no. 9 (1973): 199–214.

———. "Introduction." In *Between God
and Man: An Interpretation of Judaism
from the Writings of Abraham J. Heschel,*
edited by Fritz Rothschild, 7–32. New
York: Free Press, 1959.

Rubenstein, Mary-Jane. *Strange Wonder:
The Closing of Metaphysics and the
Opening of Awe.* New York: Columbia
University Press, 2008.

Rundle, Bede. *Why There Is Something
Rather Than Nothing.* Oxford: Clarendon Press, 2004.

Sagi, Avi, ed. *Yeshayahu Leibowitz: His
World and His Thought* [Hebrew]. Jerusalem: Keter, 1995.

Sanders, J. A. "Apostle to the Gentiles."
Conservative Judaism 28, no. 1 (Fall
1973): 61–63.

Sarot, Marcel. "Omnipotence and Self-
Limitation." In *Christian Faith and
Philosophical Theology: Essays in Honor
of Vincent Brümme,* edited by Gijsbert
van den Brink, Luco J. van den Brom,
and Marcel Sarot, 172–185. Kampen:
Kok Pharos, 1992.

Sauter, Gerhard. "Argue Theologically
with One Another: Karl Barth's Argument with Emil Brunner." In *Theology
as Conversation: The Significance of
Dialogue in Historical and Contemporary Theology: A Festschrift for Daniel
L. Migliore,* edited by Bruce L. McCor-
mack and Kimlyn J. Bender, 30–47.
Grand Rapids, Mich.: William B. Eerdmans, 2009.

Scheler, Max. *The Nature of Sympathy.*
Translated by Peter Heath. New Haven,
Conn.: Yale University Press, 1954.

Schiffman, Pinchas. "The Detaching of

the Ethical from the Religious Consciousness: An Unconscious Contribution to Secularization, Chauvinistic
Nationalism, and Ultra-Orthodoxy"
[Hebrew]. In Ravitzky, *Yeshayahu Leibowitz,* 59–73.

Schlimm, Matthew R. "Different Perspectives on Divine Pathos: An Examination of Hermeneutics in Biblical Theology." *Catholic Biblical Quarterly* 69,
no. 4 (2007): 673–694.

Scholem, Gershom. "Devekut or Com-
munion with God." In *The Messianic
Idea in Judaism and Other Essays on
Jewish Spirituality,* 203–227. New York:
Schocken Books, 1971.

———. *Major Trends in Jewish Mysticism.*
1st Schocken paperback ed. New York:
Schocken Books, 1961.

Schwartz, Baruch J. "The Ultimate Aim
of Israel's Restoration in Ezekiel." In
*Birkat Shalom: Studies in the Bible,
Ancient Near Eastern Literature, and
Postbiblical Judaism Presented to Shalom
M. Paul on the Occasion of His Seven-
tieth Birthday,* edited by Chaim Cohen
and Shalom M. Paul, 305–319. Winona
Lake, Ind.: Eisenbrauns, 2008.

Schweid, Eliezer. *Prophets to Their People
and to Humanity: Prophecy and Prophets in Twentieth-Century Jewish Thought*
[Hebrew]. Jerusalem: Magnes Press,
1999.

Seeskin, Kenneth. *Searching for a Distant
God: The Legacy of Maimonides.* New
York: Oxford University Press, 2000.

Shannon, William H. *Thomas Merton: An
Introduction.* Rev. ed. Cincinnati: St.
Anthony Messenger Press, 2005.

———. *Thomas Merton's Dark Path: The
Inner Experience of a Contemplative.*
New York: Farrar, Straus, and Giroux,
1987.

———. *Thomas Merton's Paradise Journey:
Writings on Contemplation.* Cincinnati:
St. Anthony Messenger Press, 2000.

Shatz, David. "Maimonides' Moral

Theory." in *The Cambridge Companion to Maimonides*, edited by Kenneth Seeskin, 167–192. Cambridge: Cambridge University Press, 2005.

Simon, Derek. "'No One, Not Even God, Can Take the Place of the Victim': Metz, Levinas, and Practical Christology after the Shoah." *Horizons* 26, no. 2 (1999): 191–214.

Solomon, Norman. "Heschel in the Context of Modern Jewish Religious Thought." *European Judaism* 41, no. 1 (2008): 4–15.

Soloveitchik, Joseph. "The Crisis of Human Finitude." In *Out of the Whirlwind: Essays on Mourning, Suffering, and the Human Condition*, edited by David Shatz, Joel B. Wolowelsky, and Reuven Ziegler, 151–178. Hoboken, N.J.: Ktav, 2003.

———. "*Kol dodi dofek*." In *Divre hagut veha'arakhah*, 9–55. Jerusalem: World Zionist Organization, 1962. Translated by Lawrence Kaplan as *Fate and Destiny: From the Holocaust to the State of Israel*. Hoboken, N.J.: Ktav, 2000.

———. "Prayer as Dialogue." In *Reflections of the Rav: Lessons in Jewish Thought*, adapted by Abraham R. Besdin, 71–88. Hoboken, N.J.: Ktav, 1979.

———. "Redemption, Prayer, Talmud Torah." *Tradition: A Journal of Orthodox Jewish Thought* 17, no. 2 (1978): 55–72.

Soskice, Janet Martin. "Theological Realism." In *The Rationality of Religious Belief: Essays In Honour of Basil Mitchell*, edited by William J. Abraham and Steven W. Holtzer, 105–120. Oxford: Clarendon Press, 1987.

Tamburello, Dennis, O.F.M. *Ordinary Mysticism*. New York: Paulist Press, 1996.

Tanenzapf, Sol. "Abraham Heschel and His Critics." *Judaism* 23, no. 3 (1974): 279–285.

Taylor, Charles. *A Secular Age*. Cambridge, Mass.: Harvard University Press, 2007.

Teshima, Jacob Y. "My Teacher." In *No Religion Is an Island: Abraham Joshua Heschel and Interreligious Dialogue*, edited by Harold Kasimow and Byron L. Sherwin, 63–67. Maryknoll, N.Y.: Orbis, 1991.

Tillich, Paul. *Biblical Religion and the Search for Ultimate Reality*. Chicago: University of Chicago Press, 1955.

———. *Systematic Theology*. Chicago: University of Chicago Press, 1951.

Tracy, David. *Blessed Rage for Order: The New Pluralism in Theology*. New York: Seabury Press, 1975.

Tucker, Gordon. "A. J. Heschel and the Problem of Religious Certainty." *Modern Judaism* 29, no. 1 (February 2009): 126–137.

———. "Heschel's *Torah min ha-shamayim*: Ancient Theology and Contemporary Autobiography." *Conservative Judaism* 50, no. 2–3 (1998): 48–55.

Turner, Denys. *Faith Seeking*. London: SCM Press, 2002.

Underhill, Evelyn. *Collected Papers of Evelyn Underhill*. Edited by Lucy Menzies. New York: Longmans, Green, 1946.

———. *The Essentials of Mysticism and Other Essays*. London: J. M. Dent & Sons, 1920.

———. *Evelyn Underhill: Modern Guide to the Ancient Quest for the Holy*. Edited by Dana Greene. Albany: State University of New York Press, 1988.

———. *Mysticism: The Nature and Development of Spiritual Consciousness*. Oxford: Oneworld Publications, 1993.

———. *Practical Mysticism: A Little Book for Normal People*. New York: E. P. Dutton, 1915.

———. *Practical Mysticism and Abba*. Edited by John F. Thornton and Susan B. Varenne. New York: Vintage Books, 2003.

———. *The Spiritual Life.* New York: Harper & Brothers, 1937.

———. *The Ways of the Spirit.* Edited and with an introduction by Grace Adolphsen Brame. New York: Crossroad, 1990.

———. *Worship.* London: Nisbet, 1936.

Volz, Paul. *Das Dämonische in YHWH.* Tübingen: Mohr, 1924.

von Balthasar, Hans Urs. *Explorations in Theology I: The Word Made Flesh.* San Francisco: Ignatius Press, 1989.

von Harnack, Adolf. *Marcion: The Gospel of the Alien God.* Translated by John E. Steely and Lyle D. Bierma. Durham, N.C.: Labyrinth Press, 1990.

Waldoks, Moshe. *Hillel Zeitlin: The Early Years (1894–1919).* Ann Arbor, Mich.: University Microfilms International, 1985.

Ward, Keith. *Religion and Creation.* Oxford: Clarendon Press, 1996.

Webb, Stephen H. *Re-Figuring Theology: The Rhetoric of Karl Barth.* Albany: State University of New York Press, 1991.

Webster, John. *Barth.* New York: Continuum, 2000.

Weger, Karl-Heinz. *Karl Rahner: An Introduction to His Theology.* New York: Seabury Press, 1980.

Weinandy, Thomas G., O.F.M. *Does God Suffer?* Notre Dame, Ind.: University of Notre Dame Press, 2000.

Westphal, Merold. "Onto-theology, Metanarrative, Perspectivism, and the Gospel." In *Christianity and the Postmodern Turn: Six Views,* edited by Myron B. Penner, 141–153. Grand Rapids, Mich.: Brazos, 2005.

———. "Overcoming Onto-Theology." In *God, the Gift, and Postmodernism,* edited by John D. Caputo and Michael J. Scanlon, 146–169. Bloomington: Indiana University Press, 1999.

———. "Prayer as the Posture of the Decentered Self." In *The Phenomenology of Prayer,* edited by Bruce Ellis Benson and Norman Wirzba, 13–31. New York: Fordham University Press, 2005.

———. "A Reader's Guide to 'Reformed Epistemology.'" *Perspectives* 7, no. 9 (1992): 10–13.

Wiesenthal, Simon. *The Sunflower.* New York: Schocken Books, 1969.

Wilken, Robert L. "Marcion." In *The Encyclopedia of Religion,* edited by Mircea Eliade, 8: 5700–5702. 2nd ed. Detroit: Macmillan Reference, 2005.

Wilson, Stephen G. "Marcion and the Jews." In *Anti-Judaism in Early Christianity,* Vol. 2, *Separation and Polemic,* edited by Stephen G. Wilson, 45–58. Waterloo, Ont.: Wilfred Laurier University Press, 1986.

Wolpe, David. "Hester Panim in Modern Jewish Thought." *Modern Judaism* 17, no. 1 (1997): 25–56.

Work, Telford. *Living and Active: Scripture in the Economy of Salvation.* Grand Rapids, Mich.: William B. Eerdmans, 2002.

Wright, Tamra. "Beyond the 'Eclipse of God': The Shoah in the Jewish Thought of Buber and Levinas." In *Levinas and Buber: Dialogue and Difference,* edited by Peter Atterton, Matthew Calarco, and Maurice Friedman, 203–225. Pittsburgh: Duquesne University Press, 2004.

Zeitlin, Hillel. *Be-hevyon ha-neshamah* [Hebrew]. In *Netivot,* 205–235. Warsaw: Ahisefer, 1913.

INDEX

Holocaust, 10, 14, 21, 43, 95, 149, 174–179,
181, 185, 187, 189, 190, 191, 193, 224, 229,
270n87, 289n22, 290n35, 293n77
Hosea, 147, 164–167, 286n209, 287n218
humanity: capacity for knowledge of
God, 18, 73, 76–80, 176; cruelty of, 14,
24, 182, 239n84, 267n9; indifference of,
7, 8, 24, 222, 232; in need of God, 9, 15,
21, 88, 96, 102, 190; in need of religion,
45, 62; power of, 14–16, 45, 96, 201–202,
223, 230, 233; turning away from God,
218–219, 221, 222, 224. *See also* God: in
need of humanity
human nature, 72, 76, 80, 81, 249n92
Husserl, Edmond, 256n273

immanence. *See* God: immanence of
immanent frame, 61, 63
indebtedness, 17, 37, 43, 66, 230, 231,
246n80
indifference, 8, 24, 157, 171–173, 221, 229,
232, 246n98; of God, 5, 172, 173, 182, 188,
189; to God, 59, 133, 172, 222; to others,
7, 8, 149, 172, 179, 230; to wonder, 30,
39, 172
Ineffable Name of God: Man, The, 187–189
insight. *See* intuition
inspiration, divine, 25, 115–117, 130
intuition, 18, 33, 53–54, 56, 58, 66, 68,
70–71, 74–77, 79, 108, 252n206, 252n209,
254n256, 254n265, 254n271, 274n154
Irenaeus, 152
Isaiah, 145, 146, 154, 223
Ishmael, Rabbi, 161, 162, 168, 170, 192, 193,
284n175, 284n181
Islam, 11–13, 50
Israel: An Echo of Eternity, 174

James, William, 67–68
Jeremiah, 145–146, 148, 272n116, 283n161
Jewish law, 104–105
"Jewish Theology," 13
Jewish theology, 50, 69, 104, 115, 135, 136,
138, 141, 161, 244n63; Hellenization of,
135–136, 142–143, 232. *See also names of
individual theologians*
Jewish thought, 1, 110, 112, 118, 135, 162, 192

Job, 175–179, 182–183, 185, 186, 189, 291n43,
292n54
Judaism, 9, 76, 88, 95, 115, 118, 123, 129,
136, 141–142, 144, 151, 161, 164, 199,
218, 229, 245n63, 281n111, 289n22; and
Christianity, 149, 151, 260n29, 280n106,
290n31, 304n128; and Islam, 12–13,
304n128; and revelation, 101, 103–105
(*see also* revelation)
justice, 20, 23, 46, 48, 121, 147, 155, 160–161,
172–173, 177–178, 204n109, 272n116,
281n111; of God, 11, 96, 97, 122, 139, 148,
153, 155, 161, 168, 178, 195, 233

Kabbalah, 164
Kadushin, Max, 241n18
Kant, Immanuel, 53, 54, 57, 139, 256n273
Kaplan, Edward, 26, 264n248, 293n58,
293n77
Kaplan, Mordecai, 113–115
Katz, Steven, 241n115
Kaufman, William, 2, 261n48, 266n116,
274n154
Kavka, Martin, 239n84
Kepnes, Steven, 224
Kierkegaard, Søren, 65, 116, 241n115
Koretz, Rabbi Pinhas of, 224
Kotzk, Rabbi Menahem Mendl of, 11,
29, 124, 174–180, 182–183, 186, 189–191,
193–194, 197–201, 228, 241n115, 253n242,
288nn1–2, 288n3, 289n5, 289n16, 292n53,
298n62, 309n29
"Kotzker and Job," 175–179

Lamm, Norman, 113–115, 133
Leibowitz, Yeshayahu, 306n144
Levenson, Jon, 125–126, 197, 271n102,
273n135, 276n11, 295n114, 310n41
literalism, 105–108, 109, 156–157, 158
liturgy, 195, 197, 204–205, 211, 297n40,
297n45. *See also* prayer

Mackler, Aaron, 264n80
Magid, Shaul, 239n84, 311n1
Maimonides, 136–137, 140, 142–143, 151,
157–158, 232, 268n40, 276n7, 277n37
Malits, Elena, 213

SHAI HELD is Co-Founder, Dean, and Chair in Jewish Thought at Mechon Hadar (The Hadar Institute) in New York City. He received the Covenant Award for excellence in Jewish education in 2011.

CPSIA information can be obtained at www.ICGtesting.com
Printed in the USA
LVOW08*0819031113

359796LV00001B/1/P